# UK Sanctions Law and Practice

# UK Sanctions Law and Practice

*Edited by*

AMANDA PINTO KC

ALEXANDRE HAINES

SOPHIE O'SULLIVAN

OXFORD
UNIVERSITY PRESS

OXFORD
UNIVERSITY PRESS

Great Clarendon Street, Oxford, OX2 6DP,
United Kingdom

Oxford University Press is a department of the University of Oxford.
It furthers the University's objective of excellence in research, scholarship,
and education by publishing worldwide. Oxford is a registered trade mark of
Oxford University Press in the UK and in certain other countries.



Published in the United States of America by Oxford University Press
198 Madison Avenue, New York, NY 10016, United States of America.

British Library Cataloguing in Publication Data
Data available

Library of Congress Control Number: 2025951471

ISBN 978–0–19–896417–9

DOI: 10.1093/oso/9780198964179.001.0001

Printed and bound by
CPI Group (UK) Ltd., Croydon, CR0 4YY

MIX
Paper | Supporting
responsible forestry
FSC® C013604

The manufacturer's authorised representative in the EU for product safety is
Oxford University Press España S.A. of Parque Empresarial San Fernando de Henares,
Avenida de Castilla, 2 – 28830 Madrid (www.oup.es/en or product.safety@oup.com).
OUP España S.A. also acts as importer into Spain of products made by the manufacturer.

*To Chris*
*Christopher Jack de Vos Meiring, 1992–2024*

# Foreword

'Jaw, jaw,' Harold Macmillan famously said, 'is better than war, war.' That is undoubtedly true but in recent years international institutions and governments across the world have tried to find a way of responding to hostile states that falls somewhere between those alternatives. When 'jaw' is clearly not working and 'war' cannot be contemplated, the imposition and enforcement of sanctions on states and on individuals connected with them are an important part of that response.

The legislation which governs the various sanctions regimes discussed in this book is very long and very complicated. That is perhaps inevitable given the complexity of modern trade in goods and finance. Legal historians living a hundred years from now will find a wealth of information about our society—and our place in the world—from a careful examination of both the primary and secondary legislation which makes up the sanctions framework. In the Sanctions and Anti-Money Laundering Act 2018 (SAMLA) they will find an interesting illustration of how nation-states cooperate through the United Nations and of the obligations that membership of the international community brings with it. That act could also be used as a case study for a future student's dissertation on Brexit, since it provides a good example of how to bring about the shift from the incorporation of EU sanctions via the European Communities Act 1972 to the post-Brexit domestic legal landscape.

Future economists or social scientists will find a wealth of information about the way we live now in, for example, the Russia (Sanctions) (EU Exit) Regulations 2019. They would get a useful insight into the scale and scope of international commodities trade, with over 70 distinct regulations dealing with preventing supply of goods, finance, trade, energy, transport, and services. They may be bewildered by the list of products which must not be imported to or from the Russian Federation ranging from after-shave to jet fuel to radiation hardened TV cameras and quantum computing goods. On a lighter note, they would also learn the kinds of things that we value from the list of 'luxury items' in Schedule 3A to SAMLA 2018: horses, caviar and truffles, diamonds and hand-woven tapestries, bayonets and butter-knives, sun loungers and personal weighing machines. Pity the man who can no longer purchase his £250 false beard. They would certainly learn something about our professional services industry from the very detailed provisions in which the legislature tries to anticipate the ingenuity of those who may be instructed to help people circumvent the prohibitions.

Anyone considering the sanctions framework needs to study not only the enactments but also the body of case law that is rapidly building up around the enforcement of sanctions. That is also discussed in this timely and important new book. In studying that they would, I hope, come to understand what it means in the early twenty-first century to say that the United Kingdom is a country governed by the rule of law. The legal issues thrown up by the sanctions framework have generated case law which revisits and explains the respective remits of Parliament, the Executive, and the Judiciary—an appreciation of which is vital to the operation of our constitution. These cases are proving to be a springboard for the broader development of key concepts in judicial review such as the test for assessing the proportionality of a measure in *Bank Mellat* in 2014 and the disclosure of sensitive material in closed material procedure in *R (Sarkandi) v FCO* in 2015. Perhaps most important, the challenges brought by people on the receiving end of a sanctions measure require the courts to perform their age-old constitutional role. That is the role of protecting the rights of individuals by ensuring that Ministers act lawfully within the powers Parliament has conferred on them and in compliance with the human rights norms that Parliament has said must govern this aspect, as they govern all other aspects, of the state's conduct.

Looking at the world around us, it seems clear that sanctions will continue to be needed to help keep the citizens of this country safe and to ensure that the United Kingdom plays its part in shaping world events. The authors of this book have created an invaluable resource for current and future practitioners in this fast-moving area.

**Lady Rose of Colmworth DBE**<br>
Justice of the Supreme Court of the United Kingdom<br>
31 October 2025

# Preface

The majority of existing sanctions texts and guidance—many written from an academic perspective—focus either on the *why* of sanctions, their effectiveness as instruments of foreign policy, or on compliance-related matters. Few focus on *how* sanctions operate in a legal context, resulting in a lacuna for practitioners, especially those working in the UK. Those texts that have focused on the *how* have quickly become outdated due to the speed at which the sanctions landscape—political, legislative, and judicial—is developing. To give some perspective on the rate of change, at the start of 2023, there were no Administrative Court judgments on section 38 SAMLA challenges; at the time of writing, however, there are eight such judgments (including an interim relief decision),[1] as well as two Court of Appeal judgments[2] and one Supreme Court judgment.[3]

The Commercial Court and Chancery Division have been equally busy, having handed down a number of important judgments impacting on sanctions law in the last few years, including *Mints*,[4] *Celestial Aviation*,[5] *Litasco*,[6] *Vneshprombank*,[7] *Hellard*,[8] and *Eurochem*.[9] A number of those judgments have been appealed to the Court of Appeal, with one Supreme Court decision pending.[10]

[1] *LLC Synesis v Secretary of State for Foreign, Commonwealth and Development Affairs* [2023] EWHC 541 (Admin) (14 March 2023); *Mazepin v Secretary of State for Foreign, Commonwealth and Development Affairs* [2023] EWHC 1777 (Admin) (8 June 2023); *Dalston Projects Ltd v Secretary of State for* Transport [2023] EWHC 1885 (Admin) (21 July 2023); *Shvidler v Secretary of State for Foreign, Commonwealth and Development Affairs* [2023] EWHC 2121 (Admin) (18 August 2023); *Mikhail Fridman, R (on the application of) v HM Treasury* [2023] EWHC 2657 (Admin) (26 October 2023); *Phillips v Secretary of State for Foreign, Commonwealth Affairs* [2024] EWHC 32 (Admin) (12 January 2024); *Khan v Secretary of State for Foreign Commonwealth, and Development Affairs* [2024] EWHC 361 (Admin) (23 January 2024); and *Dana Astra IOOO v Secretary of State for Foreign, Commonwealth and Development Affairs* [2025] EWHC 289 (Admin) (11 February 2025). On 19 December 2024, the Administrative Court handed down judgment in *PJSC VTB Bank v HM Treasury* [2025] EWHC 3359 (Admin).

[2] *Shvidler v Secretary of State for Foreign, Commonwealth and Development Affairs* and *Dalston Projects Ltd v Secretary of State for Transport* [2024] EWHC Civ 172 (27 February 2024) (both appeals heard together); and *Khan v Foreign, Commonwealth and Development Affairs* [2025] EWCA Civ 41 (24 January 2025).

[3] *Shvidler v Secretary of State for Foreign, Commonwealth and Development Affairs* and *Dalston Projects Ltd v Secretary of State for Transport* [2025] UKSC 30 (29 July 2025).

[4] *PJSC National Bank Trust v Mints* [2023] EWHC 118 (Comm) (27 January 2023).

[5] *Celestial Aviation v UniCredit Bank AG* [2023] EWHC 663 (Comm) (23 March 2023).

[6] *Litasco SA v Der Mond Oil and Gas Africa SA* [2023] EWHC 2866 (Comm) (15 November 2023).

[7] *Vneshprombank LLC v Georgy Ivanovich Bedzhamov* [2024] EWHC 1048 (Ch) (3 May 2024).

[8] *Hellard v OJSC Rossiysky Kredit Bank* [2024] EWHC 1783 (Ch) (10 July 2024).

[9] *LLC Eurochem North-West-2 v Société Générale SA* [2025] EWHC 1938 (Comm) (31 July 2025).

[10] *Mints v PJSC National Bank Trust* [2023] EWCA Civ 1132, 6 October 2023: in *Mints*, the High Court dismissed the Appellants' application for an indefinite stay but granted permission to appeal to the Court of Appeal. The Court of Appeal dismissed the Appellants' appeal. The Appellants then sought permission to appeal to the Supreme Court, but withdrew their Supreme Court appeal against the Court of Appeal decision in May 2025; and *Celestial Aviation v UniCredit Bank AG* [2024] EWCA Civ 628, 11 June 2024: permission to appeal to the Supreme Court was granted on 1 November 2024, with a hearing listed for 8 December 2025.

Case law aside, the sanctions 'regulatory' landscape in the UK is virtually unrecognizable compared to the start of the decade: not only are there new dedicated sanctions offices, but the number of staff employed in those offices has also expanded exponentially.

Moreover, the Trade, Aircraft and Shipping Sanctions (Civil Enforcement) Regulations 2024 (TASSCER) came into force on 10 October 2024, empowering the Secretary of State to enforce trade, aircraft, and shipping sanctions, ensuring that prohibitions or requirements are adhered to. If the framework to regulate and enforce trade, aircraft, and shipping sanctions was considerably less developed in 2020 than the equivalent financial sanctions framework, any gap between the two has been dramatically reduced in the last 12 months. Responsibility for the implementation of enforcement powers in the context of trade sanctions falls to the newly established Office of Trade Sanctions Implementation (OTSI) which sits within the Department for Business and Trade (DBT). For aircraft and shipping-related sanctions, civil enforcement will rest primarily with the Department for Transport (DfT) rather than OTSI. An illustration of an added complication is that applications for licences to provide sanctioned professional and business services and other standalone services should be submitted to OTSI through its new online application service, whereas applications to export goods to sanctioned destinations or to provide sanctioned ancillary services should be submitted to the Export Control Joint Unit (ECJU) (which also sits within DBT) using its Export Control Organisation's online export licensing (or SPIRE) system. Meanwhile, His Majesty's Revenue and Customs (HMRC) continues to play a role in enforcing export controls within the UK. How did the sanctions landscape in the UK become so complicated so quickly?

Two colossal geopolitical events triggered the need for and focus of this book: (1) the UK's 31 January 2020 withdrawal from the EU following the 23 June 2016 referendum; and (2) Russia's 24 February 2022 full-scale invasion of Ukraine, in an escalation of the Russo-Ukrainian conflict that started in 2014. The former has had a direct de jure effect on UK sanctions law whilst the latter has had a de facto effect on UK foreign policy, which utilizes the new legal sanctions framework to achieve its aims. With this in mind, this book seeks to serve as a practical guide to how economic sanctions operate in the UK in terms of law and procedure since Brexit. It reflects the UK's legal sanctions framework as fully as possible as of October 2025, focusing on the Russia (Sanctions) (EU Exit) Regulations 2019 (the 'Russia Regulations') as a model, since they accurately reflect the wider UK sanctions panorama.

In order to maximize its practical use, the scope of this book has been deliberately narrowed in the six following ways.

First, rather than sanctions compliance, and the purpose of sanctions more generally, including their attendant geopolitical motive and effectiveness, this book concentrates on sanctions *law* and *practice*. As a result, it will likely be most useful to practitioners, although we anticipate those working in relevant industries will find certain chapters useful—in particular, Chapters 4, 6, and 10, as well as the narrative on key sanctions law aspects (for example, ownership and control addressed in Chapter 9). The book addresses some compliance challenges (for example, at the end of Chapter 3) and a number of subsections throughout several chapters deal with licencing developments which may be relevant to industry (for example, specific trade prohibitions and related licences in Chapter 5).

Second, the context is *UK* law, as opposed to the law of international organizations and supranational unions (such as the UN and OSCE;[11] and EU respectively) and, indeed, the law of other sovereign states such as the US. Where international and EU law is relevant to the creation of the UK's sanctions framework as it exists today, it has been addressed in Chapter 1. That said, and bearing in mind the inextricable relationship between the respective sanctions frameworks of the EU and the UK, where there are important distinctions and similarities, or interesting comparative elements, the EU position has been addressed.

Third, the book's emphasis is on economic sanctions, including financial and trade sanctions. As such, it leaves out immigration sanctions (Part 4 of the Russia Regulations). We note that on 9 January 2025, the UK Government announced its intention to develop a new sanctions regime targeting irregular migration and organized immigration crime, as part of its efforts to 'smash the gangs profiting from the vile trade in people-smuggling. This new regime will boost our ability to prevent, combat, deter, and distrust irregular migration and hold smugglers and their enablers accountable'.[12] On 23 July 2025, the Global Irregular Migration and Trafficking in Persons Sanctions Regulations 2025 came into force, and the first 25 designations were made against individuals and entities involved in people-smuggling networks across multiple regions.[13] These measures, now extended to Crown Dependencies such as Guernsey, impose asset freezes, travel bans, and exclusion from the UK financial system, making the regime fully operational.

Fourth, the book is concerned with sanctions in the context of foreign policy as opposed to national security; sanctions concerned with the prevention of terrorism have, therefore, been left out notwithstanding that financial sanctions may apply to persons designated under terrorism legislation. As such, the Anti-Terrorism, Crime and Security Act 2001 (ATCSA), Counter-Terrorism Act 2008 (CTA), and Terrorist Asset-Freezing Act 2010 (TAFA) are not addressed in detail.

Fifth, in order to make the book as user-friendly as possible, when considering sanctions regulations, the focus is on the UK's Russia regime. The Russia Regulations are by

[11] Organization for Security and Co-operation in Europe.

[12] Foreign, Commonwealth and Development Office (FCDO), 'UK to Launch World First Sanctions Regime to Snare People Smugglers Travelling Upstream' (Press release, 8 January 2025) <https://www.gov.uk/government/news/uk-to-launch-world-first-sanctions-regime-to-snare-people-smugglers-travelling-upstream> accessed 31 August 2025.

[13] Office of Financial Sanctions Implementation (OFSI), 'Consolidated List of Financial Sanctions Targets in the UK' (HM Treasury 2025) <https://ofsistorage.blob.core.windows.net/publishlive/2022format/ConList.html> accessed 31 August 2025.

far the most complex regulations to have come out of SAMLA. A cursory comparison between the most recent version of the Russia Regulations and the legislative text as originally enacted highlights an eight-fold increase in volume. The original Russia Regulations have been amended on 30 occasions between 2020 and 2025.[14] Moreover, (1) the guidance available on the Russia Regulations (now plentiful on gov.uk) as well as (2) case law; (3) developments in licensing, law, and practice; and (4) enforcement action in the Russia context are considerably more advanced when compared to other UK sanctions regimes. (See, for example, the recent monetary penalty of £465,000 against Herbert Smith Freehills CIS LLP by OFSI for breaches of UK financial sanctions on Russia.)[15] Lastly, the sheer scope of industries affected by the UK's Russia regime overshadows the impact of other sanctions regimes such as those imposed on North Korea and Myanmar. It can be said with confidence that whatever legal issue non-Russia sanctions regimes might raise, they are likely to have already been addressed by the vast material to have come out of the Russia Regulations than any other regime. This is so whether by government agency guidance, legal commentary, and/or Administrative Court, Court of Appeal, or Supreme Court judgment(s). As an illustration, the FCDO's March 2024 Post-Legislative Scrutiny Memorandum: Sanctions and Anti-Money Laundering Act 2018 includes a case study at section 10 entitled 'Russia sanctions'.[16] The same is true of the EU's sanctions regime against Russia.

Sixth, export controls—the legislative framework by which the UK Government controls the export of a range of military and 'dual-use' items—although often considered as falling under trade sanctions, is not addressed. Instead, the focus is on economic sanctions including financial and trade sanctions insofar as they are used as tools of foreign policy as opposed to controls that originate in international humanitarian law. As such, we have not focussed on the Export Control Act 2002 and Export Control Order 2008. That said, Part 5 of the Russia Regulations goes beyond the mere inclusion of prohibitions that mirror those set out in the export control framework; the scope of many prohibited products is often wider and, as a result, the Russia Regulations are stricter than the UK's export control framework. This is not surprising as the Russia Regulations are not a creature of international humanitarian law; instead, they are a foreign policy tool designed to encourage Russia to cease actions destabilizing Ukraine or undermining or threatening its territorial integrity, sovereignty, or independence.

At its root, sanctions law and practice are inextricably bound to geopolitics. UK sanctions law, despite its statutory complexity and interaction with administrative, commercial, human rights, and criminal law, remains a foreign policy instrument aimed

[14] Export Control Joint Unit, 'Russia Sanctions: Guidance' (Statutory guidance, 2025) <https://www.gov.uk/government/publications/russia-sanctions-guidance/russia-sanctions-guidance> accessed 31 August 2025.

[15] OFSI, 'HSF Moscow Penalty: Key Lessons for Industry' (*OFSI Blog*, 4 April 2025) <https://ofsi.blog.gov.uk/2025/04/04/hsf-moscow-penalty-key-lessons-for-industry/> accessed 31 August 2025.

[16] FCDO, 'Post-Legislative Scrutiny Memorandum: Sanctions and Anti-Money Laundering Act 2018' (CP 1024, 4 March 2024) <https://www.gov.uk/government/publications/post-legislative-scrutiny-memorandum-sanctions-and-anti-money-laundering-act-2018> accessed 31 August 2025.

squarely at achieving political objectives. Its effectiveness has always hinged on the degree of international coordination: sanctions bite hardest when allies move in step, and are generally less effective when they do not. In the past year, mounting global instability, the advance against multilateralism, and the erosion of traditional alliances have sharpened this challenge, creating further obstructions to how much sanctions can shape global outcomes in practice.

Lastly, two very recent developments—one geopolitical and the other affecting legal practice—merit a reference.

First, on 15 October 2025, the UK designated Russia's two largest oil companies. Until that date—and despite UK, EU and US sanctions having denied Russia access to hundreds of billions of US dollars since February 2022 and the UK having sanctioned approximately 1,800 individuals and more than 1,000 entities and shadow fleet vessels—Russia's largest oil companies remained undesignated, demonstrating how inextricably linked sanctions are to the geopolitical status quo and the desire for global energy stability. On 15 October 2025, the UK announced 90 new sanctions, targeting PJSC Rosneft and PJSC Lukoil—two of the world's biggest energy companies, which together export 3.1 million barrels of oil per day—and 88 other entities, individuals, and ships. Rosneft alone produced nearly half of Russia's oil and was responsible for 6 per cent of oil production globally. The Government's published list of Russia sanctions targets includes all entities involved in supporting the Russia energy sector, individuals and entities involved in supporting Russia's defence sector, entities involved in supporting the Russian financial services sector, and ships involved in the transportation of Russian liquefied natural gas.[17] Although the UK had previously sanctioned Gazprom Neft and Surgutneftegas, it only did so in January 2025.

Second, on 29 October 2025—following the expiration of OFSI Legal Services General Licence INT/2025/6160920 on 28 October 2025—OFSI issued its new Legal Services General Licence INT/2025/7323088 under the UK Autonomous Sanctions Regimes (see Annex 1 of the General Licence for the list of regimes covered). Between the issuance of the first Legal Services General Licence on 31 October 2022 and the expiry of the last one on 28 October 2025, payment of legal fees for the provision of particular legal services was only permitted if the client was designated pursuant to the Russia and Belarus Regulations. However, from 29 October 2025, UK legal firms and counsel can—subject to conditions therein—receive payment from persons designated under *any* of the regulations listed in the General Licence. The current Legal Services General Licence expires on 28 April 2026.

[17] FCDO, 'List of Russia Sanctions Targets, 15 October 2025' (Policy paper) <https://www.gov.uk/government/publications/list-of-russia-sanctions-targets-15-october-2025/list-of-russia-sanctions-targets-15-october-2025> accessed 31 October 2025. See also Claire Mills, 'Sanctions Against Russia: What Has Changed in 2025?' (Briefing Paper No CBP 10342, House of Commons Library 4 November 2025) <https://researchbriefings.files.parliament.uk/documents/CBP-10342/CBP-10342.pdf> accessed 10 November 2025.

The two October 2025 developments set out above demonstrate both the timeliness and relevance of this book and highlight the likely breadth of UK sanctions practice to come. At the time of writing, new data revealed on 15 October 2025 that UK sanctions have now frozen £28.7 billion of Russian assets since February 2022.[18]

Beyond the 15 October 2025 designations and the issuance of the new OFSI Legal Services General Licence, two UK licence-related developments are also worth mentioning: on 15 October 2025, OFSI introduced General Licence INT/2025/7539056 (the Energy Entities Wind-down) which permits the winding down from any transactions involving a listed Designated Person; and, on 16 October 2025, the UK ECJU extended the General Trade Licence authorizing the provision of some business software and technology to Russia which would otherwise be prohibited.

Despite the corrosion of multilateralism, the UK did not act alone: on 22 October 2025, the US's OFAC designated Russian oil giants Rosneft and Lukoil[19] and, on 23 October 2025, the European Council adopted the EU's 19th sanctions package against Russia,[20] which included a ban on imports of Russian Liquified Natural Gas from 1 January 2027 and narrowed the exemptions benefiting Rosneft and Gazprom Neft's oil imports into the EU.

Any errors are entirely our own. We have endeavoured to state the law as of 31 October 2025.

Amanda Pinto KC
Alexandre Haines
Sophie O'Sullivan
October 2025

[18] FCDO, The Rt Hon Yvette Cooper MP, and The Rt Hon Rachel Reeves MP, 'Huge Blow for Putin's War Machine as UK Sanctions Russian Oil' (Press release, 15 October 2025) <https://www.gov.uk/government/news/huge-blow-for-putins-war-machine-as-uk-sanctions-russian-oil> accessed 31 October 2025.

[19] US Department of the Treasury, 'Treasury Sanctions Major Russian Oil Companies, Calls on Moscow to Immediately Agree to Ceasefire' (Press release, 22 October 2025) <https://home.treasury.gov/news/press-releases/sb0290> accessed 31 October 2025.

[20] Council of the EU, '19th Package of Sanctions against Russia: EU Targets Russian Energy, Third-Country Banks and Crypto Providers' (Press release, 23 October 2025) <https://www.consilium.europa.eu/en/press/press-releases/2025/10/23/19th-package-of-sanctions-against-russia-eu-targets-russian-energy-third-country-banks-and-crypto-providers/> accessed 31 October 2025.

# Acknowledgements

We wish to thank OUP, particularly Fiona Briden for commissioning the book, and Lindsay Glick and Lisa Butts for being splendid editors.

We want to thank all the contributors who have made this book such a pleasure to write and Rosa Bennathan for stepping in to help.

Amanda, Alexandre, and Sophie

# Contents

# Table of Cases

# Table of Statutes

# Table of Foreign Statutes

# Table of Statutory Instruments

# Table of European Conventions

# Table of European Legislation

# Table of International Conventions

# List of Abbreviations

| | |
|---|---|
| 2020 Regulations | Global Human Rights Sanctions Regulations 2020 |
| ATCSA | Anti-Terrorism, Crime and Security Act 2001 |
| Belarus Regulations | Republic of Belarus (Sanctions) (EU Exit) Regulations 2019 |
| CAA | Civil Aviation Authority |
| CDDA | Company Directors Disqualification Act 1986 |
| CEMA | Customs and Excise Management Act 1979 |
| CFA | Criminal Finances Act 2017 |
| CPR | Civil Procedure Rules |
| CTAT | Counter-Terrorism Act 2008 |
| DBT | Department for Business and Trade |
| DD | director disqualification |
| DD-DP | director disqualification-designated person |
| DfT | Department for Transport |
| DP | designated person |
| DPA | Deferred Prosecution Agreement |
| ECA | European Communities Act 1972 |
| ECCTA | Economic Crime and Corporate Transparency Act 2023 |
| ECHR | European Convention on Human Rights |
| ECJU | Export Control Joint Unit |
| ECTEA | Economic Crime (Transparency and Enforcement) Act 2022 |
| EO | executive order |
| FCA | Financial Conduct Authority |
| FCDO | Foreign, Commonwealth and Development Office |
| FSMA | Financial Services and Markets Act 2000 |
| Global Magnitsky Act | Global Magnitsky Human Rights Accountability Act (US) |
| HMRC | His Majesty's Revenue and Customs |
| HMT | His Majesty's Treasury |
| ICC | International Criminal Court |
| IEEPA | International Emergency Economic Powers Act (US) |
| Iran Regulations | Iran (Sanctions) Regulations 2023 |
| Magnitsky Act | Russia and Moldova Jackson-Vanik Repeal and Sergei Magnitsky Rule of Law Accountability Act (US) |
| NCA | National Crime Agency |
| North Korea Regulations | Democratic People's Republic of Korea (Sanctions) (EU Exit) Regulations 2019 |
| OFAC | Office of Foreign Assets Control (US) |
| OFSI | Office of Financial Sanctions Implementation |
| OTSI | Office of Trade Sanctions Implementation |
| PCA | Policing and Crime Act 2017 |
| POCA | Proceeds of Crime Act 2017 |
| PSC | person with significant control |

| | |
|---|---|
| Russia Regulations | Russia (Sanctions) (EU Exit) Regulations 2019 |
| SAMLA | Sanctions and Anti-Money Laundering Act 2018 |
| SCPO | Serious Crime Prevention Order |
| TAFA | Terrorist Asset-Freezing Act 2010 |
| TASSCER | Trade, Aircraft and Shipping Sanctions (Civil Enforcement) Regulations 2024 |
| TEU | Treaty on European Union |
| TFEU | Treaty on the Functioning of the European Union |
| U.S.C. | US Code |

# List of Contributors

**Stephen Bailey**, Barrister, Three Raymond Buildings

**Rachel Barnes KC**, Barrister, Three Raymond Buildings

**John Binns**, Partner, BCL Solicitors

**Francis Bond**, Senior Associate, Macfarlanes

**Tom Cornell**, Counsel, Debevoise & Plimpton

**Alexandre Haines**, Barrister, 4 Pump Court

**Jessica Hocking**, Barrister, Three Raymond Buildings

**Salomé Lemasson**, Avocate, SL Avocat; Professional Associate, Outer Temple Chambers

**Charles McCombe**, Barrister, Three Raymond Buildings

**Robert Morris**, Barrister, Three Raymond Buildings

**Mohamed Naleemudeen**, Associate, BCL Solicitors

**Sophie O'Sullivan**, Barrister, Outer Temple Chambers

**Amanda Pinto KC**, Barrister, Three Raymond Buildings

**Charles Steele**, Professional Associate, Outer Temple Chambers

**Victoria Turner**, Partner, Eversheds Sutherland

# Overview

The need for a comprehensive practitioner text on the now-embedded UK sanctions framework and its interpretation by the courts cannot be overstated. This book aims to provide a practical guide to how sanctions law operates in the UK today, as well as an EU and global perspective of which UK practitioners should be aware. The book is broken down into 10 chapters as follows:

Chapter 1 introduces sanctions, including their purpose and types, gives a brief historical perspective, and details the sources of UN and EU[1] sanctions law and their implementation, in order to give an overview of the UK sanctions framework pre-Brexit and before the coming into force of the Sanctions and Anti-Money Laundering Act 2018 (SAMLA).

Chapter 2 sets out the post-Brexit sanctions framework and sets the stage for how sanctions law operates in the UK today.

Chapters 3 to 7 reflect the substantive law and framework relating to financial sanctions, director disqualification sanctions, trade sanctions, shipping and aircraft sanctions, and human rights sanctions respectively.

Chapter 8 addresses sanctions designations and challenges to them, including the procedure and grounds for such challenges.

Chapter 9 addresses sanctions in commercial disputes, both in litigation and arbitral proceedings.

Chapter 10 looks ahead and provides a global perspective from a US standpoint.

[1] For the sake of simplicity, the acronym EU will be used throughout this book to refer to both the European Community and the European Union.

# 1

# Introduction

*Amanda Pinto KC, Alexandre Haines, and Sophie O'Sullivan*



## A. Introduction to Sanctions

Both states and international organizations use sanctions as part of a political and diplomatic strategy to achieve a desired outcome. They may be imposed to apply pressure on the target—be it state, organization, or individual—in order to: **1.01**

(i) coerce it into changing its behaviour by increasing the cost on the target, so that it decides to cease the offending behaviour;
(ii) constrain it by denying it access to key resources needed to continue its offending behaviour (including the financing of terrorism or nuclear proliferation);
(iii) signal disapproval as a method of stigmatization and isolation or as a way of sending broader political messages nationally or internationally; and
(iv) protect the value of assets that have been misappropriated from a country, until these assets can be repatriated.[1]

Following the Cold War, the use of sanctions as an instrument of foreign policy increased, due most notably to the alignment of the permanent members of the UN Security Council. Sanctions have since become an increasingly popular international tool. While the extent of their success is a matter of debate, they have certainly become more targeted towards specific individuals or entities. **1.02**

[1] Office of Financial Sanctions Implementation (OFSI), 'UK Financial Sanctions General Guidance' (13 February 2024) s 1.1 <https://www.gov.uk/government/publications/financial-sanctions-general-guidance/uk-financial-sanctions-general-guidance> accessed 18 August 2025.

Amanda Pinto KC, Alexandre Haines, and Sophie O'Sullivan, *Introduction* In: *UK Sanctions Law and Practice*.
Edited by: Amanda Pinto KC, Alexandre Haines, and Sophie O'Sullivan, Oxford University Press.
 DOI: 10.1093/oso/9780198964179.003.0001

1.03 Despite their widespread use, there is no legal definition of 'sanctions' under international law.[2] Indeed, historically, the EU referred to sanctions as 'restrictive measures'. Nonetheless, the EU, UN, and UK now all refer to these measures as sanctions, as do many other domestic and international systems.

1.04 Sanctions that require some form of legal implementation generally fall into four broad categories:

1. Financial sanctions are restrictions that can limit the provision of certain financial services or restrict access to trade, financial markets, funds, and economic resources.[3] The primary type of financial sanction is an asset freeze, applicable to named individuals and entities restricting access to funds and economic resources.[4] Other financial sanctions may also prohibit the provision of insurance and reinsurance or financing either for specific sectors or target entities, for example investment bans, restrictions on access to capital markets, and directions to cease banking relationships and activities.
2. Trade sanctions are measures imposing restrictions on import and export. They are generally imposed against a state, the most extreme form of which is a comprehensive trade embargo amounting to a total blockade on trade. Trade sanctions usually prohibit specific activities, and a common example is an arms embargo, which is a sanction against the export of weaponry and dual-use items (goods which have both a civil and military use). Developments in trade sanctions include the 2023 prohibition—in the Russia context—on the provision of certain legal advisory services.
3. Immigration sanctions, known as travel bans, restrict the movement to or through the territory of the sanctioning state of identified individuals associated with regimes or groups whose behaviour is considered unacceptable by the international community.[5]
4. Aircraft and shipping sanctions, including de-registering or controlling the movement of aircraft and ships.

1.05 Sanctions were traditionally agreed and coordinated at an international level. The two international organizations that have used them the most are the UN and the EU. Of note, their objectives are somewhat differently framed.

1.06 In the UN, the main objective of sanctions is to maintain international peace and security,[6] although the Security Council's sanctions decisions must also be taken in

[2] Jeremy Farrall, *UN Sanctions and the Rule of Law* (CUP 2007). See also Clara Portela, *EU Sanctions and Foreign Policy* (Routledge 2010).

[3] Policing and Crime Act 2017 (PCA), s 143. See also 'UK Financial Sanctions General Guidance' (n 1) s 1.1. See Sanctions and Anti-Money Laundering Act 2018 (SAMLA), s 3, for a comprehensive list of all prohibitions and requirements that amount to financial sanctions.

[4] 'UK Financial Sanctions General Guidance' (n 1) s 1.3.

[5] UK Visas and Immigration, *International Travel Bans* (Version 10.0, Home Office, 16 October 2023).

[6] UN Charter, Arts 1(1), 25, 39, and 41.

accordance with the promotion of human rights.[7] Sanctions measures available to the Security Council encompass a broad range of enforcement options that do not involve the use of armed force.[8]

In the EU—a supernational political and economic union comprised of 27 Member States—the primary aim of sanctions is to support and further its Common Foreign and Security Policy (CFSP) objectives. These objectives are to support democracy, the rule of law, human rights, and the principles of international law, as well as to preserve peace, prevent conflicts, and strengthen international security.[9] The difficulty at the EU level has often been to adopt sanctions in a timely manner, given unanimity is required across all Member States. **1.07**

Although the UN sanctions framework prioritizes peace and security whereas the EU framework prioritizes the rule of law, there is a clear overlap between their respective objectives, namely that both legal frameworks should support human rights and the rule of law. **1.08**

There is also considerable overlap between UN and EU sanctions themselves, not least because the EU adopts measures to implement *all* sanctions imposed by Security Council resolutions,[10] ensuring consistency of the implementation of UN sanctions across EU Member States. This is done through EU decisions and regulations, the latter having direct legal effect in all EU Member States, which included the UK before Brexit. **1.09**

Further, the EU can impose its own sanctions (referred to as EU 'autonomous' or 'independent' sanctions) in the absence of Security Council resolutions. Certain sanctions regimes originally imposed by the EU have been superseded by Security Council sanctions where the UN has later passed resolutions.[11] The EU has also imposed additional sanctions on countries already subject to Security Council sanctions. **1.10**

The terms 'sanctions system' or 'sanctions framework' denote the UN's, EU's, or UK's overreaching sanctions structure or framework. The term 'sanctions regime', on the other hand, refers to an individual sanctions regime aimed at a specific state, organization, or individual (such as the UN's Syria sanctions regime or the UK's Russia sanctions regime). **1.11**

In addition to UN and EU sanctions, the Organization for Security and Co-operation in Europe ('OSCE')—of which the UK and all EU Member States are members—can also impose sanctions, although most OSCE sanction demands have historically been covered by sanctions imposed by the EU.[12] While there is overlap in their aims and **1.12**

[7] UN Charter, Art 1(2) and (3).

[8] UN Charter, Art 41.

[9] TEU Art 21(2), especially paras (b) and (c).

[10] Article 215, Treaty on the Functioning of the European Union ('TFEU') (ex Art 301 TEC) which requires any restrictive measure imposed by the EU to be based on a CFSP decision.

[11] See, for example, Ethiopia/Eritrea (UNSC Res 1767 (2007)), Yugoslavia (UNSC Res 713 (1991)), Iraq (UNSC Res 660 (1990)), and Libya (UNSC Res 1970 (2011)).

[12] An example arose in response to the armed conflict between Armenia and Azerbaijan over the area of Nagorno-Karabakh. In 1992, OSCE requested its Member States to impose an embargo on supplying arms to

objectives and both collaborate on a range of issues, OSCE is a regional, security-oriented intergovernmental organization. Its mandate includes arms control.

1.13 At a national level, the UK used to make statutory instruments (UK regulations) to impose penalties for breaches of EU regulations. The Sanctions and Anti-Money Laundering Act 2018 (SAMLA) was one of the first government bills to go through Parliament following the triggering of Article 50 of the Treaty on European Union, whereby the UK formally gave notice of its intention to withdraw from the EU.[13] Until SAMLA came into force, the UK's domestic sanctions framework (as opposed to the international and regional sanctions frameworks created by the UN and the EU respectively) was confined to terrorism legislation; the UK could only impose its own financial sanctions and restrictions under terrorism legislation, namely the Anti-Terrorism, Crime and Security Act 2001 (ATCSA), Counter Terrorism Act 2008 (CTA), and the Terrorist Asset-Freezing Act 2010 (TAFA). (See paragraph 1.35 below.)

1.14 Post-Brexit, the UK continues to be bound by international law,[14] but it is no longer bound by European law and EU instruments thereunder (including EU council decisions and regulations).[15] Now UN sanctions have to be implemented directly by UK regulations under SAMLA,[16] giving the government new powers to introduce secondary legislation.

1.15 The UK Government summarizes UK sanctions as follows:

- 'Sanctions are restrictive measures that can be put in place to fulfil a range of purposes. In the UK, these include complying with UN and other international obligations, supporting foreign policy and national security objectives, as well as maintaining international peace and security, and preventing terrorism'.[17]

forces from both states engaged in the combat. The UK's Foreign and Commonwealth Office has confirmed that the UK continues to apply OSCE's embargo. See HC Deb 2 July 2014 vol 583, col 57WS <https://publications.parliament.uk/pa/cm201415/cmhansrd/cm140702/wmstext/140702m0001.htm> accessed 18 August 2025. See also FCDO and Export Control Joint Unit (ECJU), 'UK Arms Embargo on Armenia and Azerbaijan' (31 December 2020) <https://www.gov.uk/guidance/arms-embargo-on-armenia> accessed 18 August 2025.

[13] SAMLA's first reading was on 18 October 2017. While SAMLA received royal assent on 23 May 2018, only a handful of provisions entered into force on that date: ss 32 (Periodic reports on exercise of power to make regulations under s 1), 50 (Reports on progress towards register of beneficial owners of overseas entities), 52–6 (supplementary and transitory provisions), and 60–5 (definitions, interpretation, extent, commencement, and title). The remaining substantial provisions of the Act came into force at 23:00 on 31 December 2020, at the end of the Brexit transition period.

[14] International law governs relations between independent nation states and consists of international treaty law and international customary law. Post-Brexit, the UK remains bound by the international treaties and conventions it has ratified in the past, whether bilaterally or multilaterally, with the obvious exception of the EU treaties. The UK retains its status as a member of the UN and as a member of the UN Security Council; it therefore remains bound by UN Security Council resolutions.

[15] Under s 3 of the EU (Withdrawal) Act 2018, all direct EU legislation, including EU regulations and EU decisions, became part of the UK's domestic law after 'exit day' (29 March 2019), subject to statutory exceptions.

[16] SAMLA 2018, s 1(1)(a).

[17] FCDO, OFSI, Office of Trade Sanctions Implementation (OTSI), HMRC, and Department for Transport (DfT), 'UK Sanctions' (Collection, 5 June 2025) <https://www.gov.uk/government/collections/uk-sanctions> accessed 16 October 2025.

- 'The UK implements a range of UK sanctions regimes through regulations established under the Sanctions and Anti-Money Laundering Act 2018 [or SAMLA]. [SAMLA] provides the main legal basis for the UK to impose, update and lift sanctions. These regimes apply to the whole of the UK, including Northern Ireland'.[18]
- 'Sanctions regulations apply to:
  - any individual, business or organisation undertaking activities anywhere in the UK (including the territorial sea)
  - any business or organisation incorporated or constituted under the law of any part of the UK undertaking activities anywhere in the world
  - any UK national, wherever they are in the world'.[19]

It is beyond doubt that in 2025, the UK's sanctions framework is virtually unrecognizable compared with the position pre-Brexit and even just before the 2022 Russia invasion of Ukraine. **1.16**

## B. Historical Perspective

The UK's sanctions framework has relatively recently come into being. In the context of the UK's prior central role (both legally and politically) within the EU sanctions framework—both as an EU member and by virtue of its position as a permanent member of the UN Security Council—current UK sanctions law can only be understood in the context of how sanctions developed in the UN and the EU. **1.17**

Between the end of the Second World War in 1945 and the fall of the Berlin Wall in 1989, the UN Security Council imposed sanctions regimes only twice: against Southern Rhodesia in December 1966, in response to the declaration of independence by the illegal white minority regime, and against South Africa in November 1977, in response to its apartheid system, nuclear ambitions, and regional military aggression.[20] The Cold War had a substantial impact on the UN Security Council's ability to exercise its sanctions powers because of the veto power belonging to its five permanent members. By contrast, in the next 27 years, the UN Security Council imposed more than 30 additional sanctions regimes, predominantly against states, but also against terrorist organizations. The majority of sanctions-related UN Security Council resolutions have amounted to economic and trade sanctions and more targeted measures such as arms embargoes, travel bans, and financial or commodity restrictions. Today, there are 14 **1.18**

[18] Department for Business and Trade (DBT) and ECJU, 'Trade Sanctions, Arms Embargoes, and Other Trade Restrictions' (Guidance, 3 August 2012) <https://www.gov.uk/guidance/current-arms-embargoes-and-other-restrictions> accessed 16 October 2025.

[19] FCDO, OFSI, OTSI, DfT, HM Treasury, and DBT, 'Starter Guide to UK Sanctions' (Guidance, 22 September 2025) <https://www.gov.uk/guidance/starter-guide-to-uk-sanctions> accessed 16 October 2025.

[20] Southern Rhodesia: SC Res 232 (16 December 1966), para 2, later strengthened by SC Res 253 (29 May 1968), paras 3–6; and South Africa: SC Res 518 (4 November 1977), paras 2, 4.

ongoing sanctions regimes which focus on supporting political settlement of conflicts, nuclear non-proliferation, and counter-terrorism.[21]

1.19 Since 1990, perhaps unsurprisingly, EU sanctions have been implemented more frequently than UN sanctions. Where the UN Security Council could not unanimously agree, the EU could still impose its own sanctions. The EU's practice of imposing sanctions on states in the absence of UN Security Council resolutions started in 1980 when it imposed a sanction against the USSR following the Soviet invasion of Afghanistan. Further autonomous EU sanctions were imposed in 1981, following the imposition of martial law in Poland, and in 1982, with the invasion of the Falkland Islands by Argentina. In October 2025, there were 40 EU sanctions regimes in force[22] as against 14 imposed by the UN Security Council.[23] All of the UN sanctions regimes are necessarily included in the list of EU sanctions regimes. It follows that more than 60 per cent of EU sanctions regimes are autonomous.

1.20 The similarity of the UN and EU sanctions frameworks and the sanctions themselves is due, in part, to the desire of the EU to be consistent with UN sanctions, in order to increase the effectiveness of sanctions regimes as a whole and, also, to the fact that, pre-Brexit, two of its members were permanent members on the Security Council (the UK and France).

1.21 Nonetheless, despite the similarities between the UN and the EU sanctions systems and their parallel evolution, one obvious difference is that, because the UN requires unanimous approval of the Security Council, it cannot impose sanctions against its permanent members. The UN will not, therefore, follow the EU by imposing sanctions against China, Russia, or the US. Moreover, there are substantial differences between the objectives of their sanctions (peace and security for the UN, and rule of law concerns for the EU), the manner in which they are administered, and the judicial review process in each system.

1.22 Originally, both UN and EU sanctions regimes were applied against entire nations. This approach was criticized for causing disproportionate hardship to civilian populations. Such concerns influenced a shift in the manner in which sanctions were applied, resulting in more focused sanctions (often called 'smart sanctions') where specific individuals, entities, or groups (such as terrorist organizations) were targeted instead of entire populations. Both the UN Security Council and the Council of the EU now tend to employ targeted sanctions measures such as arms embargoes, asset freezes, and travel bans against specific individuals and entities.[24]

21 UN Security Council, 'Sanctions' <https://www.un.org/sc/suborg/en/sanctions/information> accessed 14 October 2025.

22 European Commission, 'EU Sanctions Tracker' https://data.europa.eu/apps/eusanctionstracker/ accessed 14 October 2025.

23 European Commission, 'Overview of Sanctions and Related Resources' https://finance.ec.europa.eu/eu-and-world/sanctions-restrictive-measures/overview-sanctions-and-related-resources_en> 14 October 2025.

24 Not to be confused with the European Council, the Council of the EU is the EU institution that negotiates and adopts EU legislation in coordination with the EU Parliament.

## C. Sources of Sanctions Law and Implementation of Sanctions

### 1. UN

The UN imposes sanctions, and requires member states to implement them, through resolutions passed by its Security Council. Like all states which have signed up to the UN Charter, the UK is obliged under international law to implement UN sanctions.[25] 1.23

#### (i) The legal basis for the UN's sanctions framework

The legal basis for the UN sanctions regime is found in Chapters V–VIII of the UN Charter. In Chapter V, Article 24 grants the Security Council primary responsibility for the maintenance of peace and security, and Article 25 provides that Security Council decisions are binding on all UN Member States. In Chapter VII, Article 39 requires the Security Council to take appropriate action (either through non-forcible sanctions under Article 41 or through the use of force under Article 42, if the measures under Article 41 are inadequate) in order to maintain or restore international peace and security.[26] Article 41 gives the Security Council the power to decide what measures to employ in order to give effect to its decisions, and to call upon UN Member States to apply such measures: '[t]he Security Council may decide what measures not involving the use of armed force are to be employed to give effect to its decisions, and it may call upon the Members of the United Nations to apply such measures'.[27] The measures listed include, but are not limited to, 'complete or partial interruption of economic relations and of rail, sea, postal, telegraphic, radio, and other means of communication and the severance of diplomatic relations'.[28] 1.24

#### (ii) The implementation of UN sanctions

There is no specific guidance in the UN Charter on how UN sanctions ought to be implemented and administered. However, Article 29 sets out that the Security Council may establish subsidiary bodies as needed for the performance of its functions.[29] The Security Council has created two administrative bodies to administer and monitor the implementation of sanctions, namely, sanctions committees and sanctions expert monitoring bodies. 1.25

Sanctions committees, which traditionally undertook the task of sanctions monitoring, are comprised of the 15 members of the Security Council. Each UN sanctions regime is usually administered by a sanctions committee chaired by a non-permanent member 1.26

[25] UN Charter, Art 25, Ch V: 'The Members of the United Nations agree to accept and carry out the decisions of the Security Council in accordance with the present Charter'.

[26] UN Charter, Art 39, Ch VII: 'The Security Council shall determine the existence of any threat to the peace, breach of the peace, or act of aggression and shall make recommendations, or decide what measures shall be taken in accordance with Articles 41 and 42, to maintain or restore international peace and security'.

[27] UN Charter, Art 41, Ch VII.

[28] ibid.

[29] Also reflected in Rule 28 of the Security Council's Provisional Rules of Procedure.

of the Security Council. Sanctions committees report to the Security Council on implementation and administering exemptions of sanctions, as well as administering blacklists of targets subjected to sanctions measures.[30]

1.27 Sanctions expert monitoring bodies which have taken various shapes over the years, including monitoring mechanisms,[31] monitoring teams,[32] and monitoring groups,[33] provide independent analysis of particular sanctions regimes and make recommendations to strengthen sanctions implementations. They assist sanctions committees, undertake fieldwork investigations to identify how sanctions are being applied and violated, and make recommendations on how sanctions might be strengthened.[34]

## 2. EU

### (i) The legal basis for the EU's sanctions framework

1.28 Sanctions are one of the EU's tools to promote the objectives of the CFSP. They are imposed in order to 'bring about a change in policy or activity by the target country, part of country, government, entities or individuals, in line with the objectives set out in the Common Position'.[35] All CFSP decisions must aim to support democracy, the rule of law, human rights, and the principles of international law.[36] The legal basis for EU sanctions originates in the 1957 TFEU, which included a provision allowing Member States to deviate from Community measures in order to comply with other international obligations (including UN sanctions). This was illustrated in 1965 when EC Member States were first confronted with the requirement to implement UN sanctions imposed against Rhodesia. It was only in the 1992 Treaty on European Union (TEU or Maastricht Treaty) that the procedure for imposing sanctions in the EU was first codified.

1.29 Pursuant to Article 215 of TFEU, restrictive measures can be adopted by the Council of the EU following a joint proposal by the High Representative of the Union for

[30] Jeremy Farrall, 'Sanctions' in Jacob Katz Cogan, Ian Hurd, and Ian Johnstone (eds), *The Oxford Handbook of International Organizations* (OUP 2016).

[31] See, for example, the UNITA (National Union for the Total Independence of Angola) Monitoring Mechanism and the Afghanistan/Taliban/Al-Qaeda Monitoring Mechanism.

[32] See, for example, the Analytical Support and Sanctions Monitoring Team—SC Res 1526 (30 January 2004).

[33] See, for example, the Somalia Monitoring Group established in December 2003.

[34] Farrall, 'Sanctions' (n 30). For example, the Sanctions Monitoring Team pursuant to Resolutions 1526 (2004) and 2253 (2015) concerning ISIL (Da'esh), Al-Qaida, and the Taliban is comprised of 10 experts assisting two Security Council Committees. The mandate of the Monitoring Team includes the submission of reports on implementation of the sanctions measures to each Committee: <https://www.un.org/sc/suborg/en/sanctions/1267/monitoring-team/work-and-mandate> accessed 18 August 2025.

[35] Council of the EU, EU Doc 15114/05 (2 December 2005): Guidelines on implementation and evaluation of restrictive measures (sanctions) in the framework of the EU Common Foreign and Security Policy, pp 4–5 (paras 2–6), especially para 4; Council of the EU, EU Doc 11205/12 (15 June 2012): Guidelines on the implementation and evaluation of restrictive measures (sanctions) in the framework of the EU Common Foreign and Security Policy, pp 5–6 (paras 2–6), especially para 4.

[36] TEU, Art 21(2); see also Press Office of the Council of the EU, 'EU Restrictive Measures' (Factsheet, 29 April 2014) <https://www.consilium.europa.eu/uedocs/cms_data/docs/pressdata/en/foraff/135804.pdf> accessed 14 October 2025.

Foreign Affairs and Security Policy and the Commission. The EU imposes sanctions in three ways. First, it implements all sanctions imposed by the UN Security Council by adopting measures through EU regulations. These have direct legal effect in the territory of the EU on all EU nationals, residents, and operators, without the requirement for transposition into domestic law. Second, the EU may reinforce UN sanctions by applying stricter and additional measures. Third, it can impose its own sanctions which are implemented through regulations with direct effect in all Member States.[37] The latter sanctions practice is usually described as 'autonomous' or 'independent'.

Decisions on the adoption, renewal, or lifting of sanctions regimes are taken by the Council of the EU on the basis of proposals from the High Representative of the Union for Foreign Affairs and Security Policy and Vice President of the European Commission (HR/VP). The EU Council is constituted of government ministers from each EU country who regularly meet to develop the EU's CFSP. It is thus the main decision-making body in the EU.[38] The European Commission, together with the HR/VP, gives effect to these decisions into EU law through joint proposals for Council regulations that are also adopted by the EU Council.[39] These Council regulations are directly applicable in the Member States, without the need of additional transposal.[40] **1.30**

Generally speaking, unanimity is required on matters which EU Member States consider to be particularly sensitive, including but not limited to CFSP-related decisions (save under specific circumstances whereby a qualified majority is required). Interestingly, under unanimous voting, abstention does not prevent a decision from being taken.[41] **1.31**

### (ii) The implementation of EU sanctions

The mechanisms the EU has put in place for sanctions administration and monitoring are 'less institutionalized and less substantial than those of the UN sanctions system',[42] most notably because they do not operate the equivalent of the UN's sanctions committees and sanctions expert monitoring bodies. It is through the Council of the EU's Foreign Relations Counsellors Working Party (RELEX and Coreper II) and, specifically, the Sanctions Formation, that EU sanctions are administered and monitored.[43] **1.32**

[37] 'EU Restrictive Measures' (n 36).

[38] Not to be confused with the Council of Europe, a group of 46 Member States, including Turkey and other countries who are not part of the EU. (Until 15 March 2022 Russia was part of the Council of Europe.) Also not to be confused with the European Council, which is constituted by the heads of the Member States and determines the general political direction and priorities of the EU.

[39] EU Commission, 'Sanctions (Restrictive Measures)' <https://ec.europa.eu/info/business-economy-euro/banking-and-finance/international-relations/restrictive-measures-sanctions_en> accessed 14 October 2025.

[40] Article 288(1) of TFEU.

[41] The EU Council also has to vote unanimously in relation to EU membership, citizenship (i.e. the granting of new rights to EU citizens), harmonization of national legislation on indirect taxation, social security and social protection, EU finance, and certain provisions in the field of justice and home affairs (e.g. European Public Prosecution Office etc.). Council of the EU, 'Voting System: Unanimity' <https://www.consilium.europa.eu/en/council-eu/voting-system/unanimity/> accessed 14 October 2025.

[42] Farrall, 'Sanctions' (n 30).

[43] RELEX/SANCTIONS; see Council of the EU, 'Preparatory Bodies: Working Party of Foreign Relations Counsellors (RELEX)' <http://www.consilium.europa.eu/en/council-eu/preparatory-bodies/working-party-foreign-relations-counsellors/> accessed 14 October 2025.

The Sanctions Formation was set up to develop best practices and exchange experiences regarding sanctions implementation,[44] although it has been criticized for its limited ability to respond to geopolitical developments.[45]

1.33 When the Council of the EU notifies persons and entities targeted by an asset freeze or travel ban of the measures taken against them, it must also inform them of the two available legal remedies. The targeted person or entity can ask the Council of the EU to reconsider its decision[46] and they can also challenge the decision before the EU's General Court.[47] Both processes can be launched in parallel, and one is not the prerequisite for the other (unlike in the UK). Challenges brought before the EU's General Court seek to obtain the annulment of the decision based on five limited grounds: (i) lack of competence of the EU institution that adopted the contested act; (ii) infringement of an essential procedural requirement; (iii) infringement of the Treaties; (iv) infringement of any rule of law relating to the application of the Treaties; and (v) misuse of powers.

## D. UK Sanctions Framework Pre-Brexit

1.34 Before the UK left the EU, when sanctions were imposed by the UN or the EU, the UK had to give effect to the sanctions in UK law because of its international obligations. As stated, UN sanctions are implemented by the EU and, once implemented through EU regulation, they took direct legal effect in the UK. In order to enforce sanctions, the UK had, traditionally, enacted statutory instruments to criminalize the breach of financial sanctions and to impose penalties for breaches of EU regulations. The European Communities Act 1972 (ECA) limited the maximum penalty for offences created by regulations,[48] including offences related to breaching financial sanctions, to two years' imprisonment upon conviction on indictment and three months upon summary conviction.[49]

1.35 Following the enactment of ATCSA in 2001, CTA in 2008, and TAFA in 2010, the UK was able to impose its own sanctions and restrictions unilaterally and independently of the EU. Originally this power was limited to terrorism-related offences. The maximum term of imprisonment for offences created under both ATCSA 2001 and CTA 2008 was two years' imprisonment on conviction on indictment, or six months on summary conviction. In contrast, the offences created under TAFA 2010 carried a maximum penalty

[44] European Council, EU Doc 8666/1/08 REV 1 (24 April 2008), annex: Update of the EU Best Practices for the effective implementation of restrictive measures; EU Doc 15114/05 (2005), para 82; EU Doc 11205/12 (2012), para 94.

[45] Farrall, 'Sanctions' (n 30).

[46] Council of the EU, 'How the EU Adopts and Reviews Sanctions' (Explainers) <http://www.consilium.europa.eu/en/policies/sanctions/adoption-review-procedure/> accessed 14 October 2025.

[47] 'EU Restrictive Measures' (n 36); and in accordance with the conditions laid down in Arts 275 and 263 of TFEU. Proceedings shall be instituted within two months of the publication of the measure, or of its notification to the plaintiff, or, of the day on which it came to their knowledge.

[48] Made under s 2(2) of ECA.

[49] ECA 1972, sch 1(1)(d).

of seven years' imprisonment. This created an anomalous inconsistency between the penalties for breaching sanctions based on the one hand on an EU financial sanctions regulation and sanctions provided for in the domestic ATCSA 2001 and CTA 2008, and the higher penalties for breaches of the UK's TAFA 2010 sanctions regimes on the other.

There was a further issue in relation to the enforcement measures available for breaches of financial sanctions. The measures set out in the UK legislation were limited to criminal prosecution or an administrative warning letter. **1.36**

In order to address both the inconsistency in punishment across the relevant statutes and the limited enforcement powers, two steps were taken: first, the Chancellor announced the creation of the Office of Financial Sanctions Implementation (OFSI), established within the Treasury on 31 March 2016. The aim of OFSI was to 'help ensure that financial sanctions are properly understood, implemented and enforced'.[50] Second, the Policing and Crime Act in 2017 (PCA)[51] introduced new measures covering sentencing, enforcement, and implementation. Part 8 'Financial sanctions' of the PCA increased the UK authorities' powers, thereby supporting the work of OFSI by strengthening the enforcement regime and providing for tougher penalties for breaches of sanctions. **1.37**

The most significant developments under Part 8 of the PCA are: **1.38**

- the increased maximum custodial sentence to seven years' imprisonment on conviction for criminal breaches of financial sanctions, resulting in the harmonization of penalties across existing sanctions legislation;[52]
- the expansion of the range of civil enforcement powers by creating a new monetary penalties regime for breaches of financial sanctions;[53] and
- the inclusion of financial sanctions in the list of offences in relation to which Deferred Prosecution Agreements (DPAs) may be entered into and Serious Crime Prevention Orders (SCPOs) may be made.[54]

Once OFSI had established that a breach of sanctions may have occurred, it could: (i) make a request for details of how the relevant person proposes to improve its compliance practices; (ii) refer that person to the relevant regulatory body; (iii) impose a fine; or (iv) refer the case to the relevant agencies for investigation and, thereafter, prosecution. **1.39**

The basis for challenging unilateral UK sanctions measures pre-SAMLA in the terrorism legislation context was through judicial review and that remains so today. See, **1.40**

[50] HM Treasury, Summer Budget 2015 (Policy paper, 8 July 2015). Although OFSI was created in 2016 (i.e. before Brexit), both its role and size have vastly expanded by 2025.
[51] The PCA came into force on 1 April 2017.
[52] PCA 2017, s 145.
[53] PCA 2017, s 146.
[54] PCA 2017, ss 150 and 151.

for example, *Bank Mellat v HM Treasury*, the leading case on challenging unilateral sanctions measures imposed under CTA 2008.[55]

**1.41** When the UK was a member of the EU, both UN and EU sanctions had a direct legal impact within its jurisdiction. But following its departure from the EU, had there been a legislative vacuum, the UK would have been at risk of breaching its international obligations. With that in mind, SAMLA received royal assent on 23 May 2018. Until its provisions came into force, the UK's domestic sanctions regimes remained confined to terrorism legislation. SAMLA filled the legislative lacuna created by the UK's departure from the EU, enabling the UK to impose, for the first time, sanctions independent of the international community (other than sanctions related to terrorism offences). SAMLA was, therefore, a significant legislative milestone following the 23 June 2016 referendum.

**1.42** The Brexit Transition Period ran from 31 January 2020 to 31 December 2020. During that period, the UK continued to be bound by EU-derived sanctions and UN sanctions continued to be implemented in the UK through EU regulations. At the end of the Brexit Transition Period, EU law (including sanctions measures) no longer applied in the UK, subject to any provisions retained by the European Union (Withdrawal) Act 2018. It is with that history in mind that the UK's sanctions framework must be viewed.

[55] [2013] UKSC 39 (*Bank Mellat I–2*).

# 2

# The Post-Brexit UK Sanctions Framework

*Amanda Pinto KC, Alexandre Haines, and Sophie O'Sullivan*



## A. Introduction

After the UK left the EU, the Sanctions and Anti-Money Laundering Act 2018 (SAMLA) provided the UK with a domestic framework of powers to continue to meet its international obligations under the UN Charter by enabling the implementation of UN sanctions directly in the UK.[1] SAMLA was designed, in part, to fill the legislative lacuna that would have otherwise been created by the UK's departure from the EU because those UN sanctions implemented by the EU would no longer take direct legal effect in the UK. SAMLA enabled, inter alia, the UK to implement UN sanctions regimes immediately and to use sanctions to meet national security and foreign policy objectives.[2] Without SAMLA, the UK would not be able to add, amend, or lift sanctions regimes in response to UN requirements. As set out in Chapter 1, SAMLA was a significant legislative milestone following the 23 June 2016 referendum. **2.01**

The UK currently has 26 geographical sanctions regimes and nine thematic regimes in force.[3] Some of these regimes give effect to the UK's obligations under Security Council resolutions; the majority, however, are autonomous UK sanctions regimes. **2.02**

[1] Sanctions and Anti-Money Laundering Act 2018 (SAMLA), s 1(1)(a).
[2] SAMLA 2018, s 1(2).
[3] FCDO, 'Current UK Sanctions Regimes' (Collection, 31 January 2020) <https://www.gov.uk/government/collections/uk-sanctions-regimes-under-the-sanctions-act> accessed 22 August 2025. The following countries are subject to two UK sanctions regimes: Iran (standard regime, and one concerned with nuclear weapons),

Amanda Pinto KC, Alexandre Haines, and Sophie O'Sullivan, *The Post-Brexit UK Sanctions Framework* In: *UK Sanctions Law and Practice*. Edited by: Amanda Pinto KC, Alexandre Haines, and Sophie O'Sullivan, Oxford University Press.
 DOI: 10.1093/oso/9780198964179.003.0002

2.03 Every UK sanctions regime, whether it gives effect to a Security Council resolution or is an autonomous UK regime, operates in accordance with its own set of regulations which are brought into force by secondary legislation. There are 38 sets of regulations in effect.[4] The Russia (Sanctions) (EU Exit) Regulations 2019—which fully came into force on 31 December 2020—are the longest set of regulations pursuant to SAMLA and the ones that have been amended the most by far (28 times in under five years).

2.04 This chapter gives an overview of the post-Brexit UK sanctions framework.[5]

## B. The UK's Power to Make Sanctions Regulations

2.05 Section 1 of SAMLA empowers the Secretary of State for the relevant ministry and the Treasury[6] (the 'appropriate Minister') to make sanctions regulations they consider 'appropriate' for the following purposes:

- to comply with a UN obligation;[7]
- to comply with any other international obligations (including the UK's membership of other international organizations such as the OCSE);[8] or
- to address/achieve one or more of the following purposes:
  (a) furthering the prevention of terrorism both in the UK and elsewhere;
  (b) the interests of national security;
  (c) the interests of international peace and security;
  (d) furthering a foreign policy objective of the UK Government;
  (e) promoting the resolution of armed conflicts or the protection of civilians in conflict zone;
  (f) providing accountability for, or deterring, gross violations of human rights, or otherwise promoting compliance with international human rights law or respect for human rights;[9]
  (g) promoting compliance with international humanitarian law;

Lebanon (standard regime, and one concerned with the assassination of Rafiq Hariri and others), and Syria (standard regime, and one concerned with cultural property). Thematic regimes include sanctions relating to chemical weapons, counter-terrorism, cyber activity, global anti-corruption, and global human rights.

[4] ibid.

[5] The term 'framework' is used to describe the overarching sanctions system operating in the UK (or elsewhere). The term 'regime' refers to a particular package of sanctions measures adopted in relation to a particular state or situation (for example, the UK's Russia regime). In the US, sanctions regimes are commonly referred to as sanctions 'programs'.

[6] SAMLA 2018, s 1(9).

[7] SAMLA 2018, s 1(1)(a).

[8] SAMLA 2018, s 1(1)(b).

[9] Also referred to as the 'Magnitsky amendment'. The name derives from the case of Sergei Magnitsky, a Russian tax lawyer who, while working for London-based Hermitage Capital in 2007, uncovered a $230 million fraud committed by tax officials in the Russian Interior Ministry. Jailed in Russia in 2008 on charges of tax evasion, he refused to withdraw his testimony and died in prison in 2009, having suffered human rights violations while in detention. Following the Magnitsky Act passed by US Congress in 2012 which named the Russians involved (later broadened to the Global Magnitsky Act 2016), there was pressure on the UK to follow suit. Two major pieces of legislation had 'Magnitsky' elements added to them: the Proceeds of Crime Act 2002 (POCA) and SAMLA. The Criminal Finances Act 2017 amended POCA 2002 to expand the definition of 'unlawful conduct' to include gross human rights abuse or violation and SAMLA includes gross human rights violation as a reason for imposing sanctions

(h) contributing to multilateral efforts to prevent the spread and use of weapons and materials of mass destruction; or
(i) promoting respect for democracy, the rule of law, and good governance.[10]

All sanctions regulations must set out the purpose for which they have been made.[11] The Russia Regulations are made for the purposes of 'encouraging Russia to cease actions destabilising Ukraine or undermining or threatening the territorial integrity, sovereignty or independence of Ukraine' and 'promoting the payment of compensation by Russia for damage, loss or injury suffered by Ukraine on or after 24 February 2022 as a result of Russia's invasion of Ukraine'.[12] **2.06**

As originally enacted, SAMLA required two conditions to be fulfilled before a person could be designated under the relevant regulation: there must be reasonable grounds to suspect that the person in question is an 'involved person' as defined,[13] and the Minister must consider that it is appropriate to make the designation in the light of the regulatory purposes as set out in section 1(3) and the likely significant effects of the designation on that person.[14] Notably, this two-pronged test set a lower threshold than the EU framework's 'necessity' test. However, the bar was lowered further on 15 March 2022, when the Economic Crime (Transparency and Enforcement) Act 2022 (ECTEA) came into force. By section 58 ECTEA, the appropriateness criterion set out in section 11(2)(b) of SAMLA was removed, thereby reducing the Minister's designation requirements. Subsections 61(1) and (3)(c) ECTEA deemed all 'pre-commencement regulations' to omit any reference to the appropriateness test; it follows that regulation 6(1)(b) of the Russia Regulations, for example, no longer applies. **2.07**

The changes under ECTEA further marked the contrast between the UK's pre-Brexit sanctions framework and SAMLA. The current framework gives far greater discretion to the appropriate Minister, with the result that sanctions may be used far more extensively than before. The previous government's reassurances that it did not intend to alter how sanctions were implemented in practice are arguably a show of intent and not binding. But since the relevant ECTEA amendments, that difference is even more marked. Assuming HRA compliance and proportionality are considered by the Minister in relation to a designation, the abolition of the appropriate test may make little difference in practice. It does, however, likely show the direction of travel, namely the pursuit of a more draconian framework that affords substantial latitude to ministerial discretion. **2.08**

SAMLA in its current form requires regulations to make provision for the Minister to be able to choose whether to designate a person under the standard procedure or the **2.09**

on a person or an entity. The UK Government announced the first new Magnitsky sanctions in July 2022 under the Global Human Rights Sanctions Regulations 2020. The UK imposed asset freezes and travel bans on 20 Saudi citizens alleged to have been involved in the murder of Jamal Khashoggi, the Saudi journalist murdered in the Saudi Embassy in Istanbul. Also targeted were 25 Russian officials allegedly involved in the mistreatment of Sergei Magnitsky (see Chapter 7.B, 'Background to the UK's Human Rights Legislation: The "Magnitsky Affair"'.)

[10] SAMLA 2018, s 1(2).
[11] SAMLA 2018, s 1(3).
[12] The Russia (Sanctions) (EU Exit) Regulations 2019, reg 4(a) and (b).
[13] SAMLA 2018, original s 11(2)(a).
[14] SAMLA 2018, original s 11(2)(b).

urgent procedure.[15] Moreover, the regulations must provide that under the standard procedure the Minister is prohibited from designating a person by name except where condition A is met.[16] Condition A is that the Minister has reasonable grounds to suspect that that person is 'an involved person'.[17] The urgent procedure for designation is set out at section 11(2B)–(2F). Section 11(3) defines 'an involved person' as a person who:

(a) is or has been involved in an activity specified in the regulations;[18]
(b) is owned or controlled directly or indirectly by a person who is or has been so involved;[19]
(c) is acting on behalf of or at the direction of a person who is or has been so involved;[20] or
(d) is a member of, or associated with, a person who is or has been so involved.[21]

2.10 Significant differences in due process also arise. Persons designated pursuant to UN sanctions are able to challenge their designations through the EU General Court but, in the UK under SAMLA, individual rights are reduced and those on the UN list are deprived of the rights they enjoyed under EU law. For example, the EU General Court can declare designations unlawful even when they originate from a Security Council decision, but this is not an available option under SAMLA.[22] In other words, there is no judicial review process of UN sanctions measures in the UK. SAMLA instead provides a mechanism whereby a person designated on a UN sanctions list may 'request the Secretary of State to use [their] best endeavours' to secure the removal of the person's name from the relevant UN list.[23] The result is that, from a due process perspective, there is a distinction between UK unilateral designations and the effect UN designations have domestically in the UK, whereby the former are subject to judicial review but the latter are not.

## C. UK Government Departments and Agencies Involved in Sanctions

2.11 The UK sanctions space is complicated and somewhat disjointed because of the numerous bodies involved.[24] Although not legally defined, in practical terms, different UK government departments have a specific role within the sanctions framework, both in the domestic and international regimes.

2.12 The Foreign, Commonwealth and Development Office (FCDO) is responsible for directing the UK's sanctions policy, including all international sanctions regimes and

15 SAMLA 2018, s 11(1A).
16 SAMLA 2018, s 11(2).
17 SAMLA 2018, s 11(2A).
18 SAMLA 2018, s 11(3)(a).
19 SAMLA 2018, s 11(3)(b).
20 SAMLA 2018, s 11(3)(c).
21 SAMLA 2018, s 11(3)(d).
22 *European Commission v Kadi* EU:C:2013:518.
23 SAMLA 2018, s 25(2).
24 A similar observation can be made for EU sanctions, considering that each Member State is required to designate one or several national competent authorities who are tasked with issuing authorizations, gathering

designations.[25] HM Treasury's Office of Financial Sanctions Implementation (OFSI), which implements financial sanctions, is the body responsible for ensuring that they are properly understood and enforced in the UK, undertaking investigations and enforcement of civil breaches of sanctions and imposing monetary penalties. OFSI reports the most serious cases to the National Crime Agency (NCA) for criminal investigation, and issues licences to allow humanitarian aid or the payment of legal fees which would otherwise be unlawful.[26] Financial sanctions prosecutions are dealt with by the NCA together with the CPS; His Majesty's Revenue and Customs (HMRC) will likely prosecute criminal breaches of trade sanctions (because HMRC already prosecutes breaches of export control). The Export Control Joint Unit (ECJU), which is part of the Department for International Trade, administers the UK's system of export controls and licensing for military and dual-use items subject to arms embargoes.[27] The Home Office implements travel bans which are administered by the UK Border Agency.[28]

**2.13** On 11 December 2023, the government announced the creation of the Office of Trade Sanctions Implementation (OTSI), part of the Department for Business and Trade (DBT). OTSI is responsible for: the civil enforcement of trade sanctions, including the power to issue civil monetary penalties (criminal enforcement of trade sanctions offences remains HMRC's responsibility); licensing relating to the provision of standalone services, including professional and business services which would otherwise be prohibited under UK sanctions regimes; and trade sanctions business engagement and issuing guidance and monitoring of compliance with trade sanctions to detect breaches.[29] OTSI's civil enforcement powers are set out in the Trade, Aircraft and Shipping Sanctions (Civil Enforcement) Regulations 2024 (TASSCER), which came into effect on 10 October 2024. OTSI can levy penalties up to £1 million or 50 per cent of the value of the breach, whichever is higher. It can also issue warning letters where monetary penalties are not deemed appropriate. Where there is 'evidence of circumvention or high levels of recklessness and serious evasion', OTSI can refer such matters to HMRC for consideration of criminal prosecution.[30] For an overview of Government department and agency sanctions responsibilities, please see Table 2.1.

information on asset freeze measures and other ad hoc sectoral restrictions, and ensuring the effective enforcement of sanctions decisions, alongside national judiciary bodies.

[25] FCDO et al., 'UK Sanctions' (Collection, 5 June 2025) <https://www.gov.uk/government/collections/uk-sanctions> accessed 22 August 2025.

[26] NCA, 'Bribery, Corruption and Sanctions Evasion' <https://www.nationalcrimeagency.gov.uk/what-we-do/crime-threats/bribery-corruption-and-sanctions-evasion> accessed 26 October 2025; Rena Lalgi, 'Office of Financial Sanctions Implementation: an introduction' (*OFSI Blog*, 1 March 2018) <https://ofsi.blog.gov.uk/2018/03/01/office-of-financial-sanctions-implementation-an-introduction/> accessed 22 August 2025.

[27] ibid and ECJU, 'About Us' <https://www.gov.uk/government/organisations/export-control-organisation/about> accessed 22 August 2025.

[28] Home Office, *International Travel Bans* (Version 10.0, 16 October 2023) <https://assets.publishing.service.gov.uk/government/uploads/system/uploads/attachment_data/file/674861/international-travel-bans-v8.0ext.pdf> accessed 22 August 2025; and OFSI, 'UK Financial Sanctions General Guidance' (13 February 2024) <https://www.gov.uk/government/publications/financial-sanctions-general-guidance/uk-financial-sanctions-general-guidance> accessed 22 August 2025.

[29] OTSI, 'About Us' <https://www.gov.uk/government/organisations/office-of-trade-sanctions-implementation/about> accessed 22 August 2025.

[30] OTSI, 'Introducing OTSI' (*OTSI Blog*, 11 October 2024) <https://otsi.blog.gov.uk/2024/10/11/introducing-otsi/> accessed 22 August 2025.

**Table 2.1** Sanctions Responsibilities of Government Departments and Agencies

| Department or Agency | Sanctions Responsibilities |
|---|---|
| Foreign, Commonwealth and Development Office (FCDO) | FCDO is 'responsible for the UK's international sanctions policy and decisions, including all international sanctions regimes and designations as well as ship specifications. [It] negotiates all international sanctions.'[a] For specific queries about sanctions regimes, email fcdo.correspondence@fcdo.go.uk. |
| HM Treasury | HM Treasury leads on designations under the UK's domestic counter-terrorism sanctions regime. |
| Office of Financial Sanctions Implementation (OFSI) | OFSI is 'responsible for implementing the UK's financial sanctions on behalf of HM Treasury.'[b] OFSI undertakes investigations and civil enforcement of breaches of financial sanctions, and it is responsible for issuing licences. If civil enforcement action is not appropriate, OFSI will refer cases to the NCA and CPS or SFO. OFSI is also responsible for the implementation and enforcement of the Oil Price Cap on Russian oil. For specific queries about financial sanctions, email ofsi@hmtreasury.go.uk. |
| Department for Business and Trade (DBT) | DBT leads on trade sanctions which include prohibitions on 'the import, export, transfer, movement, making available or acquisition of goods and technology'; 'the provision or procurement of services related to goods and technology'; and 'the provision or procurement of certain other non-financial services'.[c] DBT's Import Controls and Sanctions team implements trade sanctions relating to imports. For information on import controls and prohibitions, see 'Notices to importers'.[d] For specific queries, email importsanctions@businessandtrade.gov.uk. |
| Office of Trade Sanctions Implementation (OTSI) | OTSI—launched in October 2024—is responsible for civil implementation and enforcement of certain trade sanctions including services and the movement of goods involving UK companies and persons which do not cross the UK border. OTSI's priorities are (i) 'raising awareness of trade sanction'; (ii) 'supporting businesses with trade sanctions compliance'; (iii) 'issuing licences'; and (iv) 'detecting and responding to suspected breaches, including taking appropriate and proportionate enforcement action where necessary'.<br><br>OTSI works in partnership with HMRC to enforce trade sanctions. OTSI is responsible for civil enforcement concerning the (a) 'provision or procurement of sanctioned trade services'; (b) 'movement, making available or acquisition of sanctioned goods outside the UK'; (c) 'transferring, making available or acquisition of sanctioned technology outside the UK'; (d) 'providing ancillary services to the movement, making available or acquisition of sanctioned goods outside the UK'; and (e) 'providing ancillary services to the transfer, making available or acquisition of sanctioned technology outside the UK'.[e]<br><br>OTSI is also responsible for licencing relating to the provision of standalone services, including professional and business services, which are otherwise prohibited under UK sanctions regimes. The licencing of ancillary services to the movement of goods continues to be the responsibility of the Export Control Joint Unit (ECJU).[f]<br><br>For specific queries about trade services sanctions within OTSI's remit, use the OTSI enquiry form.[g] |
| The Insolvency Service | The Insolvency Service is an executive agency sponsored by DBT. It administers bankruptcies and debt relief orders, investigates trading companies and the conduct of directors, and works to disqualify unfit company directors. It is responsible for investigating and prosecuting individuals who are suspected of breaching director disqualification sanctions and also issues licences.[h] |

| | |
|---|---|
| Department for Transport (DfT) | The DfT is 'responsible for the implementation and civil enforcement of sanctions in the aviation and shipping sectors', including controlling movement of ships and aircraft in UK waters and airspace.[i] For specific queries, email transportsanctions@dft.gov.uk. |
| Home Office | 'The Home Office implements and enforces immigration sanctions, also known as travel bans. Those subject to travel bans will be refused leave to enter or remain in the UK. Any applications they make for a visa to travel to the UK, including for transit purposes, will be refused. Any foreign national who is subject to a travel ban, and who is currently in the UK, will have their permission to stay in the UK cancelled and steps will be taken to remove them from the UK. For specific enquires, email public.enquiries@homeoffice.gov.uk.'[j] |
| HM Revenue and Customs (HMRC) | HMRC is responsible for the criminal enforcement of all trade sanctions measures, and enforces trade sanctions on goods crossing UK borders in line with its role as the UK's customs body. Specifically, it is responsible for export controls and breaches of trade sanctions where they relate to (a) 'import or export of goods to, or from, the UK'; (b) 'transfer of technology to, or from, the UK'; and (c) 'provision of ancillary services relating to the import and export of goods and the transfer of technology to, or from, the UK.'[k]<br>Report breaches of export controls and trade sanctions to HMRC—exports.strategic@hmrc.gov.uk.[l] |
| National Crime Agency (NCA) | The NCA is responsible for investigating and prosecuting criminal breaches of financial sanctions and criminal breaches of transport sanctions. |
| Crown Prosecution Service (CPS) | The CPS typically prosecutes cases referred by the NCA and HMRC. |
| Serious Fraud Office (SFO) | The SFO may investigate and prosecute cases in which sanctions offences are within its remit. The power of the Director of the SFO to accept cases for investigation and prosecution is limited to those of serious or complex fraud, or bribery and corruption.[m] In practice, certain sanctions offences intersect with international bribery or serious fraud. |
| Ofcom | Ofcom is the regulator of communications services in the UK. 'Ofcom is responsible for monitoring compliance with trade sanctions in relation to internet services, and for assessing suspected breaches. Ofcom has published guidance on how to complain to UK internal providers about possible sanctioned content.'[n] |
| Department for Science, Innovation and Technology (DSIT) | DSIT is a ministerial department, supported by 16 agencies and public bodies. It prioritizes innovation, investment, and productivity through science, research, and development. DSIT has published guidance on complying with technology transfer sanctions.[o] |

[a] OFSI, 'UK Financial Sanctions General Guidance' (13 February 2024) <https://www.gov.uk/government/publications/financial-sanctions-general-guidance/uk-financial-sanctions-general-guidance> accessed 22 August 2025.

[b] ibid.

[c] FCDO et al., 'UK Sanctions' (Collection, 5 June 2025) <https://www.gov.uk/government/collections/uk-sanctions> accessed 22 August 2025.

[d] DBT and DIT, 'Import Controls' (Guidance, 12 December 2012) 'Notices to importers' <https://www.gov.uk/guidance/import-controls#notices-to-importers> accessed 22 August 2025.

[e] OTSI, 'About Us' <https://www.gov.uk/government/organisations/office-of-trade-sanctions-implementation/about> accessed 22 August 2025.

*(continued)*

**Table 2.1** Continued

[f] 'Contact the Office of Trade Sanctions Implementation (OTSI)' <https://submit.forms.service.gov.uk/form/3576/contact-otsi/12324> accessed 22 August 2025.

[g] FCDO et al., 'UK Sanctions'.

[h] ibid.

[i] ibid.

[j] ibid.

[k] OTSI, 'About Us'.

[l] ECJU, DIT, and DBT, 'Export Controls: Military Goods, Software and Technology' (Guidance, 6 September 2019) 'Breaches of export control and trade sanctions legislation' <https://www.gov.uk/guidance/export-controls-military-goods-software-and-technology#breaches-of-export-control-and-trade-sanctions-legislation> accessed 22 August 2025.

[m] CJA 1987, ss 1(3) and 2A(5).

[n] FCDO et al., 'UK Sanctions'. See also Ofcom, 'Content or Services Provided by TV-Novosti or Rossiya Segodnya' (4 May 2022) <https://www.ofcom.org.uk/make-a-complaint/complain-about-a-video-sharing-platform-vsp/content-or-services-provided-by-tv-novosti-or-rossiya-segodnya> accessed 22 August 2025.

[o] DBT, OTSI, and DSIT, 'Complying with Technology Transfer Sanctions' (Guidance, 24 April 2025) <https://www.gov.uk/government/publications/complying-with-technology-transfer-sanctions> accessed 22 August 2025.

## D. Types of Sanctions

Sections 3 to 8 of SAMLA set out the types of sanctions that the Minister can impose in sanctions regulations: financial sanctions;[31] director disqualification sanctions;[32] immigration sanctions;[33] trade sanctions;[34] aircraft sanctions;[35] shipping sanctions;[36] and other sanctions for the purpose of complying with a UN obligation.[37] Section 3 of SAMLA sets out the types of financial sanctions that can be imposed, including: **2.14**

- targeted asset freezes;[38]
- restrictions on a wide range of financial markets and services;[39]
- preventing persons from owning, controlling, or having a prescribed interest in businesses which are connected to a prescribed country or of a prescribed description.[40]

The director disqualification sanctions at section 3A[41] provide that if a designated person subject to this measure acts as a director of or in the management of a company, they commit a separate criminal offence under section 11A of the Company Directors Disqualification Act 1986, punishable by up to two years imprisonment.[42] **2.15**

Section 5 provides for trade sanctions and refers to Schedule 1 ('Trade Sanctions')[43] which sets out the types of trade sanctions that can be imposed and their effect. This includes controls on the provision and procurement of certain goods, technology, land, and non-financial services and on the involvement of UK persons in a number of activities. **2.16**

## E. Territorial Application

SAMLA provisions apply to conduct *in* the UK,[44] and to all UK persons, *wherever* they are in the world.[45] Sanctions regulations enacted under SAMLA apply to conduct and **2.17**

31 SAMLA 2018, s 3. See also Chapter 3, 'Financial Sanctions'.
32 SAMLA 2018, s 3A. See also Chapter 4, 'Director. Disqualification Sanctions'.
33 SAMLA 2018, s 4.
34 SAMLA 2018, s 5. See also Chapter 5, 'Trade Sanctions'.
35 SAMLA 2018, s 6. See also Chapter 6.B.2, 'Aircraft Sanctions'.
36 SAMLA 2018, s 7. See also Chapter 6.B.1, 'Shipping Sanctions'.
37 SAMLA 2018, s 8.
38 SAMLA 2018, s 3(1)(a).
39 SAMLA 2018, s 3(1)(b)–(f).
40 SAMLA 2018, s 3(1)(g).
41 Added to SAMLA by s 35 of the Economic Crime and Corporate Transparency Act 2023 ('ECCTA'). See also Chapter 4.
42 Company Directors Disqualification Act 1986, s 13.
43 SAMLA 2018, s 5(1) and (2).
44 SAMLA 2018, s 21(1)(a).
45 SAMLA 2018, s 21(1)(b).

individuals that are 'connected' to the UK. Application of the UK sanctions framework therefore has wide extra-territorial effect.[46]

**2.18** A UK person is a UK national or a body incorporated or constituted under the law of any part of the UK.[47] UK nationals are British citizens and nationals, and British overseas territories citizens and nationals.[48] OFSI's guidance states:

> A UK nexus might be created by such things as a UK company working overseas, transactions using clearing services in the UK, actions by a local subsidiary of a UK company (depending on the governance), action taking place overseas but directed from within the UK, or financial products or insurance brought on UK markets but held or used overseas.[49]

**2.19** The conduct itself need not be active; conduct includes omissions so those with the requisite UK nexus are also caught.[50]

## F. The Impact of SAMLA on the PCA

**2.20** The Policing and Crime Act 2017 (PCA) received Royal Assent on 31 January 2018. In terms of sanctions, the PCA 2017 significantly increased penalties for financial sanctions violations and introduced new enforcement measures.[51] Part 8 of the PCA 2017 was amended by SAMLA in three substantive ways: first, the meaning of financial sanctions legislation was expanded to include sanctions regulations made under section 1 of SAMLA.[52] This means that more sanctions offences may attract a Deferred Prosecution Agreement (DPA) or Serious Crime Prevention Order. Further, the power in section 146 of the PCA 2017 to impose a civil monetary penalty applies to financial sanctions made under SAMLA. Second, sections 152 to 156 of the PCA 2017 ('avoidance of delay: temporary regulations') are omitted.[53] These powers were initially necessary to enable the government to make temporary provisions to implement UN financial sanctions so that there was no gap between the UN imposing the sanctions and the UK adopting them. When SAMLA came into force, it required the UK to implement UN sanctions directly, so these temporary powers were no longer necessary.

[46] Similarly, although it does not theoretically apply extraterritorially, the EU sanctions framework has significant extra-territorial *effect*, as it also applies to so-called 'EU Operators', namely entities that are not necessarily incorporated in the EU but that conduct part or whole of their business activities within the EU.

[47] SAMLA 2018, s 21(2)(b).

[48] SAMLA 2018, s 21(3).

[49] OFSI and HM Treasury, 'Financial Sanctions Enforcement and Monetary Penalties Guidance' (3 April 2017) s 3.9 <https://www.gov.uk/government/publications/monetary-penalties-for-breaches-of-financial-sanctions> accessed 22 August 2025.

[50] SAMLA 2018, s 21(5).

[51] See Chapter 3.J, 'Enforcement and Defences'.

[52] SAMLA 2018, sch 3, para 8(2) ('Consequential Amendments'): 'In section 143(4) (meaning of "financial sanctions legislation") after paragraph (e) insert – (f) a provision of regulations made under section 1 of [SAMLA] that contains a prohibition or requirement imposed for a purpose mentioned in section 3(1) or (2) of that Act'.

[53] SAMLA 2018, sch 3, para 8(4).

Third and notably, SAMLA allows sanctions regulations to create criminal offences punishable with up to a maximum of 10 years' imprisonment, thereby increasing the maximum sentence of seven years' imprisonment for breaches of financial sanctions.[54]

## G. Sentencing Increases in Criminal Proceedings

### 1. The Background

Prior to the PCA 2017, the maximum penalties for sanctions offences in the context of terrorism under Schedule 3 of the Anti-Terrorism, Crime and Security Act 2001 (failure to comply with freezing orders) and Schedule 7 to the Counter-Terrorism Act 2008 (failure to comply with requirements such as undertaking customer due diligence, or limiting or ceasing certain types of business) was two years' imprisonment. Sections 144 and 145 PCA 2017 provided for an uplift in the criminal penalties for sanctions offences. Section 144 modified the application of the European Communities Act 1972 (ECA) to increase the maximum term of imprisonment for offences relating to financial sanctions, bringing them into line with breaches of the UK domestic and EU terrorist asset-freezing regimes.[55] The sentence limitations originally provided for in the ECA of two years on indictment or three months on summary conviction were disapplied.[56] **2.21**

The PCA 2017 harmonized the maximum term of imprisonment for breach of sanctions between EU and domestic sanctions regimes. The maximum sentences for offences relating to EU financial sanctions were thus extended to seven years' imprisonment on indictment (applying to all of the UK) and, on summary conviction, to six months' imprisonment in England, Wales, and Northern Ireland and 12 months' imprisonment in Scotland.[57] Section 144 of the PCA 2017, however, was omitted on 31 December 2020 by regulation 128 of the Law Enforcement and Security (Amendment) (EU Exit) Regulations 2019. **2.22**

### 2. The Current Position

Under SAMLA, the maximum term of imprisonment for sanctions breaches was further increased to 10 years, bringing it in line with the maximum sentence for trade sanctions and export control breaches.[58] Currently, the 10-year maximum applies to **2.23**

[54] SAMLA 2018, s 17(4) and (5).
[55] PCA 2017, s 144(1).
[56] PCA 2017, s 144(2).
[57] PCA 2017, s 144(3).
[58] SAMLA 2018, s 17(5)(a).

trade sanctions,[59] and financial sanctions breaches attract a maximum term of seven years' imprisonment.[60]

## H. Civil Penalties

2.24 In addition to the breach of UK sanctions prohibitions being a criminal offence,[61] there are some sanctions regimes which provide for the imposition of a civil monetary penalty for breach of certain prohibitions. For example, the Russia Regulations give Ofcom the power to impose a monetary penalty for offences related to internet services[62] and the Treasury a similar power for offences including those related to maritime transportation of certain oil and oil products,[63] reporting obligations,[64] and investments.[65] Procedural rights with respect to Treasury monetary penalties include the obligation of the Treasury to explain the grounds for imposing the penalty, to specify the amount in question, to explain that the person is entitled to make representations, and to specify the period within which any such representations must be made.[66]

2.25 At the conclusion of an investigation into sanctions violations, the following outcomes are available to HMRC, OFSI, and OTSI:

- criminal prosecution;
- a DPA;
- referral to a sectoral regulator where appropriate, such as the Financial Conduct Authority (FCA);
- imposing a civil monetary penalty (in the case of OFSI and OTSI) or a compound penalty in lieu of criminal prosecution (HMRC), often in the context of export control cases;
- issuing a warning letter with no further action;
- making a finding that there was no breach.

### 1. OFSI's Powers

2.26 Section 146 of the PCA 2017 provides that the Treasury (OFSI, in practice) may impose a monetary penalty on a person if it is satisfied, on the balance of probabilities, that the

59 See, for example, Russia Regulations 2019, reg 80(2)(d).
60 See, for example, Russia Regulations 2019, reg 80(1)(d).
61 Of note: in the EU, and despite the enactment of Directive 2024/1226 of 24 April 2024, breach of EU sanctions does not automatically amount to a criminal offence, as some Member States have opted for administrative or civil penalties instead. However, the harmonization introduced by the Directive (currently under transposition) aims at granting similar deterrence effects to both criminal and civil/administrative penalties.
62 Russia Regulations 2019, reg 88A. See reg 88B for procedural rights following the imposition of monetary penalties.
63 Russia Regulations 2019, reg 88C(1).
64 Russia Regulations 2019, reg 88C(1A).
65 Russia Regulations 2019, reg 88C(1B).
66 Russia Regulations 2019, reg 88D.

person has breached a prohibition, or failed to comply with an obligation, that is imposed by or under financial sanctions legislation. The amount is determined by the Treasury.[67] Where it is possible to estimate the value, the penalty can range from 50 per cent of the estimated value of the funds or economic resources or £1 million, whichever is the greater.[68] Since 15 June 2022, when ECTEA 2022 inserted section 146(1A) into the PCA 2017,[69] OFSI can impose monetary penalties for financial sanctions breaches on a strict liability basis, meaning that neither knowledge nor suspicion of a breach is required for a penalty. Any monetary penalty payable is recoverable by the Treasury as a civil debt and, once received by the Treasury, it must be paid into the Consolidated Fund.[70]

OFSI provides guidance on its approach to the enforcement of monetary penalties.[71] **2.27**
OFSI takes several 'case factors' into account when determining the 'fair and proportionate' amount of a monetary penalty.[72] In its assessment, OFSI first looks at the severity of the breach, which involves an assessment of circumvention of sanctions, the value of the breach, and the harm or risk of harm to the sanction regime's object.[73] OFSI then assesses the conduct of the person in breach, including: intent, knowledge, and reasonable cause to suspect; compliance systems in place; the extent of ownership and control; failure to apply for a licence or any breach of a licence term; professional facilitation; isolated or repeated breaches; reporting of breaches;[74] and degree of co-operation.[75] OFSI also considers the public interest in pursuing enforcement action, and in determining the type of enforcement action to pursue.[76]

OFSI's monetary penalty decision process consists of three parts: (1) penalty threshold; **2.28**
(2) baseline penalty matrix; and (3) penalty recommendation.[77] Following OFSI's case assessment, it will "likely assess that the penalty threshold is reached if one or more of the following is demonstrated:

- the case meets the tests in section 146(1), PCA 2017 – that is, on the balance of probabilities, there has been a breach;
- the breach has involved funds or economic resources being made available to a designated person. The financial sanctions regimes are designed to prevent this;

[67] PCA 2017, s 146(2).

[68] PCA 2017, s 146(3). The UK's single largest financial penalty to date was imposed on Standard Chartered Bank on 18 February 2021, amounting to £20.47 million for making funds available to a designated person. Of note, the financial institution self-reported and was deemed to have acted in good faith.

[69] Section 146(1A) of the PCA 2017 reads: 'In determining for the purposes of subsection (1) whether a person has breached a prohibition, or failed to comply with an obligation, imposed by or under financial sanctions legislation, any requirement imposed by or under that legislation for the person to have known, suspected or believed any matter *is to be ignored*' (emphasis added).

[70] PCA 2017, s 146(11) and (12).

[71] OFSI, 'Financial Sanctions Enforcement and Monetary Penalties Guidance' (n 49).

[72] ibid s 3.3.

[73] ibid s 3.4.1.

[74] OFSI 'values voluntary disclosure' which may be a mitigating factor when OFSI assesses the case and impact on any subsequent decision to apply a monetary penalty. If multiple parties are involved, OFSI expects voluntary disclosure from each party. ibid s 3.4.1(J).

[75] ibid s 3.4.2.

[76] ibid s 3.6.

[77] ibid s 4.

- the breach has involved a person dealing with the funds or economic resources of a designated person or entity in breach of an asset freeze;
- there is evidence of circumvention. By making arrangements to circumvent the law, a person not only breaches the law but attacks the integrity of the system;
- a person has not complied with a requirement to provide information; and/or OFSI considers that a monetary penalty is appropriate and proportionate.

> OFSI will assess these matters on a case-by-case basis. If the penalty threshold is reached, we may impose a penalty. We have discretion not to do so and in practice decide what enforcement response is appropriate depending on whether the case is of lesser or moderate severity enough to justify imposing a monetary penalty".[78]

2.29 In terms of the baseline monetary penalty, OFSI will generally impose a level of monetary penalty that is clearly and consistently related to its view of the impact of the case and the value of the breach (which may be estimated if it cannot be calculated accurately).[79] OFSI's baseline monetary penalty matrix encourages prompt and complete voluntary disclosure of the facts of the case, which may be a mitigating factor in its assessment and reduce the level of monetary penalty imposed.[80] OFSI first works out the statutory maximum monetary penalty it could impose. Within the maximum, OFSI then decides the level of monetary penalty on the basis of reasonableness and proportionality based on its view of the seriousness of the case:

> 'Reasonable' means an ordinary reasonable person would regard the proposed penalty as appropriate to the offence
>
> 'Proportionate' means there is a relationship between the value of the proposed penalty and a holistic assessment of all the other factors present in the case. This does not mean that a penalty should necessarily be either a specific percentage or multiple of the breach amount. It only means it must be neither an insufficient nor excessive amount.[81]

2.30 Once OFSI has a baseline penalty level, it applies the following penalty matrix: OFSI makes up to a 50 per cent reduction in the final monetary penalty amount to a person who gives a prompt and complete voluntary disclosure of a breach of financial sanctions. If OFSI assesses the case as 'serious', it may make reductions of up to 50 per cent for voluntary disclosure. If OFSI assesses a case as 'most serious', it may make reductions of up to 30 per cent for voluntary disclosure. If OFSI assesses a series of breaches where only some were voluntarily disclosed, it takes that into account when determining any reduction. There is, therefore, an emphasis on the value OFSI places

[78] ibid s 4.1.
[79] ibid s 4.2.
[80] ibid.
[81] ibid.

on voluntary disclosure and it is likely that voluntary disclosure will always trigger a benefit, even in the most serious cases. Any voluntary disclosure will be assessed on a case-by-case basis, and a reduction may not be given if it transpires that the person has not made a complete disclosure in the course of the investigation. For example, a reduction may not be given if the person self-disclosed to OFSI only because it believed OFSI was already aware, or if the person refused to provide information upon request.

Finally, OFSI's penalty process follows this approach: 2.31

- determine the estimated value of the transactions which breach the regulations
- determine the maximum monetary penalty—this is £1 million or 50% of the estimated value of the breach, whichever is higher
- apply the seriousness determination—either 'serious' or 'most serious', depending on the facts
- determine the baseline: this is also based on the facts of the case and what level of monetary penalty under the relevant maximum would be reasonable and proportionate
- determine if a reduction applies—if so, determine an appropriate percentage reduction and apply it to the baseline

In the event that there is no transaction value to base a calculation on (for example, if a penalty is imposed for an information offence) OFSI will impose such monetary penalty as seems reasonable and proportionate to the facts of the case. The permitted maximum in such cases is £1 million. This initial process creates a monetary penalty recommendation.

This recommendation is then considered by a decision maker, who can decide to agree, change or reject the recommendation. If OFSI is minded to impose a monetary penalty, this is then communicated to the person on whom OFSI intends to impose the penalty. They have a right to make representations (see Chapter 5) 'which could change OFSI's view on whether a monetary penalty should be imposed, or the value of any penalty.'[82]

OFSI also has the power to impose monetary penalties for information offences and will treat a failure to provide requested information as an aggravating factor in a case. For relevant firms—as defined in the various regulations made under SAMLA—a failure to provide information on a breach of financial sanctions may be a criminal offence. Moreover, for all 'persons' as defined in regulations made under SAMLA, a failure to comply with the annual frozen asset review reporting requirement, without reasonable excuse, may be a criminal offence. Lastly, OFSI has broad powers to require information from anyone, and it may be a criminal offence in its own right not to provide it. 2.32

[82] ibid s 4.3.

**2.33** The FCA also has the power to impose fines on regulated entities for breaches of financial regulations, commonly occurring where there has also been a breach of sanctions by the FCA-regulated entity.[83]

## 2. OTSI's Powers

**2.34** OTSI's civil enforcement powers are set out in TASSCER 2024 which came into effect on 10 October 2024.[84] OTSI, part of DBT, has powers to enforce certain trade sanctions. When OTSI assesses a suspected breach of trade sanctions, it first seeks to establish whether there has been a breach of a prohibition or a failure to comply with an obligation.[85] Once OTSI is satisfied that there has been a breach, it then determines the severity of the breach: Lesser Severity, Medium Severity, or High Severity—a distinction drawn to ensure that the enforcement outcome is proportionate to the seriousness of the breach. Where non-compliance has been identified, the aim of the enforcement outcome is to change behaviour and to improve future compliance. Indicators of a Lesser Severity breach may include: (i) low or no culpability; (ii) lower harm to the purposes of the sanctions regime; and (iii) lower financial value, where there are no other relevant indicators. Indicators of a Medium Severity breach may include: (i) failure to prevent a breach through behaviours such as negligence or recklessness; (ii) significant or moderate harm to the purposes of the sanctions regime; and (iii) moderate financial value, where there are no other relevant indicators. Indicators of a High Severity breach may include: (i) a significant level of culpability, which could include intentional actions or significant negligence; (ii) extensive or sophisticated planning, such as efforts being taken to conceal the breach; (iii) serious harm to the purpose of the sanctions regime; and (iv) high financial value, where there are no other relevant indicators.[86]

**2.35** Strict liability applies to most breaches of trade sanctions. Regulation 6 of TASSCER 2024 requires OTSI to ignore any defence that a person did not know and had no reasonable cause to suspect that an offence had been committed under trade sanctions regulations.

**2.36** Once OTSI has determined the severity of the breach, the potential outcomes are:

- Warning letter: this may include a requirement that a person comply with a continuing obligation to keep OTSI informed about certain information as circumstances change, such as the improvement of due diligence processes.

[83] S.206(1) Financial Services and Markets Act 2000.
[84] Trade, Aircraft and Shipping Sanctions (Civil Enforcement) Regulations 2024.
[85] DBT and OTSI, 'How Suspected Breaches of Trade Sanctions are Assessed by the Office of Trade Sanctions Implementation (OTSI)' (Guidance, 12 September 2024) s 3 <https://www.gov.uk/guidance/how-suspected-breaches-of-trade-sanctions-are-assessed-by-the-office-of-trade-sanctions-implementation-otsi> accessed 22 August 2025.
[86] ibid s 4.

- Referral to the relevant regulator: OTSI may refer the case to the person's regulator, for example the FCA.
- Referral to other organizations: if a UK registered company is involved in the breach, or if the breach involves a director of a UK registered company, OTSI may refer the case to Companies House or the Insolvency Service.
- Public disclosure: where OTSI decides that it would be in the public interest to share information about a breach, it may publicize those details.
- Monetary penalty: OTSI can levy penalties up to £1 million or 50 per cent of the value of the breach, whichever is higher.
- Referral to HMRC: OTSI may refer the case to HMRC where it determines that the breach merits criminal enforcement. HMRC, as a criminal enforcement authority, can use its powers to offer a compound penalty (often the outcome in cases of export control violations) or refer the matter to the CPS to consider prosecution.

Once OTSI has established that there has been a breach and determined the severity of the case, it considers a range of factors in determining the enforcement outcome. Mitigating and aggravating factors determine whether the monetary penalty is reduced (or imposed at all) or increased.[87] Where a monetary penalty is being considered, for Low and Medium Severity cases, OTSI will make up to a 50 per cent reduction to the final monetary penalty if prompt and comprehensive voluntary disclosure of the breach has been made. For High Severity cases, OTSI will make up to a 30 per cent reduction to the final monetary penalty if prompt and comprehensive voluntary disclosure of the breach has been made.[88] **2.37**

OTSI cannot issue monetary penalties if criminal proceedings are ongoing (or have taken place) against a business or person for the same breach or where the business or person has already been convicted of an offence in respect of that breach. **2.38**

Before OTSI can impose a civil monetary penalty, the person in breach must be informed that OTSI intends to impose a penalty, the reason for the penalty, the amount in question, the right of the person to make representations, and the date by which those representations must be made. OTSI considers those representations and reviews both the reasons for the decision to impose a monetary penalty and the amount. Outcomes may include reaffirming the decision to impose the monetary penalty, changing the amount of the monetary penalty, or cancelling the decision to impose the monetary penalty. OTSI will then communicate its final decision having considered the representations made. If OTSI's decision remains to impose a monetary penalty, it will inform the recipient of its decision; the right to seek a review; and the date by which the recipient must request OTSI reviews the decision. All monetary penalties are paid into the Consolidated Fund and are recoverable as civil debts. **2.39**

[87] ibid s 6.
[88] ibid.

**2.40** OTSI may publish a report about breaches including naming the individual or business who has committed the breach and providing facts about the breach. The report may include information about specific risks and broader trends to assist other individuals and businesses to comply with sanctions.

## I. Right of Review

### 1. Against OFSI

**2.41** Once OFSI has notified the person that it intends to impose a monetary penalty,[89] there are three opportunities to seek review of the decision: review by the Treasury itself before the penalty is imposed, followed by a review by a Minister of the Crown, and then an appeal to the Upper Tribunal.[90]

**2.42** Before imposing a monetary penalty, the Treasury must notify a person of its intention to do so.[91] At that point, the Treasury must explain the grounds for imposing the penalty, specify the amount of the penalty, explain that the recipient is entitled to make representations, and specify the period within which any such representations must be made.[92] The Treasury appears to have unfettered discretion regarding the time period it imposes for representations to be submitted.

**2.43** The opportunity to make representations by the person regarding their conduct and the amount of any penalty is similar to a response to a US-style 'show cause letter'.[93] The Treasury must consider the representations before making a final decision to impose a monetary penalty and, if it decides to impose one, it must inform the person of its decision, explain that the person is entitled to seek a review by a Minister of the Crown, and specify the period within which the person must inform the Treasury that they seek such a review.[94] Again, the Treasury appears to have unfettered discretion when setting the period within which the person must seek review. 'Minister' means the holder of an office in the UK Government.[95]

**2.44** If, notwithstanding the person's representations as part of the first stage of review, the Treasury imposes a monetary penalty, the person has the right to request a review of the decision by a Minister, currently the Economic Secretary to the Treasury. The Minister

[89] As it must in accordance with PCA 2017, s 147.

[90] See the Tribunal Procedure (Upper Tribunal) Rules 2008, SI 2008/2698 <http://www.legislation.gov.uk/uksi/2008/2698/contents> accessed 22 August 2025.

[91] PCA 2017, s 147(1).

[92] PCA 2017, s 147(2).

[93] See, for example, the practice of the World Bank Group's Integrity Vice Presidency of issuing 'show cause letters' when investigating a respondent for sanctionable practices. Office of Suspension and Debarment, 'Global Directory, Exclusion Summary of WBG Sanctions System' (World Bank Group, July 2021) <https://www.worldbank.org/content/dam/documents/sanctions/office-of-suspension-and-debarment/other-documents/WBG%20Sanctions%20System.pdf> accessed 22 August 2025.

[94] PCA 2017, s 147(3).

[95] PCA 2017, s 147(8).

has the power to uphold the decision to impose the penalty and its amount, uphold the decision but substitute a different amount of penalty, or cancel the decision to impose the penalty altogether.[96]

The outcome of a Ministerial review can be appealed on any ground to the Upper Tribunal.[97] In this third and final stage of review, the Upper Tribunal may quash the Minister's review and, if it does so, it may also quash the Treasury's decision to impose the penalty in the first place. The Upper Tribunal may uphold the Minister's decision but substitute a different amount for that determined by the Treasury or, in a case where the Minister substituted a different amount, by the Minister.[98] The Upper Tribunal procedure rules govern procedure.[99] A notice of appeal must be made in writing and received by the Upper Tribunal no later than 28 days after notice was given of the decision under challenge. Schedule 4 of the Upper Tribunal procedure rules sets out what must be stated in and provided with the notice of appeal. Upper Tribunal decisions may be appealed to the Court of Appeal with permission.[100] **2.45**

Once a monetary penalty is finalized and payable, OFSI will inform the person concerned how they should pay. Payment should be made within 28 working days of the date the penalty has been imposed and should not be unreasonably delayed. **2.46**

The Treasury is under a statutory obligation to publish reports about the imposition of monetary penalties under sections 146 or 148 PCA 2017.[101] OFSI's practice is to publish details of all monetary penalties it imposes, as well as a summary of the case, to help increase awareness, deter future non-compliance, and promote good practice. **2.47**

OFSI may also choose to publish details of breach cases where no monetary penalty has been imposed.[102] **2.48**

## 2. Against OTSI

The procedure for appealing a civil monetary penalty for a breach of trade sanctions is similar to that relating to a breach of financial sanctions. OTSI is under an obligation to tell the appellant what the decision is, the existence of the right to seek a review, and the date by which OTSI must be told that a review has been requested. If a review is requested, the Secretary of State (or delegated authority such as a minister or a senior official who is unconnected with the original decision) will review the monetary penalty and may decide: (i) to uphold the decision to impose a penalty and its amount; **2.49**

[96] PCA 2017, s 147(4).
[97] PCA 2017, s 147(6).
[98] PCA 2017, s 147(7).
[99] Upper Tribunal Procedure Rules 2008 (n 90).
[100] See OFSI, 'Financial Sanctions Enforcement and Monetary Penalties Guidance' (n 49) at ss 6 and 7, for guidance on the process for review and the right to appeal.
[101] PCA 2017, s 149(2).
[102] See OFSI, 'Financial Sanctions Enforcement and Monetary Penalties Guidance' (n 49) at ss 9.2 and 10.

(ii) uphold the decision to impose a penalty, but increase or lower the amount; or (iii) cancel the decision to impose a penalty. Once a review has been sought, an appeal to the Upper Tribunal can be made if the appellant is dissatisfied with the Secretary of State's decision. (See paragraph 2.45.)

## J. Officer of a Body Corporate, Partnership, or Unincorporated Body

**2.50** Where financial sanctions have been breached by a corporate or other 'body', the Treasury may also impose a monetary penalty on an officer of the body if it is satisfied, on the balance of probabilities, that the breach or failure in respect of which the monetary penalty is payable by the body, occurred with the consent or connivance, or was attributable to neglect of an officer.[103]

**2.51** A 'body' is defined as a body corporate, a partnership, or an unincorporated body other than a partnership.[104] In a body corporate, an 'officer of a body' means a director, manager, secretary, or other similar officer of the body or a person purporting to act in any such capacity;[105] in a partnership, it means a partner or a person purporting to act as a partner;[106] and in relation to an unincorporated body other than a partnership, a person who is concerned in the management or control of the body or purports to act in the capacity of a person so concerned.[107]

## K. Licences

**2.52** The power to issue a licence is contained in the sanctions regulations made under SAMLA and can permit otherwise prohibited transactions and prohibited activity to take place in certain circumstances.[108]

**2.53** A licence is a written permission from, for example, OFSI or OTSI[109] allowing an act that would otherwise breach prohibitions imposed by financial and trade sanctions respectively.[110] A licence is not to be confused with an exception to a prohibition that applies automatically in certain defined circumstances, as set out in the regulations.[111]

[103] PCA 2017, s 148(1).
[104] PCA 2017, s 148(2).
[105] PCA 2017, s S.148(2)(a).
[106] PCA 2017, s 148(2)(b).
[107] PCA 2017, s 148(2)(c).
[108] SAMLA 2018, s 15(2)(b) and (3).
[109] See para 2.61 below for a DBT general licence.
[110] See OFSI, 'UK Financial Sanctions General Guidance' (n 28) s 6, particularly s 6.4.
[111] See, for example, reg 58(3) of the Russia Regulations 2019 that disapplies the prohibitions at regs 11 to 13 when a financial institution credits a frozen account with interest of other earnings due on the account.

There are two types of licences: general and specific. A general licence allows multiple parties to undertake specified activities which would otherwise be prohibited by sanctions legislation, without the need for a specific licence. General licences cannot be applied for: they are issued by OFSI on behalf of HM Treasury or DBT and can be varied, suspended, or revoked at any time. Each general licence includes requirements for reporting and record-keeping. Specific licences must be applied for and can only be granted on one or more of the grounds listed in, for example, Schedule 5 of the Russia Regulations in the case of licences relating to financial sanctions (including, for example, basic needs, legal services, extraordinary expenses, and pre-existing judicial decisions). **2.54**

OFSI guidance states that specific licences cannot be granted retroactively, but nothing in the regulations prevents OFSI from issuing a licence with retroactive effect; so, the guidance likely reflects a strategic decision on their part. The policy arguments for OFSI's position are clear: OFSI seeks to avoid the situation where a person falls foul of the prohibitions and seeks retroactive permission for the actions or omissions. Nonetheless, as a matter of law, nothing expressly prevents OFSI from issuing retroactive general licences in order to reduce its workload. **2.55**

In the context of legal fees and financial sanctions (as opposed to legal advisory services and trade sanctions), a licence is not required to provide legal advice to, or to act for, a designated person, subject to cases where the advice could be deemed to constitute an economic resource or fund; a licence is, however, a requirement for any person or organization involved in a transaction with those subject to financial sanctions. Lawyers therefore need a licence in order to receive payment for any work and any related disbursements from or on behalf of a designated person so that they are not in breach of, inter alia, regulation 11 of the Russia Regulations (i.e. dealing with funds owned by a designated person).[112] **2.56**

Over the last three years, a general licence was routinely issued by OFSI to permit payments for legal fees and disbursements incurred in connection with the representation of persons designated under the Russian and Belarusian sanctions regime. This development was unsurprising given the high volume of legal representation required in respect of individuals and entities designated as a result of the UK sanctions regimes against Russia and Belarus. For all other UK sanctions regimes, specific licences had to be sought in order to be paid for legal services. **2.57**

At the time of writing, the latest legal fees general licence was issued on 29 October 2025 (INT/2025/7323088).[113] Previously, the legal services General Licence—the last **2.58**

[112] A similar analysis applies under the EU sanctions framework, whereby lawyers need to obtain a specific licence from the relevant national competent authorities before receiving funds from designated persons.

[113] OFSI and HM Treasury, 'OFSI General Licences' (Collection, 1 January 2021) <https://www.gov.uk/government/collections/ofsi-general-licences> accessed 28 October 2025; General Licence – Legal Services, INT/2025/7323088 <https://assets.publishing.service.gov.uk/media/68f8da6f25d7d8af156dc2ab/INT.2025.7323088_GL.pdf> accessed 26 October 2025.

one being General Licence INT/2025/6160920 which expired on 28 October 2025—applied only to the Russia and Belarus Regulations. General Licence INT/2025/7323088, however, was issued under the UK Autonomous Sanctions Regulations allowing, inter alia, lawyers to receive payment from persons designated under *any* regulations listed in the General Licence for the provision of legal advice, provided that they have met the terms of the licence. General Licence INT/2025/7323088 expires on 28 April 2026. Legal services are defined as those 'provided to a designated person, including legal advice and/or representation in court, whether provided within the UK or another jurisdiction, in relation to any matter except a claim for defamation or malicious falsehood'. A person providing legal services or advice to a DP (designated person) is covered by the definition of a 'Law Firm' within the provisions. The legal services General Licence specifies that any payment must be in relation to legal services which have been provided, or are being provided, by the Law Firm/lawyer to a DP. In other words, the general licence does not on its face authorize receipt of payments from DPs that relate to legal services provided to non-DPs. Where a Law Firm relies upon the general licence, it is subject to a reporting obligation and must, within 14 days of receiving payment for legal services, comply with the requirements at paragraph 9 for Part A or paragraph 12 for Part B.[114]

**2.59** There are separate conditions for payment obligations that predate or post-date designation (each defined as Part A and Part B respectively of the legal fees general licence). Both categories are subject to a total cap of £2,000,000 paid by a designated person on professional legal fees, including counsel's fees[115] for the duration of the licence. It is therefore vital that barristers and solicitors coordinate, so that the cap is not breached.[116]

**2.60** Where a legal services general licence does not apply (for example, where the amounts in question have been exhausted), an application can be made for a specific legal fees licence. The application form is available online.[117] For specific licences, OFSI will expect the instructed law firm to provide a schedule demonstrating the anticipated legal fees and/or those incurred to date. When issuing a licence to permit the payment of professional fees and expenses for the provision of legal services, OFSI is obliged under SAMLA to ensure that those fees and expenses are reasonable. The burden of proving they are reasonable falls on the applicant.[118]

[114] General Licence – Legal Services (n 113).

[115] Inclusive of VAT, should it apply.

[116] Bar Standards Board, 'Sanctions' <https://www.barstandardsboard.org.uk/for-barristers/compliance-with-your-obligations/sanctions.html> accessed 22 August 2025.

[117] OFSI and HM Treasury, 'Licenses That Allow Activity Prohibited by Financial Sanctions' (4 August 2017) <https://www.gov.uk/guidance/licences-that-allow-activity-prohibited-by-financial-sanctions> accessed 22 August 2025.

[118] OFSI, 'Reasonableness in Licensing' (*OFSI Blog*, 30 June 2021) <https://ofsi.blog.gov.uk/2021/06/30/reasonableness-in-licensing/> accessed 22 August 2025.

Other examples of general licences issued by OFSI in the financial sanctions context include the Russian Oil Majors Wind Down[119] and Continuation of Business of PJSC Rosneft Oil Company's German Named Subsidiaries General Licences.[120] OFSI also issued a general licence allowing Arbitrators and Arbitration Associations, including the London Court of International Arbitration, to process payments from designated persons subject to the Russia and Belarus sanctions regimes: INT/2025/5787748. 2.61

In the context of legal advisory services and trade sanctions, the Russia Regulations impose a general prohibition on 'legal advisory services'. The DBT issued its General Trade Licence (Russia sanctions—Legal Advisory Services)[121] on 11 August 2023, which was revoked on 6 September 2024 following a change to the Russia Regulations whereupon it was no longer required.[122] Specifically, the regulatory changes expanded the scope of permitted legal advisory services to include compliance with any UK or non-UK sanctions, Russian counter-measures, and any criminal legislation imposed by any jurisdiction.[123] 2.62

In the trade sanctions context, there are three licensing bodies in DBT responsible for administering licences on behalf of the Secretary of State to carry out activity otherwise prohibited under UK trade sanctions. The relevant body depends on the activity that is to be carried out. From 10 October 2024, OTSI is responsible for licensing relating to the provision of standalone services, including professional and business services. The Import Controls and Sanctions team is responsible for administering licences for the import of goods and associated activities—for example, the provision of ancillary services—that are prohibited under UK import controls or sanctions. Finally, the ECJU is responsible for licensing the export of goods, software and technology from the UK. 2.63

A crucial component of the UK's sanctions framework is the two-tier public law process of review, found in Chapters 2 (Review by appropriate Minister, and other reviews) and 4 (Court reviews) of Part 1 of SAMLA. This process—including the Administrative Court and appellate court decisions to have come out of section 38 of SAMLA (Court reviews of decisions)—is addressed in Chapter 8 of this book. 2.64

[119] INT/2025/7539056 <https://assets.publishing.service.gov.uk/media/68ef66b0e7b6794c076bbe6c/INT-2025-7539056_GL.pdf> accessed 29 October 2025.

[120] INT/2025/7598960 <https://assets.publishing.service.gov.uk/media/68f8794bb391b93d5aa39a38/INT.2025.7598960_.pdf> accessed 29 October 2025.

[121] <https://assets.publishing.service.gov.uk/government/uploads/system/uploads/attachment_data/file/1177398/russia-sanctions-legal-advisory-services-general-trade-licence__1_.pdf> accessed 22 August 2025.

[122] <https://www.gov.uk/government/publications/general-trade-licence-russia-sanctions-legal-advisory-services> accessed 22 August 2025.

[123] Russia Regulations 2019, reg 60DB.

Another key area of the UK sanctions framework, and one that raises many questions in practice, relates to the applicable offences, in particular the financial sanctions offences found in Chapters 1 (Asset freeze etc.) and 2 (Other financial and investment restrictions) of the Russia Regulations. The scope of these key offences is addressed in Chapter 3 of this book. Finally, director disqualification sanctions, trade sanctions, shipping and aircraft sanctions, and human rights sanctions are addressed in Chapters 4, 5, 6, and 7, respectively.

# 3

# Financial Sanctions

*Sophie O'Sullivan and Victoria Turner*



## A. Introduction

Financial sanctions have evolved over time from simple asset freezes into a complex and multifaceted toolbox. In the UK, such measures are imposed either to give domestic effect to UN Security Council (UNSC) Resolutions, or to pursue the Government's own foreign policy and national security objectives. **3.01**

The Foreign, Commonwealth and Development Office (FCDO) is responsible for formulating the UK's international sanctions policy, including financial sanctions. It also drafts legislation to implement these sanctions in the UK, either in compliance with the UK's commitments to the UN, or pursuant to its autonomous powers as set out in the Sanctions and Anti-Money Laundering Act 2018 (SAMLA), as amended. SAMLA sets out the purposes of financial sanctions.[1] **3.02**

[1] Sanctions and Anti-Money Laundering Act 2018 (SAMLA), s 3.


Sophie O'Sullivan and Victoria Turner, *Financial Sanctions* In: *UK Sanctions Law and Practice*. Edited by: Amanda Pinto KC, Alexandre Haines, and Sophie O'Sullivan, Oxford University Press. © Oxford University Press 2026. DOI: 10.1093/oso/9780198964179.003.0003

3.03 The purposes of financial sanctions are stated in OFSI's Financial Sanctions General Guidance[2] to include coercing a regime, or individuals within a regime, into changing their behaviour; constraining a target by denying them access to key resources required to continue their offending behaviour; signalling disapproval and potentially isolating the target by stigmatizing their activity; and protecting misappropriated assets.[3]

3.04 OFSI is responsible for enforcing financial sanctions as well as providing guidance on their implementation. It also issues licences to authorize acts which would otherwise give rise to a breach of financial sanctions measures.

3.05 Financial sanctions will generally:[4]

- target specific individuals or entities—'designated persons'—with asset freezes to restrict their access to funds and economic resources;
- impose restrictions which limit the provision of certain financial services or access to financial markets, funds, and economic resources by designated or named persons, and persons 'connected to' a geographical location, specified groups, or sectors; or,
- make directions to cease all business or dealings with a specified person, group, sector, or country.

3.06 At the time of writing, the most expansive and comprehensive set of financial sanctions imposed by the UK under SAMLA is contained in The Russia (Sanctions) (EU Exit) Regulations 2019 (as amended) (the 'Russia Regulations'). This sanctions regime was first imposed in the UK pursuant to EU legislation in 2014,[5] in response to Russia's annexation of Crimea, and its provisions have substantially expanded over time—particularly since Russia's invasion of Ukraine in February 2022. Given the breadth and complexity of the Russia Regulations, along with their wide and onerous impact on persons and entities with a nexus to the UK, most of the case law, legal guidance, and commentary addressing the UK's autonomous (post-Brexit) sanctions laws has focused on this regime. For these reasons, this chapter examines the UK's financial sanctions framework primarily through the lens of the Russia Regulations, as the legal issues and analysis will (for the most part) be relevant and applicable to all other UK sanctions regimes.

[2] Office of Financial Sanctions Implementation (OFSI), 'UK Financial Sanctions General Guidance' (updated 13 November 2024) <https://www.gov.uk/government/publications/financial-sanctions-general-guidance/uk-financial-sanctions-general-guidance> accessed 4 September 2025.

[3] ibid s 1.1.

[4] ibid. OFSI, 'UK Financial Sanctions General Guidance' (n 2) s 1.3. See also Foreign, Commonwealth and Development Office (FCDO), 'Post-Legislative Scrutiny Memorandum: Sanctions and Anti Money Laundering Act 2018' (CP 1024, March 2024) 9.

[5] Council Regulation (EU) 833/2014 and Council Regulation (EU) 269/2014.

## B. Types of Financial Sanctions

UK financial sanctions are typically categorized by 'regime', each of which comprises a collection of sanctions measures which are imposed for a specific target or set of purposes. A sanctions regime will either target a specific 'geographical issue' and relate primarily to a particular country or region, for example, Russia, Iran, or Libya; or be 'thematic' and relate to a particular issue, such as global anti-corruption, chemical weapons, or cyber activity.[6] 3.07

As each sanctions regime is implemented in response to a particular event or issue, the restrictions set out in regulations are necessarily specific to the purposes they seek to achieve. That said, there is a basket of measures that are collectively termed the 'asset freeze and making available provisions' which are imposed across every UK financial sanctions regime.[7] 3.08

Whilst UK financial sanctions have historically been dominated by the application of asset freezes, there has been a growth of other types of financial sanctions measures, most notably in the Russia Regulations, the Belarus Regulations,[8] the Syria Regulations,[9] and the North Korea Regulations,[10] which include 3.09

- correspondent banking restrictions;
- investment restrictions;
- restrictions relating to the provision of loans and credit;
- insurance and reinsurance related restrictions;[11]
- restrictions relating to transferable securities and money market instruments;
- restrictions on the provision of trust services; and
- restrictions in respect of the provision of financial services relating to foreign exchange reserve and asset management.

These more innovative financial sanctions measures are aimed at targeting specific sectors of economies and the specific revenue streams of those who are the ultimate target of the sanctions programmes.

[6] See FCDO, 'Post-Legislative Scrutiny Memorandum' (n 4) Annex A, for a list of statutory instruments made pursuant to SAMLA. Thematic sanctions regimes are generally inherited from the EU pre-Brexit. Importantly, the EU has enacted a fifth thematic sanctions regime concerning restrictive measures against serious human rights violations and abuses, enacted in December 2020 and currently applicable until 8 December 2026 (unless renewed).

[7] See below at section D, 'Asset Freezes and "Making Available" Restrictions'.

[8] The Republic of Belarus (Sanctions) (EU Exit) Regulations 2019 (as amended).

[9] The Syria (Sanctions) (EU Exit) Regulations 2019 (as amended).

[10] The Democratic People's Republic of Korea (Sanctions) (EU Exit) Regulations 2019 (as amended).

[11] The insurance and reinsurance restrictions can be categorized as either financial or trade restrictions. For example, in the North Korea Regulations they are categorized as financial sanctions measures, whereas in the Russia Regulations they are categorized as trade sanctions measures.

## C. Application of Financial Sanctions

3.10 UK sanctions laws apply to (i) all conduct by any person within the territory of the United Kingdom (including Northern Ireland) or in its territorial sea; and (ii) the conduct of all UK persons, wherever they are in the world.[12]

3.11 The term 'UK persons' encompasses all UK nationals and all bodies incorporated or constituted under the law of any part of the UK, including branches of UK companies operating overseas.[13] The term 'UK nationals' is further defined to include

- British citizens;
- citizens of British Overseas Territories;
- British nationals (overseas) or British Overseas citizens;
- persons who are British subjects;[14] and
- British protected persons.[15]

3.12 UK sanctions may also be imposed, by way of an Order in Council, on companies incorporated or constituted under the law of any of the Channel Islands, the Isle of Man, and any of the British Overseas Territories.

3.13 OFSI guidance is clear that a breach of sanctions does not have to occur within the UK for OFSI to have authority to enforce it.[16] The jurisdictional limit of the UK's sanctions laws is often described in the context of a 'UK nexus', which is to say that the relevant person/activity must have a connection to the UK to be within the enforcement remit of UK authorities. Whilst the OFSI guidance is not prescriptive as to what can constitute a 'UK nexus', it provides some insights. In particular, a 'UK nexus' is likely to be present if (i) an activity takes place (partially or fully) in the UK; (ii) if a UK person is involved in the activity or approves such activity; (iii) if a non-UK company engages in financial transactions using clearing services in the UK; (iv) if an activity takes place overseas but is directed from a company or person within the UK; and (v) if a financial product bought on UK markets is held or used overseas.[17] In its monetary penalty notice in respect of Tracerco Limited in May 2022,[18] OFSI imposed a penalty in relation to activity which took place in the UAE and specifically noted that 'UK financial sanctions can also apply to the actions of UK companies abroad. All companies with a UK

[12] SAMLA 2018, s 21.
[13] ibid.
[14] Pursuant to the British Nationality Act 1981.
[15] ibid.
[16] OFSI, 'Financial Sanctions Enforcement and Monetary Penalties Guidance' (updated 14 November 2024) s 3.2 <https://www.gov.uk/government/publications/financial-sanctions-enforcement-and-monetary-penalties-guidance/financial-sanctions-enforcement-and-monetary-penalties-guidance> accessed 4 September 2025.
[17] ibid s 3.2.
[18] OFSI, Report of Penalty for Breach of Financial Sanctions Regulations (section 149(2) PACA 2017 report), 'Imposition of Monetary Penalty – Tracero Limited' <https://assets.publishing.service.gov.uk/government/uploads/system/uploads/attachment_data/file/1086645/29.06.22_Tracerco_monetary_penaly_notice.pdf> accessed 4 September 2025.

nexus [including through its parent company being a UK incorporated entity] must make sure they comply with the restrictions in place, and this is especially important when operating internationally.'[19] Similarly, in its monetary penalty notice in respect of Herbert Smith Freehills CIS LLP (HSF Moscow),[20] OFSI imposed a penalty on HSF Moscow for payments made in Russia and which related to activity in Russia, the UK nexus being that HSF Moscow was incorporated in the UK.

## D. Asset Freezes and 'Making Available' Restrictions

The most common forms of financial sanctions measures are asset freeze and 'making available' restrictions.[21] In broad terms, these restrictions state that a person within the jurisdiction of UK sanctions (as set out above in paragraphs 3.10–13) must not **3.14**

- deal with funds or economic resources that are owned, held, or controlled by a designated person if they know or have reasonable cause to suspect that they are dealing with such funds or economic resources. This essentially means that a designated person's funds and economic resources must be frozen. It is important to note that the application of an asset freeze does not change the ownership of the funds and economic resources—they remain the asset of the designated person and are not confiscated or seized by OFSI;[22]
- make funds available (i) directly or indirectly, to a designated person; or (ii) to any person for the benefit of a designated person, if they know or have reasonable cause to suspect that they are making such funds available;
- make economic resources available directly or indirectly, to a designated person if they know or have reasonable cause to suspect that they are making such economic resources available, and that the designated person would be likely to exchange the economic resources for (or use them in exchange for), funds, goods, or services; and
- make economic resources available to any person for the benefit of a designated person, if they know or have reasonable cause to suspect that they are making such economic resources available.

There are several components to these restrictions which we examine in further detail in section D.1 on 'Designation Criteria'.

[19] ibid para 14.
[20] OFSI, 'Imposition of Monetary Penalty: Herbert Smith Freehills CIS LLP (HSF Moscow)' (20 March 2025) <https://assets.publishing.service.gov.uk/media/67dae19a1a60f79643028472/200325_HSF_PENALTY_NOTICE.pdf> accessed 4 September 2025.
[21] See for example, the Russia (Sanctions) (EU Exit) Regulations 2019, regs 11–15.
[22] OFSI, 'UK Financial Sanctions General Guidance' (13 February 2024) <https://www.gov.uk/government/publications/financial-sanctions-general-guidance/uk-financial-sanctions-general-guidance> accessed 4 September 2025.

## 1. Designation Criteria

3.15 The asset freeze and making available restrictions are targeted at designated persons. Designated persons are individuals and entities that are designated pursuant to the specific designation criteria set out in each UK sanctions programme. Designations are made by the Secretary of State and typically take place by way of designating a specific person or entity directly by name.[23] However, in the Russia Regulations, the Secretary of State is also given the power to designate by description,[24] enabling all members of a specified group to be designated. The power to enable designation by description is set out in section 12 of SAMLA and was first used by the UK Government in March 2022, when the Russia Regulations were amended to reflect the inclusion of designation by description.[25]

## 2. Sanctions Lists

3.16 The FCDO decides on a person or entity's designation. Once this is done, the designated person or entity is added to the FCDO's 'UK Sanctions List'.[26] The UK Sanctions List is a comprehensive list of all persons, entities, aircraft, and ships that are designated or specified under UK sanctions. As such, the list is broader than those that are subject to the asset freeze and making available provisions.

3.17 OFSI also maintains a 'Consolidated List' of asset freeze targets.[27] This list contains the names of all persons and entities that have been identified as designated persons and which are subject to the asset freeze and making available restrictions. From 28 January 2026, the UK Sanctions List will be the only sanctions list which details sanctions designations published by the UK Government, and the Consolidated List will be made redundant.[28]

3.18 Both the FCDO's UK Sanctions List and OFSI's Consolidated List detail all designated persons; however, the information contained within each list may vary. (For example, alternative aliases may be listed.)

23 See for example, the Yemen (Sanctions) (EU Exit) (No 2) Regulations 2020, reg 5.

24 Russia Regulations, reg 5(1A).

25 See the Russia (Sanctions) (EU Exit) (Amendment) (No 7) Regulations 2022, reg 5. See also Chapter 8, 'Designations and Challenges', paras 8.16–18.

26 FCDO, 'The UK Sanctions List' (6 July 2020) <https://www.gov.uk/government/publications/the-uk-sanctions-list> accessed 4 September 2025.

27 OFSI and HM Treasury, 'Financial Sanctions Targets: List of All Asset Freeze Targets' <https://www.gov.uk/government/publications/financial-sanctions-consolidated-list-of-targets/consolidated-list-of-targets> accessed 4 September 2025.

28 FCDO, HM Treasury, and OFSI, 'Moving to a Single List for UK Sanctions Designations, 28 January 2026' (Guidance, 13 October 2023) <https://www.gov.uk/guidance/moving-to-a-single-list-for-uk-sanctions-designations-28-january-2026> accessed 21 October 2025.

## 3. Definitions

There are a number of key definitions to be aware of when considering the asset freeze and making available provisions. 3.19

'Funds' is very broadly defined in SAMLA as meaning 'financial assets and benefits of every kind, including (but not limited to)—(a) cash, cheques, claims on money, drafts money orders and other payment instruments; (b) deposits, balances on accounts, debts and debt obligations; (c) publicly and privately traded securities and debt instruments, including stocks and shares, certificates representing securities, bonds, notes, warrants, debentures and derivative products; (d) interest, dividends and other income on or value accruing from or generated by assets; (e) credit, rights of set-off, guarantees, performance bonds and other financial commitments; (f) letters of credit, bills of lading and bills of sale; (g) documents providing evidence of an interest in funds or financial resources; (h) any other instrument of export financing'.[29] 3.20

'Economic resources' means 'assets of every kind, whether tangible or intangible, movable or immovable, which are not funds but can be used to obtain funds, goods or services'.[30] This may include things like property, vehicles, aircraft, antiques, precious metals, jewellery, etc. OFSI also clarified in its enforcement action against Hong Kong International Wine and Spirits Competition Limited that bottles of wine are tangible economic resources and, interestingly, that the provision of publicity is an intangible economic resource.[31] This was on the basis that providing publicity to a designated person gives them the opportunity to generate funds. In addition, the definition of 'economic resources' is wide and needs to be considered in a broad sense, particularly in the context of intangible economic resources. OFSI determined in its enforcement action against Telia Carrier UK Limited that the provision of international telephone calls to a designated person (in this case a corporate entity) amounted to the provision of an economic resource on the basis that it could be used to generate income.[32] 3.21

The 'freezing' of funds and economic resources is defined as preventing such funds or economic resources from being dealt with.[33] 3.22

Funds are 'dealt with' if '(a) they are used, altered, moved, transferred or if access to them is allowed, (b) they are dealt with in any other way that would result in any change in volume, amount, location, ownership, possession, character or destination, or 3.23

[29] SAMLA 2018, s 60(1).
[30] SAMLA 2018, s 60(2).
[31] OFSI, Report of Penalty for Breach of Financial Sanctions Regulations (section 149(2) PACA 2017 report), 'Imposition of Monetary Penalty – Hong Kong International Wine and Spirits Competition Ltd' <https://assets.publishing.service.gov.uk/government/uploads/system/uploads/attachment_data/file/1106745/Notice_of_Imposition_of_MP_-_HKIWSC.pdf> accessed 4 September 2025.
[32] OFSI, Report of Penalty for Breach of Financial Sanctions Regulations (section 149(2) PACA 2017 report), 'Imposition of Monetary Penalty – Telia Carrier UK Limited' <https://assets.publishing.service.gov.uk/government/uploads/system/uploads/attachment_data/file/842548/Telia_monetary_penalty.pdf> accessed 4 September 2025.
[33] SAMLA 2018, s 60(3) and (4).

(c) any other change is made that would enable [the funds to be used], including portfolio management'.[34] However, it is worth noting the potential conflict between judicial interpretation of what might include 'dealing with funds' in the context of a debt: in *Libyan Investment Authority v Maud*—a case decided before SAMLA 2018—the Court of Appeal found that '[p]aying the debt is not dealing with the instrument itself in any real sense; it is simply performing the obligation to which it gives rise. That can be seen as providing funds which are otherwise not available to the recipient'.[35] In contrast, Bright J in *LLC Eurochem v Société Générale SA*—having determined that *Maud* had not been decided under UK domestic regulations—'confess[ed] that [he found] the reasoning of the Court of Appeal in [Maud] difficult to follow at some points' and that he found 'it quite difficult not to see these banking processes as a form of dealing with the instrument'.[36] *Eurochem* sets out a number of distinguishing factors that go a certain way to resolving any conflict, including that the issues in *Maud* arose in relation to the EU Libya Regulation, not the Russia Regulations.

**3.24** Economic resources are 'dealt with' if they are exchanged for (or used in exchange for) funds, goods, or services, including by being pledged as security or otherwise.[37] However, '[t]he everyday use by a designated person of their own economic resources for personal consumption is not prohibited'.[38]

**3.25** References to funds and economic resources being 'owned, held or controlled' by a person include

- where a 'person has any legal or equitable interest, regardless of whether the interest is held jointly with another person and regardless of whether any other person holds an interest in the funds or economic resources;'[39]
- 'any tangible property (other than real property), or bearer security, that is comprised in funds or economic resources and is in the possession of the [designated] person';[40]
- funds or economic resources that are owned, held, or controlled by a person who is in turn owned or controlled (directly or indirectly) by a designated person.[41]

**3.26** The notion of 'making available' is not defined in UK sanctions legislation. The Council of the EU General Secretariat has, however, published guidance on the effective implementation of restrictive measures, in which it broadly defined 'making available' in the following terms:[42]

[34] SAMLA 2018, s 60(3).
[35] *Libyan Investment Authority v Maud* [2016] EWCA Civ 788 [18].
[36] *LLC Eurochem v Société Générale SA* [2025] EWHC 1938 (Comm) [395]–[6].
[37] SAMLA 2018, s 60(4).
[38] OFSI, 'UK Financial Sanctions General Guidance' (n 2) s 3.1.3.
[39] Russia Regulations 2019, reg 11(6).
[40] ibid.
[41] Russia Regulations 2019, reg 11(7).
[42] Council of the EU, EU Doc 11623/24 (3 July 2024): EU Best Practices for the effective implementation of restrictive measure <https://data.consilium.europa.eu/doc/document/ST-11623-2024-INIT/en/pdf> accessed 4 September 2025.

- 'Making funds available to a designated person or entity, be it by way of payment for goods and services, as a donation, in order to return funds previously held under a contractual arrangement, or otherwise, is generally prohibited unless it is authorized by the competent authority pursuant to the relevant derogation provided for in the Regulation.'[43]
- 'Making economic resources available to a designated person or entity, including by gift, sale, barter, or returning economic resources held or controlled by a third party to a designated owner, is prohibited.'[44] This does not include 'assets which are only suitable for personal use or consumption' which cannot, therefore, 'be used by a designated person to obtain funds, goods or services.'[45]

The term 'made available' has also been interpreted by the European Court of Justice (ECJ) as having a 'wide meaning' in that 'it encompasses all the acts necessary under the applicable national law if a person is effectively to obtain full power of disposal' in relation to the economic resource concerned.[46] The fact that economic resources are made available against payment of a consideration which may be regarded as adequate is, therefore, irrelevant.[47] **3.27**

In the context of the 'making funds or economic resources available for the benefit of a designated person' provisions, funds/economic resources are deemed to be 'made available for the benefit of a designated person only if that person obtains, or is able to obtain, a significant financial benefit.'[48] 'Financial benefit includes the discharge (partial or full) of a financial obligation for which the designated person is wholly or partly responsible,'[49] however, the term 'significant' is not defined in the legislation. In addition, the concept of making funds or economic resources 'available indirectly to a designated person' includes 'making them available to a person who is owned or controlled directly or indirectly [ ... ] by a designated person.'[50] **3.28**

The courts have considered the concepts of 'making available' and 'dealing with' in specific contexts, as well as the asset freeze provisions more generally, and have confirmed the following: **3.29**

- A judgment can be lawfully entered into for a designated person, and creating a judgment debt as a result does not 'make funds available' to a designated person (although enforcing the debt would).[51]
- UK sanctions do not curtail the right of access to the court, including the right to obtain a money judgment.[52]

43 ibid para 49. Emphasis added.
44 ibid para 57. Emphasis added.
45 ibid para 58.
46 Judgment in *Möllendorf*, EU:C:2006:596, s 51.
47 ibid ss 51, 56, 58, and 59.
48 See Russia Regulations 2019, reg 15(4).
49 See Russia Regulations 2019, reg 13(4).
50 See e.g. Russia Regulations 2019, reg 14(4).
51 *Mints v PJSC National Bank Trust and PJSC Bank Otkritie Financial Corporation* [2023] EWCA Civ 1132.
52 ibid.

- The imposition of an asset freeze does not prevent a designated person from having access to justice, even if it makes paying legal representatives more difficult.[53]
- Designated persons retain all their civic rights, including full access to the courts and entitlement to have their rights determined by the court.[54]
- When exercising its discretion on whether to grant an order in favour of a designated person, such as an order for security for costs, the courts should take into account that such an order may create a risk to a party subject to that order of breaching sanctions prohibitions in other jurisdictions, such as the EU, and thereby a risk of civil or criminal penalties overseas.[55]
- Administration proceedings, including access to insolvency proceedings, do not give rise to a breach of sanctions as they do not, in and of themselves, involve 'dealing with' the funds or economic resources of designated persons. Similarly, the appointment of administrators by a court does not, in and of itself, make funds or economic resources available to or for the benefit of a designated person,[56] albeit the underlying activities required for the insolvency/administration activity to occur would involve such dealings and a licence would be required for such actions.
- Financial obligations owed to a designated person (e.g. rental payments) remain owed and payable where the contract or agreement which established the payment obligation was entered into before the date of designation. This is pursuant to the prior obligations exception in UK sanctions regulations (e.g. section 58(5) of the Russia Regulations), which should be read consistently with the corresponding exception in EU sanctions legislation which was transposed into UK law after Brexit.[57]

**3.30** The courts have also considered the impacts of asset freeze measures and whether the measures are proportionate when they infringe on fundamental rights granted by the European Convention on Human Rights (ECHR), notably Article 1 of Protocol No 1 (right to peaceful enjoyment of personal property) and Article 8 (right to private and family life). The Supreme Court, in handing down its first judgment addressing UK sanctions laws under SAMLA 2018 in *Shvidler (Appellant) v Secretary of State for Foreign, Commonwealth and Development Affairs (Respondent)*,[58] has stated that 'in deciding whether the [asset freeze] measures are proportionate the court has to consider the balance to be struck between two incommensurate values: the Convention rights engaged and the interests of the community relied on to justify interfering with them'.[59] The Supreme Court held that the court is able to assess the impact of sanctions

[53] *Barclays Bank Plc v VEB.RF* [2024] EWHC 1074 (Comm) para 51.
[54] *Sergey Taruta v Jsc Vtb Bank* [2022] BVIHCMAP2021/0043.
[55] *LLC Eurochem North-West-2 v Societe Generale SA* [2023] EWHC 2720 (Comm) para 30.
[56] *KRF Services (UK) Ltd* [2024] EWHC 2978 (Ch) paras 97–9.
[57] *Chanana v Khan* [2025] EWHC 1472.
[58] *Shvidler (Appellant) v Secretary of State for Foreign, Commonwealth and Development Affairs (Respondent)* [2025] UKSC 30.
[59] ibid para 126.

on those made subject to them. However, the court also noted that the UK Government has 'special constitutional responsibilities, by contrast with those of a court, in relation to steps taken in an effort to respond to and contain Russia's invasion of Ukraine. They also have superior institutional competence to make the relevant assessment whether the sanctions imposed in these cases may serve some useful purpose in responding to and containing Russia's actions.'[60] Therefore, the government 'should be accorded a wide margin of appreciation' when imposing sanctions and making judgments as to whether the objective of an asset freeze (or other sanctions measures) is 'sufficiently important to justify the limitation of a fundamental right'.[61] (Also see Chapter 8, 'Designations and Challenges' at paragraphs 8.43–5.)

In addition, the majority of the Supreme Court held that asset freezes have to be 'severe and open-ended if they are to be effective'.[62] Those made subject to an asset freeze should be prevented from enjoying their assets and while the effect can be devastating and disrupting, and a previously luxurious lifestyle can be impacted, this does not lead to a breach of human rights.[63] 3.31

By contrast, Leggatt LJ, in his dissenting judgment on *Shvidler*, stated: 3.32

> Making it a criminal offence for an individual who has done nothing unlawful to deal with any of his own assets without the government's permission, and imposing this sanction without any geographical or temporal limit, is a serious invasion of liberty. The court on an application for judicial review of such a measure should require cogent reasons to justify it.[64]

## 4. Ownership and Control

As detailed above at paragraph 3.25, in addition to the prohibitions and restrictions expressly relating to designated persons, the asset freeze and making available restrictions also apply to any entity that is 'owned or controlled' by a designated person. Whilst the UK Government has indicated that it will look to designate owned and controlled entities in their own rights where possible,[65] such entities are often not directly designated. When that is the case, these entities will not appear on the FCDO's 'UK Sanctions List' or OFSI's 'Consolidated List' even though they are subject to the asset freeze and making available restrictions.[66] 3.33

Unlike EU legislation, SAMLA does not provide a definition for ownership and control, but section 62(5) of SAMLA permits specific definitions of ownership and control 3.34

[60] ibid para 127.
[61] ibid para 130.
[62] ibid para 213.
[63] ibid paras 210–11.
[64] ibid para 254. (See also Chapter 8, 'Designations and Challenges' at paragraphs 8.51–8.)
[65] OFSI, 'UK Financial Sanctions General Guidance' (n 2) s 4.1.
[66] The same holds true under EU sanctions regimes. However, the ownership and control test differs in the EU.

to be inserted into each sanctions regulation.[67] The definitions provided in specific regulations to date have adopted identical provisions, which set out the meaning of ownership and control of an entity by a designated person. These definitions are repeated and expanded upon in OFSI's 'UK Financial Sanctions General Guidance'.

**3.35** In essence, an entity is determined to be owned or controlled by a person if either the ownership or control condition is met.

(i) Ownership

**3.36** Ownership is the first of the two conditions, and this is established by one or more of the following being demonstrated:[68]

- the person holds (directly or indirectly) more than 50 per cent of the shares in an entity;
- the person holds (directly or indirectly) more than 50 per cent of the voting rights in an entity; or
- the person has the right (directly or indirectly) to appoint or remove a majority of the board of directors of the entity.

**3.37** Each sanctions regulation has a schedule which contains additional information on how to interpret the ownership conditions.[69] This additional information generally covers the following:

- If two or more persons hold a share or a voting right jointly, then each of them is treated as holding the share or voting right.
- If shares or rights held by a person are subject to a joint arrangement with another person who holds shares or rights in the entity, then each individual is treated as holding the combined shares or rights. A joint arrangement is defined as any arrangement (including any scheme, agreement, or understanding, whether or not it is legally enforceable) between the two parties that they will exercise all or substantially all their rights in a way that is pre-determined by their arrangement.
- Shares held by a person ('A') as a nominee for another person ('B') are treated as held by the other person (B) and not the nominee (A). In addition, if a right is held by one person but is controlled by a designated person, the designated person is treated as holding the right. (Note that if both parties have a joint arrangement in place, both parties will be deemed to hold the right.)
- The calculation of the required shareholding is specifically in relation to a holding of more than 50 per cent of the shares in the issued share capital. If the entity does

[67] The EU published detailed guidance on the notions of ownership and control. See Council of the EU, EU Doc 11623/24 (n 42); EU Commission consolidated FAQs on the implementation of EU Regulation No 833/2014 and No 269/2014, as regularly updated.

[68] See e.g. Russia Regulations 2019, reg 7.

[69] See e.g. Russia Regulations 2019, sch 1.

not have a share capital then a reference to 'holding shares' is to holding a right or rights to share in the capital or profits of the person.

- It is important to note that OFSI has stated that, when making an assessment in relation to ownership and whether the 50 per cent threshold is exceeded, OFSI would not aggregate different designated persons' holdings in a company, unless they are subject to a joint arrangement, as described above.[70] As such, if two individual designated persons each hold 30 per cent of the share capital of an entity, then the threshold for ownership will not necessarily be met as neither individual owns more than 50 per cent. However, if those two individuals had entered into a joint arrangement, or one controlled the rights conferred on the other, or the shares were in fact held jointly between the two, then the entity would be captured by the ownership rules and therefore be subject to the asset freeze and making available restrictions.
- Adopting a difference approach, the EU aggregates holdings of different designated persons and, although not binding, the European Commission's FAQs on Russian sanctions explicitly state: 'One should take into account the aggregated ownership of the entity. For example, if one listed person owns 30% of the entity and another listed person owns 25% of the entity, the entity should be considered as owned by listed persons.'[71] Although the UK and EU were historically aligned on this issue with the UK's stance derived from its pre-Brexit guidance, it is not anticipated that the EU's position on this issue will soon be adopted by the UK. The UK's stance on aggregated ownership is long established and it would be a material shift for the UK courts to now adopt the EU approach.
- Shares or rights can be held directly or indirectly. If the designated person holds a share or right in one entity, which in turn holds shares/rights in a second entity (or in a longer chain of persons), such shares or rights are held indirectly. Where a majority stake is held at each level in the chain, the designated person is deemed to indirectly hold the shares or rights of each entity in the chain.
- The right to appoint or remove a majority of the board of directors is defined as meaning the right to appoint or remove directors that hold the majority of voting rights at board meetings on all or substantially all matters. If there is no board of directors, then the equivalent management body would apply.

Whilst ownership is often thought of as the easiest of the two conditions for ownership and control to be demonstrated, it can often require detailed analysis of corporate structures and arrangements between shareholders. Complex arrangements can require detailed analysis and review, and careful consideration of the requirements of the regulations and their accompanying schedules is likely to be required. **3.38**

[70] OFSI, 'UK Financial Sanctions FAQs' (1 May 2024) question 4 <https://www.gov.uk/government/publications/uk-financial-sanctions-faqs/uk-financial-sanctions-faqs> accessed 4 September 2025.

[71] EU FAQs (n 67) s B.1 'Asset Freeze', question 8.

(ii) Control

**3.39** Control is the second of the two conditions by which an entity may be caught by the regulations. Where a designated person has a minority (or no apparent) interest in an entity such that the ownership condition is not met, it is still necessary to consider whether the designated person controls the entity.[72]

**3.40** At the time of writing, the control condition is typically stated within each sanctions regulation as follows:[73]

> It is reasonable, having regard to all the circumstances, to expect that P [a person] would (if P chose to) be able, in most cases or in significant respects, by whatever means and whether directly or indirectly, to achieve the result that affairs of [the company] are conducted in accordance with P's wishes.

**3.41** The definition of control is broad and can cause significant difficulty when assessing whether an entity is captured by an asset freeze on an individual designated person. Control requires an assessment beyond the corporate structure and can require evaluation of a range of information. OFSI's 'Financial Sanctions General Guidance' has set out what control could include, but it is not an exhaustive list:

- appointing, solely by exercising one's voting rights, a majority of the members of the administrative, management or supervisory bodies of an entity, who have held office during the present and previous financial year
- controlling alone, pursuant to an agreement with other shareholders in, or members of an entity, a majority of shareholders' or members' voting rights in that entity
- having the right to exercise a dominant influence over an entity, pursuant to an agreement entered into with that entity, or to a provision in its Memorandum or Articles of Association, where the law governing that entity permits it being subject to such agreement or provision
- having the right to exercise a dominant influence referred to in the point above, without being the holder of that right (including by means of a front company)
- having the ability to direct another entity in accordance with one's wishes. This can be through any means, directly or indirectly. For example, it is possible that a designated person may have control or use of another person's bank accounts or economic resources and may be using them to circumvent financial sanctions.[74]

**3.42** Since 2022, significant judicial consideration has been given to the concept of control in this context. This has led to the development of judicial commentary on the scope and application of the ownership and control test and further, more specific guidance from the UK Government.

[72] OFSI, 'UK Financial Sanctions General Guidance' (n 2) s 4.1.2.
[73] See e.g. Russia Regulations 2019, reg 7(4).
[74] OFSI, 'UK Financial Sanctions General Guidance' (n 2) s 4.1.

(iii) OFSI guidance

Assessments of ownership and control can be difficult and complex. Getting it wrong can result in sanctions breaches being committed because asset freeze measures are not implemented or adhered to. Comprehensive due diligence is often required. The level of due diligence that should be undertaken is not prescribed in legislation or guidance and will vary depending on the relationship with the entity (or designated person) in question. In response to industry requests for clarity on OFSI's expectations in this regard, OFSI set out further guidance relating to ownership and control in its 'Financial Sanctions Enforcement and Monetary Penalties Guidance'.[75] **3.43**

OFSI's guidance on ownership and control states that where a breach of sanctions arises as a result of an incorrect assessment of ownership and control, OFSI will consider the degree of due diligence carried out as well as the quality of that due diligence. OFSI will consider appropriate due diligence conducted on the ownership and control of an entity to be a mitigating factor where the ownership and control determination reached was made in good faith and was a reasonable conclusion to draw from such due diligence. OFSI may also consider a failure to carry out appropriate due diligence on the ownership and control of an entity, or the carrying out of any such due diligence in bad faith, as an aggravating factor. **3.44**

OFSI has stated in its 'Financial Sanctions Enforcement and Monetary Penalties Guidance' that demonstration of the following due diligence efforts will potentially amount to mitigating factors when a breach arises: **3.45**

- an examination of the formal ownership and control mechanisms of an entity to establish whether there is available evidence of ownership and control by a designated person
- an examination of actual, or the potential for, influence or de facto control over an entity by a designated person
- open-source research on an entity and any persons with ownership of, or the ability to exercise control over, the entity, together with an examination of whether such persons are, or have links to, designated persons such that further investigation may be warranted
- direct contact with the entity and/or other relevant entities to probe into indirect or de facto control, including, where appropriate, seeking commitments by UK persons as to the role of any designated person or person with links to a designated person [It should be noted that OFSI will consider a party's contractual or commercial relationship with a designated person, or the entity that may be owned or controlled by the designated person, when considering whether the level of due diligence conducted is reasonable. Where there is a direct relationship with the party in question, greater direct engagement will be expected.]
- regular checks and/or ongoing monitoring of the above where appropriate.[76]

[75] OFSI, 'Financial Sanctions Enforcement and Monetary Penalties Guidance' (n 16) s 3F.
[76] OFSI, 'Financial Sanctions Enforcement and Monetary Penalties Guidance' (n 16) s 3F.

3.46 In addition, OFSI has set out examples of the types of information that could be gathered and areas of enquiry which could be made when assessing whether ownership or control is established:

## Formal ownership and/or control

1. the percentage of shares and/or voting power of shareholders
2. the ownership and distribution of other shares in a company
3. whether ownership / shareholding has recently been altered or divested, including in possible anticipation or response to the imposition of financial sanctions. If so, consideration of whether this warrants further investigation into the possibility of joint arrangements or indirect or de facto control
4. the composition of shares, and whether shares have been split into different classes, or other structural changes made
5. whether changes to ownership and/or control were part of a pre-planned or wider business/financial strategy
6. corporate constitutional documents, including articles of association or constitution
7. any commercial justifications for complex ownership and control structures
8. agreements between shareholders or between any shareholders and the entity (for example, shareholders, joint venture, operating, or guarantee agreements)[77]

## Indirect or de facto control

1. indications of continued influence (or the potential for it) by a designated person, including through personal connections and financial relationships
2. the presence or involvement of proxies, including persons holding assets on behalf of a designated person
3. ownership, holdings of shares, or control by trusts associated with a designated person
4. if shares or other ownership interests of a designated person have been divested, the nature of any relationships and prior involvement of the person benefitting
5. if applicable, how recent transfers of shares were funded and whether this was done at an accurate and true valuation
6. any operational steps taken to ensure that the designated person cannot exercise control over the entity and/or that the designated person cannot benefit from, or use, corporate assets

[77] ibid.

7. information relating to the circumstances of board and/or management appointments, including the backgrounds, relevant experience, and relationships with designated persons
8. the running of board meetings and governance processes, including board or shareholders' meeting minutes concerning recent changes in the entity's ownership and control relating to the designated person
9. ongoing financial liabilities directly related to a designated person, for example, personal loans, loan guarantees, property holdings, equipment etc.
10. other shareholder agreements, voting agreements, put or call options or other coordination agreements in place between the entity and the designated person or controlled entities
11. whether there are any benefits conferred to the designated person by the entity or transactions between the entity and the designated person[78]

The above factors are intended to be a guide and are not an exhaustive list of all areas of due diligence which could be relevant. Each ownership and control assessment must be based on its own facts and merits. In addition, ownership and control assessments are made at a specific point in time and therefore must be kept under review and be subject to on-going monitoring. **3.47**

### (iv) Case law and further guidance

Since 2022, the application of the concepts of ownership and control has been subject to greater judicial scrutiny. **3.48**

#### *a)* Hmicho v Barclays Bank Plc

One of the first court judgments to consider concepts of ownership and control related to the concept of control between spouses, rather than in the context of a corporate organization.[79] **3.49**

In the case of *Hmicho*, the claimant, Elaine Hmicho, sought an interim mandatory injunction to restore access to her three personal bank accounts, which the bank had frozen. The bank had frozen the accounts due to suspicions that payments made into them by her husband were made with the intention of circumventing sanctions imposed on him via the UK's sanctions programme in relation to Syria. The claimant's husband had been made subject to an asset freeze and, having identified this, the bank took action to freeze the accounts it held for Mr Hmicho.[80] The bank also identified the following: **3.50**

[78] ibid.

[79] *Hmicho v Barclays Bank Plc* [2015] EWHC 1757 (QB).

[80] At this time, EU sanctions were applicable in the UK, and the asset freeze was imposed via Council Implementing Regulation 2015, SI 2015/375 and Council Implementing Regulation 2015, SI 2015/780. It is noted that the asset freeze was later removed.

- the designated person (Mr Hmicho) had third-party rights over his wife's account as well as online banking access to her accounts;
- the majority of funds into the claimant's accounts appeared to originate from the designated person, with some deposits taking place immediately before and after his designation in the EU; and
- there were substantial and unexplained cash deposits into the claimant's accounts as well as some unexplained bank transfers to the claimant's accounts held at another bank.

**3.51** As a result, the bank froze the claimant's accounts on the basis that (i) there was evidence that the designated person had transferred funds to his wife in order to circumvent sanctions; (ii) there were concerns that the unexplained withdrawals of funds to her account at another bank were an attempt to make funds available to or for the benefit of the designated person; and (iii) there were reasons to suspect that the funds in her accounts in fact belonged to, or were controlled by, the designated person. The claimant sought to argue that the funds transferred to her were gifts and her husband did not own or control them.

**3.52** The court refused the claimant's application. The following key points are worthy of note:

- The court could not 'have the necessary "high degree of assurance" that [the bank's] suspicion is unreasonable'[81] and could not 'have a high degree of assurance that were [the bank] to unfreeze [the accounts] and release the funds in those accounts, [the bank] would not thereby be making the funds available, directly or indirectly to' a designated person or for their benefit.[82]
- The court could not 'have the necessary "high degree of assurance" that [the bank] is not entitled to hold the reasonable suspicion that the funds in the accounts [ … ] belong to, or are owned or controlled by' a designated person.[83]
- Being a spouse of a designated person doesn't automatically mean that funds belonging to the spouse can be assumed to be owned or controlled by the designated person—there must be more than just marital status to evidence ownership and control.
- The 'balance of convenience [ … ] rests very firmly on [the bank's] side rather than [the claimant's]' and it was not appropriate for the court to make an order requiring the bank to take action (unfreezing the accounts) which might render it criminally liable for a sanctions breach.[84] As such, the risk for a party, such as financial institution, committing a criminal offence outweighs the inconvenience to a person whose funds are frozen in compliance with sanctions legislation.

[81] *Hmicho* (n 79) para 65.
[82] *Hmicho* (n 79) para 68.
[83] *Hmicho* (n 79) para 69.
[84] *Hmicho* (n 79) para 69.

### *b)* Mints v PJSC National Bank Trust and PJSC Bank Otkritie Financial Corporation

The Court of Appeal judgment in *Mints* is significant as it considered, amongst other matters, the scope and application of the ownership and control provisions in the context of the Russia Regulations.[85] **3.53**

The judgment followed a long-running commercial dispute which commenced in 2019, before the Russian invasion of Ukraine in 2022. The defendants, PJSC National Bank Trust (NBT) and PJSC Bank Otkritie ('Bank Otkritie') brought civil proceedings against a number of individuals, including Boris Mints, Dmitry Mints, Alexander Mints, Igor Mints, and others (together referred to as 'Mints'). The case had been progressing in the UK High Court at the time of Russia's invasion of Ukraine. Following the invasion, the UK Government designated a number of Russian individuals and entities pursuant to the Russia Regulations. Importantly, this included Vladmir Putin (designated on 25 February 2022), Bank Otkritie (designated on 28 February 2022), and Elvira Nabiullina (the governor of the Central Bank of Russia, designated on 30 September 2022). **3.54**

NBT was not listed as a designated person. Both Bank Otkritie and NBT were majority owned by the Central Bank of Russia, which was not listed as a designated person. Instead, the Central Bank was subject to other targeted financial sanctions (as discussed later, in paragraph 3.124). **3.55**

One of the issues which the court had to consider was whether NBT was caught by an asset freeze restriction. On 27 January 2023, the UK High Court determined that NBT was not 'owned or controlled' by a designated person.[86] Mints had sought to argue that NBT was owned or controlled by either Vladmir Putin or Elvira Nabiullina and as such the asset freezes they were subject to extended to NBT. The question turned on the interpretation of the control test and whether a designated person can be deemed to control an entity through their political office. The High Court determined that the asset freeze provisions which applied to Vladmir Putin or Elvira Nabiullina appeared to be primarily designed to operate at a personal level and that control through political office was unlikely to be the intention of the sanctions regulations.[87] **3.56**

The issue of how the control test should be interpreted was considered by the Court of Appeal which made a number of key observations, albeit obiter: **3.57**

- The High Court's conclusion that the control test (regulation 7(4) of the Russia Regulations) had a carve-out for political office was not borne out by the clear and plain language of the regulation. There is nothing in the regulation which limits 'control' to only a personal capacity, and finding that 'control' is not interpreted as being exercised through public office or a political position would involve 'reading into the rule words which are simply not there'.[88]

[85] *Mints v PJSC National Bank Trust* [2023] EWCA Civ 1132.
[86] *PJSC National Bank Trust v Mints* [2023] EWHC 118 (Comm).
[87] ibid para 238.
[88] *Mints* (n 85) para 226.

- If it was intended that there should be a carve-out so that an asset freeze on an individual would not extend through their political office, then the legislation should expressly address this.[89]
- If the consequence of giving the control test its correct meaning (based on its language) was that every company in Russia could be considered to be controlled by Vladmir Putin, the remedy for this would be for the executive and parliament to amend the legislation to avoid such a consequence. It is not for the courts to 'put a gloss on the language' to avoid the consequence.[90]
- Any absurd consequences of the application of the asset freeze and making available restrictions, via the ownership and control rules, were created not from the interpretation of the rules but from the UK Government designating Vladimir Putin without giving thought to the potential consequences. The Court of Appeal noted that 'Putin is at the apex of a command economy' and 'in a very real sense [...] could be deemed to control everything in Russia'.[91] Similarly, the court noted that Elvira Nabiullina could be deemed to control either of the banks involved in the litigation due to the fact the Central Bank of Russia, of which she was governor, held majority stakes in them.

**3.58** This judgment gave a very broad (albeit *obiter* and therefore not binding) view of the application and interpretation of the ownership and control rules and raised significant questions about how the asset freeze and making available restrictions should be applied. It is notable that the court did not appear to consider that the control test at regulation 7(4) of the Russia Regulations (and indeed in all UK sanctions regimes) requires it to be 'reasonable, having regard to all the circumstances' to determine that a designated person controls another person or entity. Further, the judgment did not clarify the basis upon which it had determined that Vladimir Putin could *reasonably* be said to control everything in Russia such that all of its affairs are conducted in accordance with his wishes.

*c)* Litasco SA v (i) Der Mond Oil and Gas Africa SA & (ii) Locafrique Holding SA

**3.59** Adding to the ambiguity was the judgment in the High Court matter of *Litasco*.[92] This case arose from a commercial and contractual dispute between the parties, with the claimant making an application for summary judgment for sums it said were due to it under agreements made in November 2022.

**3.60** Litasco SA was not a designated person. It was a Swiss company owned by PSJC Lukoil, which was also not a designated person. However, Lukoil was partly owned by Vagit Alekperov ('Alekperov') who was designated in the UK on 13 April 2022.

[89] *Mints* (n 85) para 231.
[90] *Mints* (n 85) para 225.
[91] *Mints* (n 85) para 233.
[92] *Litasco SA v Der Mond Oil and Gas Africa SA* [2023] EWHC 2866 (Comm).

The comments made in the *Mints* judgment were considered along with the interpretation and application of the control test. In this case, the court determined that Lukoil was not subject to the asset freeze that was in place in respect of Alekperov as there was no evidence that he controlled the company. The defendants also sought to rely on the findings in *Mints* that Lukoil (and in turn Litasco) must be controlled by Vladimir Putin and therefore were subject to an asset freeze. **3.61**

The judge in this case held that it was 'wholly improbable'[93] that any funds paid to Litasco for the payment of the debt owed would be used in accordance with Vladimir Putin's wishes, such that he could be said to be in control of the company and its assets. In relation to the comments made by the Court of Appeal in *Mints*, the judge in *Litasco* stated: **3.62**

> I believe the better interpretation of Regulation 7(4) is that it is concerned with an existing influence of a designated person over a relevant affair of the company [ . . . ] not a state of affairs which a designated person is in a position to bring about. Were matters otherwise, it would follow that President Putin was arguably in control, for Regulation 7(4) purposes, of companies of whose existence he was wholly ignorant, and whose affairs were conducted on a routine basis without any thought of him. Further, I note that the Chancellor endorsed part of Mr Rabinowitz KC's summary of the effect of Regulation 7(4), namely that it applies 'when the designated person "calls the shots"' ([229], [232]), not the wider formulation at [114] ('if the designated person calls the shots, or can call the shots'). While I accept that the Chancellor at [233] lends some limited support to a view that being 'at the apex of a command economy' might be sufficient for Regulation 7(4) purposes, and that 'Mr Putin could be deemed to control everything in Russia', these observations were couched in tentative terms, and, in my view, necessarily reflected the particular context in which they were made (see [67]).[94]

According to *Litasco*, an 'existing influence' is needed to demonstrate control rather than a hypothetical one as suggested by *Mints*. **3.63**

Following *Litasco* (although likely written prior to judgment being handed down) the FCDO and OFSI published joint guidance on 17 November 2023 which states that the UK Government: **3.64**

- 'does not generally consider designated public officials to exercise control over a public body in which they hold a leadership function';
- 'does not intend for sanctions measures targeting public officials to prohibit routine transactions with public bodies, including (but not limited to) taxes, fees, import duties, the purchase or receipt of permits, licences, or public utility services; or any other ordinary and incidental payments'; and

[93] ibid para 68.
[94] ibid para 70.

- 'would look to designate the relevant public body if it considers that the designated public official exercises control'.[95]

**3.65** However, the joint guidance further states that 'if there was sufficient evidence to demonstrate that the designated individual exercises control over the public body within the meaning of the relevant regulations, then the relevant legal test under UK sanctions regulations may be met'.[96] A relevant consideration as part of that assessment will be 'whether the designated person derives a significant personal benefit from payments to the public body, such that they amount to payments to that person rather than the public body'.[97]

**3.66** With regard to control of private entities, the joint guidance states that there is 'no presumption on the part of the UK Government that a private entity is subject to the control of a designated public official simply because that entity is based or incorporated in a jurisdiction in which that official has a leading role in economic policy or decision-making'.[98]

*d)* Hellard v OJSC Rossiysky Kredit Bank

**3.67** The High Court case of *Hellard* in July 2024 added to the judicial commentary on the application of the ownership and control test in the context of the Russian Regulations.[99]

**3.68** In this case the High Court suggested it would be useful to break the concept of control into four categories, for each of which different thresholds would apply. The four categories were as follows:[100]

1. De jure control, which exists where there is an absolute legal right to exercise control, as found, for example, in the constitutional documents of a company.
2. Actual present de facto control, which exists where a party lacks the legal right to control an entity but is still 'calling the shots'. Such control would be demonstrated where the individual has exercised a decisive influence.
3. Potential future de jure control, which applies in circumstances where a designated person has the legal means to obtain ownership or control in the future, e.g. where the designated person has an option or a forward contract to acquire a majority shareholding in a company.
4. Potential future de facto control, which applies in circumstances where, although there is no evidence that the person is currently exercising de facto control, there is a reasonable belief that they could, if they wished, exercise control in some

[95] OFSI and FCDO, 'Ownership and Control: Public Officials and Control Guidance' pt 2 <https://www.gov.uk/government/publications/ownership-and-control-public-officials-and-control-guidance/ownership-and-control-public-officials-and-control-guidance> accessed 4 September 2025.
[96] ibid pt 2.
[97] ibid pt 2.
[98] ibid pt 3.
[99] *Hellard v OJSC Rossiysky Kredit Bank* [2024] EWHC 1783 (Ch).
[100] ibid paras 76–7.

manner. The judge in *Hellard* did state it was difficult to conceive of a way this type of control could be demonstrated since, by definition, there would be no legal right or power indicating control and no evidence of control being exercised. He expected them to be very rare.

The concepts of ownership and control continue to give rise to practical difficulties for those seeking to comply with sanctions. There will doubtless be further developments in this area. **3.69**

*e)* Tonzip Maritime Ltd v 2Rivers Pte Ltd

This case involved a dispute over a voyage charterparty agreement for a vessel, 'Catalan Sea', to transport oil from Primorsk, Russia, to Aliaga, Turkey.[101] Tonzip Maritime Ltd (the vessel owners) refused the charterers' (2Rivers Pte Ltd) orders to load cargo, citing sanctions risks based on a screening report that linked ownership and control of the cargo company to a person designated by the EU and UK. The owners invoked the charterparty's sanctions clause, which permitted refusal of orders if, in their reasonable judgment, performance would expose them to sanctions risks. **3.70**

The High Court, confirming *Litasco*, ruled in favour of the charterers, finding that the claimant's refusal was not justified under the sanctions clause. The court held that the owners' assessment was speculative and not objectively reasonable, as it relied on outdated or incomplete information without adequately considering contradictory evidence showing the absence of ongoing control by the designated person. The court held that 'reasonable cause to suspect' requires more than speculative or indirect associations; it demands objective evidence of a real possibility of a sanctions violation.[102] The decision emphasized that sanctions risk evaluations must be evidence-based rather than presumptive, highlighting the risks and limitations in relying solely on automated screening tools. Of particular note is the fact the court concluded that reliance on third-party sanctions screening vendors is not, in and of itself, sufficient evidence on which to base a reasonable assessment of ownership and control; without evidence to support alleged links between an entity and a designated person the conclusion reached can only be speculation. In order for an assessment of ownership and control to be reasonable, it must be supported by evidence or documents. **3.71**

## E. Exceptions

Section 15 of SAMLA provides UK ministers with the power to create general exceptions to any prohibition or requirement contained within sanctions legislation, **3.72**

[101] *Tonzip Maritime Ltd v 2Rivers Pte Ltd* [2025] EWHC 2036 (Comm). See also Chapter 8 at para 8.20; Chapter 9 at para 9.22 on *Vneshprombank LLC v Bedzhamov* [2024] EWHC 1048 (Ch) and interpretation of reg 7 [73]–[8]; on reg 11 requiring actual ownership/control [92]–[100]; and on reasonable cause to suspect [120]–[31].

[102] For further discussion on 'reasonable cause to suspect', see J 3.134–8.

including financial sanctions measures. All such exceptions, once created, apply automatically to all persons and entities who would ordinarily be affected, the restrictions do not apply, and the specified activity may be undertaken without the need to obtain a specific licence from OFSI or risk UK enforcement proceedings.[103] In contrast, generally speaking, exceptions and derogations provided for by EU Regulations still require the applicant to file an application for a specific authorization to be given by the national competent authority of the relevant Member State.

**3.73** The nature and extent of any UK exception is specific to each sanctions regime and is set out in the relevant sanctions regulation. There are, however, some common exceptions found across financial sanctions legislation in relation to the asset freeze and making available restrictions which include

- a relevant institution crediting a frozen account with interest or other earnings due on the frozen account, so long as those funds are frozen immediately;[104]
- a relevant institution crediting a frozen account where it receives funds transferred to it for crediting to the frozen account;[105]
- a transfer of funds to a relevant institution for crediting to an account held or controlled (directly or indirectly) by a designated person, where those funds are transferred in discharge (or partial discharge) of obligations which arose before the date the person became a designated person;[106] and
- allowing independent persons to transfer their legal or equitable interests in frozen funds or economic resources to another person, where immediately before the transfer (i) the independent person is not a designated person, (ii) the independent person holds the interest in the funds or economic resources, (iii) the independent person does not hold the interest jointly with a designated person, and (iv) the independent person is not owned or controlled, directly or indirectly by a designated person. For this exception to apply, all four of these preconditions (i)–(iv) must apply to the relevant transfer.[107]

**3.74** UK sanctions also generally contain an exception to allow large financial institutions to transfer funds held or controlled by a designated individual to comply with the ring-fencing requirements imposed under the Financial Services (Banking Reform) Act 2013.[108]

**3.75** In some cases, exceptions for the provision of humanitarian assistance are also captured in the legislation. Since 2023, the Sanctions (Humanitarian Exception) (Amendment) Regulations 2023 ensure that the UK can fulfil its obligations to implement UNSC resolution 2664, which provides for a standardized humanitarian exception to all asset

[103] For licences, see below at paras 3.100–21.
[104] See e.g. Russia Regulations 2019, reg 58(3).
[105] See e.g. Russia Regulations 2019, reg 58(4).
[106] See e.g. Russia Regulations 2019, reg 58(5).
[107] See e.g. Russia Regulations 2019, reg 58(1).
[108] See e.g. Financial Services (Banking Reform) Act 2013, reg 58(6).

freezes imposed under UN sanctions regimes, which must be implemented into UK domestic legislation. The humanitarian exemption is not present in sanctions regimes that do not derive from the UN and it does not apply to the Afghanistan (Sanctions) (EU Exit) Regulations 2020 which has a bespoke humanitarian exemption to address the humanitarian crisis in Afghanistan.[109]

## F. Other Examples of Financial Sanctions

As previously noted, whilst asset freeze and making available restrictions are at the heart of the UK's financial sanctions toolkit, growth of other types of financial sanctions measures—most notably in the Russia Regulations, the Belarus Regulations, and the North Korea Regulations—means that financial sanctions now have the potential to be highly targeted to specific activities, which are separate and distinct from the restrictions applying to designated persons. This enables financial sanctions to be broader in their application and to impact areas where asset freeze measures may not be appropriate. **3.76**

Whilst this chapter does not address every type of financial sanctions measure, it considers the key provisions from a banking and finance perspective. **3.77**

### 1. Correspondent Banking and Payment Processing Restrictions

Both the North Korea Regulations and the Russia Regulations contain restrictions relating to correspondent banking and payment processing, albeit they are different in their scope and application. **3.78**

In the North Korea Regulations,[110] it is prohibited for a UK credit or financial institution to (i) open a bank account with or (ii) establish a correspondent banking relationship with a DPRK credit or financial institution,[111] if they know or have reasonable cause to suspect that the bank account or correspondent banking relationship is with a DPRK credit or financial institution. UK credit and financial institutions are also required to close any bank accounts and terminate any existing correspondent banking relationships with such parties.[112] It is also prohibited for a person to make or receive a transfer of funds which they know or have reasonable cause to suspect is to or from the DPRK,[113] unless the payment is a personal remittance valued at £4,000 or less[114] **3.79**

[109] See The Afghanistan (Sanctions) (EU Exit) Regulations 2020, reg 25A.

[110] North Korea Regulations 2019, reg 18.

[111] Including (i) a credit or financial institution domiciled in the DPRK, (ii) a branch or subsidiary, wherever located, of a credit or financial institution domiciled in the DPRK, and (iii) a credit or financial institution that is not domiciled in the DPRK but is owned or controlled (directly or indirectly) by a person domiciled in the DPRK.

[112] North Korea Regulations 2019, reg 18.

[113] North Korea Regulations 2019, reg 28.

[114] North Korea Regulations 2019, reg 83(3).

or is of a value of £13,000 or less and is for a specified reason[115] (which includes, but is not limited to where it relates to foodstuffs, healthcare, or medical equipment; is for agricultural or humanitarian purposes; or is for specific projects funded by the UK Government). Another example is regulation 16 of the Syria Regulations, containing similar correspondent banking restrictions.

**3.80** By contrast, the correspondent banking and payment processing restrictions in the Russia Regulations[116] are connected to designated persons, whereas the North Korea and Syria restrictions are broader. The Russia Regulations prohibit UK credit and financial institutions from establishing or continuing a correspondent banking relationship with (i) a designated person, (ii) a UK credit or financial institution which is owned or controlled by a designated person, and (iii) a non-UK credit or financial institution which is owned or controlled by a designated person, if they know or have reasonable cause to suspect that the correspondent banking relationship is with a designated person. In addition, UK credit and financial institutions must not process a payment to, from, or via the parties previously described at (i) to (iii) if they know or have reasonable cause to suspect that payment is to, from or via such a person (with very limited exceptions).[117] This restriction was amended to close a perceived gap in the application of the asset freeze measures which did not legally address a scenario where a UK person may receive funds from a non-designated financial institution which in turn received it from a designated person who was further up the payment chain.

**3.81** The Russia Regulations define a 'correspondent banking relationship' as the provision of banking services by a correspondent to a respondent, including providing a current or other liability account and related services such as cash management, international funds transfers, cheque clearing, providing customers of the respondent with direct access to accounts with the correspondent (and vice versa), and providing foreign exchange services.[118]

## 2. Investment Restrictions

**3.82** The North Korea Regulations, Syria Regulations, and Russia Regulations also contain different forms of investment ban restrictions.[119] They broadly comprise of a range of measures which may restrict UK persons from:

- acquiring any ownership interest in land located in the relevant jurisdictions;
- acquiring any ownership interest or control over companies incorporated in such jurisdictions;

[115] North Korea Regulations 2019, regs 18, 83(1), and (2).
[116] Russia Regulations 2019, reg 17A.
[117] Russia Regulations 2019, reg 59A.
[118] Russia Regulations 2019, reg 17A(6).
[119] See Russia Regulations 2019, regs 18 and 18B; North Korea Regulations 2019, regs 18–27; and Syria Regulations 2019, regs 16–18.

- establishing a joint venture over companies incorporated in such jurisdictions; or
- opening a representative office or establishing a branch in such jurisdictions.

The North Korea Regulations also contain specific requirements to close representative offices, branches, and subsidiaries of UK credit and financial institutions in the DPRK.[120] There are additional restrictions targeting investment by the Government of DPRK, the Worker's Party of Korea, any national of the DPRK, and any entity incorporated or constituted under the law of the DPRK.[121] **3.83**

It is worth noting that the Russia Regulations contain investment ban restrictions both in relation to Russia (regulation 18B) and the non-government controlled Ukrainian territory[122] (regulation 18). **3.84**

These restrictions are subject to various exceptions captured within the relevant regulations—see, for example, regulation 60ZZA of the Russia Regulations. **3.85**

## 3. Restrictions Relating to the Provision of Loans and Credit

The Russia Regulations and Belarus Regulations have a unique set of restrictions relating to the provision of loans and credit. There are various nuances within the restrictions but, essentially, a person must not (unless an exemption applies)[123] directly or indirectly grant a loan, enter into an arrangement to grant a loan, or make funds or economic resources available to enable another to grant a loan.[124] **3.86**

The definition of 'loan and credit' varies. A number of the financial restrictions under these provisions depend upon (i) the loan or credit having a maturity exceeding 30 days, (ii) the date the loan or credit was granted, (iii) the identity (direct or indirect) of the recipient of the loan or credit, or person in control of the recipient, and (iv) where the loan or credit relates to an investment or purchase, the location or purpose of that investment.[125] With regard to the date on which a credit or loan was granted, for the purposes of this prohibition, any rollover of an existing debt obligation is considered a new transaction.[126] **3.87**

The restrictions apply in numerous ways in different circumstances. The UK Financial Sanctions FAQs provide many examples:[127] **3.88**

[120] North Korea Regulations 2019, reg 19.
[121] North Korea Regulations 2019, reg 26.
[122] Defined at the time of writing as Crimea and non-government controlled areas of Donetsk, Kherson, Luhansk, and Zaporizhzhia oblasts. See Russia Regulations 2019, reg 2.
[123] See e.g. Russia Regulations 2019, reg 59.
[124] See e.g. Russia Regulations 2019, reg 17.
[125] As per Russia Regulations 2019, regs 17 and 18B(2).
[126] OFSI, 'UK Financial Sanctions FAQs' (n 70) question 21.
[127] OFSI's FAQs are updated with new examples regularly.

- In contrast to the similar restrictions that the US imposes,[128] the UK's loans and credit restrictions do not apply to payment terms for goods or service. However, the provision of payment terms/delayed payment may not be used to circumvent the prohibition to provide new loans or credit.[129]
- Payment and settlement services, including through correspondent banking, are to be construed as directly or indirectly 'making' or 'being part of an arrangement to make' a relevant loan or credit to a person subject to the loan and credit prohibitions.[130]
- Financial institutions can confirm or advise letters of credit and provide discounting or post financing for them. However, if the maturity exceeds 30 days and the applicant of the letter of credit is a person subject to the loans and credit restrictions, this would be prohibited as it would constitute extension of a loan.[131]

## 4. Restrictions Relating to Transferable Securities and Money Market Instruments

**3.89** The Russia Regulations and Belarus Regulations also contain targeted restrictions which prohibit UK persons from dealing with specific transferable securities and money market instruments. The restrictions vary depending on the issuer of the transferable security/money market instrument, the nature of the transferable securities, and money market instruments and their date of issue.

**3.90** The term 'transferable security' means a security, negotiable on the capital market, of any of the following kinds, but excluding instruments of payment—

(a) shares in companies and other securities equivalent to shares in companies, partnerships or other entities, and depositary receipts in respect of shares;
(b) bonds or other forms of securitised debt, including depositary receipts in respect of such securities;
(c) any other securities giving the right to purchase or sell any security of a kind mentioned in paragraph (a) or (b).[132]

**3.91** The term 'money market instrument' is defined as 'an instrument of a kind normally dealt in on the money market, such as treasury bills, certificates of deposit and commercial papers, excluding instruments of payment'.[133]

128 See e.g. Administration of Barack Obama, Executive Order 13662, 'Blocking Property of Additional Persons Contributing to the Situation in Ukraine' (2014) Dir 1.
129 OFSI, 'UK Financial Sanctions FAQs' (n 70) question 20.
130 OFSI, 'UK Financial Sanctions FAQs' (n 70) question 114.
131 OFSI, 'UK Financial Sanctions FAQs' (n 70) question 117.
132 See e.g. Russia Regulations 2019, reg 16(10).
133 ibid.

'Dealing with' is defined broadly and applies to both primary and secondary market trading of transferable securities or money-market instruments.[134] In contrast, asset freeze restrictions do not impact the secondary market trading of transferable securities or money market instruments issued by designated persons. 'A reference to "dealing with" includes a reference to purchasing or selling the security or instrument, providing investment services relating to the security or instrument, or assisting in the issuance of the security or instrument.'[135] The term 'investment services' is also broadly defined.[136] **3.92**

Some of the financial prohibitions under this provision relate to dealing with transferable securities or money market instruments which are owned, controlled, or otherwise under the direction of a person 'connected with Russia or Belarus'.[137] A person 'connected with Russia/Belarus' is defined to mean an individual who is 'ordinarily resident' or otherwise 'located' in Russia/Belarus; or, where the person is a company or other entity, a person who is domiciled in, or incorporated or constituted under the law of Russia/Belarus.[138] **3.93**

'Ordinarily resident' is not further defined in the Russia Regulations and there is no UK case law defining the phrase 'ordinarily resident in Russia' in a sanctions context. However, as per Lord Scarman in *R v Barnet London Borough Council ex parte Shah* (the leading case involving the term) **3.94**

> Unless, therefore, it can be shown that the statutory framework or the legal context in which the words are used requires a different meaning, I unhesitatingly subscribe to the view that 'ordinarily resident' refers to a man's abode in a particular place or country which he has adopted voluntarily and for settled purposes as part of the regular order of his life for the time being, whether of short or of long duration.[139]

'Domiciled' is a term applied on a case-by-case basis where OFSI states that it will consider all evidence available when forming its view. In a 10 July 2025 FAQ response, OFSI provided the following guidance: **3.95**

> During an assessment we will attach significant weight to an entity's place of incorporation and constitution, as we consider this to represent a substantial connection between the entity and a given jurisdiction. However we would also take into account additional factors such as the location of an entity's i) registered office, ii) controlling shareholders or directors, iii) central management or control, and/or iv) primary business operations, taking a balanced view of the facts of a case. Lastly, we consider the domicile of a subsidiary company to be independent to the domicile of its parent company.[140]

[134] OFSI, 'UK Financial Sanctions FAQs' (n 70) question 10.
[135] See e.g. Russia Regulations 2019, reg 16(9).
[136] See e.g. Russia Regulations 2019, reg 16(10)(a)–(h).
[137] See e.g. Russia Regulations 2019, reg 16(4D) and Belarus Regulations 2019, reg 15A.
[138] Russia Regulations 2019, reg 19A and Belarus Regulations 2019, reg 2.
[139] [1983] 2 AC 309, para 343. See also *Anthony Mackay v HMRC* [2018] UKUT 378 (TCC).
[140] OFSI, 'UK Financial Sanctions FAQs' (n 70) question 153.

## G. Circumvention

3.96 It is prohibited for a person to circumvent sanctions. Each UK sanctions regime contains provisions which makes it an offence to intentionally participate in activities knowing that the object or effect of them is (whether directly or indirectly) to circumvent financial sanctions.[141]

3.97 'Circumvent' is not defined in any of the UK's sanctions legislation or government guidance.[142] The case of *R v R* [2015] EWCA 796—although a family law case and referring to a previous UK Russia sanctions regime—is useful. It is the most recent and relevant instance in which the Court of Appeal has considered circumvention offences in a sanctions context, although the court declined to formulate the meaning of 'circumvent' for the purposes of the Council Regulation (EU) 269/2014 (EU Regulation).

3.98 In *R v R*, the issue was whether an English court order to pay an interim maintenance allowance in linked family proceedings amounted to a breach of anti-circumvention provisions, where the party being ordered to pay was a designated person. Lord Pannick, representing the husband, argued that, as the ex-wife lived in the UK, she must remit the money to the UK once it had been transferred to her Russian bank account pursuant to the court order. He argued that the court order inevitably leading to this series of transfers was itself both 'dealing with funds' and a circumvention of the sanctions prohibitions, because the object and effect of the court order was to prevent the funds from being frozen. The Court of Appeal disagreed and held that there was no circumvention because the EU Regulation did not have the objective of preventing an English court from ordering a Russian husband to make maintenance payments to his Russian ex-wife's account in Russia. Arden LJ, in her leading judgment, held that the court order did not itself transfer funds and therefore could not amount to 'dealing with funds'. In her view, the order merely provided for the payment by the husband of monies to a Russian bank account.[143] Briggs LJ stated that the payment in Russia of interim maintenance by a divorced husband to his former wife was beyond the scope of the EU Regulation unless it was put into effect by conduct or involved assets within the EU. Briggs LJ further stated that it was not the purpose of the EU Regulation to regulate the making of court orders. In his view, even if the court took an 'abnormal' route to achieving that objective, it would simply be taking a lawful route to a lawful objective and would thus be circumventing nothing. *R v R* also emphasized that when a court comes to grapple with the term 'circumvent', it will be a fact-sensitive and context-driven exercise.

[141] See e.g. Russia Regulations 2019, reg 19.

[142] In contrast, the EU recently enacted Directive No 2024/1226 of 24 April 2024 relating to the definition of criminal offences and penalties for the violation of Union restrictive measures. It provides a list of prohibited conduct characterizing violation or circumvention of EU sanctions. As for all directives, this text must be transposed into domestic law before being enforceable, in distinction to EU regulations which are of direct binding effect.

[143] In *R v R* [2015] EWCA 796, Arden LJ at [29] rejected the appellant's submission that the court order was 'dealing with funds'.

The UK authorities have published a series of guidance notes (Red Alert Notices) relating to financial sanctions, from which it is clear that the UK authorities interpret 'circumvention' and 'evasion' as analogous terms, and that *attempted* circumvention, or actions *intended* to facilitate circumvention, are sufficient to breach the circumvention prohibition such that *actual* circumvention need not be established.[144] **3.99**

## H. Licensing

Breaches of financial sanctions give rise to offences unless an exception or licence applies. A sanctions-related licence, issued pursuant to section 15 SAMLA, authorizes behaviour which would otherwise amount to a breach of sanctions. Financial sanctions-related licences are issued by OFSI. **3.100**

These licences only apply to conduct subject to UK jurisdiction. So, should the intended transaction or payment involve or pass through another jurisdiction, parties will need to consider whether sanctions prohibitions apply in that jurisdiction. If so, they must also apply for a licence, where available, from the relevant country's competent authority. **3.101**

In the UK, there are two types of licences—general and specific.[145] Licences must be specifically applied for in advance from OFSI, unless a general licence can be relied upon in relation to the relevant conduct. **3.102**

### 1. General Licences

A list of general licences is publicly available.[146] They are available for any person to rely on and where a general licence authorizes a particular activity, a person can only apply for a specific licence if they cannot make use of the general licence for some reason or it is deficient in some way.[147] General licences cannot be applied for but are issued by OFSI under such conditions as HM Treasury deems appropriate and 'will best support the Government's policy priorities'. In practice, they are often issued to address situations where a sanctions measure impacts a wide group. For example, general licences can be issued in respect of the payment of legal fees by designated persons,[148] following **3.103**

144 National Crime Agency, OFSI, Joint Money Laundering Intelligence Taskforce, and National Economic Crime Centre, 'Financial Sanctions Evasions Typologies: Russian Elites and Enablers' (0697-NECC, July 2022) p 4 <https://nationalcrimeagency.gov.uk/who-we-are/publications/605-necc-financial-sanctions-evasion-russian-elites-and-enablers/file> accessed 4 September 2025; ibid, 'Gold-based Financial and Trade Sanctions Circumvention' (0731-NECC, November 2023) p 4 <https://www.nationalcrimeagency.gov.uk/who-we-are/publications/679-necc-red-alert-gold-sanctions-circumvention/file> accessed 4 September 2025.

145 There is no general licence system in the EU.

146 OFSI and HM Treasury, 'OFSI General Licences' (Collection, 1 January 2021) <https://www.gov.uk/government/collections/ofsi-general-licences> accessed 4 September 2025.

147 OFSI, 'UK Financial Sanctions General Guidance' (n 2) s 6.9.

148 At the time of writing, the current version of this licence, which came into force on 29 October 2025, is INT/2025/7323088. It will expire on 28 April 2026. For the first time, the legal services general licence has been granted

OFSI receiving a significant number of specific licence applications for legal fees, or in response to unforeseen circumstances (e.g. the general licence issued following the designation of the National Settlement Depository in Russia[149]—which was not issued at the time of the designation but later, when the impact on non-Russian parties holding Russian-based securities became apparent).

**3.104** Each general licence may include requirements that are unique to that licence. These could include prior notification of use and recordkeeping and reporting requirements.[150] It is the responsibility of the person relying on a general licence to ensure the activities they undertake fall within the terms of the licence and that they comply with any of its conditions. Failure to comply with the terms of a licence can give rise to a breach for which a monetary penalty can be imposed.[151]

**3.105** Once a licence is issued, any specified conduct undertaken will not be in breach of UK sanctions law, but OFSI will not issue licences retrospectively. If a person or entity carries out an act that was not permitted under a general licence, and a specific licence had not been obtained beforehand, it may have breached financial sanctions. Therefore, if, for example, person 'P' undertakes a prohibited activity that is later a permitted activity by way of an OFSI licence, this does not offer P a defence to the sanctions breach, because the licence had not been issued at the time the prohibited activity took place. The fact that a relevant licence was issued after the prohibited conduct may, however, provide mitigation.

**3.106** Breach of a general licence is a serious offence, punishable by a maximum of seven years' imprisonment and/or an unlimited fine (see section J, 'Enforcement and Defences', below).

## 2. Specific Licences

**3.107** Where a general licence does not exist, persons within the jurisdiction of the UK sanctions regime can apply for a specific licence. By contrast to a general licence, a specific licence is not publicly available, and it is issued to an applicant for a specific act or set of acts. Only the persons detailed in the specific licence may rely on it.

**3.108** Specific licences will only be granted by OFSI where one or more of the statutory licencing grounds has been met.[152] Therefore, the applicant must provide evidence to

under the UK Autonomous Sanctions Regulations meaning it applies to all sanctions regimes except those imposed under United Nations sanctions obligations. See FAQ 170 <https://www.gov.uk/government/publications/uk-financial-sanctions-faqs/uk-financial-sanctions-faqs?> accessed 10 November 2025.

[149] General licence INT/2024/4919848, which expired on 12 October 2024.

[150] OFSI, 'UK Financial Sanctions General Guidance' (n 2) s 6.9.

[151] OFSI, 'Financial Sanctions Enforcement and Monetary Penalties Guidance' (n 16) ss 3G and 4.4.

[152] While sanctions are adopted at the EU level, licences and authorizations are granted by the national competent authorities (NCAs) designated in each Member State, and are only applicable in the concerned Member State. Theoretically, NCAs are encouraged to communicate and adopt harmonized positions on the concrete

support their licence application, demonstrating that the relevant criteria have been met. Insufficient evidence will result in the application being deemed incomplete and returned for the applicant to resubmit.[153] An application for a specific licence should be made using the OFSI application form.[154]

Applications will be prioritized where there is a genuine and evidenced need for urgency, such as for humanitarian purposes or where there may be a risk to life. **3.109**

Each financial sanctions regime has its own specific licencing grounds.[155] That said, the following are common licencing grounds featured across most sanctions regimes:[156] **3.110**

- Expenditure to meet the basic needs of the designated person (or any financially dependent family member)—such as payments of tax, utility bills, rent or mortgage, insurance costs, property management fees, etc. This ground does not necessarily enable a person to continue the lifestyle they had before being designated.
- Fees for the provision of legal services (provided that such fees and disbursements are reasonable) and reasonable professional fees.
- Payment of fees for the routine maintenance of frozen funds and economic resources.
- Payment of extraordinary expenses where such expenses are unexpected, unavoidable, and/or not recurring. This provision cannot be used where other licensing grounds are more suitable or as a way of avoiding limitations on other grounds.
- Payments required by a court order made prior to the date of designation and only to satisfy a pre-existing judicial decision or lien.[157]
- Payments due as a result of a prior obligation such as under contracts, agreements, or obligations that were entered into prior to the imposition of the relevant sanctions. However, the payment cannot relate to trade provisions specified in the regulations nor can it result in funds or economic resources being made available to a designated person directly or indirectly.
- Transactions which enable humanitarian assistance activity—this includes the work of international and non-governmental organizations carrying out relief activities for the benefit of the applicable civilian population.
- To enable payments relating to the insolvency of a designated person.

implementation of sanctions' authorizations and licences. In practice, however, responses from NCAs may very well differ and are in any event not binding on other Member States, thus undermining the harmonized enforcement of EU sanctions and creating significant legal uncertainty for business operators.

153 OFSI, 'UK Financial Sanctions General Guidance' (n 2) s 6.10.

154 OFSI and HM Treasury, 'Licences that Allow Activity Prohibited by Financial Sanctions' (Guidance, 4 August 2017) <https://www.gov.uk/guidance/licences-that-allow-activity-prohibited-by-financial-sanctions> accessed 4 September 2025.

155 See e.g. Russia Regulations 2019, sch 5.

156 OFSI, 'UK Financial Sanctions General Guidance' (n 2) s 6.6.

157 It should be noted that this ground varies depending on whether the designated person is designated pursuant to a UN obligation or not.

3.111 In the context of the Russia Regulations, there is also a divestment licensing ground. The divestment and enabling others to divest licensing grounds set out in Part 1ZA of Schedule 5, and the insolvency grounds set out in Part 1ZB of Schedule 5, apply to the asset freeze etc. prohibitions, loans and credit arrangements prohibitions, dealing with transferable securities or money market instruments prohibitions, correspondent banking relationships etc. prohibitions, provision of financial services relating to foreign exchange reserve and asset management prohibitions and trust services prohibitions. A UK entity or representative (on their behalf) may apply for a licence from OFSI to allow the divestment activities. Part 1ZA sets out the purposes pursuant to which, or for which, activities OFSI may grant an individual licence.[158]

3.112 It is worth noting, however, as Saini LJ highlighted in *R (on the application of Mikhail Fridman) v HM Treasury*[159] that, even where the applicant has satisfied a relevant licencing ground, OFSI nonetheless retains a discretion to refuse an application:

> [E]ven if that threshold is satisfied, HMT has a further embedded discretion to refuse the licence. That follows from the statutory language in Regulation 64(2): the Russia Regulations provide that HMT 'may' issue a licence when 'appropriate' for one of the specified purposes. This requires the exercise of classic discretionary judgement.[160]

3.113 As well as evidence in support of a financial sanctions licence application, the applicant should also provide OFSI with:

- what the UK nexus (UK link) is
- a detailed explanation of why you think the licensing ground applies (licensing grounds are listed in the form)
- a detailed explanation of the sanctions regime which you are applying under, the sanctions which you believe are engaged, the licensing ground which you believe applies, and how all the requirements of the licensing ground are met
- detailed information about the transactions (for example the value of the goods or services, parties to the contract, dates of future transactions, the amounts of intended payments; the payment currency; the intended payment route(s), details of all parties, including the sender, receiver of funds, intermediaries and beneficiaries)
- the intended purpose of the transaction/funds/activity
- explanation of the reasonableness of any proposed payment (where relevant)
- for frozen assets, bank details - payment method, account details, payment route details and whether funds are available for payments

158 FCDO, Export Control Joint Unit, OFSI, and OTSI, 'Russia Sanctions: Guidance' (Statutory guidance, 9 May 2019) s 3.2.
159 *R (on the application of Mikhail Fridman) v HM Treasury* [2023] EWHC 2657 (Admin).
160 ibid [9]. Also see *Mints* (n 85) [219]. (For further discussion of *Fridman* see s H.3.115, 'Refusal of a Licence and licence appeals'.)

- copies of documents to support your application - for example, retainer agreement or letter of engagement, memoranda or articles of association, trust deeds, lease agreements, contracts, quotations from suppliers.[161]

Specific licences will usually be issued for a finite period. It is the responsibility of all parties relying on a specific licence to ensure that their activity complies with the specific terms of the licence and that any reporting and record-keeping requirements are adhered to. It should be noted that whilst OFSI may grant a licence in respect of financial sanctions, a transaction may also require a trade sanctions licence which must be applied for separately. **3.114**

### 3. Refusal of a Licence and Licence Appeals

Where OFSI refuses to issue a specific licence, it must provide written reasons for its decision. Where a licence has been refused, applicants have the following options: **3.115**

- to re-apply, with new or supplementary evidence or new supporting arguments;
- re-apply under a different derogation/ground (where applicable); or
- seek to challenge the decision in court.[162]

A court challenge must be lodged with the High Court[163] in accordance with section 38(2) of SAMLA. The claim is brought under Part 8 of the Civil Procedure Rules (CPR) and is governed by Part 79 of the CPR. In deciding whether the licence decision ought to be set aside, the court must apply the principles applicable in judicial review.[164] **3.116**

The first (and, at the time of writing, only) court challenge under SAMLA against a refusal by OFSI to grant a licence was pursued by Mikhail Fridman.[165] Mr Fridman, a designated person under the Russia Regulations, challenged OFSI's decision to refuse him a specific licence to access frozen funds in order to pay (i) a £30,000 monthly management fee due under contract to the managing agent of a substantial property he owned in London, UK; (ii) a £1,850 monthly fee to the same managing agent relating to the technology in the property (phone lines, audio equipment, etc.); and (iii) household staff costs. **3.117**

Mr Fridman sought a specific licence on the grounds of prior obligations, basic needs, and routine holding and maintenance. The court dismissed Mr Fridman's application on all grounds. The following key points arose from the judgment: **3.118**

[161] OFSI and HM Treasury, 'Licences that Allow Activity Prohibited by Financial Sanctions' (n 154), updated 1 September 2025.
[162] OFSI, 'UK Financial Sanctions General Guidance' (n 2) s 6.13.
[163] Or the Court of Session in Scotland, as applicable.
[164] SAMLA 2018, s 38(4).
[165] *Fridman* (n 159).

- OFSI retains a residual discretion to refuse to grant a licence, even if the conditions for granting a licence are met. The discretion must be exercised consistently and rationally, by reference to the overall statutory regime. It was 'not at large'.[166]
- The applicant is responsible for providing all relevant information for licensing applications and OFSI is not required to identify gaps or act as an advisor.[167]
- A licence cannot be granted under the Prior Obligations Derogation ground of the Russia Regulations,[168] if the payment will be made directly or indirectly to another designated person. This includes where the payment is made to a person or entity which is owned or controlled by that designated person.[169]
- Review proceedings under section 38 of SAMLA are to be conducted in accordance with judicial review principles and should not be used as a vehicle to pursue a 'rolling' application for a licence, with iterative updates and new information as the proceedings move towards a hearing.[170]

**3.119** Saini LJ recommended that OFSI consider making public its internal licensing guidance as a matter of good administrative practice,[171] and, on 27 February 2024, OFSI published further guidance: 'OFSI Designated Individuals Licensing Principles'[172] and 'Guidance: Licensing Delegation Framework'.[173] The first provided further guidance on the fundamental and general principles OFSI applies to licencing applications and the specific principles it applies to applications which relate to basic needs, frozen assets, and issues of ownership and control. The second set out the framework used by OFSI to determine whether a decision is contentious and therefore should be taken by a Minister.

**3.120** As further court challenges to OFSI's licencing decisions come through the UK courts, it will be interesting to see the extent of judicial deference—meaning an appreciation of the expertise and knowledge of the primary decision-maker—afforded to the Government should it seek to argue that, even where the conditions to grant a licence are met by the applicant, it was nonetheless right to refuse the licence on the grounds that it undermined the policy objectives of the sanctions regime.[174]

**3.121** For 'Court Challenges', also see Chapter 8, section D.2.

[166] *Fridman* (n 159) [59]–[60].
[167] *Fridman* (n 159) [69].
[168] Russia Regulations 2019, sch 8, para 5.
[169] *Fridman* (n 159) [75].
[170] *Fridman* (n 159) [65].
[171] *Fridman* (n 159) [48].
[172] 'OFSI Designated Individuals Licensing Principles' (Guidance, updated 6 June 2025) <https://www.gov.uk/government/publications/financial-sanctions-licensing/ofsi-licensing-designated-individuals-licensing-principles--2> accessed 4 September 2025.
[173] 'Licensing Delegation Framework' (Guidance, updated 6 June 2025) <https://www.gov.uk/government/publications/financial-sanctions-licensing/licensing-delegation-framework> accessed 4 September.
[174] For further discussion on judicial deference to court challenges under section 38 of SAMLA, see Chapter 8, s E.3.

# I. Reporting Obligations

## 1. Relevant Firms

Financial sanctions generally include reporting obligations which apply to relevant firms.[175] **3.122**

Broadly speaking, these reporting requirements require a relevant firm to inform OFSI as soon as practicable if it knows, or has reasonable cause to suspect: **3.123**

- that a person is a designated person; or
- that a person has breached a prohibition or failed to comply with an obligation relating to financial sanctions or a relevant licensing offence; and
- the 'information or other matter on which the knowledge or cause for suspicion' is received in the course of carrying out its business.[176]

There are specific reporting requirements attached to certain regimes and types of restrictions. For example, in the Russia Regulations the following additional reporting requirements apply: **3.124**

- A relevant firm must inform OFSI as soon as practicable if it knows, or has reasonable cause to suspect, that it holds funds or economic resources for a prohibited person (at the time of writing defined as being the Central Bank of the Russian Federation, the National Wealth Fund of the Russian Federation, the Ministry of Finance of the Russian Federation, and any person owned or controlled or acting at the direction of such persons[177]) and the information or other matter on which the knowledge or cause for suspicion is received in the course of carrying out its business.[178]
- A relevant firm must report where it has knowledge or reasonable cause to suspect that a person has breached the requirements relating to the maritime transportation of certain oil and oil products.[179]

The relevant firm's report to OFSI must include: **3.125**

[175] 'Relevant firm' is defined in each regulation. Under regulation 71 of the Russia Regulations, a 'Relevant firm' is defined as (i) a party with permission under Part 4A of the Financial Services and Markets Act 2000; (ii) a money service business; (iii) a statutory or local auditor; (iv) an accountancy firm, law firm, or person providing tax advice or trust services; (v) an estate agent; (vi) a holder of a casino operating licence; (vii) a person engaged in making supplying, selling, or exchanging certain precious stones and metals; (viii) a crypto exchange provider; and (ix) a custodian wallet provider. From 14 May 2025, pursuant to The Sanctions (EU Exit) (Miscellaneous Amendments) (No 2) Regulations 2024, high value dealers, art market participants, insolvency practitioners, and letting agents are also included in the definition.

[176] Syria Regulations 2019, reg 69.

[177] Russia Regulations 2019, reg 70(7).

[178] Where a relevant firm holds such funds or economic resources, an annual report must be filed with OFSI by no later than 31 October of each calendar year, in respect of such funds and economic resources that were held as of 30 September of that year.

[179] Namely the restrictions at regulations 46Z9B to 46Z9D of the Russia Regulations.

- the information or other matter on which the knowledge or suspicion is based;
- any information held about the person by which they can be identified; and
- if the relevant firm knows or has reasonable cause to suspect that a person is a designated person or prohibited person, and that person is a customer of the relevant firm, the report must also state the nature and amount or quantity of any funds or economic resources that the relevant firm held for that customer when it first had the knowledge or suspicion.[180]

**3.126** There is also generally an obligation for a relevant institution (i.e. a person with permission under Part 4A Financial Services and Markets Act 2000 (FSMA)) to inform OFSI without delay if it

- credits a frozen account or relevant account (as defined in the applicable UK regulations) or where it receives funds transferred to that institution for crediting that account; or
- transfers funds from a frozen account or relevant account with a relevant institution conducting excluded activity (within the meaning of section 142D FSMA) to an account with a ring-fenced body (within the meaning of section 142A FSMA) when both accounts are held or controlled, directly or indirectly, by the same designated person in relation to whom the exception permitting this transfer under the application regulation applies.[181]

**3.127** It is advisable for individuals and entities to refer to the 'Information and Records' part of the statutory instrument for the relevant sanctions regime, for the specific scope of their reporting obligations.

**3.128** For the avoidance of doubt, information to which legal professional privilege attaches does not need to be reported to OFSI. This exception must be carefully applied. OFSI's 'Financial Sanctions General Guidance' provides: 'OFSI expects legal professionals to carefully ascertain whether legal privilege applies, and which information it applies to. OFSI may challenge a blanket assertion of legal professional privilege where it is not satisfied that such careful consideration has been made.'[182]

## 2. Designated Persons

**3.129** Some sanctions regimes, including the Russia Regulations, contain additional reporting obligations on designated persons.[183]

180 See e.g. Syria Regulations 2019, reg 69.
181 OFSI, 'UK Financial Sanctions General Guidance' (n 2) s 5.1.3.
182 OFSI, 'UK Financial Sanctions General Guidance' (n 2) s 5.4.
183 See Russia Regulations 2019, pt 9.

One significant example of this is a further reporting requirement that was imposed by the Russia (Sanctions) (EU Exit) (Amendment) (No 4) Regulations 2023,[184] on persons designated under the Russia Regulations. Regulation 70A(1) imposes reporting obligations on designated persons who are 'a United Kingdom person'[185] to disclose to OFSI within 10 weeks of designation any funds or economic resources they own, hold, or control and the nature, value, and location of those funds or economic resources in any jurisdiction. Going even further, regulation 70A(2) requires a designated person who is *not* a 'United Kingdom person' to report to OFSI (within the same timeframe) the nature, value, and location of their UK funds and economic resources. 3.130

Regulation 70A(2) arguably raises questions over the proper extra-territorial scope of UK sanctions laws given regulation 70A(2) purports to have the power to demand reporting requirements of persons who would otherwise fall outside the UK's jurisdiction. The provision is presumably predicated on the basis that having funds or economic resources in the UK amounts to 'conduct in the United Kingdom' for the purposes of section 21(1)(a) of SAMLA. 3.131

## J. Enforcement and Defences

OFSI is responsible for monitoring compliance with financial sanctions and for assessing suspected breaches. It has the power to impose monetary penalties for breaches of financial sanctions and to refer cases to law enforcement agencies for investigation and potential prosecution under powers provided in Part 8 of the Policing and Crime Act 2017 (PCA). 3.132

Where a financial sanctions breach has been identified, OFSI has a range of options as to what, if any, enforcement proceedings to pursue: 3.133

- issue a warning letter (but taking no further enforcement action);
- impose a civil monetary penalty (OFSI);
- refer for criminal prosecution;
- refer to a relevant sectoral regulator where appropriate (for example, the Financial Conduct Authority (FCA)); or
- enter into a Deferred Prosecution Agreement (DPA).

As can be seen across all of the financial sanctions prohibitions implemented by regulations made under SAMLA, the prohibition or restriction stated in each regulation is made out where the person 'knows, or has reasonable cause to suspect' that they are undertaking the prohibited activity. As such, for a breach of financial sanctions to be proved, in addition to the relevant *act* being carried out, that person must also have the 3.134

[184] Which came into force on 26 December 2023.
[185] Within the meaning of SAMLA 2018, s 21(2) and (3).

requisite level of *knowledge or suspicion* in connection with that act. For example, regulation 16(1) of the Russia Regulations states that, 'A person ("P") must not, directly or indirectly, deal with a transferable security or money-market instrument falling within paragraph (2) *if P knows, or has reasonable cause to suspect,* that P is dealing with such a transferable security or money-market instrument'; or regulation 11(1) of the Syria Regulations, which states that, 'A person ("P") must not deal with funds or economic resources owned, held or controlled by a designated person *if P knows, or has reasonable cause to suspect,* that P is dealing with such funds or economic resources.'[186]

**3.135** In criminal law, this knowledge or reasonable cause to suspect component is called the 'mental element of the offence', or the *mens rea.* In sanctions breaches, the mental element of the offence can be proved either subjectively or objectively; subjectively through evidence of the person's actual knowledge that their actions would contravene a financial sanctions measure, or, objectively, that, in all the circumstances, the person had reasonable cause to suspect that this would be the case. In the latter situation, it is irrelevant if the person honestly considered he was not in breach of the regulations if, in all the circumstances, a reasonable person knowing what the person knew, would so conclude.

**3.136** When first enacted, in any enforcement proceedings for breaches of financial sanctions under PCA 2017, whether criminal or civil, it was not enough that the person had done the prohibited act; it was also necessary to prove they knew or suspected that they were in breach. However, in the context of civil enforcement for financial sanctions breaches, since 15 June 2022 (as a result of changes made by the Economic Crime (Transparency and Enforcement) Act 2022 (ECTEA)), financial sanctions have been subject to strict liability, meaning that when determining whether a person has breached financial sanctions, OFSI need only prove the breach has occurred and need not prove any mental element. No defence is available.[187]

**3.137** OFSI's 'Enforcement and Monetary Penalties for Breaches of Financial Sanctions Guidance' provides this commentary with respect to the strict liability amendment:

> On 15 March 2022 the Economic Crime (Transparency and Enforcement) Act 2022 amended the powers in the 2017 Act [...] adding subsection 1A. This removed the requirement for OFSI to demonstrate that a person had knowledge or reasonable cause to suspect they were in breach of a financial sanction to issue a monetary penalty. This amendment applies only to consideration of civil liability and the imposition of a monetary penalty and is not relevant to any assessment of whether a criminal offence has been committed under sanctions regulations.[188]

**3.138** As such, the defences available to a person for a breach of financial sanctions differ, depending on whether criminal or civil enforcement proceedings are being pursued.

186 Emphasis added.
187 Policing and Crime Act 2017 (PCA), s 146(1A).
188 OFSI, 'Financial Sanctions Enforcement and Monetary Penalties Guidance' (n 16) s 1.2.

If civil enforcement is pursued, a breach is subject to strict liability and all that OFSI must prove, on the balance of probabilities, is that the relevant activity took place (for example, that a UK person, as a matter of fact, dealt with funds owned or controlled by a designated person).[189] It is irrelevant that the person knew or ought reasonably to have suspected that they were in violation of the particular prohibition. If *criminal* proceedings are pursued, however, the prosecuting authority must also demonstrate beyond reasonable doubt that the person knew or had reasonable cause to suspect that they were involved in the prohibited activity.

## 1. Penalties for Non-Compliance

### (i) Criminal penalties

Section 17 of SAMLA enables the UK Government to implement criminal penalties within each set of sanctions regulations. Whilst SAMLA states that the maximum penalty on indictment cannot exceed 10 years' imprisonment, most sanctions regulations provide for a penalty following criminal conviction for a UK financial sanctions offence of up to seven years' imprisonment and/or a fine on conviction on indictment; 12 months' imprisonment on summary conviction in England, Wales, and Scotland; and six months' imprisonment in Northern Ireland. However, the specific penalty for any given offence is set out in the particular applicable regulation. **3.139**

From 26 December 2023, a body corporate can be found liable for a criminal offence for a breach of financial sanctions if a 'senior manager of a body corporate or partnership acting within the actual or apparent scope of their authority' commits an offence pursuant to financial sanctions measures.[190] This provision has significantly extended those through whom a corporate can be criminally liable for a sanctions breach. Before it came into force, liability could only attach if a person who was the directing mind and will of the company had committed the offence. Now corporate criminal liability can attach through a broader category of person. **3.140**

### (ii) Civil penalties

OFSI has the power to impose monetary penalties for breaches of financial sanctions, as well as for breaches of supplemental provisions such as reporting requirements and information offences. The calculation of the penalty depends on the nature of the restriction but generally can be broken down as follows: **3.141**

- where a prohibition relates to particular funds or economic resources which can be estimated in value, the penalty can range from 50 per cent of the estimated value of each breach or up to £1 million, whichever is the greater;[191]

[189] PCA 2017, s 146(1A), as amended.
[190] Economic Crime and Corporate Transparency Act 2023 (ECCTA), s 196 and sch 12, para 20.
[191] PCA 2017, s 146(3).

- in any other case, the permitted maximum applies, which at the time of writing is £1 million.[192]

**3.142** A civil monetary penalty may be imposed on both individuals and entities. Further, where a monetary penalty is imposed on an entity, OFSI may also impose a monetary penalty on any of its officers[193] if it is satisfied on the balance of probabilities that the breach or failure in respect of which the monetary penalty is payable, took place with the consent or connivance of the officer or was attributable to neglect on their part.[194]

**3.143** OFSI's 'Enforcement and Monetary Penalties Guidance'[195] provides some insight into its approach towards compliance, enforcement, and penalties. It provides a list of common factors it will take into account to determine the gravity of the breach identified and the appropriate penalty, including:

- the severity of the breach;
- the value of the breach;
- the harm, or risk of harm, to the sanctions regime's objectives by the breach;
- whether there is intentional circumvention of sanctions;
- the party's knowledge of sanctions and compliance systems;
- the party's behaviour, including evidence of deliberate breach, wilful neglect, failure to take reasonable care and mistake;
- the extent of ownership and control assessments;
- failure to apply for a licence or breach of a licence;
- evidence of professional facilitation;
- repeated, persistent, or prolonged breaches; and
- the level of co-operation with authorities.[196]

**3.144** Voluntary disclosure and co-operation with the investigation by each party involved in the breach is expected and will generally be treated as a mitigating factor by OFSI in assessing the suitability or quantum of any monetary penalty.

**3.145** It is important to note that failure to provide information on sanctions breaches can be a criminal offence in its own right. In some circumstances, financial sanctions regulations require relevant firms to give information.[197] In other circumstances HM Treasury, through OFSI, can use statutory powers to require the provision of information. In both cases, failure to provide information 'without reasonable excuse' may amount to an offence attracting a monetary penalty.

192 PCA 2017, s S.146(4).
193 Officer is defined to include a director, manager, secretary, partner, or in the case of an unincorporated body, a person who is concerned in the management or control of the body.
194 PCA 2017, s 148(1).
195 OFSI, 'Financial Sanctions Enforcement and Monetary Penalties Guidance' (n 16).
196 OFSI, 'Financial Sanctions Enforcement and Monetary Penalties Guidance' (n 16) s 3 on 'Case assessment'.
197 See s I, 'Reporting Obligations', in this chapter.

In the EU, penalties incurred for sanctions violation or circumvention differ from one Member State to the other. In certain Member States, criminal penalties are incurred, whereas in other Member States they are administrative only. This disparity in enforcement has been identified as jeopardizing the effectiveness of EU sanctions and has led to the EU recently enacted Directive No 2024/1226 on the harmonization of definitions and penalties incurred for sanctions violations and circumvention. The deadline for transposition into domestic law was 20 May 2025. 3.146

### 2. Deferred Prosecution Agreements

Financial sanctions breaches can now be subject to court-approved Deferred Prosecution Agreements[198] made between prosecutors in England and Wales and organizations, where the prosecution is satisfied 'that there is sufficient evidence to prove beyond reasonable doubt that a criminal offence has been committed by the organisation'.[199] 3.147

A DPA can be entered into once the organization is charged with an offence. Once a DPA has been entered into proceedings are automatically suspended subject to certain conditions. If the conditions of the DPA are breached, the prosecution may resume. 3.148

### 3. Serious Crime Prevention Orders (SCPOs)

A SCPO is a protective measure designed to prevent a person from engaging further in serious crime. An order is made pursuant to the Serious Crime Act 2007 (as amended). Breaches of financial sanctions are included in the list of offences for which a SCPO can be made.[200] 3.149

## K. Compliance Challenges

The development and complexity of financial sanctions means that compliance with them has never been more complex. Whilst the practical methods of complying with financial sanctions are outside the scope of this chapter, most relevant firms deploy sophisticated sanctions screening tools and stringent compliance procedures. However, the impact of sanctions on business relationships requires expert knowledge of how the financial sanctions regimes operate in practice and their impact on specific transactions. The operational burden that financial sanctions compliance creates may be significant: businesses must complete sanctions related risk assessments, maintain up to 3.150

[198] PCA 2017, s 150.
[199] OFSI, 'Financial Sanctions Enforcement and Monetary Penalties Guidance' (n 16) s 7.3.2.
[200] Serious Crime Act 2007, sch 1, pt 1, para 13B.

date sanctions policies and procedures, provide sanctions related training, and keep up to date with the frequent changes to financial sanctions measures and legislation whilst assessing the practical impact of such changes. Even without improper *mens rea*, they may still be at significant risk of breach and consequent penalty.

**3.151** Following its review of sanctions systems and controls in firms it regulates, the FCA issued guidance[201] in September 2023 which set out key themes and examples of good and poor practice. Some points of general application to note are:

- Governance, oversight, and the ability to monitor and review the effectiveness of sanctions implementation through management information is key.
- Resources for sanctions teams need to be sufficient to adapt and react to sanctions risks.
- Sanctions screening tools need to be properly calibrated and tailored to the risks faced by the business using them, with sufficient oversight over third-party providers of such tools.
- Customer due diligence and 'know your customer' procedures are vital to ensuring sanctions compliance.

**3.152** Non-compliance with financial sanctions can lead to severe penalties. Although the enforcement of financial sanctions in the UK to date has been limited, the reputational impact of getting it wrong can be significant. The pressure to comply with evolving financial sanctions, whilst managing the cost and compliance burdens that they create, is a constant challenge for relevant firms to balance appropriately.

[201] FCA, 'Sanctions Systems and Controls: Firms' Response to Increased Sanctions Due to Russia's Invasion of Ukraine' (updated 20 March 2024) <https://www.fca.org.uk/publications/good-and-poor-practice/sanctions-systems-and-controls-firms-response-increased-sanctions-due-russias-invasion-ukraine> accessed 4 September 2025.

# 4

# Director Disqualification Sanctions

*Amanda Pinto KC, John Binns, and Mohamed Naleemudeen*



## A. Introduction

Director disqualification (DD) sanctions prohibit a person designated for these purposes from acting as a director of a UK company or taking part in its promotion, formation, or management.[1] **4.01**

In summary, the DD sanctions power applies the pre-existing prohibition and enforcement framework of the Company Directors Disqualification Act 1986 (CDDA) into sanctions regulations. The power to do this, and to designate persons for these purposes, was inserted into the Sanctions and Anti-Money Laundering Act 2018 (SAMLA) by the Economic Crime and Corporate Transparency Act 2023 (ECCTA). **4.02**

As of 20 August 2025, the UK Government has incorporated DD sanctions into 29 of its 38 sanctions regimes (as discussed below),[2] and has imposed DD sanctions on 3,963 **4.03**

[1] Sanctions and Anti-Money Laundering Act 2018 (SAMLA), s 3A.

[2] The Sanctions (EU Exit) (Miscellaneous Amendments and Revocations) Regulations 2024; the Sanctions (EU Exit) (Miscellaneous Amendments) 2024; the Iran (Sanctions) Regulations 2023; the Global Irregular Migration and Trafficking in Persons Sanctions Regulations 2025. Note: DD sanctions have not yet been incorporated into sanctions regimes flowing from UN sanctions (Afghanistan, Haiti, Iraq, ISIL (Da'esh) and Al-Qaida, Lebanon and Lebanon (Hariri), Libya, Syria in relation to cultural property, and Yemen) and arms embargoes (Armenia and Azerbaijan, and China and Hong Kong). See further para 4.51 below.

Amanda Pinto KC, John Binns, and Mohamed Naleemudeen, *Director Disqualification Sanctions* In: *UK Sanctions Law and Practice*. Edited by: Amanda Pinto KC, Alexandre Haines, and Sophie O'Sullivan, Oxford University Press.

DOI: 10.1093/oso/9780198964179.003.0004

individuals and entities.[3] However, with the first DD sanctions having only been imposed on 9 April 2025, it is still too early to understand the full consequences and effects of the measure.

## B. Background

### 1. The White Paper

4.04 On 26 October 2023, ECCTA inserted DD sanctions into SAMLA[4] and provisions to give effect to the DD sanctions into the CDDA. These provisions came into force on 4 March 2024.

4.05 ECCTA was part of the previous Conservative Government's legislative package that intended to tackle economic crime by reforming the UK's corporate transparency and corporate structure frameworks.[5]

4.06 This legislative reform was spurred by the Conservative Government's Corporate Transparency and Register Reform White Paper, which was published in February 2022 (the 'White Paper').[6] The White Paper proposed measures to tackle economic crime, support national security and anti-corruption measures, improve Companies House, and boost enterprise, after four rounds of Government consultation with stakeholders.[7]

4.07 The White Paper proposed DD sanctions as part of proposed restrictions on the use of corporate directors,[8] to increase transparency of corporate structures and to make register information more reliable.[9] The restrictions included the power 'to void the appointment, and prevent the registration, of individuals acting as directors (and equivalents in other entities) who are disqualified (without the permission of the court), undischarged bankrupts (without the permission of the court) or a designated person under section 9 of the Sanctions and Anti-Money Laundering Act 2018'.[10]

4.08 ECCTA incorporates the White Paper's proposed reforms to director identity verification and restrictions to director identity, including DD sanctions. The Explanatory Notes to ECCTA state that a key objective of the act is to 'prevent organised criminals, fraudsters, kleptocrats and terrorists from using companies and other corporate entities

[3] Foreign, Commonwealth and Development Office (FCDO), 'The UK Sanctions List' <https://search-uk-sanctions-list.service.gov.uk/> accessed 20 August 2025.
[4] Economic Crime and Corporate Transparency Act 2023 (ECCTA), s 35.
[5] Explanatory Notes to the ECCTA 2023 (56-EN, 2024) <https://www.legislation.gov.uk/ukpga/2023/56/pdfs/ukpgaen_20230056_en.pdf> accessed 20 August 2025.
[6] Department for Business, Energy and Industrial Strategy (BEIS), Corporate Transparency and Register Reform White Paper (CP 68, February 2022) p 13, para 13.
[7] ibid p 15.
[8] ibid p 43, para 139.
[9] ibid p 43, para 136.
[10] ibid p 45, para 149.

to abuse the UK's open economy'.[11] ECCTA intends to protect the UK's national security, consumers, and business by making it harder for the aforementioned persons/groups 'to engage in money laundering, corruption, terrorism-financing, illegal arms movements and ransomware payments'.[12]

ECCTA intends to achieve its objectives by strengthening transparency and registration requirements, introducing new criminal offences, and broadening the Registrar of Companies' and law enforcement's investigatory and enforcement powers.[13] **4.09**

The Explanatory Notes to ECCTA note that the DD sanctions are 'a completely new type of sanctions measure'; and they set out that an individual subject to DD sanctions 'will commit an offence if they act as a director of a company or directly or indirectly take part in or be concerned in the promotion, formation or management of a company'.[14] **4.10**

The purpose of DD sanctions is further elaborated in the Explanatory Memorandum to the Sanctions (EU Exit) (Miscellaneous Amendments and Revocations) Regulations 2024, which incorporated DD sanctions into several of the UK's existing sanctions regimes.[15] **4.11**

The Explanatory Memorandum states that, previously, designated persons (DPs) 'subject to an asset freeze, have not been prevented from acting as a UK company director as a result of their designation. This is because acting as a director of a UK company does not necessarily require the provision of funds or economic resources by UK persons.'[16] However, under DD sanctions, DPs subject to an asset freeze can be prohibited from acting as directors of UK companies. DD sanctions also intend to further prevent DPs 'from accessing or deriving benefit from the UK economy'.[17] **4.12**

## 2. The Company Directors Disqualification Act 1986

Under the Company Directors Disqualification Act 1986 (CDDA), a person (including a body corporate) may be disqualified, for a specified period, from (1) acting as a director or, (2) directly or indirectly, being concerned or taking part in the promotion, formation or management of a company.[18] The grounds for disqualification include **4.13**

[11] Explanatory Notes to ECCTA (n 5), p 13, para 2(a).
[12] Explanatory Notes to ECCTA (n 5), p 14, para 5.
[13] Explanatory Notes to ECCTA (n 5), p 13, para 3.
[14] Explanatory Notes to ECCTA (n 5), p 18, para 11(b)(ii).
[15] Explanatory Memorandum to the Sanctions (EU Exit) (Miscellaneous Amendments and Revocations) Regulations 2024/643 (CO/EM/2024.1) <https://www.legislation.gov.uk/uksi/2024/643/pdfs/uksiem_20240643_en_001.pdf> accessed 20 August 2025; Venezuela, Guinea-Bissau, Belarus, Zimbabwe, Syria, Russia, Burundi, Guinea, Bosnia and Herzegovina, Nicaragua, Myanmar, Global Anti-Corruption, Global Human Rights, Unauthorised Drilling Activities, Cyber, and Chemical Weapons.
[16] ibid p 4, para 5.10.
[17] ibid p 4, para 5.10.
[18] Company Directors Disqualification Act 1986 (CDDA), s 1(1).

general misconduct in connection with companies, unfitness, promoting tax avoidance, etc.

**4.14** The CDDA defines a 'company' as a company registered under the Companies Act 2006 in Great Britain.[19] The definition of 'company' in the CDDA also includes companies and associations that are incorporated in the UK, but are not registered under the Companies Act 2006, such as limited liability partnerships and charity trustees.

**4.15** In *R v Seager (Mornington Stafford)*, Aikens LJ stated that the intention of the CDDA is to ensure that 'only reasonably competent, responsible and honest people act as company directors' in order to protect shareholders, employees, and members of the public from 'possible fraud, incompetence and regulatory failings by people who are supposedly directing companies'.[20]

**4.16** Disqualification proceedings under the CDDA are a civil process, although a disqualification order may be imposed by a criminal court (typically as part of a sentencing exercise). A disqualification order or a voluntary undertaking may have penal consequences, and the contravention of either is a criminal offence.[21]

**4.17** The CDDA extends to England, Wales, and Scotland. The Company Directors Disqualification (Northern Ireland) Order 2002 (NI Order) governs DD sanctions in Northern Ireland.

**4.18** The appropriate authority for the CDDA is the Secretary of State.[22] The Secretary's powers have been delegated to the Department of Business and Trade's Insolvency Service, which investigates, enforces, and monitors compliance with the CDDA.

## C. Director Disqualification Sanctions

**4.19** The Secretary of State is empowered to designate a person under DD sanctions (making them a 'DD-designated person' or 'DD-DP'), pursuant to section 3A of SAMLA.[23]

**4.20** Section 3A provides:

> **3A Director Disqualification Sanctions**
>
> (1) For the purposes of section 1(5)(aa) regulations 'impose director disqualification sanctions' if they provide for designated persons (see section 9) to be persons subject to director disqualification sanctions for the purposes of—
>
> (a) section 11A of the Company Directors Disqualification Act 1986, and

[19] CDDA 1986, s 22.
[20] *R v Seager (Mornington Stafford)* [2009] EWCA Crim 1303, para 67.
[21] CDDA 1986, s 13.
[22] CDDA 1986, s 1A(5).
[23] SAMLA 2018, s 3A.

(b) Article 15A of the Company Directors Disqualification (Northern Ireland) Order 2002.

(2) As to the effect of such provision, see—

(a) section 11A of the Company Directors Disqualification Act 1986, and

(b) Article 15A of the Company Directors Disqualification (Northern Ireland) Order 2002.

As is apparent, an analysis of DD sanctions requires an analysis of section 11A of the CDDA, which contains the substantive content of the measure, including its offence, penalty, defence, and liability provisions. 4.21

## 1. The Offence Provision

Under section 11A(1) of the CDDA (and equivalent NI Order provision), a disqualified person (including a DD-DP) commits an offence if they, without an exception or a licence: 4.22

a. 'act as a director of a company'; or
b. 'directly or indirectly [ ... ] take part in or be concerned in the promotion, formation or management of a company'.[24]

The prohibitions should be read broadly, as the terms 'director' and 'promotion, formation or management' have been defined, and construed, broadly. 4.23

- The CDDA defines 'director' as 'including any person occupying the position of director, by whatever name called'.[25]
- The 'promotion' of a company was defined in *Twycross v Grant* by Cockburn CJ, as occurring when a person 'undertakes to form a company with reference to a given project and to set it going, and who takes the necessary steps to accomplish that purpose'.[26]
- The 'formation' of a company references the incorporation of a company, i.e. 'the legal acts necessary to bring a company into existence'.[27] In relation to this prohibition, ECCTA has also amended the Companies Act 2006 to supplement the prohibition of persons subject to DD sanctions being involved in the formation of a company.
- Defining what is meant by the 'management' of a company is likely to be a fact-specific exercise and will be dependent on factors including the company's size, complexity, and management structure. The Insolvency Service notes that

[24] CDDA 1986, s 11A.

[25] CDDA 1986, s 22.

[26] *Twycross v Grant* (No 1) (1877) 2 CPD 469.

[27] Insolvency Service, 'Effect of a Disqualification' (Guidance, 22 May 2024) <https://www.gov.uk/government/publications/corporate-insolvency-effect-of-a-disqualification-order/effect-of-a-disqualification> accessed 20 August 2025.

'"management of a company" is not confined to management of the internal affairs of that company'.[28] Further, a manager may be someone in a position equivalent to that of a director, without having been appointed as such, or may formally be below director level. Being concerned in the management of the company may include such activities as

i. undertaking tasks in relation to the company's business, e.g. ordering or negotiating with suppliers, dealing with the company bank account;
ii. acting as a management consultant; or
iii. taking executive decisions as to the company's affairs or giving the appearance of being in a position to take such decisions.

- The broad scope of the provision is demonstrated by the second condition, which explicitly prohibits DPs from both 'directly or indirectly [ … ] taking part in or being concerned in' the promotion, formation, or management of a company. This indicates the intentionally broad scope, with the focus being less on form, and more on a person's circumstantial and factual effect on the company. In *Re Market Wizard Systems (UK) Ltd*, regarding 'a person being concerned in the management of a company', Carnwath J acknowledged the difficulty of achieving a succinct test, but emphasized that 'ultimate control' is not a necessary element. Instead, an important factor is whether the person in question's role is relevant to 'the solvency or the probity of the corporation's administration'.[29]

**4.24** Further, under section 159A of the Companies Act 2006, a DD-DP is prohibited from being appointed as a director of a company if the person is subject to DD sanctions, unless they have a licence or an exception applies. If the DP is appointed in contravention of section 159A, then their appointment is void.[30]

**4.25** Flowing on from section 159A, under section 9 of the Companies Act 2006, which sets out the registration documents required when incorporating a new company, applications must include a statement that none of the shareholders, at incorporation, are disqualified under the CDDA, which includes persons subject to DD sanctions.

**4.26** Additionally, under section 12A, applications must include a statement that no person with significant control (PSC) of the company at its incorporation is subject to DD sanctions.[31] Given that anyone with a share worth over 25 per cent of a company is a PSC (whether or not they are also a director), this provision appears

[28] ibid.
[29] *Re Market Wizard Systems (UK) Ltd* [1998] 7 WLUK 260.
[30] Companies Act 2006, s 159A(3).
[31] The Companies Act, at part 1 of Schedule 1A, defines a person with 'significant control' as a person who, directly or indirectly, (i) holds more than 25 per cent of the shares or the voting rights in the company; (ii) holds the right to appoint or remove a majority of the board of directors; and (iii) holds the right to exercise, or actually exercises, significant influence or control over the company, including influence or control over a trust or partnership with 'significant control' of the company.

to broaden the impact of DD designations substantially. DD-DPs would not only be prevented from controlling UK companies, but also from owning significant stakes in them. As the company's obligation to make the statement applies on incorporation, and there is no ongoing obligation to confirm the absence of DD-DP PSCs, this appears only to affect companies incorporated after the DD designation of the PSC concerned.

## 2. Penalties

Under section 13 of the CDDA (or equivalent NI Order provision), a DD-DP who acts as a director (or who, directly or indirectly, is involved in the promotion, formation, or management) of a company is liable: **4.27**

(a) on conviction on indictment, to imprisonment for not more than 2 years or a fine, or both; and
(b) on summary conviction, to imprisonment for not more than 6 months or a fine not exceeding the statutory maximum, or both.[32]

Further, under section 15 of the CDDA, the DD-DP will be personally responsible for all relevant debts of a company if the person is involved in its management while subject to DD sanctions.[33] However, the DD-DP will not be liable for the relevant debts if they were incurred at a time when the person did not know and could not reasonably have been expected to know that they were subject to DD sanctions.[34] **4.28**

A person who acts under the instructions of a DD-DP, without a licence, will also be personally liable for the company's relevant debts.[35] However, the person who acted on instructions will not be liable if they can show they reasonably believed that the instructions were authorized by a licence (issued by virtue of section 15(3A) of SAMLA: see paragraphs 4.40–4 below).[36] **4.29**

## 3. Defences

It is a defence for a person 'to prove that they did not know and could not reasonably have been expected to know that they were subject to director disqualification sanctions at the time at which they engaged in that conduct'.[37] **4.30**

[32] CCDA 1986, s 13.
[33] CDDA 1986, s 1.
[34] CDDA 1986, s 3A.
[35] CDDA 1986, s 1.
[36] CDDA 1986, s 15.
[37] ECCTA 2023, s 36(2).

## 4. Corporate and Officers' Liability

4.31 Corporations may be held criminally liable for contravening these prohibitions through the actions of their 'directing minds'. This is not one of the offences for which corporations can be liable through the actions of their senior managers under section 196 and Schedule 12 of ECCTA (though it should be noted that Schedule 12 can be amended by regulations).

4.32 If a corporation is guilty of the offence and it is proved that 'the offence occurred with the consent or connivance of, or was attributable to any neglect on the part of any director, manager, secretary or other similar officer of the body corporate, or any person who was purporting to act in any such capacity',[38] such officers will also be personally liable. An 'officer' is defined by reference to the Companies Act 2006, section 1173, which includes 'a director, manager or secretary'.

4.33 Regarding the penalty, the provision states the officer is liable to be 'punished accordingly'.[39] In other words, the officer will be subject to the same sentence as if they had committed the offence themselves.

## 5. Territorial Scope/Jurisdiction

4.34 If a person is designated under DD sanctions, it is an offence for them to act as a director or take part directly or indirectly in the promotion, formation, and management of all registered and unregistered companies formed in England, Wales, Scotland, and Northern Ireland.[40]

### (i) Overseas acts by UK persons

4.35 The relevant offence will, however, be committed contrary to the CDDA rather than SAMLA regulations, which means that the general rules governing the territorial application of criminal offences apply. In contrast to breaches of financial sanctions or trade sanctions, the offence *does not* therefore extend to acts overseas by 'UK persons' (as defined in section 21 of SAMLA).[41] A prosecution of any DD-DP (whether a 'UK person' or not) located overseas for acting as a director of a UK company would therefore have to proceed on the basis that a 'substantial measure' of their conduct had taken place in the UK, applying ordinary, non-SAMLA principles of jurisdiction (as articulated in *R v Wallace Duncan Smith*).[42] That may well be clear where the company's assets, operations, and/or personnel are in the UK, but less so where the company's only link to the UK is the fact of its registration here. Depending on where the DD-DP is located (and where they travel), there may also be practical difficulties with extraditing them to the UK for such a prosecution.

[38] CDDA 1986, s 14.
[39] CDDA 1986, s 14(1).
[40] CDDA 1986, ss 22 and 24.
[41] SAMLA 2018, s 21.
[42] *R v Smith (Wallace Duncan) (No 4)* [2004] EWCA Crim 631.

**4.36** Licensing offences, in contrast, have the territorial scope of offences under sanctions regulations, so would apply to acts overseas by UK persons.

(ii) Extra-territorial jurisdiction

**4.37** The Insolvency Service's guidance on DD sanctions notes that a person subject to DD sanctions may still be committing an offence in the UK if they (directly or indirectly) continue 'being a director of a foreign company that has sufficient connection to the UK, even if it is not registered here. For example, if it carries out business or has assets here'.[43]

**4.38** In the Insolvency Service's guidance, the interpretation of DD sanctions appears to stem from the CDDA's definition of 'company',[44] which includes companies that may be wound up under Part 5 of the Insolvency Act 1986. Foreign companies that conduct business in the UK come within that category.[45]

**4.39** This purported extra-territorial reach of DD sanctions is not expressly set out in SAMLA or the CDDA and thus would not appear legally binding. Nevertheless, it indicates that a person subject to the DD sanctions may potentially be committing an offence under UK law if they continue acting as the director of a foreign company with a 'sufficient connection' to the UK (or may be considered to have acted as such). In any event, an activity that breaches the prohibition *and* that takes place in the UK would constitute such an offence.

## 6. Licensing and Exceptions

**4.40** Similar~~ly~~ to other sanctions measures, SAMLA section 15 (exceptions and licences) allows for the creation of exceptions and the issuance of licences to authorize DD-DPs to do acts that may be otherwise ~~be~~ prohibited under DD sanctions.

**4.41** The Secretary of State may issue a licence to a DD-DP, authorizing them to carry out acts (or omissions) that would otherwise have been prohibited by the DD sanctions.[46]

**4.42** The Insolvency Service is responsible, on behalf of the Secretary of State, for assessing and granting/refusing licences to persons designated under DD sanctions.[47]

**4.43** If the Insolvency Service grants a licence, then the licence will specify the act(s) it authorizes. A licence may be subject to conditions. It may also be varied or revoked, and any such changes will be communicated to the DD-DP or their authorized representative.[48]

[43] The Insolvency Service, 'Director Disqualification Sanctions' (Guidance, 8 April 2025) <https://www.gov.uk/guidance/director-disqualification-sanctions> accessed 20 August 2025.

[44] CDDA 1986, s 22(2).

[45] Insolvency Act 1986, s 225.

[46] Explanatory Notes to ECCTA (n 5), p 50, paras 288–9.

[47] The Insolvency Service, 'Licence Application for Directors Subject to Director Disqualification Sanctions' (Guidance, 9 April 2025) <https://www.gov.uk/guidance/licence-application-for-directors-subject-to-director-disqualification-sanctions> accessed 20 August 2025.

[48] See e.g. Russia (Sanctions) (EU Exit) Regulations 2019 (Russia Regulations), reg 66.

**4.44** It is an offence if a person obtains a licence, for themselves or others, by knowingly or recklessly providing information that is false in a material respect, or by providing or producing a document that is not what it purports to be.[49] A person also commits an offence if they purport to act under the authority of a DD licence but fail to comply with any condition of the licence.[50] Both offences are punishable with up to two years' imprisonment on indictment.[51] In both instances, the licence is to be treated as void from the time at which it was issued.[52]

### 7. Relevant Agencies and Authorities

**4.45** The Secretary of State is responsible for implementing and overseeing the DD sanctions. The Secretary's responsibilities have been delegated to the Insolvency Service and Companies House.

**4.46** The Insolvency Service is responsible for overseeing the DD sanctions licensing regime, and investigation and enforcement of breaches of DD sanctions.

**4.47** The Insolvency Service also has the power to bring prosecutions for breaches of DD sanctions, or, where appropriate, to refer cases to law enforcement agencies for potential prosecution. The Insolvency Service also monitors compliance with DD sanctions and for assessing suspected breaches of the main prohibitions and the licensing prohibitions.

**4.48** Companies House (and the Department for the Economy in Northern Ireland) is responsible for recording information about DD sanctions in its respective Disqualified Director Register. Companies House is also responsible for annotating the Companies Register and preventing registration of a disqualified director's appointments.[53]

## D. Which Sanctions Regulations Have Given Effect to the DD Sanctions?

**4.49** The UK Government has incorporated DD sanctions into 29 of its 38 sanctions regimes, originating from domestic, United Nations, and other international sanctions.

**4.50** The UK first incorporated DD sanctions into the Iran (Sanctions) Regulations 2023—which entered into force on 14 December 2023—as part of that new regime's original regulations. More recently, the UK also incorporated DD sanctions into The Global Irregular Migration and Trafficking in Persons Sanctions Regulations 2025 (entered into force on 23 July 2025), as part of the new regime's original regulations.

**4.51** For 27 regimes, the UK incorporated DD sanctions through two amendments to the respective existing regimes' regulations:

[49] Russia Regulations 2019, reg 67A (3).
[50] Russia Regulations 2019, reg 67A (2).
[51] Russia Regulations 2019, reg 80(3).
[52] Russia Regulations 2019, reg 67A (3).
[53] CDDA 1986, s 18.

i. The Sanctions (EU Exit) (Miscellaneous Amendments and Revocations) Regulations 2024 (entered into force on 16 May 2024) in respect of Belarus, Bosnia and Herzegovina, Guinea-Bissau, Guinea, Myanmar, Nicaragua, Russia, Syria, Venezuela, Zimbabwe; Chemical Weapons, Cyber, Global Anti-Corruption, Global Human Rights, and Unauthorized Drilling Activities in the Eastern Mediterranean.
ii. The Sanctions (EU Exit) (Miscellaneous Amendments) Regulations 2024 (entered into force on 5 June 2024) in respect of the Central African Republic, Democratic People's Republic of Korea, Democratic Republic of the Congo, Libya, Mali, Somalia, South Sudan, Sudan, Yemen, Domestic Counter-Terrorism, International Counter-Terrorism, and in relation to Iran's nuclear weapons programmes.[54]

The DD sanctions provisions inserted into each regime are consistent with each other, flowing from the relevant SAMLA provisions. Each provision states that a person within the designation criteria may be designated under DD sanctions, and will then be subject to DD sanctions for the purposes of section 11A of the CDDA and article 15A of the NI Order.[55] Further provisions then state that, under a licence, DD-DPs may be authorized to engage in acts (or omissions) otherwise prohibited by the DD sanctions. The regulations also provide offences in relation to obtaining or operating the licences (as above, paragraphs 4.40–6).[56] **4.52**

## E. Enforcement

At the time of writing, no enforcement actions have been commenced or taken. **4.53**

## F. Similar Sanctions Measures in Other Jurisdictions

There are currently no comparable sanctions measures elsewhere. The European Union, United States, Australia, and New Zealand do not have DD sanctions. **4.54**

## G. Issues with Director Disqualification Sanctions

### 1. Purposes of DD Sanctions

Disqualification under the CDDA can arise in various circumstances, including as a result of misconduct, unfitness, promoting tax avoidance, competition infringements, participation in wrongful trading, and bankruptcy.[57] The logical case for extending this **4.55**

[54] The DD sanctions in the UK's sanctions regimes relating to Mali, domestic counter-terrorism, and international counter-terrorism were further amended to include licensing provisions: Mali (Sanctions) (EU Exit) (Amendment) and Sanctions (Miscellaneous Amendments) Regulations 2024.

[55] See e.g. Sanctions (EU Exit) (Miscellaneous Amendments and Revocations) Regulations 2024, pt 4.

[56] ibid.

[57] See e.g. CDDA 1986, ss 2, 6, and 10.

to the broad class of 'involved persons', as defined in various regulations made under SAMLA for assorted purposes (ranging from combating nuclear proliferation to protecting human rights),[58] is not immediately obvious. Someone classified as an 'involved person' does not necessarily present either an internal risk to UK companies or a risk of exploiting companies externally for nefarious purposes.

**4.56** The policy imperative of DD sanctions, however, seems clear. In the aftermath of Russia's full-scale invasion of Ukraine, various initiatives concerned with corporate transparency, 'dirty money', economic crime, kleptocracy, and 'oligarchs' became conflated. In seeking to address these issues the government could at least arguably point to a class of DPs who should not be allowed to have (or, pertinently, be allowed to retain) access to important aspects of the UK's economy.

## 2. Trust Services: A Comparison

**4.57** A comparison to the trust services ban, so far unique to the Russia sanctions regime, is instructive.[59] In both cases, the UK Government has identified an aspect of its economy to which it says DPs (or some DPs) should be denied access. In the case of the trust services ban, however, the UK's facility for this was already 'baked in' to the framework of financial sanctions—'trust services' being included within the definition of financial services in SAMLA.[60] The UK's use of the tool to target DPs (and Russian residents) under the Russia regime was coordinated with its allies, and coherently expressed as part of the effort to coerce, constrain, and send a signal to the Russian government.[61]

**4.58** On this basis, the UK Government took a decision to designate all DPs who were already designated for other purposes under Russia sanctions (asset freeze, etc.), under the new trust services ban as well from 21 March 2023.[62] At a stroke, all 1,730 DPs on the Russia list became subject to these new prohibitions, thereby proscribing the provision of trust services for their benefit. And similarly, on 9 April 2025, with no prior warning, the UK Government imposed DD sanctions on 2,996 individual DPs and 818 entity DPs, exposing them and the companies they direct to potential criminal consequences.

**4.59** Importantly, however, the impact of the trust services ban was mitigated by a combination of exceptions and general licences, which allowed for a staged and orderly withdrawal of services, including an effective 'grace period' to allow such services to be wound down.[63] In the regulations themselves, exceptions were made, for instance,

[58] See e.g., Russia Regulations 2019, reg 6(1); the Iran (Sanctions) (Nuclear) (EU Exit) Regulations 2019, reg 6(1); the Global Human Rights Sanctions Regulations 2020, reg 6(1).
[59] Russia Regulations 2019, reg 18C.
[60] SAMLA 2018, s 61(1)(b)(ix).
[61] OFSI, 'Trust Services Sanctions Update' (*OFSI Blog*, 21 March 2023) <https://ofsi.blog.gov.uk/2023/03/21/trust-services-sanctions-update/> accessed 20 August 2025.
[62] ibid.
[63] Russia Regulations 2019, reg 60ZZB; OFSI and HM Treasury, General Licence INT/2023/2589788, 'Wind-down of Trust Services Provided to Designated Persons' (21 March 2023).

where trust services were provided for the purposes of complying with asset freeze provisions, to charities or pension schemes, or solely to benefit people aged under 18.

In practice, too, the overlap between dealing with DPs' assets, providing funds or resources to DPs (as already prohibited by asset freeze provisions), and providing trust services for their benefit (as covered by the new ban), while often complicated, sent a clear enough message about what was prohibited, and what would be allowed in the short and longer term. Broadly speaking, the UK Government wanted to prevent anyone subject to the UK's jurisdiction from helping DPs with 'their' assets, not just by 'dealing' with direct assets of DPs and their companies, but also by managing assets with which DPs were involved indirectly (as settlors and/or beneficiaries of trusts). 4.60

Some would argue there are legitimate distinctions between dealing with assets and holding assets on trust on the one hand, and, on the other, between assets 'owned, held or controlled' by DPs and assets held in a trust for which the DP was a settlor or is a beneficiary. Nonetheless, when the government instituted the trust services ban, it was at least clear what it was aiming for, and why. It was also apparent that it had taken into account (at least to some extent) the practicalities of bringing the ban into force. Both the aim and the practicalities are unclear in respect of DD sanctions. 4.61

## 3. Unanswered Questions

At the time of writing, DD sanctions have been wielded indiscriminately against individuals and entities that were previously designated under all financial sanctions regimes. Rather than being imposed to further the purposes of targeting specific actors or any specific sanctions regime, the DD sanctions seem to be directed at 'cleaning up' the UK's corporate landscape by excluding people who (for very different purposes) the UK Government has deemed worth targeting with asset freezes and travel bans. 4.62

When DD sanctions were first imposed on 9 April 2025, there was no grace period, no exceptions, and minimal guidance to ameliorate any collateral impact the prohibitions may have. While still too early to understand the full impact of DD sanctions, such impromptu designations are bound to have a bigger impact than just removing directors. They will lead to some companies collapsing and assets losing value or, at worst, being destroyed. It is notable that, unlike other sanctions regimes, there is no provision for monetary penalties or any reporting requirements. What we do have, nonetheless, are officers of UK companies, in a state of uncertainty about how to respond. This has had most effect on those caught under the Russia Regulations, because of the integration of Russian monies into the UK economy (resulting in the potential for UK companies to be used as vehicles for Russian money) and because of the conflation of the sanctions agenda with broader issues around economic crime, kleptocrats, and oligarchs. 4.63

One distinction worth bearing in mind is between UK companies where a DP is engaged purely as a director (or one of several directors), and those (perhaps more 4.64

common) where the DP also owns and/or controls the company. In the latter case, the company itself would already be subject to asset freeze provisions broadly as if it were the DP itself, including prohibitions on dealing with its assets and on providing funds or economic resources to it or for its benefit (as set out in Chapter 3, 'Financial Sanctions').

**4.65** For companies in the former category, the impact of a director becoming a DD-DP would seem relatively straightforward. The DD-DP must cease acting as a director or face criminal liability (subject to jurisdiction—as discussed in paragraphs 4.37–9 above). The company itself also faces liability, which its other officers should take steps to ensure does not also extend to them personally. If other directors remain, or replacements can be found, then the company can continue to operate, and—depending on the connections, expertise and skills the DD-DP brought to the role—experience little adverse impact (though the negotiation of an exit package might prove daunting).

**4.66** Even in this less complicated scenario, there may still be issues. Some transitional provisions (perhaps in the form of a general licence) will surely have to cater for the fact that resignations and the handover of control cannot realistically be instantaneous. The other methods of disqualification under the CDDA generally involve a process of orders being applied for and taking effect,[64] which gives time for those involved to be replaced as directors. The designation schemes under SAMLA regulations typically involve DPs being 'notified' of their status by way of a public statement, and the relevant prohibitions taking effect immediately. The latter practices are not readily adaptable to the purposes of DD sanctions.

**4.67** For companies which are owned or controlled by the DP, the requirement on a DP to step down as director is practically complicated and unsatisfactory. The DD-DP designation may leave no one in effective control, although the DP remains the company's owner (and their assets remain subject to financial sanctions). This situation has no obvious benefit and will clearly cause manifold problems. Few are likely to volunteer for the position of replacement director in such a scenario. Moreover, the lack of formal control is likely to prompt disorderly dissolutions and complex, urgent applications to OFSI to licence divestments, liquidations, and receiverships, none of which is in the public interest.

**4.68** All that, of course, is to assume that DPs and their companies will have both the ability and the desire to do the 'right thing' (however that is best defined) according to UK law. Many will not. Part of the impact of DD designations, therefore, may be an array of breaches, circumventions, and steps taken overseas that are designed to frustrate the purposes of DD sanctions. As discussed in paragraph 4.35, the jurisdictional reach of the new prohibitions may sometimes be unclear or contested, and enforcement by

[64] See e.g. CDDA 1986, ss 1A(1) and 2.

extradition may be difficult where DD-DPs are located in jurisdictions that will not extradite to the UK.

The effect of those steps will be to secure assets currently held by UK companies (and, therefore, theoretically subject to the jurisdiction of UK sanctions law) and make them available to their DP owners outside that jurisdiction. How will law enforcement address such steps to make these assets available overseas? It may be difficult for authorities in the UK to do so in practice. If, for instance, a DD-DP director transfers assets from his UK company to the UAE before resigning, the question of who can be prosecuted under what provisions of the CDDA, sanctions regulations, or both, may well prove academic. This, in turn, would make the UK Government's victory in removing DP directors from UK companies somewhat pyrrhic. It may be that a combination of pragmatic use and creative enforcement could make that victory more genuine but it remains to be seen whether this can be achieved in practice. **4.69**

# 5

# Trade Sanctions

*Alexandre Haines, Robert Morris, and Jessica Hocking*



## A. Overview

### 1. Introduction

**5.01** The first reported use of trade sanctions was in 432 BC when the Athenian Empire imposed the Megarian Decree, effectively blocking traders from Megara from harbours and marketplaces in the Athenian Empire. This was an inauspicious start to a policy aimed at avoiding conflict, as it then led to the Peloponnesian War. Swing forward a couple of millennia and trade sanctions now tend to focus upon particular sectors,

Alexandre Haines, Robert Morris, and Jessica Hocking, *Trade Sanctions* In: *UK Sanctions Law and Practice*.
Edited by: Amanda Pinto KC, Alexandre Haines, and Sophie O'Sullivan, Oxford University Press.
 DOI: 10.1093/oso/9780198964179.003.0005

goods, technologies, and services aiming to balance competing policy objectives. The most extensive package of trade sanctions is now found in the Russia (Sanctions) (EU Exit) Regulations 2019 (the 'Russia Regulations'), which forms the focus of this chapter. In general terms, trade sanctions are measures that restrict (i) 'the import, export, transfer, movement, making available or acquisition of goods and technology'; (ii) 'the provision and procurement of services related to goods and technology'; and (iii) 'the provision and procurement of certain non-financial services'.[1]

Trade sanctions apply to all individuals or businesses within the territory or territorial sea of the United Kingdom, and all UK nationals and legal entities established under UK law wherever they are in the world.[2] **5.02**

The UK's use of trade sanctions has reached unprecedented levels since the start of the Russo-Ukraine war. Trade sanctions have wide application and, since 10 October 2024, breaches can be pursued by the relevant UK authorities using criminal and civil enforcement powers, including on a strict liability basis. The creation of the Office of Trade Sanctions Implementation (OTSI) in October 2024 is a clear sign of the UK Government's desire to intensify civil enforcement of trade sanctions in the UK, particularly in response to Russia's ongoing aggression in Ukraine. **5.03**

Like all areas of sanctions, this is a changing landscape. To ensure ongoing compliance, those subject to trade sanctions (including exporters, importers, and professional service providers) must be alive to the regular changes in this area and update their systems and controls accordingly. **5.04**

## 2. Trade Sanctions and Export Controls

This chapter is focused on trade sanctions governed by the Sanctions and Anti-Money Laundering Act 2018 (SAMLA) and, in particular, the prohibitions found in the Russia Regulations. (Other trade sanctions regimes are also considered below in section H.) However, legal advisers cannot advise on trade sanctions in isolation; where there are trade sanctions issues and potential breaches, export controls will likely apply and must also be considered. **5.05**

Despite operating in parallel, trade sanctions are distinct from export controls. Export controls are restrictions adopted to deprive states of goods and raw material required for activities that threaten to breach international humanitarian law, international human rights law, and peace and security. Import controls are restrictions adopted to deprive states of sources of funding for similar reasons. **5.06**

[1] Department for Business and Trade (DBT) and Export Control Joint Unit (ECJU), 'Trade Sanctions, Arms Embargoes, and Other Trade Restrictions' (Guidance, 3 August 2012) <https://www.gov.uk/guidance/current-arms-embargoes-and-other-restrictions> accessed 26 May 2025. See also Sanctions and Anti-Money Laundering Act 2018 (SAMLA), sch 1.

[2] SAMLA 2018, s 21. See also the Russia (Sanctions) (EU Exit) Regulations 2019, reg 3.

5.07 The distinctions between trade sanctions and export controls are to be found in

1. Their use—trade sanctions tend to be adopted on the basis of foreign policy and national security objectives and are often implemented for purposes that reflect the underlying aims of a specific sanctions regime (for example, restrictions on goods that are a direct source of revenue for a government or restrictions on items relating to proliferation activities), whereas export controls regulate the export of goods, software and technology that could be used for purposes contrary to the interest of the exporting country, usually in the context of international humanitarian law or the law of armed conflict.
2. Their scope—many trade sanctions apply both to conduct taking place within the UK and conduct taking place outside the UK (albeit with a UK nexus, such as conduct involving a UK person), whereas export controls apply to the exportation of goods from the United Kingdom.
3. The texts that create them—whereas SAMLA[3] created the UK's ability to impose trade sanctions independently from the EU for one or more of the purposes mentioned in Schedule 1(1), the legal basis for domestic export controls is found in an entirely different set of statutes and regulations, namely the Export Control Act 2002 (*c.* 28), the Export Control Order 2008 (SI 2008/3231), and retained Council Regulation (EC) No 428/2009.
4. Their regulator—trade sanctions are overseen by a complex system of bodies including the Department for Business and Trade (DBT), HM Revenue and Customs (HMRC), and the Office of Trade Sanctions Implementation (OTSI) (see section B below), whereas export controls are administered by the Export Control Joint Unit (ECJU) within DBT and enforced by HMRC.

5.08 In practice, in the context of military and dual-use items, both trade sanctions and export controls under their respective regimes apply, with trade sanctions generally having a broader application (e.g. wider definitions of goods or extended list of prohibited goods). More often than not, the provision of services (as opposed to the export of goods) tends to be targeted by trade sanctions without export control provisions being engaged. However, given the overlap between the regimes, where trade sanctions are engaged, legal advisers must also consider whether export controls and financial sanctions apply.

5.09 On 28 February 2022, under Article 32 of the Export Control Order 2008, the Secretary of State for International Trade suspended all extant export licences for dual-use items to Russia.[4] This included licences with Russia as the final destination. The Russian trade sanctions regime is currently the UK's most developed system of trade sanctions law, and so is the focus of this chapter.

[3] SAMLA 2018, s 5.

[4] ECJU and Department for International Trade (DIT) (as it was then called before it became the DBT in February 2023), Notice to exporters 2022/03: licence suspensions and open general export licences revised <https://www.gov.uk/government/publications/notice-to-exporters-202203-licence-suspensions-and-ogels-revised> accessed 26 May 2025.

## B. The Regulators

The UK's system of sanctions regulation is complex. Unlike in the US, where the Office of Foreign Assets Control (OFAC) (part of the US Department of the Treasury) administers *and* enforces economic *and* trade sanctions, in the UK there are multiple government departments and bodies involved in the administration and enforcement of economic and trade sanctions. (See Chapter 2.C, 'UK Government Departments and Agencies Involved in Sanctions'.) 5.10

In very broad terms, the Foreign, Commonwealth and Development Office (FCDO) is responsible for policy and designations; HM Treasury (HMT) implements and enforces financial sanctions through its Office of Financial Sanctions Implementation (OFSI), which undertakes investigations and enforcement of civil breaches; the National Crime Agency (NCA) undertakes investigations and enforcement of criminal breaches; the Department for Transport (DfT) implements transport sanctions (including controlling movement of ships and aircraft in UK waters and airspace); the Home Office implements travel bans (immigration sanctions); DBT and the ECJU implement trade sanctions and embargoes (as well as export controls and licensing for military and dual-use items); HMRC enforces breaches of export control and is responsible for the criminal enforcement of all trade sanctions; and, finally, OTSI is responsible for the civil enforcement of certain trade sanctions breaches. 5.11

### 1. UK Agencies Involved in Trade Sanctions

The system is particularly complex for trade sanctions, where the following agencies are involved in the implementation, administration, and enforcement of trade sanctions in the UK: 5.12

1. DBT implements trade sanctions and other trade restrictions and has overall responsibility for trade sanctions licensing.
2. ECJU is part of DBT and administers the UK's system of export controls and licensing for military and dual-use items.
3. HMRC is responsible for the criminal enforcement of all trade sanctions. HMRC, as a criminal enforcement authority, can refer a matter to the Crown Prosecution Service (CPS) to consider a prosecution.[5] Although HMRC can refer cases to the CPS, in practice it often exercises its power to issue administrative penalties (known as 'compound penalties').[6] If accepted by the suspect, the case is concluded without a criminal prosecution.

[5] See DBT and OTSI, 'How Suspected Breaches of Trade Sanctions are Assessed by the Office of Trade Sanctions Implementation (OTSI)' (Guidance, 12 September 2024) s 5 <https://www.gov.uk/guidance/how-suspected-breaches-of-trade-sanctions-are-assessed-by-the-office-of-trade-sanctions-implementation-otsi> accessed 26 May 2025.

[6] The power to compound is found in the Customs and Excise Management Act 1979 (CEMA), s 152.

a. HMRC is also responsible for civil enforcement of trade sanctions relating to (i) the 'import or export of goods to, or from, the UK'; (ii) the 'transfer of technology to, or from, the UK'; (iii) the 'provision of ancillary services relating to the import and export of goods and the transfer of technology to, or from, the UK'; and (iv) 'military and dual-use goods and technology, which are subject to strategic export controls'.[7]

4. OTSI (which is part of DBT) was launched in October 2024. OTSI is responsible for issuing licences relating to the provision of standalone services (e.g. professional and business services) which are otherwise prohibited by trade sanctions.
   a. OTSI is also responsible for civil enforcement of certain trade sanctions, relating to (i) the 'provision or procurement of sanctioned trade services'; (ii) the 'movement, making available or acquisition of sanctioned goods outside the UK'; (iii) 'transferring, making available or acquisition of sanctioned technology outside the UK', (iv) 'providing ancillary services to the movement, making available or acquisition of sanctioned goods outside the UK', and (v) 'providing ancillary services to the transfer, making available or acquisition of sanctioned technology outside the UK'.[8]
   b. OTSI's role is explained further in section C. It is too early to say how effective OTSI's role will be in this complex system of regulation, but its creation is a clear sign of the UK Government's intent to increase civil enforcement of trade sanctions in the UK, particularly in response to Russia's continued aggression.

**5.13** OTSI's creation exacerbates the complexity of sanctions regulation in the UK. Practitioners will question whether a consistent approach to implementation, administration, and enforcement across economic and trade sanctions can be achieved in a regulatory system with so many stakeholder agencies. Some are of the view that a simpler system, with one authority responsible for the administration and enforcement of economic and trade sanctions, would be more likely to achieve consistency and clarity for those subject to the regimes. It would appear, however, that for the foreseeable future, this disparate group of bodies will continue to monitor the enforcement and regulation of trade sanctions.

[7] OTSI, 'About Us' <https://www.gov.uk/government/organisations/office-of-trade-sanctions-implementation/about> accessed 31 October 2025.

[8] ibid. Certain trade sanctions are excluded from OTSI's remit, pursuant to regulation 2 of the Trade, Aircraft and Shipping Sanctions (Civil Enforcement) Regulations 2024, namely

(a) Regs 18(1) of the Russia Regulations (investments in relation to non-government controlled Ukrainian territory (in so far as it concerns activity mentioned in Regulation 18(2)(a)));
(b) Reg 18B(1) (investments in relation to Russia);
(c) Regs 46Z9B to 46Z9D of the Russia Regulations (maritime transportation of certain oil and oil products);
(d) Reg 54A of the Russia Regulations (internet services);
(e) Reg 27P of the Republic of Belarus (Sanctions) (EU Exit) Regulations 2019 (preventing provision of internet services); or
(f) a provision of Russia Regulations or the Republic of Belarus (Sanctions) (EU Exit) Regulations 2019 which makes supplemental provision in connection with of these excluded trade sanctions regulations.

## C. OTSI

OTSI was launched by DBT and commenced operations on 10 October 2024. OTSI's stated purpose is to 'strengthen the United Kingdom's implementation and enforcement of trade sanctions'.[9] OTSI is primarily responsible for helping businesses comply with sanctions, investigating potential breaches, civil enforcement, and referring cases to HMRC for criminal enforcement. **5.14**

### 1. Legislative Framework

Under SAMLA, 'Ministers'[10] can make sanctions regulations when they consider it appropriate to do so for the carrying out of one or more of the purposes in section 1 of SAMLA. These purposes include compliance with UN obligations, furthering a foreign policy objective of the UK Government, and promoting respect for democracy, the rule of law and good governance.[11] Ministers are permitted to make regulations for inter alia trade, aircraft and shipping sanctions and for the corresponding enforcement of those sanctions.[12] **5.15**

The Trade, Aircraft and Shipping Sanctions (Civil Enforcement) Regulations 2024 (TASSCER) came into force on 10 October 2024 and were made pursuant to Part 1 of SAMLA.[13] TASSCER introduced important new powers relating to the administration and enforcement of trade sanctions in the UK. **5.16**

Part 2 of TASSCER introduced new civil enforcement powers which give the Secretary of State the power to impose monetary penalties on a strict liability basis if they are satisfied, on the balance of probabilities, that a person has breached an obligation under certain trade sanctions regulations.[14] (See paragraphs 5.22–4.) **5.17**

Part 3 of TASSCER introduced (a) new reporting obligations requiring relevant persons to inform the Secretary of State of potential breaches of trade sanctions (see further paragraphs 5.40–4 below), and (b) new powers for the Secretary of State to request information from persons in line for certain purposes as set out in the regulations (see further paragraphs 5.28–35 below). **5.18**

In accordance with section 43 of SAMLA, the Secretary of State for Foreign, Commonwealth and Development Affairs provided statutory guidance to assist in the implementation of, and compliance with, TASSCER.[15] The statutory guidance **5.19**

9 OTSI, 'About Us' (n 7).
10 S 1(9) of SAMLA 2018 defines 'appropriate Ministers' as the Secretary of State and the Treasury.
11 SAMLA 2018, s 1(1)–(2).
12 SAMLA 2018, s 1(5).
13 The Secretary of State made TASSCER 2024 in exercise of the powers conferred by SAMLA 2018, ss 1(1)(a) and (c), 1(2) and (3), 16, 17, 17A, 21(1), and 54(1) and (2).
14 TASSCER 2024, ss 6 and 7.
15 FCDO, DBT, DfT, and OTSI, 'Trade, Aircraft and Shipping Sanctions, Civil Enforcement: Guidance' (Statutory guidance, 12 September 2024) <https://www.gov.uk/government/publications/trade-aircraft-and-shipp

provides that where powers in TASSCER are conferred on the Secretary of State in relation to trade sanctions, it is the Secretary of State for Business and Trade who will be responsible for the exercise of those powers. The statutory guidance provides that in practice DBT, through OTSI, leads on civil enforcement in relation to trade sanctions.[16]

## 2. Jurisdiction and Approach

### (i) Extra-territoriality

**5.20** The requirements[17] of TASSCER apply to conduct in the United Kingdom or the territorial sea[18] by any person.[19]

**5.21** TASSCER also has extra-territorial application for 'United Kingdom persons' only. 'United Kingdom persons' are United Kingdom nationals or bodies incorporated or constituted under the law of any part of the United Kingdom[20]. Regulation 3 provides that TASSCER 2024 applies to conduct by a 'United Kingdom person' wherever the conduct occurs, including where it is 'wholly or partly outside the United Kingdom'.

### (ii) Strict liability in civil enforcement

**5.22** TASSCER gives the Secretary of State power to impose civil monetary penalties for trade sanctions breaches on a strict liability basis.

**5.23** Regulation 5(1) provides that the Secretary of State may impose a monetary penalty on a person if the Secretary of State is satisfied, on the balance of probabilities, that the person has breached a prohibition, or failed to comply with an obligation, imposed by or under sanctions regulations. Regulation 6 provides that 'any defence that the person did not know or had no reasonable cause to suspect that an offence had been committed under trade sanctions regulations is to be ignored'. The same applies to monetary penalties for aircraft and shipping sanctions.[21]

ing-sanctions-civil-enforcement-guidance/trade-aircraft-and-shipping-sanctions-civil-enforcement-guidance> accessed 26 May 2025.

[16] ibid.

[17] 'Relevant requirements' are defined in reg 3(3) of TASSCER 2024 as the reporting and information requirements imposed by regs 15(1)–(2), 16(1)–(2), 17(1), 18(1), 19(1), 19(3), 20(1), and 20(3).

[18] 'Territorial sea' is defined in SAMLA 2018, s 62(1) as (without more), the territorial sea adjacent to the United Kingdom.

[19] SAMLA 2018, s 21. See e.g. reg 5(4) of TASSCER 2024, which provides that monetary penalties can be imposed for breaching a prohibition or failing to comply with an obligation imposed by or under sanctions regulations, against

(a) a United Kingdom person in relation to conduct (i) in the United Kingdom or the territorial sea or (ii) wholly or partly outside the United Kingdom; and
(b) any other person in relation to conduct in the United Kingdom or the territorial sea.

Reg 3(2) of TASSCER 2024 provides that 'any person may comply, or fail to comply, with a relevant requirement by conduct in the territorial sea'. See further reg 3(4) of TASSCER 2024 which provides, 'Nothing in this regulation is to be taken to prevent a relevant requirement from applying to conduct (by any person) in the United Kingdom'.

[20] Reg 2 of TASSCER 2024 says 'United Kingdom person' has the meaning given in SAMLA 2018, s 21.

[21] See TASSCER 2024, reg 7(2).

These strict liability civil enforcement powers are similar to OFSI's civil enforcement powers for financial sanctions. They reinforce the seriousness with which the UK Government is taking sanctions compliance. For companies conducting business in the United Kingdom and all companies incorporated in the United Kingdom—particularly those with export/import operations or international supply chains—these strict liability powers exacerbate the need for robust compliance procedures and systems and controls to ensure compliance with UK trade sanctions. 5.24

(iii) Standard of proof

The civil standard of proof applies to the Secretary of State's power to impose civil monetary penalties for trade sanctions breaches.[22] 5.25

(iv) Personal liability for company officers

Under regulation 8(2), the Secretary of State has the power to impose monetary penalties on an officer of a body corporate,[23] partners of a partnership,[24] or members of an unincorporated body managed by its members,[25] where the body corporate has breached a prohibition or failed to comply with an obligation imposed by or under sanctions regulations[26] and the breach or failure was committed with the consent or connivance of the individual or is attributable to any neglect on the part of that individual.[27] 5.26

The risk of personal liability means entities should ensure their compliance procedures and systems and controls contain appropriate sanctions compliance measures to adequately mitigate against both personal and corporate liability. As its guidance states, OTSI can impose separate monetary penalties on the legal entity and the officers who run it.[28] 5.27

## 3. Information Requests

Regulations 17–19 of TASSCER introduce three information powers which are, in practice, exercised by OTSI. These powers entitle the Secretary of State to request information or documents for prescribed purposes. Failure to comply with an information request is an offence (see further paragraphs 5.36–9 below). 5.28

The first information power is set out at regulation 17(1), which provides that the Secretary of State may request a person to provide certain information if the Secretary 5.29

22 TASSCER 2024, reg 5(1).
23 This includes directors, managers, secretaries, and members of the body corporate. See TASSCER 2024, regs 8(2)(a) and 8(3).
24 TASSCER 2024, reg 8(4)(a).
25 TASSCER 2024, reg 8(4)(b).
26 TASSCER 2024, reg 8(1).
27 TASSCER 2024, reg 8(2).
28 See DBT and OTSI, 'How Suspected Breaches of Trade Sanctions are Assessed by OTSI' (n 5) s 2.

of State *believes* that the person *may* be able to provide the information.[29] The information requested must be such information as the Secretary of State 'may reasonably require' for the purpose of (a) the exercise of functions under TASSCER, (b) monitoring compliance with, or detecting evasion of, sanctions regulations, or (c) investigating a suspected breach of a prohibition, or a suspected failure to comply with an obligation, imposed by or under sanctions regulations.[30]

5.30 The second information power is set out at regulation 18(1), which provides that the Secretary of State may request a person acting under a 'trade licence'[31] to provide information about any matter to which the licence relates. The information requested must be such information as the Secretary of State 'may reasonably require' for the purpose of (a) the exercise of functions under TASSCER, (b) monitoring compliance with, or detecting evasion of, sanctions regulations, or (c) investigating a suspected breach of a prohibition, or a suspected failure to comply with an obligation, imposed by or under sanctions regulations.

5.31 The third information power is set out at regulation 19(1), which provides that the Secretary of State may request a person acting under an 'aircraft or shipping licence'[32] or a relevant 'direction'[33] to provide information about any matter to which the licence or direction relates. The information request must be for the purpose of (a) the exercise of functions under TASSCER, (b) monitoring compliance with, or detecting evasion of, sanctions regulations, (c) investigating a suspected breach of a prohibition, or a suspected failure to comply with an obligation, imposed by or under sanctions regulations, or (d) monitoring compliance with, or detecting evasion of any condition of, that licence or direction.[34]

5.32 Regulation 20(2) is remarkably broad and provides that where the Secretary of State requests that documents be produced, the Secretary of State may take copies of or extracts from any document produced and may request any person producing the document to give an explanation of it. Where the documents are produced by a body corporate, partnership or unincorporated body other than a partnership, the Secretary of State can request that the explanation of the documents comes from a present or past partner, employee, or officer.[35]

5.33 Where the Secretary of State requests a person to produce documents, that person must 'take reasonable steps to obtain the documents (if they are not already in the person's possession or control)' and they must 'keep the documents under their possession or

[29] See also s 3.1 of OTSI's 'Statutory Guidance on Civil Enforcement' (n 15).
[30] TASSCER 2024, reg 17(2).
[31] Reg 18(2) of TASSCER 2024 defines a 'trade licence' as 'an authorisation issued by the Secretary of State or the Treasury (as the case may be) providing for a prohibition imposed by trade sanctions regulations not to apply to anything done under that authorisation'.
[32] Reg 19(2) of TASSCER 2024 defines 'aircraft licence' and 'shipping licence' to mean 'an authorisation issued by the Secretary of State providing for a prohibition imposed by aircraft sanctions regulations or shipping sanctions regulations (as the case may be) not to apply to anything done under that authorisation'.
[33] Reg 19(2) of TASSCER 2024 defines 'direction' as 'a direction made under aircraft sanctions regulations or shipping sanctions regulations'.
[34] TASSCER 2024, reg 19(1) and (3).
[35] TASSCER 2024, reg 20(2)(c).

control (except for the purpose of providing them to the Secretary of State or as the Secretary of State may otherwise permit)'.[36]

Any information requested under regulations 17–19 must be provided by the requested person within the time period provided by the Secretary of State or, if no such period is specified, within a reasonable time.[37] These deadlines must be taken seriously because failure to provide the information within the specified time period is an offence. **5.34**

Regulation 29(1) states that providing information or documents to OTSI pursuant to an information request does not breach any restriction on such disclosure imposed by any other statute or otherwise. However, there are two important exceptions to this: **5.35**

1. Regulation 29(2) provides that nothing in TASSCER authorizes a disclosure of information to OTSI that contravenes data protection legislation or is prohibited by Parts 1 to 7 or Part 9, Chapter 1 of the Investigatory Powers Act 2016.[38]
2. Similarly, a person who has acted or is acting as counsel or solicitor for any person is not required to disclose any privileged information[39] in their possession in that capacity.[40]

### (i) Enforcement of information failures

Failure to comply with information requests can attract civil liability. OTSI's guidance specifically refers to its powers to enforce non-compliance with information requests using civil enforcement powers.[41] OTSI cannot issue a monetary penalty if criminal proceedings are ongoing or have taken place for the same breach, or if the person has already been convicted of an offence in respect of that breach.[42] **5.36**

Failure to comply with information requests can also attract criminal liability. Under regulation 21(1) of TASSCER, a person commits a criminal offence if that person: **5.37**

(a) without reasonable excuse, refuses or fails within the time and in the manner specified (or, if no time has been specified, within a reasonable time) to comply with any request for information or documents under regulations 17 to 19;
(b) knowingly or recklessly gives any information, or produces any document, which is false in a material particular in response to such a request;
(c) with intent to evade any provision of regulations 17 to 20, destroys, mutilates, defaces, conceals or removes any document;
(d) otherwise intentionally obstructs the Secretary of State in the exercise of the powers under regulations 17 to 20.

[36] TASSCER 2024, reg 20(3).
[37] TASSCER 2024, regs 17(3)–(4), 18(3), and 19(5).
[38] TASSCER 2024, reg 29(2).
[39] Reg 29(6) of TASSCER 2024 defines 'privileged information' as 'information with respect to which a claim to legal professional privilege (in Scotland, to confidentiality of communications) could be maintained in legal proceedings'.
[40] TASSCER 2024, reg 29(3).
[41] See DBT and OTSI, 'How Suspected Breaches of Trade Sanctions are Assessed by OTSI' (n 5) s 1.
[42] TASSCER 2024, reg 12(2); DBT and OTSI, 'How Suspected Breaches of Trade Sanctions are Assessed by OTSI' (n 5) s 8.

5.38 A person who commits an offence is liable on summary conviction in England and Wales to imprisonment for a term not exceeding six months or a fine (or both).[43] On conviction, the court may also make an order requiring the person to comply with the request for information within a specified time period.[44] Regulation 24 explains the procedure if an offence has been incorporated by an unincorporated body.

5.39 OTSI is not responsible for criminal enforcement. OTSI's guidance on 'How suspected breaches of trade sanctions are assessed by the Office of Trade Sanctions Implementation' provides that it will refer cases to HMRC 'where [OTSI] determines that the breach merits criminal enforcement'.[45] Further information about OTSI's approach to enforcement is provided at paragraphs 5.45–50 below.

## 4. Reporting Obligations

5.40 Regulation 15 of TASSCER introduced a mandatory obligation on 'relevant persons' to inform the Secretary of State as soon as practicable if they know, or have reasonable cause to suspect, that a person has breached a prohibition or failed to comply with an obligation under trade sanctions regulations.[46] A further reporting obligation applies to relevant persons in respect of known or suspected breaches of aircraft or shipping sanctions regulations.[47]

5.41 For the purpose of regulation 15, 'relevant persons' are defined as (i) persons with permission under Part 4A of the Financial Services and Markets Act 2000 (FSMA) to carry out a regulated activity, (ii) undertakings that operate currency exchange offices, transmit money (or representations of monetary value) by any means, or cash cheques that are payable to customers, or (iii) firms or sole practitioners that provide legal or notarial services to other persons by way of business.[48] This definition of 'relevant persons' is narrower than the broader category of 'relevant firms'[49] which have reporting obligations to OFSI in respect of financial sanctions breaches under regulation 70 of the Russia Regulations.

5.42 Relevant persons are only required to report their knowledge or suspicion if the information on which their knowledge or suspicion is based came to them 'in the course of carrying on their business'.[50] 'In the course of carrying on their business' is defined in broad terms in regulation 15(5). For example, in respect of relevant persons who are permitted to carry out regulated activities pursuant to Part 4A FSMA 2000, the

[43] TASSCER 2024, reg 22.
[44] TASSCER 2024, reg 21(2).
[45] See DBT and OTSI, 'How Suspected Breaches of Trade Sanctions are Assessed by OTSI' (n 5) s 5.
[46] OTSI published general guidance on reporting obligations (and voluntary disclosures): 'Report a Suspected Breach of Trade Sanctions' (10 October 2024) <https://www.gov.uk/guidance/report-a-suspected-breach-of-trade-sanctions> accessed 26 May 2025.
[47] TASSCER 2024, reg 16.
[48] TASSCER 2024, reg 15(4).
[49] Russia Regulations 2019, reg 71(1).
[50] TASSCER 2024, reg 15(1)(b).

information must come to them in the course of their carrying on the regulated activity to which their permission relates. In respect of a firm or sole practitioner that provides legal or notarial services, the information must come to them in the course of their providing legal or notarial services. (However, regulation 29 provides that a person who has acted or is acting as counsel or solicitor for any person is not required to disclose any privileged information[51] in their possession in that capacity.[52])

OTSI's guidance on 'Mandatory reporting for suspected breaches of trade sanctions'[53] says that reports should be made by relevant persons as soon as practicable using the online service.[54] This guidance provides that reports should include details of the information or other matter that the relevant person's knowledge or suspicion is based on and any information they hold about the business or person suspected of breaching trade sanctions, by which they can be identified. **5.43**

Failure to comply with the reporting obligations in regulations 15 and 16 is an offence which could result in a civil monetary penalty or criminal prosecution.[55] If a criminal prosecution is brought, a person is liable on summary conviction in England and Wales, to imprisonment for a term not exceeding six months or a fine (or both). **5.44**

## 5. Enforcement Outcomes for Breaches of Trade Sanctions

OTSI's guidance on 'How suspected breaches of trade sanctions are assessed by the Office of Trade Sanctions Implementation' provides that there are one or more potential outcomes for breaches of trade sanctions, depending on the severity of the breach: **5.45**

1. Warning letter. This may include requiring a person to comply with a continuing obligation to keep OTSI informed about certain information as circumstances change, such as the improvement of due diligence processes.
2. Referral to a regulator. OTSI may refer the case to a regulator if the person is a regulated professional.
3. Referral to other organizations. If a UK registered company is involved in the breach, or if the person is the director of a UK registered company, OTSI may refer the case to Companies House or the Insolvency Service.
4. Public disclosure. OTSI may publicize details about the breach where OTSI decides that it would be in the public interest to do so.

[51] Reg 29(6) of TASSCER 2024 defines 'privileged information' as 'information with respect to which a claim to legal professional privilege (in Scotland, to confidentiality of communications) could be maintained in legal proceedings'.

[52] TASSCER 2024, reg 29(3).

[53] DBT and OTSI, 'Mandatory Reporting for Suspected Breaches of Trade Sanctions' (Guidance, 12 September 2024) <https://www.gov.uk/guidance/mandatory-reporting-for-suspected-breaches-of-trade-sanctions> accessed 26 May 2025.

[54] See also s 3.2 of OTSI's 'Statutory Guidance on Civil Enforcement' (n 15), which contains a link to the 'Report a Breach tool'.

[55] TASSCER 2024, regs 15(3) and 16(3).

5. Monetary penalties (see further paragraph 5.51 below).
6. Referral to HMRC. Where OTSI determines that the breach merits criminal enforcement, OTSI may refer the case to HMRC. HMRC can refer the matter to the CPS to consider a prosecution.

**5.46** OTSI's guidance provides that it will determine what enforcement action is 'appropriate and proportionate on a case-by-case basis' and that OTSI 'will consider the public interest when determining what action should be taken'.[56]

**5.47** The guidance also outlines how OTSI will determine the severity of a breach. There are three categories: lesser severity (e.g. where there is low or no culpability, lower harm to the purposes of the sanctions regime, and lower financial value); medium severity (e.g. where there is failure to prevent a breach through behaviours such as negligence or recklessness, significant or moderate harm to the purposes of the sanctions regime, and moderate financial value); and high severity (e.g. where there is significant culpability (such as intentional actions or significant negligence), extensive or significant planning (such as efforts being taken to conceal the breach), serious harm to the purposes of the sanctions regime, and high financial value).

**5.48** The guidance also provides that where a monetary penalty is being considered, OTSI will consider a range of aggravating and mitigating factors which may affect whether a monetary penalty is imposed or the amount of such penalty. Mitigating factors include:

- timely voluntary disclosure of the suspected breach by the individual or business responsible. This could lead to a reduction of up to 50% of a monetary penalty imposed for the breach
- compliance with requests for information received from OTSI during the investigation
- no record of previously having breached UK sanctions
- good standards of customer due diligence and other relevant compliance systems proportionate to the size, exposure to sanctions and resources of the business
- demonstration of steps taken to address causes of the breach[57]

**5.49** Aggravating factors include:

- failure to respond to previous warning letters
- poor compliance with the investigation
- withholding or obstructing access to information during an investigation, such as attempting to conceal or destroy evidence
- failure to comply with other sanctions requirements relevant to the breach, such as recordkeeping and licensing conditions
- previous breaches by the same individual or business, having regard to the time that has elapsed since they occurred

[56] DBT and OTSI, 'How Suspected Breaches of Trade Sanctions are Assessed by OTSI' (n 5) s 4.
[57] ibid s 6.

- inadequate standards of due diligence
- attempts to wrongly blame others[58]

OTSI makes clear that it 'values and encourages voluntary disclosure' and that suspected breaches are expected to be disclosed as soon as reasonably practicable.[59] Practitioners should be mindful of this when advising their clients. 5.50

### (i) Civil monetary penalties for breaches

Regulation 5(1) gives the Secretary of State the power to impose a monetary penalty on someone if the Secretary is satisfied, on the balance of probabilities, that the person has breached a prohibition, or failed to comply with an obligation imposed by or under sanctions regulations. Monetary penalties cannot be imposed where criminal proceedings have been brought and are ongoing in respect of the same breach, or the person has been convicted of that offence in respect of the same conduct.[60] 5.51

### (ii) Maximum penalty

For trade sanctions where it is possible to estimate the value of the breach or failure, the penalty cannot exceed the greater of (a) £1,000,000, and (b) 50 per cent of the estimated value of the breach or failure to comply.[61] In any other case, the maximum penalty is £1,000,000.[62] 5.52

### (iii) Procedural requirements for imposing a monetary penalty

TASSCER 2024 set out various procedures which must take place if the Secretary of State chooses to impose a monetary penalty. Practitioners may consider the validity of the penalty in the event that these procedural requirements are not complied with. 5.53

Before imposing a monetary penalty, the Secretary of State must: 5.54

1. inform the person of their intention to do so;[63]
2. explain the grounds for imposing the penalty;[64]
3. specify the amount of the penalty;[65]
4. explain that the person is entitled to make representations;[66]
5. specify the period within which such representations must be made;[67] and
6. consider any representations made.[68]

[58] ibid s 6.
[59] ibid s 6.
[60] TASSCER 2024, reg 12.
[61] TASSCER 2024, reg 9(2). See also s 3 of OTSI's 'Statutory Guidance on Civil Enforcement' (n 15).
[62] TASSCER 2024, reg 9(3). See also s 2.2 of OTSI's 'Statutory Guidance on Civil Enforcement' (n 15).
[63] TASSCER 2024, reg 11(1).
[64] TASSCER 2024, reg 11(2)(a).
[65] TASSCER 2024, reg 11(2)(b).
[66] TASSCER 2024, reg 11(2)(c).
[67] TASSCER 2024, reg 11(2)(d).
[68] TASSCER 2024, reg 11(3).

5.55 If, having considered any representations, the Secretary of State decides to impose a penalty, the Secretary of State must:

1. inform the person of the decision;[69]
2. explain that the person is entitled to seek a review by the Secretary of State;[70] and
3. specify the period within which the person must inform the Secretary of State that the person wishes to seek such a review.[71]

(iv) Right of review to the Secretary of State

5.56 Where a monetary penalty is imposed on a person, that person is entitled to seek a review by the Secretary of State within the deadline specified in the penalty. The Secretary of State may uphold the decision to impose the penalty and its amount, substitute a different amount, or cancel the decision to impose the penalty.[72]

5.57 In practice, the Secretary of State is being asked to review its own decision to impose a penalty.

(v) Appeal to the Upper Tribunal

5.58 If the Secretary of State upholds the decision to impose a penalty (whether for the same or different amount), the person subject to the penalty may appeal on any ground to the Upper Tribunal.[73] The Upper Tribunal may quash the Secretary of State's decision to impose the penalty or uphold that decision but substitute a different amount.[74]

## 6. Information Sharing

5.59 Regulation 27 permits the Secretary of State to share relevant information obtained pursuant to TASSCER with various groups. This includes the police, other parts of government, supervisory bodies, regulators, governments of any country, and any other person to whom the Secretary of State considers it appropriate to disclose the information.[75] This information can only be shared for certain purposes, as set out in regulation 27(2), and can be shared with any person with the consent of a person who, in their own right, is entitled to the information.[76] OTSI's guidance says it will also have regard to data protection legislation and the DBT Personal Information Charter.[77]

69 TASSCER 2024, reg 11(3)(a).
70 TASSCER 2024, reg 11(3)(b).
71 TASSCER 2024, reg 11(3)(c).
72 TASSCER 2024, reg 11(4).
73 TASSCER 2024, reg 11(5).
74 TASSCER 2024, reg 11(6).
75 TASSCER 2024, reg 27(3). See also s 2.5 of OTSI's 'Statutory Guidance on Civil Enforcement' (n 15).
76 TASSCER 2024, reg 27(4).
77 DBT, 'Personal Information Charter' <https://www.gov.uk/government/organisations/department-for-business-and-trade/about/personal-information-charter> accessed 26 May 2025; DBT and OTSI, 'Mandatory Reporting for Suspected Breaches of Trade Sanctions' (n 53).

OTSI's guidance on 'How suspected breaches of trade sanctions are assessed by the Office of Trade Sanctions Implementation' provides that if OTSI believes that a suspected breach sits outside of its enforcement powers, or if a case involves breaches across multiple types of sanctions, it will disclose the suspected breach to the relevant organization responsible for enforcement.[78] 5.60

### 7. Publication of Breaches

Under regulation 13, OTSI may publish reports about breaches of trade sanctions regulations whether or not a monetary penalty has been imposed. The guidance states that these reports may name the person who committed the breach and provide facts about the breach.[79] The publication of breaches will be of concern because of its reputational impact and other wider consequences. 5.61

### 8. OTSI's Approach to Enforcement

It is not yet clear how robust OTSI's approach to enforcement will be and, more importantly, how often it will seek to impose more severe penalties or refer cases to HMRC for criminal enforcement. However, there are several factors that indicate that a more robust approach will be taken following OTSI's creation. First, the reporting obligations aim to increase transparency which could lead to an increase in enforcement action. Second, the strict liability framework increases the scope of conduct caught by the regulations. Third, the UK Government's desire to crack down on trade sanctions breaches is evident; on that basis alone, OTSI may well be under pressure to take a more vigorous approach to enforcement and use the full extent of its powers under TASSCER. Fourth, the UK's approach is in line with steps taken in the US and the EU to increase enforcement activity in respect of trade sanctions. 5.62

The very real likelihood of increased enforcement action reinforces the importance of firms and advisers carefully reviewing their sanctions compliance procedures and systems and controls to ensure compliance with all aspects of UK trade sanctions. 5.63

## D. Trade Sanctions in the Russia Regulations

The trade sanctions contained in the Russia Regulations were made pursuant to section 5(1) SAMLA which provides that '[f]or the purposes of section 1(5)(c) regulations "impose trade sanctions" if they impose prohibitions or requirements for one 5.64

[78] DBT and OTSI, 'How Suspected Breaches of Trade Sanctions are Assessed by OTSI' (n 5) s 3.
[79] DBT and OTSI, 'How Suspected Breaches of Trade Sanctions are Assessed by OTSI' (n 5) s 12.

or more of the purposes mentioned in Part 1 of Schedule 1'. The purposes set out in paragraphs 2 to 16 therein include preventing the export, import, movement, acquisition, transfer, and making available of goods, technology, or land of a prescribed description to, or for the benefit of, designated persons, persons connected with a prescribed country, or a prescribed description of persons connected with a prescribed country.

**5.65** The purposes of the Russia Regulations are contained in regulation 4:

(a) encouraging Russia to cease actions destabilising Ukraine or undermining or threatening the territorial integrity, sovereignty or independence of Ukraine.
(b) promoting the payment of compensation by Russia for damage, loss or injury suffered by Ukraine on or after 24th February 2022 as a result of Russia's invasion of Ukraine.

**5.66** Insofar as they relate to trade sanctions, the Russia Regulations are organized as follows:

1. Part 5 ('Trade') includes all of the chapters relating to trade restrictions. Of those, Chapters 4A to 4N reflect the ever-increasing pressure that the UK is applying on Russia by setting out the prohibitions that apply to a growing array of goods, technologies, and services.
2. Part 7 ('Exceptions and licences') sets out the trade exceptions in regulations 60ZA to 61ZA; regulation 65 addresses the impact of trade licences on prohibited activities; and regulation 68 contains trade licensing offences, including obtaining a licence on false information and failing to comply with a licence condition. Schedules 2A to 4 all relate to trade sanctions.

**5.67** Since Russia's 2022 invasion of Ukraine (and since mid-2023 in particular), the number of trade sanctions has grown rapidly. Part 5 of the Russia Regulations as originally enacted consisted of seven chapters, including chapters focused on military goods and technology, dual-use goods and technology, energy-related goods, and exports and imports in relation to Crimea. The prohibitions in those chapters largely reflected the UK's export control regime. By October 2025, there were 32 chapters, including chapters relating to a wide range of goods and services. This extended list of prohibitions shows how much further trade sanctions in the Russia context reach than export control provisions.

## 1. Trade Sanctions: Key Concepts

### (i) Jurisdiction

**5.68** Section 21 of SAMLA provides that the prohibitions or requirements in regulations made under that Act (which includes the trade sanctions within the Russia Regulations) can have extra-territorial effect. However, this effect only applies to conduct by a UK national or a body incorporated under the law of any part of the United Kingdom.

For non-UK nationals or bodies incorporated outside the UK, the trade sanctions in the Russia Regulations only apply to conduct within the United Kingdom. Any reference to the UK includes a reference to the territorial sea of the UK.[80] Conduct may include acts and omissions.[81] **5.69**

(ii) Connection test

The purpose of the trade prohibitions in the Russia Regulations is to prevent all services, or services of a prescribed description, from being provided, directly and indirectly, to designated persons, 'persons connected with Russia' and 'persons connected with non-government controlled Ukrainian territory'.[82] **5.70**

Regulation 21(2) defines a person connected with Russia as '(a) an individual who is, or an association or combination of individuals who are, ordinarily resident in Russia, '(b) an individual who is, or an association or combination of individuals who are, located in Russia, (c) a person, other than an individual, which is incorporated or constituted under the law of Russia, or (d) a person, other than an individual, which is domiciled in Russia'. The same test is effectively applied, *mutatis mutandis*, for a person connected with non-government controlled Ukrainian territory. **5.71**

## 2. The Prohibitions in Chapters 2–6A of the Russia Regulations

Part 5 variously prohibits the export, import, acquisition, supply, and delivery of prescribed goods and services. It also prohibits the provision of technical assistance, financial services, and brokering services in relation to those goods and services. The prescribed goods and services that the prohibitions relate to are separated into chapters in Part 5 of the Russia Regulations and are listed as follows:[83] **5.72**

1. military goods and military technology (as specified in Schedule 2 to the Export Control Order 2008);[84]
2. anything which falls within Chapter 93 of the Goods Classification Table, other than military goods;[85]
3. defence and security goods and defence and security technology (as specified in Schedule 3C) and including interception and monitoring goods and interception and monitoring technology;[86]

[80] Russia Regulations 2019, reg 21(5).
[81] SAMLA 2018, s 21(5).
[82] See SAMLA 2018, s 5 and sch 1, para 11.
[83] All references to schedule numbers refer to the Russia Regulations 2019 (unless otherwise stated). A comprehensive list is provided in FCDO, ECJU, OFSI, and OTSI, 'Russia Sanctions: Guidance' (Statutory guidance, updated 25 September 2025) s 1.6 <https://www.gov.uk/government/publications/russia-sanctions-guidance/russia-sanctions-guidance> accessed 25 September 2025.
[84] 'Restricted goods' under the Russia Regulations 2019, pt 5, ch 2.
[85] 'Restricted goods' under the Russia Regulations 2019, pt 5, ch 2.
[86] Russia Regulations 2019, ch 4D, pt 5.

4. dual-use goods and technology (as specified in Annex I to Council Regulation 428/2009 as retained by the European Union (Withdrawal) Act 2018);[87]
5. special materials and related equipment and materials processing (as specified in Parts 1A and 1B of Schedule 2A);[88]
6. critical-industry goods and technology (as specified in Schedule 2A);[89]
7. quantum computing and advanced materials goods and technology (as specified in Schedule 2E);[90]
8. aviation and space goods and technology (as specified in Schedule 2C);[91]
9. 'relevant restricted goods' in relation to non-government controlled Ukrainian territory;[92]
10. jet fuel and fuel additives (as specified in Part 8 of Schedule 2A);
11. maritime goods and maritime technology (defined by reference to Chapter 4 (Navigation Equipment) and Chapter 5 (Radio-Communication Equipment) of Annex 1 of Merchant Shipping Notice 1874(a));[93]
12. infrastructure-related goods (as specified in Part 3 of Schedule 3);[94]
13. energy-related goods (as specified in Part 2 of Schedule 3) and energy-related services;[95]
14. oil refining goods and technology (as specified in Schedule 2D);[96]
15. luxury goods (as specified in Schedule 3A);[97]
16. G7 dependency and further goods (as specified in Schedule 3E);[98]
17. goods originating in non-government controlled Ukrainian territory;[99]
18. iron and steel products (as specified in Schedule 3B) and associated ancillary services;[100]
19. iron and steel products processed in a third country (as specified in Parts 1, 2, and 3 of Schedule 3B) and associated ancillary services, from 30 September 2023;[101]
20. metals (as specified in Schedule 3BA);[102]
21. oil and oil products (as specified in Schedule 3F);[103]
22. the supply or delivery by ship of oil and oil products under the commodity codes 2709 and 2710 from Russia to and between third countries and related services;[104]

[87] 'Restricted goods' under the Russia Regulations 2019, pt 5, ch 2.
[88] 'Restricted goods' under the Russia Regulations 2019, pt 5, ch 2.
[89] 'Restricted goods' under the Russia Regulations 2019, pt 5, ch 2.
[90] 'Restricted goods' under the Russia Regulations 2019, pt 5, ch 2.
[91] 'Restricted goods' under the Russia Regulations 2019, pt 5, ch 2.
[92] Russia Regulations 2019, pt 5, ch 2A.
[93] 'Restricted goods' under the Russia Regulations 2019, pt 5, ch 2.
[94] Russia Regulations 2019, pt 5, ch 5.
[95] Russia Regulations, pt 5, ch 4.
[96] 'Restricted goods' under the Russia Regulations 2019, pt 5, ch 2.
[97] Russia Regulations 2019, pt 5, ch 4B.
[98] Russia Regulations 2019, pt 5, ch 4H.
[99] Russia Regulations 2019, pt 5, ch 5.
[100] Russia Regulations 2019, pt 5, ch 4C.
[101] Russia Regulations 2019, pt 5, ch 4CA.
[102] Russia Regulations 2019, pt 5, ch 4CB.
[103] Russia Regulations 2019, pt 5, chs 4I and 4IA.
[104] Russia Regulations 2019, pt 5, ch 4IA.

23. coal and coal products (as specified in Schedule 3H);[105]
24. liquefied natural gas (as specified in Chapter 4L);[106]
25. gold, gold jewellery, and products related to gold (as specified in Schedule 3G);[107]
26. banknotes denominated in sterling and any official currency of the European Union;[108]
27. goods which generate significant revenues for Russia (as specified in Schedule 3D and Schedule 3DA);[109]
28. diamonds and diamond jewellery (as specified in Schedule 3GA);[110]
29. certain diamonds processed in third country;[111]
30. Russia's vulnerable goods (as specified in Schedule 3I);[112]
31. sectoral software and technology (as specified in Schedule 3IA);[113]
32. provision of technical assistance, armed personnel, financial services, or funds, or associated brokering services where such provision enables or facilitates the conduct of certain military activities;
33. services relating to a relevant infrastructure sector in non-government controlled Ukrainian territory;[114]
34. services relating to tourism in non-government controlled Ukrainian territory;[115]
35. internet services.[116]

### (i) The prohibitions

The trade sanctions prohibit the export, import, acquisition, supply, and delivery of the prescribed goods and services. They also prohibit the provision of technical assistance, financial services, and brokering services in relation to those goods and services. Further details about these prohibitions are provided in the following paragraphs, 5.74–134. **5.73**

#### *a) Exports*

The export of certain prescribed goods to, or for use in, Russia is prohibited by the Russia Regulations. 'Export' retains its meaning from the Customs and Excise Management Act 1979 (CEMA) and means export from the UK.[117] Almost all regulations use the phrase 'to or for use in Russia'[118] which means that, even if the immediate destination is not Russia, the prohibition may still apply. **5.74**

105 Russia Regulations 2019, pt 5, ch 4K.
106 Russia Regulations 2019, pt 5, ch 4L.
107 Russia Regulations 2019, pt 5, chs 4J and 4JA.
108 Russia Regulations 2019, pt 5, ch 4e.
109 Russia Regulations 2019, pt 5, chs 4G and 4GA.
110 Russia Regulations 2019, pt 5, chs 4JB and 4JC.
111 Russia Regulations 2019, pt 5, ch 4JC.
112 Russia Regulations 2019, pt 5, ch 4M.
113 Russia Regulations 2019, pt 5, ch 4N.
114 Russia Regulations 2019, pt 5, ch 6.
115 Russia Regulations 2019, pt 5, ch 6.
116 Russia Regulations 2019, pt 5, ch 6A.
117 SAMLA 2018, sch 1, para 32.
118 Save where the destination is Crimea or non-government controlled Ukrainian territory.

5.75 The prohibitions apply to the export of the following goods to or for use in Russia: restricted goods (regulation 22); energy-related goods (regulation 40); luxury goods (regulation 46B(1)); banknotes (regulation 46L(1)); jet fuel and additives (regulation 46N(1)); G7 dependency and further goods (regulation 46Y(1)); and Russia's vulnerable goods (regulation 46Z30).

5.76 Similar export prohibitions apply to exports to or for use in non-government controlled Ukrainian territory of relevant restricted goods (regulation 30B) and infrastructure related goods (regulation 48(1)–(2)).

5.77 The statutory guidance provides that exporters should check the ultimate end use of goods and may apply for a licence or contact the ECJU if they know or think the items may be used in Russia or in non-government controlled Ukrainian territory.[119] The guidance provides that a sanctions licence is not required for exports of non-military goods covered by the Russia Regulations from Northern Ireland to an EU Member State where the final destination is Russia or non-government controlled Ukrainian territory. However, the exporter will have to comply with any licensing requirements that apply in the relevant EU Member State for onward exportation to Russia.[120]

5.78 The prohibitions on exports are subject to exceptions or licences in Part 7.

*b) Imports*

5.79 Importing certain prescribed goods which have originated in, or have been consigned from, Russia or non-government controlled Ukraine is prohibited. 'Import' retains its meaning from CEMA and means import into the UK but does not include goods transferred from the Isle of Man except for limited purposes.[121] The use of the phrase 'goods which originate in Russia' means that even if the immediate place the goods were shipped from was not Russia, the prohibition may still apply.

5.80 The import prohibition applies to arms and related material (regulation 23); iron and steel products (regulations 46D and 46IB); metals (regulation 46IG); Schedules 3D and 3DA revenue generating goods (regulations 46S and 46XB); oil and oil products (regulation 46Z4); gold (regulation 46Z11); gold jewellery and relevant processed gold (regulations 46Z16B and 46Z16C); diamonds and diamond jewellery (regulation 46Z16K); relevant processed diamonds (regulation 46Z16R); coal and coal products (regulation 46Z18); liquefied natural gas (regulation 46Z25); and imports from non-government controlled Ukrainian territory (regulation 47(1)). These prohibitions cover both goods that are consigned from and goods that originated in Russia.

5.81 A similar prohibition relates to the import of goods which originate in non-government controlled Ukrainian territory (regulation 47).

[119] FCDO, ECJU, OFSI, and OTSI, 'Russia Sanctions: Guidance' (n 83).
[120] FCDO, ECJU, OFSI, and OTSI, 'Russia Sanctions: Guidance' (n 83).
[121] SAMLA 2018, sch 1, paras 33–4.

The statutory guidance provides that importers should check the original place goods were consigned or exported from, and apply for a licence or contact DBT's Import Controls Team if they think the items may have originated in or have been consigned from Russia or in non-government controlled Ukrainian territory.[122] The guidance provides that a sanctions licence is not required for imports of non-military goods covered by the Russia Regulations into Northern Ireland from an EU Member State which originate in or are consigned from Russia or non-government controlled Ukrainian territory. However, the importer will have to comply with any licensing requirements that apply in the relevant EU Member State for the original import into the customs territory of the EU.[123] **5.82**

The prohibitions on imports are subject to the exceptions and licences in Part 7. **5.83**

*c) Supply and delivery of goods*

The supply and delivery prohibitions in the Russia Regulations prohibit a person from directly or indirectly supplying or delivering certain goods from a third country to a place in Russia (or, to non-government controlled Ukrainian territory in respect of Chapter 5, infrastructure-related goods), or from a place in Russia to a third country or from a third country for the placing on board of a Russian-flagged vessel.[124] **5.84**

The meaning of 'third country' depends upon the regulation in question. **5.85**

1. For the purposes of regulation 49 (on infrastructure-related goods) 'third country' means a country that is not the UK, Isle of Man, or non-government controlled Ukrainian territory.
2. For the purposes of regulation 30C (on relevant restricted goods), 'third country' means a country that is not the United Kingdom or the Isle of Man.
3. For the remaining prohibitions concerning supply and delivery of goods, 'third country' means a country that is not the United Kingdom, the Isle of Man, or Russia.

The prohibition on the direct or indirect supply and delivery from a third country to a place in Russia applies to the following goods: restricted goods (regulation 24); energy related goods (regulation 41); luxury goods (regulation 46B); jet fuel and fuel additives (regulation 46N); G7 dependency and further goods (regulation 46Y); and Russia's vulnerable goods (regulation 46Z30). **5.86**

The prohibition on the direct or indirect supply and delivery from a third country to a place in non-government controlled Ukrainian territory applies to relevant restricted goods (regulation 30C) and infrastructure-related goods (regulation 49). **5.87**

[122] FCDO, ECJU, OFSI, and OTSI, 'Russia Sanctions: Guidance' (n 83).
[123] ibid.
[124] ibid.

**5.88** The prohibition on the direct or indirect supply and delivery from a place in Russia to a third country applies to the following goods: iron and steel products (regulation 46F); metals (regulation 46II); banknotes (regulation 46L); Schedule 3DA revenue generating goods (regulation 46XD); maritime transportation of certain oil and oil products (regulation 46Z9B); and diamonds and diamond jewellery (regulation 46Z16M).

**5.89** The prohibitions on supply and delivery of goods are subject to the exceptions and licences in Part 7.

*d) Making available or acquiring goods and technology*

**5.90** The statutory guidance explains that prohibitions in the Russia Regulations (aside from those in Chapter 5) on making certain goods or technology available (e.g. through a sale) include directly or indirectly making them available for use in Russia or to a 'person connected with Russia'. Some of the prohibitions also prohibit directly or indirectly acquiring certain goods or technology which originate in Russia or which are located in Russia or from a person connected with Russia.[125]

**5.91** The direct and indirect acquisition of the following goods, which originate in and are located in Russia, with the intention of those goods entering the United Kingdom, is prohibited: Schedule 3D revenue generating goods (regulation 46T), oil and oil products (regulation 46Z5), gold (regulation 46Z12), gold jewellery (regulation 46Z16D), coal and coal products (regulation 46Z19), and liquefied natural gas (regulation 46Z26). The prohibition in relation to gold jewellery applies also in relation to gold jewellery exported from Russia after 29 October 2022.

**5.92** The direct and indirect acquisition of the following goods, which originate in and are located in Russia is prohibited, regardless of whether the person acquiring them intends to bring the goods into the United Kingdom: iron and steel products (regulation 46E), metals (regulation 46IH), Schedule 3DA revenue generating goods (regulation 46XC), and diamonds and diamond jewellery (regulation 46Z16L).

**5.93** Regulation 42 prohibits making energy-related goods available for use in Russia or to a person connected with Russia.

**5.94** Regulation 50 prohibits making infrastructure goods available directly or indirectly for use in non-government controlled Ukrainian territory or to a 'person connected with non-government controlled Ukrainian territory'.

**5.95** The prohibitions on making available or acquiring goods and technology are subject to exceptions and licences in Part 7.

*e) Transfer of technology and software*

**5.96** The trade sanctions related to technology impose restrictions on making available and the transfer of particular types of technology. The provisions typically operate to

[125] ibid.

prohibit both the making available of a type of technology to a person connected with Russia or for use in Russia, and the transfer of a type of technology to a person connected with Russia or to a place in Russia.

The prohibitions now cover restricted technology (regulations 25 and 26);[126] energy-related technology (regulations 42 and 42A); G7 dependency and further technology (regulations 46Y and 46YA); Russia's vulnerable technology (regulations 46Z30 and 46Z30A); and sectoral software and technology (regulations 46Z34 and 46Z35). 5.97

'Sectoral software and technology' is defined in Schedule 3IA and, in broad terms, covers Business Enterprise software and technology; Industrial Design software; and Oil and Gas related software and technology. 5.98

The term 'transfer' is defined in paragraph 37 of Schedule 1 to SAMLA as 'a transfer by any means (or combination of means), including oral communication and that transfer of goods on which the technology is recorded or from which it can be derived, other than the export of such goods.' 5.99

'Technology' is also defined in paragraph 37 of Schedule 1 to SAMLA as 'information (including information comprised in software) that is capable of use in connection with: (a) the development, production or use of any goods or software, or (b) the development of, or the carrying out of, an industrial or commercial activity or an activity of any other kind whatsoever.' 5.100

The statutory guidance explains that where restricted technology is contained within a good, that good would be classified, respectively, as a restricted good under the accompanying goods-related provisions. This includes information contained on USB memory devices, laptops, tablets, etc.[127] 5.101

The statutory guidance on sectoral software sanctions states that the prohibitions on sectoral software and technology include making such software and technology available by intangible means (e.g. by downloading software from the internet or providing the software by means of Software as a Service (SaaS) or accessing the software via an app). 5.102

Pursuant to regulation 21, the software and technology prohibitions do not apply to software or technology that is in the public domain or used for basic scientific research. 5.103

The prohibitions on transfer of technology are subject to exceptions and licences in Part 7. Importantly, the prohibitions under the sectoral software sanctions do not include information which is of a non-commercial nature or for personal use. 5.104

Where software is subject to both trade sanctions and export controls, an exemption or licence under each set of legislation will need to apply. 5.105

[126] Regs 25 and 26 also prohibit the transfer of military technology to persons outside the UK or to a place outside the UK, where the transfer is from a place in Russia and maritime technology to a Russian-flagged vessel. Regs 30D and E extend this to non-government controlled Ukraine.

[127] FCDO, ECJU, OFSI, and OTSI, 'Russia Sanctions: Guidance' (n 83).

5.106 A general licence ('General Trade Licence Russia Sanctions – Sectoral Software and Technology') was issued on 21 July 2025 (and valid until 20 October 2025) which provided, subject to conditions, that business enterprise software may be provided where the recipient is a multinational client headquartered outside of Russia (which have global subsidiaries and affiliates in Russia); where the obligation to provide that software or technology arose before 23 April 2025; and where the software and technology to be provided is not predominantly for the subsidiary in Russia. That general licence was revoked on 16 October 2025 and replaced the same day by a virtually identical general licence, which is valid until 17 April 2026.[128]

*f) Technical assistance*

5.107 The statutory guidance explains the technical assistance prohibitions.[129] '*Technical assistance*' in relation to goods or technology is defined in regulation 21 as:

(a) technical support relating to the repair, development, production, assembly, testing, use or maintenance of the goods or technology, or
(b) any other technical service relating to the goods or technology

5.108 These prohibitions apply parasitically to specified goods or technology.

5.109 The prohibitions apply to the direct or indirect provision of such technical assistance. The prohibitions cover the export of technical assistance: (1) to persons 'connected with Russia' and persons 'connected with non-government controlled Ukrainian territory' or; (2) for use in Russia and non-government controlled Ukrainian territory. This covers the provision of technical assistance to a third country where that technical assistance will end up being used in Russia or non-government controlled Ukrainian territory.

5.110 The statutory guidance therefore provides that, if a person is providing technical assistance, they should check whether the goods or technology may be used in Russia or non-government controlled Ukrainian territory, as appropriate, and apply for a licence or contact ECJU if so.

5.111 Regulation 46A further prohibits the direct or indirect provision of technical assistance to or for the benefit of persons designated for the purpose of this regulation, where that assistance relates to an aircraft or ship.

5.112 The prohibitions in relation to the provision of technical assistance to Russia are as follows: restricted goods and restricted technology (regulation 27); where the provision of technical assistance enables or facilitates the conduct of military activities carried on or proposed to be carried on by the Russian military or any military end-user who is a

[128] ECJU and DBT, 'General Trade Licence Russia Sanctions – Sectoral Software and Technology' (Guidance, updated 16 October 2025) <https://www.gov.uk/government/publications/general-trade-licence-russia-sanctions-sectoral-software-and-technology> accessed 4 November 2025.

[129] ibid.

person connected with Russia (regulation 30); relating to relevant restricted goods and relevant restricted technology in relation to non-government controlled Ukraine (regulation 30F); energy-related goods (regulation 43); aircrafts and ships (regulation 46A); luxury goods (regulation 46BA); iron and steel products (regulations 46G and 46IC); jet fuel and fuel additives (regulation 46O); Schedule 3D revenue generating goods (regulation 46V); Schedule 3DA revenue generating goods (regulation 46XE); G7 dependency and further goods (regulation 46Z); oil and oil products (regulation 46Z7); gold (regulation 46Z14); gold jewellery (regulation 46Z16E); relevant processed gold (regulation 46Z16F); diamonds and diamond jewellery (regulation 46Z16N); certain diamonds processed in a third country (regulation 46Z16S); coal and coal products (regulation 46Z21); liquefied natural gas (regulation 46Z27); Russia's vulnerable goods (regulation 46Z31); infrastructure-related goods in relation to non-government controlled Ukraine (regulation 51).

The prohibitions on technical assistance are subject to exceptions and licences in Part 7. **5.113**

### g) *Financial services and funds related to goods and technology*

The financial services and prohibitions in the Russia Regulations apply parasitically to the direct or indirect provision of financial services in relation to specified goods and services, and to persons connected with Russia (or non-government controlled Ukrainian territory, in respect of Chapters 2A and 5). **5.114**

'Financial services' are defined in section 61 of SAMLA. As explained in the statutory guidance, they refer to any services of a financial nature in many different forms including insurance and banking. Financial services include payment and money transmission services.[130] **5.115**

Prohibitions on the provision of financial services and funds apply to similar goods or technology as those applying to 'technical assistance' (see paragraph 5.107 above) with the exception of aircrafts and ships and with the addition of maritime transportation of certain oil and oil products (regulation 46Z9C).[131] **5.116**

The prohibitions on financial services and funds are subject to exceptions and licences in Part 7. **5.117**

### h) *Brokering services*

Regulation 21 defines brokering services as any service to secure, or otherwise in relation to, an arrangement, including (but not limited to): **5.118**

(a) the selection or introduction of persons as parties or potential parties to the arrangement,
(b) the negotiation of the arrangement,

[130] ibid.
[131] See Russia Regulations 2019, regs 28, 30, 30G, 44, 46BB, 46H, 46ID, 46P, 46W, 46XF, 46Z1, 46Z8, 46Z9C, 46Z15, 46Z16G, 46Z16H, 46Z16O, 46Z16T, 46Z22, 46Z28, 46Z32, and 52.

(c) the facilitation of anything that enables the arrangement to be entered into, and
(d) the provision of any assistance that in any way promotes or facilitates the arrangement.

**5.119** The Russia Regulations prohibit the direct or indirect provision of brokering services where they relate to similar areas as those applying to 'technical assistance' (see paragraph 5.107 above), except that the prohibitions on activity relating to restricted goods and technology and energy-related goods and technology apply to non-UK activity (regulations 29 and 45), and with the addition of maritime transportation of certain oil and oil products (regulation 46Z9D).[132]

**5.120** Practitioners should be aware that the prohibitions apply equally to the indirect provision of brokering services.

**5.121** The prohibitions on brokering services are subject to exceptions and licences in Part 7.

## 3. The Prohibitions in Chapter 6B of the Russia Regulations

### (i) Professional and business services

**5.122** Regulation 54C prohibits the direct or indirect provision of certain professional and business services to persons connected with Russia, subject to the exceptions and licences at Part 7 of the Russia Regulations. Whether a person is connected to Russia is explained at paragraph 5.71 above.[133] The services prohibitions did not go so far as to prohibit services *for the benefit of* persons connected with Russia as permitted under paragraph 11 of Schedule 1 to SAMLA. However, regulation 54C does prohibit the 'indirect' provision of these services to persons connected with Russia, so advisers will need to make sure they do not fall foul thereof.

**5.123** The purpose of these measures is to prevent the export of selected UK services to Russia or the use of these services for ongoing business activity within the Russia economy. Government guidance on 'Complying with professional and business services sanctions related to Russia'[134] explains that persons connected with Russia, including subsidiaries that are owned by UK persons, should not generally benefit from the ongoing support and expertise of UK service providers in areas of sanctioned activity unless there is a relevant exception, or a licence has been granted.

[132] See regs 30, 30H, 45, 46BC, 46I, 46IE, 46Q, 46X, 46XG, 46Z2, 46Z9, 46Z9D, 46Z16, 46Z16I, 46Z16P, 46Z16U, 46Z23, 46Z29, 46Z33, and 53.

[133] These prohibitions (as well as the legal advisory services prohibition) were inserted into the Russia Regulations on 21 July 2022: The Russia (Sanctions) (EU Exit) (Amendment) (No 14) Regulations 2022, SI 2022/850.

[134] OFSI and DBT, 'Complying with Professional and Business Services Sanctions Related to Russia' (Guidance, 2 December 2022) <https://www.gov.uk/government/publications/professional-and-business-services-to-a-person-connected-with-russia/professional-and-business-services-to-a-person-connected-with-russia> accessed 26 May 2025.

*a) Territorial scope*

The prohibition applies within the territory of the UK and in relation to the conduct of all UK nationals and all bodies incorporated or constituted under the law of any part of the UK wherever they are. Government guidance on 'Complying with professional and business services sanctions related to Russia'[135] provides that the prohibition applies to branches of UK companies operating overseas. It also advises that subsidiaries of UK companies operating overseas, with a different legal status to branches, should consider how the prohibition applies to UK nationals who they employ or work with. 5.124

The statutory guidance on Russia sanctions[136] states that the provision of services via any of modes 1, 2, 3, or 4 of supply as defined under the World Trade Organization's General Agreement on Trade in Services (GATS) to any person connected with Russia is covered by the prohibitions.[137] The statutory guidance provides that this would include the supply of such services by a UK services provider to another company incorporated under Russian law and the provision of services to Russian residents who are temporarily located in another country, including the UK.[138] 5.125

Government guidance on 'Complying with professional and business services sanctions related to Russia'[139] also provides that whether export activities are within scope of the professional and business services prohibition will depend on a number of factors including the unique organizational structure of a company and its subsidiaries or branches, the nature of the service being traded, the suppliers and recipients of the service, and the design of the measure, including the licences and exceptions that apply. 5.126

*b) Relevant services*

Regulation 54C applies to the following services: accounting, advertising, architectural, auditing, business and management consulting, engineering, IT consultancy and design, and public relations. 5.127

Each of these services is defined in Schedule 3J of the Russia Regulations. 5.128

For example, paragraph 6 of Schedule 3J defines business and management consulting services as 'advisory, guidance and operational assistance services provided for business policy and strategy and the overall planning, structuring and control of an organisation, which includes (but is not limited to) management auditing, market 5.129

135 ibid.

136 FCDO, ECJU, OFSI, and OTSI, 'Russia Sanctions: Guidance' (n 83).

137 WTO's Trade Guide on GATS summarizes each of these modes as follows: 'Mode 1, cross-border supply from the territory of one WTO member country into the territory of another (for example, an architect in the U.S. sending plans to a client in Singapore); Mode 2, consumption abroad (for example, an Australian tourist taking a vacation in Las Vegas, or an Argentine citizen coming to the United States for health care); Mode 3, commercial presence (for example, the branch of an American bank in South Africa extending loans to local entrepreneurs); and Mode 4, the presence of "natural persons" for a limited period of time in another country (for example, the representative of an American software company spending a month in France installing the firm's products on a French company's computers)'. <https://www.trade.gov/trade-guide-wto-gats> accessed 26 May 2025.

138 FCDO, ECJU, OFSI, and OTSI, 'Russia Sanctions: Guidance' (n 83).

139 OFSI and DBT, 'Complying with Professional and Business Services Sanctions Related to Russia' (n 134).

management, human resources, production management and project management consulting.' As can be readily appreciated, it is very widely defined and is based upon the definitions found in Extended Balance of Payments Services classifications.

5.130 There are separate prohibitions in relation to accounting and auditing services. Accounting and auditing services are defined on the basis of the provisional Central Product Classification Codes 1991. The accounting services prohibition does not apply to the preparation services of business tax returns (when provided as a separate service) or bookkeeping services related to tax returns.[140]

*c) Exceptions*

5.131 Exceptions to the professional and business services prohibition are set out in regulation 60DA. They apply automatically.

5.132 A general exception applies to providing accounting services, business and management consulting services, engineering services, or public relations services in relation to the discharge of statutory obligations.[141]

5.133 Specific exceptions apply to auditing services.[142] For example, there is an exception for auditing services provided by auditors of UK subsidiary undertakings[143] in relation to the discharge of, or compliance with, UK statutory or regulatory obligations where this results in the provision of those services indirectly to a parent undertaking of the subsidiary which is a person connected with Russia.[144] Government guidance on 'Complying with professional and business services sanctions related to Russia'[145] clarifies that the auditing services prohibition does apply to the audit of a UK parent undertaking with a subsidiary undertaking that is a person connected with Russia (unless the UK parent undertaking is a credit institution).[146]

*d) Licences*

5.134 Licences can be issued for certain trade activities that would otherwise be prohibited by the Russia Regulations. The Secretary of State for Business and Trade is ultimately responsible for decisions to grant or refuse trade sanctions licences in any individual cases.

5.135 The statutory guidance provides the licensing grounds that are applicable to each of the professional and business services sanctions.[147] For example, licences may be granted

[140] Russia Regulations 2019, sch 3J, paras 2(b) and (d).
[141] Russia Regulations 2019, reg 60DA(1).
[142] Russia Regulations 2019, reg 60DA(3)–(5A).
[143] UK subsidiary undertakings are defined in reg 60DA(9) of the Russia Regulations as subsidiary undertakings that are incorporated or formed under the law of the United Kingdom.
[144] Russia Regulations 2019, reg 60DA(5).
[145] OFSI and DBT, 'Complying with Professional and Business Services Sanctions Related to Russia' (n 134).
[146] Russia Regulations, reg 60DA(3); OFSI and DBT, 'Complying with Professional and Business Services Sanctions Related to Russia' (n 134).
[147] FCDO, ECJU, OFSI, and OTSI, 'Russia Sanctions: Guidance' (n 83).

for services that are necessary for non-Russian persons to divest from Russia or to wind down business operations in Russia.

Persons should not assume that a licence will be granted or engage in any activities prohibited by trade sanctions until a licence has been granted. Operating without an existing licence where an application has been made is prohibited. 5.136

*e) Offence*

It is an offence to contravene the professional and business services prohibition. However, it is a defence for a person to show that they did not know and had no reasonable cause to suspect that the person to whom the services were provided was connected with Russia.[148] 5.137

Government guidance on 'Complying with professional and business services sanctions related to Russia'[149] provides that in determining compliance with the professional and business services sanctions, relevant considerations will include who the service providers are, whether the services would fall within the scope of the definition in Schedule 3J of the Russia Regulations, who the services recipients were, and whether any relevant exceptions or licensing provisions are applicable. 5.138

(ii) Legal advisory services

On 30 June 2023, the Government introduced the legal advisory services prohibition under regulation 54D of the Russia Regulations.[150] 5.139

Regulation 54D prohibits the direct or indirect provision of certain 'legal advisory services' to a non-UK person, knowing that the object or effect of those services is to enable or facilitate any activity being carried out where: 5.140

- the activity is not being carried out, or will not be carried out, in the UK; and
- the activity would be prohibited under regulations 11 to 18C, Chapters 2 to 6, or regulation 54C of the Russia Regulations, or would contravene the circumvention measures in regulations 19 or 55, if it were carried out by a UK person or took place in the UK.

In essence, where an overseas activity is not itself prohibited by the Russia Regulations, regulation 54D prohibits UK lawyers from advising on overseas activities if (hypothetically) the activity would have been prohibited if done by a UK person and/or in the UK. Importantly, advisers should be aware that regulation 54D applies to the provision of legal advisory services directly and indirectly to non-UK persons.[151] 5.141

148 Russia Regulations 2019, reg 54C(3).
149 FCDO, ECJU, OFSI, and OTSI, 'Russia Sanctions: Guidance' (n 83).
150 The prohibition was further amended on 6 September 2024.
151 Russia Regulations 2019, reg 54D(1).

5.142 When the UK Government introduced this prohibition, the accompanying official statement described it as a 'tough new law to stop Russia accessing UK legal expertise'.[152] The policy behind this prohibition is that it plugs a perceived loophole that would otherwise potentially permit UK legal services providers to support commercial activity that advances the interests of Russia where those activities are not conducted in the UK or by UK persons.

5.143 The Government's guidance on 'Complying with professional and business services sanctions related to Russia'[153] notes that the circumvention rules in regulations 19 and 55 of the Russia Regulations already prevent a person intentionally providing legal advisory services where the object or effect of the services directly or indirectly circumvents prohibitions imposed by certain Russia Regulations, including activity that enables or facilitates the contravention of those prohibitions. However, given the territorial application of the Russia Regulations, the circumvention rules in regulations 19 and 55 generally apply only to legal advisory services provided in relation to prohibited activity undertaken in the UK or by a UK person (see further section E below). The legal advisory services prohibition in regulation 54D supplements the circumvention rules and extends them to include activity with no connection to the UK, provided the legal advice is given by a UK person to a non-UK person. The significant effect of regulation 54D is to extend the existing sanctions restrictions extra-territorially for lawyers, by prohibiting them from advising on overseas activities—such as commercial transactions—which would breach UK sanctions on Russia, were it not for the fact that the activities lack a sufficient jurisdictional connection to trigger UK sanctions.

5.144 The prohibitions in Regulation 54D apply to UK and non-UK persons within the territory of the UK and to the conduct of all UK nationals and all bodies incorporated or constituted under the law of any part of the UK wherever they are.

*a) Scope of legal services*

5.145 The prohibition applies to legal advisory services as defined in paragraph 8A of Schedule 3J. 'Legal advisory services' is broadly defined and means the provision of legal advice to a client in non-contentious matters as involving:

(i) the application or interpretation of law;
(ii) acting on behalf of a client, or providing advice on or in connection with, a commercial transaction, negotiation or any other dealing with a third party;
(iii) the preparation, execution or verification of a legal document. 'Legal document' is defined as including any document which is governed in whole or in part by law, or which satisfies a legal requirement.[154]

[152] Ministry of Justice, FCDO, Alex Chalk KC, and James Cleverly MP, 'New Law Imposes Fresh Sanctions on Russia Accessing UK Legal Expertise' (Press release, 29 June 2023) <https://www.gov.uk/government/news/new-law-imposes-fresh-sanctions-on-russia-accessing-uk-legal-expertise> accessed 26 May 2025.
[153] OFSI and DBT, 'Complying with Professional and Business Services Sanctions Related to Russia' (n 134).
[154] Russia Regulations 2019, sch 3J, para 8A(1)(a).

However, 'legal advisory services' do not include any representation, advice, preparation of documents, or verification of documents undertaken as part of legal representation services[155] provided in, or in anticipation of any proceedings before administrative agencies, courts, or other duly constituted official tribunals in any jurisdiction, or arbitral or mediation proceedings in any jurisdiction.[156] Nor do they include the provision of legal advice or other services in connection with the management of claims under a contract of insurance or reinsurance.[157] This effectively excludes from the prohibition legal advice and representation in contentious proceedings and anticipated proceedings. The Government's guidance also provides that '[t]he provision of legal advisory services relating to the protection of intellectual property is not expected to be in scope of this prohibition, but this should be assessed on a case by case basis.'[158] **5.146**

Accordingly, the prohibition is focused on the provision of legal advice in non-contentious matters (including providing advice on, or in connection with, a commercial transaction). In its guidance on 'Complying with professional and business services sanctions related to Russia', the Government explains that 'legal advisory services' do not include 'legal representation services' for the purpose of regulation 54D because 'access to legal representation is an important element of the core democratic principle of the rule of law, and this sort of legal service has therefore been excluded.'[159] **5.147**

Importantly, however, the prohibition extends beyond giving legal advice to persons connected to Russia. What must be assessed is whether the relevant activity or transaction being advised upon would breach the Russia Regulations were it to take place in the UK or involve UK persons. **5.148**

*b) Knowledge*

Until 5 September 2024, regulation 54D was silent on knowledge. However, following an amendment introduced by the Russia (Sanctions) (EU Exit) (Amendment) (No 4) Regulations 2024 (SI 2024/900), regulation 54D(1) now provides that, to be in breach of the prohibition, a lawyer must provide legal advisory services *knowing* that the object or effect of these services is to enable or facilitate an activity where the object or effect of those services is to enable or facilitate financial or trade activity which would be prohibited under the UK sanctions regime if the activity was done by a UK person or taking place within the UK. **5.149**

[155] 'Legal representation services' are defined in paragraph 8A(2)(b) of Schedule 3J as including advice given in relation to a dispute or potential dispute, and on the settlement of a dispute, whether or not proceedings referred to in paragraph 8A(1)(b) of Schedule 3J are commenced in relation to the dispute.

[156] Russia Regulations 2019, sch 3J, para 8A(1)(b). Paragraphs 8A(1)(b)(i) and (ii) were amended by the Russia (Sanctions) (EU Exit) (Amendment) (No 4) Regulations 2024, SI 2024/900 to include proceedings in any jurisdiction (effective 6 September 2024).

[157] Russia Regulations 2019, sch 3J, para 8A(1)(c). This was added by the Russia (Sanctions) (EU Exit) (Amendment) (No 4) Regulations 2024 (effective 6 September 2024).

[158] OFSI and DBT, 'Complying with Professional and Business Services Sanctions Related to Russia' (n 134).

[159] ibid.

*c) Exceptions*

5.150 Regulation 60DB provides the following exceptions to the legal advisory services prohibitions in regulation 54D:

(1) The prohibitions [...] are not contravened by any act done by a person that is necessary for the official purposes of a diplomatic mission[160] or consular post[161] in Russia, or of an international organisation enjoying immunities in accordance with international law.

(2) The prohibitions [...] are not contravened by any act done by a person for the purpose of providing legal advisory services in relation to the discharge of or compliance with UK statutory or regulatory obligations.

(3) The prohibitions [...] are not contravened by any act done by a person for the purposes of providing legal advisory services to any person as to whether an act or a proposed act complies with [the Russia Regulations].

(3A) The prohibitions [...] are not contravened by any act done by a person for the purpose of providing legal advisory services to any person on or in connection with—[162]

(a) compliance with, or the consequences of non-compliance with, any relevant law,

(b) the discharge of obligations under any relevant law,[163] or

(c) the potential, or actual, application of punitive measures.[164]

(4) The prohibitions [...] are not contravened by any act done by a person ('P') in satisfaction of an obligation arising under a contract concluded before 30th June 2023, or an ancillary contract necessary for the satisfaction of such a contract, provided that—

(a) the act is carried out before the end of 29th September 2023, and

(b) P notifies the Secretary of State of the provision of the services, before or after the act is carried out, by the end of 29th September 2023.

5.151 Prior to 6 September 2024, the exceptions in regulation 60DB appeared to permit advice only in respect of whether an act complied with the UK's Russia Regulations, therefore excluding advice on compliance with foreign sanctions regimes or non-sanctions compliance, such as money laundering issues. A number of professional

[160] Reg 60DB(5) provides that 'diplomatic mission' is to be read in accordance with the Vienna Convention on Diplomatic Relations done at Vienna on 18th April 1961.

[161] Reg 60DB(5) provides that 'consular post' has the same meaning as in the Vienna Convention on Consular Relations done at Vienna on 24th April 1963.

[162] Reg 60DB(3A) was added by the Russia (Sanctions) (EU Exit) (Amendment) (No 4) Regulations 2024 (effective 6 September 2024).

[163] Reg 60DB(5) provides that 'relevant law' means (a) any sanction, imposed by any jurisdiction; (b) any law of Russia that has as its primary object or effect the frustration of any sanctions referred to in paragraph (a); or (c) any criminal law imposed by any jurisdiction.

[164] Reg 60DB(5) provides that 'punitive measures' mean any sanction which may be applied by a country in relation to a person ('P') in retaliation for P engaging, or proposing to engage, in conduct which would render P liable to penalties under the law of that country if P were subject to its jurisdiction.

bodies (such as the Law Society and various law firms) raised their concerns with the UK Government, emphasizing the inherently cross-border nature of sanctions compliance. As a result, the UK Government admitted in Parliament that this not what was intended.[165]

On 11 August 2023, DBT issued a Legal Advisory Services General Trade Licence in order to address this unintended consequence.[166] Regulation 60DB was then amended by the Russia (Sanctions) (EU Exit) (Amendment) (No 4) Regulations 2024 to make clear that legal advisory services are permitted on or in connection with compliance with global sanctions, Russian counter-sanctions and global criminal law. The amendment also clarified that legal advisory services are permitted in relation to the application of punitive measures, as well as in relation to compliance with UK statutory or regulatory obligations.[167] These amendments to regulation 60DB came into force on 6 September 2024. The Legal Advisory Services General Trade Licence was revoked on the same day as it was deemed no longer required.[168] **5.152**

*d) Licences*

For legal advisory services which are prohibited under regulation 54D and not excepted under regulation 60DB, advisers can apply for a licence. The statutory guidance provides that '[a] licence may be granted for the provisions of legal advisory service where a licencing ground would apply to the activity in relation to which the legal advisory services are being provided [ . . . ] if the relevant activity was done by a UK person or taking place in the UK'.[169] **5.153**

The Government's guidance on 'complying with professional and business services sanctions related to Russia' provides that, on applying for licences, it would be 'helpful' to: **5.154**

- provide details of the activity that the legal advice relates to and for what reason
- provide details of other licence applications and licensing grounds that apply to the activity the legal advice relates to
- provide details on the service provider(s) and the recipient(s) of the services

[165] HL Deb 19 July 2023, vol 831, col 315GC. Lord Ahmad said: '[ . . . ] this legislation can be interpreted as having the unintended consequence of prohibiting persons in the UK and British nationals abroad from providing legal advice to clients seeking to comply with the sanctions regimes of our international partners. Let me assure noble Lords that it is not the intent of these regulations to prohibit this type of legal service. UK lawyers should be able to support their clients to be sanctions-compliant beyond UK law as we work closely with our allies to tighten the net on Russia's economy.'

[166] DBT, 'General Trade Licence (Russia sanctions—Legal Advisory Services)' (11 August 2023) <https://assets.publishing.service.gov.uk/media/66d6cedc9084b18b95709f11/Revoked-russia-sanctions-legal-advisory-services-general-trade-licence.pdf> accessed 26 May 2025.

[167] See ECJU, Ministry of Justice, and DBT, 'NTE 2024/21: Update on Russia Sanctions Legal Services and Revocation of Legal Advisory Services General Trade Licence' (Notice, 6 September 2024) <https://www.gov.uk/government/publications/notice-to-exporters-202421-update-on-russia-sanctions-legal-services-and-revocation-of-legal-advisory-services-general-trade-licence/nte-202421-update-on-russia-sanctions-legal-services-and-revocation-of-legal-advisory-services-general-trade-licence> accessed 26 May 2025.

[168] DBT, 'General Trade Licence (Russia sanctions—Legal Advisory Services)' (n 166).

[169] FCDO, ECJU, OFSI, and OTSI, 'Russia Sanctions: Guidance' (n 83).

- provide information on the relationship between the service provider(s) and recipients
- explain how the continued provision of such services is consistent with the aims of the sanctions and the impact/implications if the services could not be provided.[170]

*e) Offence*

5.155 It is an offence to contravene the legal advisory services prohibition.[171]

5.156 Until 5 September 2024, it was a defence for a person to show that they did not know and had no reasonable cause to suspect that the relevant activity satisfied the conditions in regulation 54D(2) (namely, that the relevant activity would be prohibited under regulations 18 to 18C, Chapters 2 to 6, or Chapter 6B of the Russia Regulations if it was done by a UK person or if it took place in the UK). This was removed on 6 September 2024 because the prohibition now only applies where the services were provided with the requisite knowledge that the condition was satisfied.

5.157 Government guidance on 'Complying with professional and business services sanctions related to Russia' provides that in determining compliance with the prohibitions, relevant considerations will include 'who the service providers are', 'whether the services would fall in scope of the definition in Schedule 3J [of the Russia Regulations]', 'who the services recipients are', and 'whether any relevant exceptions or licensing provisions are applicable'.[172]

## E. Circumventing the Prohibitions Offence in the Russia Regulations

5.158 Regulation 55 is a circumventing provision (similar to the financial sanctions circumventing provision at regulation 19) which applies to trade prohibitions. It provides that it is an offence to intentionally participate in activities knowing that the object or effect of them is, whether directly or indirectly, to circumvent any of the prohibitions in Chapters 2 to 6 and 6B of Part 5 (or to enable or facilitate their circumvention).

5.159 It can conveniently be classified as a prohibition involving conduct and a plan. It precludes:

i. intentionally participating in activities ('the conduct');
ii. knowing that the object/effect is directly/indirectly to circumvent or facilitate ('the plan').

[170] OFSI and DBT, 'Complying with Professional and Business Services Sanctions Related to Russia' (n 134).
[171] Russia Regulations 2019, reg 54D(4).
[172] OFSI and DBT, 'Complying with Professional and Business Services Sanctions Related to Russia' (n 134).

The conduct requires intention. The plan requires knowledge. **5.160**

Unlike other prohibitions in the Russia Regulations this prohibition expressly requires knowledge as an element of the offence. **5.161**

The Government issued guidance on 25 February 2025 entitled 'Countering Russian Sanctions Evasion – Guidance for Businesses' which emphasizes that it remains the responsibility of UK businesses to fully determine the extent of their specific sanctions risk exposure and to develop an appropriate set of safeguards.[173] The guidance highlights 'Circumvention Red Flags' which it breaks down into four categories: product; customer; transaction; and export destination. The guidance highlights particular goods, stemming from the Common High Priority List, which are at a higher risk of being involved in circumvention and higher risk third countries where there is an increased risk of re-export to Russia. Companies are advised to conduct enhanced due diligence when exporting at risk products to certain countries. **5.162**

The guidance further recommends due diligence best practice, focusing upon strategic risk assessment, enhanced due diligence, screening tools, and ongoing monitoring. **5.163**

## F. Criminal Liability

Breach of the trade sanctions can result in criminal liability. The Russia Regulations set down prohibitions, breach of which is an offence under sections 50, 68, or 170 of CEMA. The Russia Regulations also create distinct criminal offences in relation to certain prohibitions. **5.164**

### 1. Imports

Prohibitions on imports are expressed in strict terms with no mental element specified either in the elements of the prohibition or in a defence. **5.165**

Breach of the import prohibitions is a criminal offence under section 50 of CEMA. Section 50(2) creates offences of intending to evade a prohibition or restriction relating to imports. The offences are triable either way. On summary conviction, a person guilty of an offence under section 50(2) is liable to a penalty of the prescribed sum or three times the value of the goods (whichever is greater) or to imprisonment for a term not exceeding six months, or to both. Following the amendments to CEMA introduced by section 32(1) of the Finance Act 2024, the maximum sentence on conviction on indictment is 14 years or a penalty of any amount, or both. Regulation 86(2) of the Russia **5.166**

[173] DBT and OFSI, 'Countering Russian Sanctions Evasion - Guidance for Businesses' (7 January 2025) <https://www.gov.uk/government/publications/countering-russian-sanctions-evasion-and-circumvention/countering-russian-sanctions-evasion-guidance-for-exporters> accessed 26 May 2025.

Regulations had specified a maximum sentence of 10 years, but this has been overtaken by the amendments to CEMA in the Finance Act 2024.[174]

5.167 Criminal liability may also arise in relation to a breach of the import prohibitions specified above under section 170 of CEMA in three ways. Section 170(1)(a) creates an offence of knowingly acquiring goods which are subject to an importation or exportation prohibition or restriction. Section 170(1)(b) creates an offence of being knowingly concerned with carrying, removing, depositing, harbouring, keeping, concealing, or in any manner dealing with any such goods with intent to evade any prohibition. Section 170(2)(b) creates an offence of being knowingly concerned in any fraudulent evasion or attempt at evasion of any prohibited goods. On summary conviction, a person guilty of an offence under section 170 is liable to a penalty of the prescribed sum or three times the value of the goods (whichever is greater) or to imprisonment for a term not exceeding six months, or to both. Following the amendments to CEMA introduced by section 32(1) of the Finance Act 2024, the maximum sentence on conviction on indictment is 14 years or a penalty of any amount, or both.[175]

## 2. Exports

5.168 Prohibitions on exports (with the exception of regulations 30B and 48(2), see further paragraph 5.172 below) are expressed in strict terms with no mental element specified in either the elements of the prohibition or in a defence.

5.169 Breach of the export prohibitions is a criminal offence under section 68 of CEMA which provides for two offences.

5.170 Under section 68(1), the exporter or intending exporter of prohibited goods and any agent of theirs who is concerned in the exportation or shipment of the goods commits a strict liability, summary only offence. The maximum sentence is three times the value of the goods or a fine of £1,000, whichever is the greater.

5.171 Under section 68(2), a triable either way offence is created. Any individual who is knowingly concerned in the exportation of such goods with intent to evade the prohibition commits an offence. Following the amendments to CEMA introduced by section 32(1) of the Finance Act 2024, the maximum sentence is 14 years.

[174] Whilst reg 86(1) of the Russia Regulations does not include regs 46IG, 46Z16K, or 46Z16R as prohibitions to which the 10-year sentence for an offence under section 50(2) CEMA applies, this has been superseded by the 14-year sentence introduced by the amendments to section 50(4)(b) CEMA by the Finance Act 2024 (effective 22 February 2024).

[175] Whilst reg 86(5) of the Russia Regulations only lists regs 22(1), 23, 30B, 40(1), 46B(1), 46D, 46N(1), 46S, 46XB, 46Y(1), 46Z4, 46Z11, 46Z1847(1), and 48 as prohibitions to the 10-year sentence for an offence under section 170(2) CEMA, there is no longer a need to update the applicable list of import/export prohibitions in reg86(5) because reg 86(6) has been superseded by the amendments to section 170(3)(b) CEMA by the Finance Act 2024 (effective 22 February 2024).

Regulation 30B(2) of the Russia Regulations prohibits 'the export of restricted goods to, or for use in, non-Government controlled areas of the Donetsk, Kherson, Luhansk and Zaporizhzhia oblasts'. For breaches of regulation 30B(2), regulation 30B(4) provides that it is a defence for a person charged under section 68(1) CEMA 'to show that they did not know and had no reasonable cause to suspect that the export was, or would have been, to, or the goods were for use in, non-government controlled areas of the Donetsk, Kherson, Luhansk and Zaporizhzhia oblasts'. Similarly for a breach of regulation 48(2) ('export of infrastructure-related goods to, or for use in, non-government controlled areas of the Donetsk, Kherson, Luhansk and Zaporizhzhia oblasts'), regulation 48(4) provides that it is a defence for the accused 'to show that they did not know and had no reasonable cause to suspect that the export was, or would have been, to, or the goods were for use in, non-government controlled areas of the Donetsk, Kherson, Luhansk and Zaporizhzhia oblasts'. **5.172**

Regulation 53A also provides a general defence for breach of prohibitions which, according to Schedules 2A, 3, or 3C, apply to items exported to non-government controlled Ukrainian territory as well as Russia. Regulation 53A(3) provides that where a person is charged with an offence under section 68(1) of CEMA 'in relation to exportation of goods to, or for use in, non-government controlled areas of the Donetsk, Kherson, Luhansk and Zaporizhzhia oblasts' which is or would be contrary to regulation 22(1) (export of restricted goods) by virtue of regulation 53A, it is a defence to show that they 'did not know and had no reasonable cause to suspect that the export was, or would have been, to, or the goods were for use in, non-government controlled areas of Donetsk, Kherson, Luhansk and Zaporizhzhia oblasts'. **5.173**

Criminal liability may also arise in relation to a breach of the export prohibitions specified above under section 170 of CEMA (see paragraph 5.167 above). On summary conviction, a person guilty of such an offence is liable to a penalty of the prescribed sum or three times the value of the goods (whichever is greater) or to imprisonment for a term not exceeding six months, or both. The maximum sentence on conviction on indictment is 14 years or an unlimited fine, or both.[176] **5.174**

## 3. Other Prohibitions

In addition to the above offences which relate to direct importation and exportation of goods, regulation 24 creates an offence relating to the direct or indirect supply or delivery restricted, military, and maritime goods from or to Russia through a third country.[177] It is a defence for a person to show that they did not know and had no reasonable cause to suspect that the goods were (ultimately) destined for or were from a **5.175**

[176] See s 32(1) of the Finance Act 2024.

[177] Under reg 24(4) of the Russia Regulations, 'third country' means a country that is not the UK, the Isle of Man, or Russia.

place in Russia, or were for placing on board a Russian-flagged vessel, whether directly or indirectly.[178]

**5.176** Further offences have also been created relating to, for example, making available or acquiring restricted goods and technology (regulation 25), the transfer of restricted technology (regulation 26), the provision of technical assistance relating to restricted goods and technology (regulation 27), the provision of financial services and funds relating to restricted goods and services (regulation 28), and the provision of brokering services relating to restricted goods and services (regulation 29).[179] These prohibitions provide a similar defence for the accused to show that they did not know and had no reasonable cause to suspect that the person was connected with Russia (or, where applicable, non-government controlled Ukrainian territory) or that the goods or technology were for use in or located in Russia (or, where applicable, non-government controlled Ukrainian territory).[180]

**5.177** Notably, the prohibitions vary in terms of the mental element required to commit an offence. Prohibitions of exports of certain goods, such as restricted goods and energy related goods (regulations 22 and 40) are expressed as strict liability offences (subject to Part 7 exceptions and licences). In contrast, other offences, such as under regulation 41 (on the supply and delivery of energy-related goods), provide a defence for the charged person to show that they 'did not know and had no reasonable cause to suspect that the goods were destined (or ultimately destined) for Russia.'[181] Thus, a person who did not have reasonable cause to suspect that the goods were ultimately destined for Russia will not be in breach. It is worth noting that the test is objective so, even if a person neither knew nor genuinely had any suspicion about the destination of the goods, if a reasonable person would have suspected that they were destined for Russia, the defence would not be made out.

**5.178** Where an individual relies upon such a defence, regulation 56 provides that if evidence is adduced which is sufficient to raise an issue with respect to the defence, the court must assume that the defence is satisfied unless the prosecution proves beyond reasonable doubt that it is not.[182] This is unusual in the context of regulatory offences as it creates merely an evidential burden upon the accused. However, the prosecution can negate the defence by proving that the accused had reasonable grounds to suspect that the goods were destined or ultimately destined for Russia.

[178] Russia Regulations 2019, reg 24(3).
[179] See also the prohibitions in Chapter 2A of the Russia Regulations, relating to goods and technology to non-government controlled Ukrainian territory.
[180] Defences are found in regs 25(3), 26(3), 27(3), 28(7), and 29(3) of the Russia Regulations.
[181] Russia Regulations 2019, reg 41(3).
[182] Russia Regulations 2019, reg 56(2).

## G. Licences

Licences may be issued for certain trade activities that would otherwise be prohibited by the Russia Regulations. Regulation 65 provides that the prohibitions do not apply to anything done under the authority of a licence issued by the Secretary of State (see above at paragraph 5.106 for the current general licence in place relating to software and technology). **5.179**

There are three separate bodies in DBT which are responsible for administering licences on behalf of the Secretary of State:[183] **5.180**

1. The Import Controls and Sanctions team is responsible for administering licences for the import of goods and associated activities.
2. ECJU is responsible for licensing the export of goods, software, and technology from the UK.
3. OTSI is responsible for licensing relating to the provision of standalone services (e.g. professional and business services) which are otherwise prohibited under the Russia Regulations.

Further, as an exception within the trade sanctions regime, OFSI is responsible for issuing licences relating to the supply or delivery by ship of oil and oil products under the commodity codes 2709 and 2710 from Russia to and between third countries and services associated with that supply or delivery (such as financial services and brokering).[184]

### 1. Applications for Licences

Applications for an import licence can be made through the online licensing system (the Import Case Management System, or ICMS).[185] The application process is managed by DBT's Import Controls Team, and guidance states that they will, to the extent that it is possible, aim to inform the trader of the application outcome within 30 days. **5.181**

Applications for an export licence can be made through the online export licensing system SPIRE.[186] Extra information on the activities proposed to be carried out can be included in a cover letter attached with any other documentation to the application. **5.182**

[183] OFSI, ECJU, and DBT, 'How to Apply for a Trade Sanctions License' (Guidance, 10 October 2024) <https://www.gov.uk/guidance/how-to-apply-for-a-trade-sanctions-licence> accessed 26 May 2025.

[184] OFSI can be contacted by emailing oilpricecap.ofsi@hmtreasury.gov.uk. OFSI and HM Treasury have also provided guidance on this specific exception: 'Maritime Services Ban and Oil Price Cap: Licences and Reporting Forms' (4 December 2022) <https://www.gov.uk/government/publications/russian-oil-services-ban> accessed 26 May 2025.

[185] <https://apply-for-an-import-licence.service.gov.uk/login-start/> accessed 26 May 2025.

[186] <https://www.spire.businessandtrade.gov.uk> accessed 26 May 2025.

5.183 When making an application for a licence, it is important to consider any potential overlap between trade sanctions and financial sanctions. Licences may need to be obtained from OFSI as well as ECJU and OTSI or DBT's Import Controls Team.

5.184 No one should assume that a licence will be granted or engage in any activities prohibited by trade sanctions until the requisite licence has been granted.

## 2. Licensing Decisions

5.185 In making decisions on whether to grant a licence to permit something which would otherwise be prohibited under Part 5 of the Russia Regulations, the Secretary of State for Business and Trade will consider each application on a case-by-case basis to determine whether granting a licence would be consistent with the stated purposes of the sanctions regime and any UN or other relevant international law obligations.

5.186 DBT guidance indicates that for each of the prohibitions, there are certain activities which will likely be licensable on the basis that the activities are consistent with the aims of the sanctions. Whilst not an exhaustive list, it is likely to be used as a basis for most decisions on trade licences. If it is considered that a proposed activity falls within one of these specific descriptions, the licence application should make this clear and explain why this is believed to be the case. A full table of the relevant considerations for trade sanctions licences has been produced on the government guidance page.[187]

## 3. Offences

5.187 Regulation 68 of the Russia Regulations creates two offences in relation to trade licences.

1. It is an offence for a person 'knowingly or recklessly' to provide information that is false in a material respect, or provide or produce a document that is not what it purports to be, for the purpose of obtaining a trade licence (for themselves or another).[188]
2. It is an offence for a person to fail to comply with any condition of the trade licence granted to them.[189]

[187] FCDO, ECJU, OFSI, and OTSI, 'Russia Sanctions: Guidance' (n 83) s 3.4.

[188] Russia Regulations 2019, reg 68(1). By reg 68(3), where such an offence is committed, the licence is to be treated as void from its issue.

[189] Russia Regulations 2019, reg 68(2).

## H. Other Trade Sanctions Regimes

In addition to the Russia Regulations, the UK implements a range of other trade sanctions regimes through regulations established under SAMLA. The UK Government publishes a list of countries in relation to which UK trade sanctions are in place.[190] At the time of writing, UK trade sanctions are in place (to varying degrees) in relation to Afghanistan, Belarus, Burma (Myanmar), the Central African Republic, the Democratic People's Republic of Korea, the Democratic Republic of the Congo, Iran, Iraq, Lebanon, Libya, Somalia, South Sudan, Sudan, Syria, Ukraine, Venezuela, Yemen, and Zimbabwe. **5.188**

### 1. Belarus

Trade sanctions were introduced by the Republic of Belarus (Sanctions) (EU Exit) Regulations 2019 (the 'Belarus Regulations') and significantly increased in response to the Russo-Ukraine war. The wide-ranging purposes of this sanctions regime include encouraging the Government of Belarus (i) 'to cease actions destabilising Ukraine or undermining or threatening the territorial integrity, sovereignty or independence of Ukraine, including by supporting or facilitating Russia's actions in respect of Ukraine', and (ii) 'to refrain from any other action which undermines or threatens peace, security or stability in Europe'.[191] **5.189**

The trade sanctions in the Belarus Regulations are comprehensive, broad, and similar to those imposed by the Russia Regulations. Prohibitions are imposed in relation to: military goods and military technology; anything which falls within Chapter 93 of the Goods Classification Table, other than military goods; the provision of technical assistance, armed personnel, financial services, or funds, or associated brokering services where such provision enables or facilitates the conduct of certain military activities; dual-use goods and technology; internal repression goods and technology; interception and monitoring goods and technology; interception and monitoring services; technical assistance relating to aircraft and ships; tobacco industry goods; potash; mineral products; iron and steel products; critical industry goods and technology; luxury goods; oil refining goods and technology; quantum computing and advanced materials goods and technology; chemical and biological weapons-related goods and technology; machinery-related goods and technology; banknotes; cement; gold, gold jewellery and relevant processed gold; rubber; wood; and aluminium.[192] **5.190**

[190] DBT and ECJU, 'Trade Sanctions, Arms Embargoes, and Other Trade Restrictions' (Guidance, 3 August 2012) <https://www.gov.uk/guidance/current-arms-embargoes-and-other-restrictions> accessed 26 May 2025.
[191] The Republic of Belarus (Sanctions) (EU Exit) Regulations 2019, reg 4(e)–(f).
[192] Belarus Regulations 2019, pt 5.

5.191 Practitioners should review the statutory guidance on the Belarus Regulations which is regularly updated.[193]

## 2. Iran

5.192 Trade sanctions are imposed against Iran under Part 6 of The Iran (Sanctions) Regulations 2023 (the 'Iran Regulations'). The purposes of the Iran Regulations include encouraging the Government of Iran to comply with international human rights law and deterring the Government of Iran or any armed group backed by them from conducting hostile activity against the UK or any other country.[194]

5.193 The trade sanctions in the Iran Regulations are less comprehensive than those imposed by the Russia Regulations or the Belarus Regulations. The Iran Regulations impose trade sanctions in relation to: (a) goods and technology which might be used for internal repression; (b) goods and technology which might be used for monitoring and interception of telecommunications; (c) the provision of interception and monitoring services; and (d) ancillary services such as financial services and brokering services provided in relation to those goods and services.[195]

5.194 Practitioners should review the statutory guidance relating to the Iran Regulations, which is regularly updated.[196]

[193] FCDO, DfT, Home Office, ECJU, OFSI, and OTSI, 'Republic of Belarus Sanctions: Guidance' (Statutory guidance, 15 January 2020) <https://www.gov.uk/government/publications/republic-of-belarus-sanctions-guidance/the-republic-of-belarus-sanctions-guidance> accessed 26 May 2025.

[194] The Iran (Sanctions) Regulations 2023, reg 4(1).

[195] Iran Regulations 2023, pt 6.

[196] FCDO, ECJU, OFSI, and OTSI, 'Iran Sanctions: Guidance' (Statutory guidance, 15 December 2023) <https://www.gov.uk/government/publications/iran-sanctions-guidance/iran-sanctions-guidance> accessed 26 May 2025.

# 6

# Aircraft and Shipping Sanctions

*Rachel Barnes KC and Stephen Bailey*



## A. Introduction

Transport is vital. It 'creates links between regions and economic activities, between people and the rest of the world, generating value'.[1] Sanctions target these links. Doing so to interrupt trade as part of economic warfare is not new—during the Napoleonic Wars, the UK, with its superior naval power, imposed a blockade and a series of trade restrictions upon neutral ships engaged in transatlantic and continental trade, prohibiting under pain of detention and seizure their trade with Continental Europe without a licence issued by the British authorities (which included a requirement to pay customs duties to the British).[2] France had instituted a similar blockade.[3] Similarly, during the First and Second World Wars, the UK introduced measures to restrict shipping trade by neutrals, establishing a sophisticated licensing system of 'navicerts' and ships' warrants **6.01**

[1] Jean-Paul Rodrigue, *The Geography of Transport Systems* (6th edn, Routledge 2024) 8.

[2] Orders in Council made on 11, 18, and 25 November 1807 and 18 December 1807, published in the *London Gazette* in issues 16087, 16090, 16091, and 16097. The Order in Council made on 18 December 1807 (issue 16097 in the *London Gazette*) declared general reprisals against all Russian vessels.

[3] The French blockade is described in the recitals to an Order in Council made on 11 November 1807 (see issue 16090 in the *London Gazette*).

Rachel Barnes KC and Stephen Bailey, *Aircraft and Shipping Sanctions* In: *UK Sanctions Law and Practice*. Edited by: Amanda Pinto KC, Alexandre Haines, and Sophie O'Sullivan, Oxford University Press. © Oxford University Press 2026. DOI: 10.1093/oso/9780198964179.003.0006

which enabled licensed neutral ships to avoid seizure of their cargo and to utilize the facilities of British controlled ports.[4]

**6.02** In the UK today, the Sanctions and Anti-Money Laundering Act 2018 (SAMLA) empowers the Secretary of State and the Treasury to make sanctions regulations which impose shipping and aircraft sanctions (collectively, transport sanctions):[5]

- Shipping sanctions impose prohibitions or requirements for one or more of a number of prescribed purposes, which include detaining ships, ensuring that ships do not enter or leave the UK, and controlling ownership and registration of ships.[6]
- Similarly, aircraft sanctions impose prohibitions or requirements for one or more of a number of prescribed purposes, which include detaining aircraft, ensuring aircraft do not overfly the UK or leave the airspace over the UK, and controlling ownership and registration of aircraft.[7]

**6.03** As of August 2025, the Secretary of State has made five sanctions regulations (or 'regimes') which impose transport sanctions (the 'five regimes').[8] Specifically, the Democratic People's Republic of Korea regime,[9] the Belarus regime,[10] the Russia regime,[11] and the Libya regime[12] impose shipping and aircraft sanctions; and the Iran regime[13] imposes shipping sanctions.[14] Each regime creates exceptions to the sanctions imposed.[15] Save for the Iran regime, each regime also provides that the Secretary of State may issue licences in respect of shipping and/or aircraft sanctions.[16] Where a

[4] For a contemporaneous description of the UK's shipping restrictions and control by navicerts and ships' warrants, see *The Ole Wegger and Other Vessels* (German Supreme Prize Tribunal) (1943) 12 ILR 532.

[5] Sanctions and Anti-Money Laundering Act 2018 (SAMLA), s 1(1), (5)(d)–(e), and (9).

[6] SAMLA 2018, s 7(1). Sanctions regulations also impose shipping sanctions where they (1) authorize certain directions to be given by the Secretary of State or a harbour authority or (2) make particular provision relating to ships designated for the purpose of a UN Security Council resolution (SAMLA 2018, s 7(2)–(6)).

[7] SAMLA 2018, s 6(1). Sanctions regulations also impose aircraft sanctions where they authorize certain directions to be given by the Secretary of State, the Civil Aviation Authority (CAA), a person who holds a licence to provide air traffic services, or an airport operator (s 6(2)–(5)).

[8] A power to restrict or prohibit flying is also contained in article 239 of the Air Navigation Order 2016 (ANO), SI 2016/765. For an example of where this power has been used in a sanctions-related context, see regulation 2 of the Air Navigation (Restriction of Flying) (Russian Aircraft) Regulations 2022, SI 2022/183.

[9] Democratic People's Republic of Korea (Sanctions) (EU Exit) Regulations 2019, SI 2019/411 (the 'North Korea Regulations'), pts 7–8.

[10] Republic of Belarus (Sanctions) (EU Exit) Regulations 2019, SI 2019/600 (the 'Belarus Regulations'), pts 5A–5B.

[11] Russia (Sanctions) (EU Exit) Regulations 2019 (the 'Russia Regulations'), SI 2019/855 pts 6–6A.

[12] Libya (Sanctions) (EU Exit) Regulations 2020, SI 2020/1665 (the 'Libya Regulations'), pts 6–7.

[13] Iran (Sanctions) Regulations 2023, SI 2023/1314 (the 'Iran Regulations'), pt 7.

[14] Part 6 of the Syria (Sanctions) (EU Exit) Regulations 2019, SI 2019/792 (the 'Syria Regulations') imposed aircraft sanctions until 24 April 2025. However, these sanctions were 'removed as the former Assad regime no longer controls Syrian Arab Airlines and cannot use its aircraft to enable its oppression of the Syrian people and, therefore, the sanctions are no longer considered necessary,' demonstrating how sanctions respond to the realpolitik (Explanatory Memorandum to the Syria (Sanctions) (EU Exit) (Amendment) Regulations 2025, SI 2025/507, para 5.6).

[15] North Korea Regulations 2019, regs 85–7; Belarus Regulations 2019, regs 31 and 31H–I; Russia Regulations 2019, regs 61A, 61B, and 63; Libya Regulations 2020, regs 44–7; Iran Regulations 2023, regs 57 and 59. The creation of exceptions is enabled by s 15(2)(a) of SAMLA.

[16] The Department for Transport (DfT) has overall responsibility for transport sanctions licensing.

licence is issued, any prohibition imposed by a regime does not apply to anything done under the authority of that licence.[17]

Unsurprisingly, the UK seeks to detect breaches of transport sanctions. It has therefore imposed obligations on various persons, including harbour authorities and airport operators, in certain circumstances to report breaches (or suspected breaches) of transport sanctions to the Secretary of State.[18] Reporting obligations are supplemented by the power of the Secretary of State to request information (which may include a request to produce documents).[19] **6.04**

The five regimes also make provision for the enforcement of shipping and/or aircraft sanctions,[20] including by way of criminal prosecution.[21] Provision for the enforcement of transport sanctions is also made in the Trade, Aircraft and Shipping Sanctions (Civil Enforcement) Regulations 2024 (TASSCER), including by providing the Secretary of State with the power to impose monetary penalties.[22] **6.05**

This chapter discusses the foregoing in detail and draws on different transport sanctions regulations by way of illustration. In particular, section B addresses the nature and scope of transport sanctions; section C discusses reporting obligations and information requests from the Secretary of State; and section D addresses the enforcement of transport sanctions.[23] Lastly, although maritime enforcement powers are broadly concerned with the enforcement of trade sanctions, we briefly discuss these powers in section E. **6.06**

## B. Nature and Scope of Transport Sanctions

Sanctions regulations impose prohibitions and requirements, and establish related offences, in relation to (1) conduct in the UK or its territorial sea by any person and (2) conduct elsewhere by a 'United Kingdom person'.[24] **6.07**

[17] North Korea Regulations 2019, regs 91–2; Belarus Regulations 2019, reg 33A; Russia Regulations 2019, reg 65A; Libya Regulations 2020, reg 50. The issuance of licences is enabled by s 15(2)(b) of SAMLA 2018.

[18] Trade, Aircraft and Shipping Sanctions (Civil Enforcement) Regulations 2024 (TASSCER), SI 2024/948, reg 16. The imposition of reporting obligations is enabled by s 16(1)(a)(i) of SAMLA 2018.

[19] TASSCER 2024, regs 17 and 19–20. The power to request the provision of information (including the production of documents) is enabled by s 16(1)(b) of SAMLA 2018.

[20] The enforcement of transport sanctions is enabled by ss 17–17A of SAMLA 2018.

[21] North Korea Regulations 2019, regs 67, 69–71, 72(4), 73(7), 74, 76, 78, and 97; Belarus Regulations 2019, regs 29D, 29F, 29G(4) and (6), 29H(3) and (5), and 36A; Russia Regulations 2019, regs 57, 57A, 57B(4) and (6), 57C(3) and (5), 57N, and 68A; Libya Regulations 2020, regs 35–7, 38(3), 39(2) and (4), 42, and 54; Iran Regulations 2023, regs 46(4), 47(4) and (6), and 48(3) and (5).

[22] TASSCER 2024, regs 5 and 8.

[23] We do not consider transport-related trade sanctions, such as the prohibitions relating to the supply and delivery of Russian-related oil and oil products (Russia Regulations 2019, pt 4IA (see Chapter 5 para 5.72)) or the prohibition on providing insurance or reinsurance services relating to aircraft to a person connected with Russia or for use in Russia (Russia Regulations 2019, reg 29A; see *Zephyrus Capital Avation Partners 1D Ltd v Fedelis Underwriting Ltd* [2024] EWHC 734 (Comm), [2024] 4 WLR 47).

[24] SAMLA 2018, s 21(1). A 'United Kingdom person' is defined as a 'United Kingdom national' (which includes British citizens, British subject, and British-protected persons) or a body incorporated or constituted under the law of any part of the UK (s 21(2)(3)). Jurisdiction may be specifically extended to include bodies incorporated or

**6.08** This section considers, in turn, prohibitions and requirements imposed in shipping sanctions regulations and aircraft sanctions regulations.

## 1. Shipping Sanctions

**6.09** The shipping sanctions in the Russia regime are among the most expansive. They have also led to significant litigation. This section accordingly focuses on the Russia regime to illustrate the nature and scope of shipping sanctions.

**6.10** Save for the narrow application of the Russia regime to particular cruise ships,[25] shipping sanctions in the Russia regime only apply to 'Russian' ships[26] (or a subset of them) and/or 'specified' ships. The sanctions do not apply to other ships, even if they set sail from, or are destined for, Russian ports.[27]

**6.11** The expression 'Russian' ship is not used in the Russia regime, but is used in this chapter as shorthand to mean:

- a ship owned,[28] controlled,[29] chartered,[30] or operated[31] by a designated person;[32]

constituted under the laws of any of the Channel Islands, the Isle of Man, or any of the British overseas territories (s 21(4)).

[25] See the text to nn 86–9 below.

[26] The term 'ship' includes 'every description of vessel (including a hovercraft) used in navigation, except the naval, military or air-force ships of any country' (SAMLA 2018, s 7(14); Russia Regulations 2019, reg 57I(6)).

[27] Foreign, Commonwealth and Development Office (FCDO), Export Control Joint Unit (ECJU), Office of Financial Sanctions Implementation (OFSI), and Office of Trade Sanctions Implementation (OTSI), 'Russia Sanctions: Guidance' (Statutory guidance, 9 May 2019) s 1.7. Updated 25 September 2025.

[28] A ship is 'owned' by a person if '(i) the legal title to the ship, or to any share in the ship, is vested in the person, or in a person who is owned or controlled directly or indirectly [ . . . ] by that person, or (ii) the person, or a person who is owned or controlled directly or indirectly [ . . . ] by that person, has a beneficial interest in the ship or in any share in the ship' (Russia Regulations 2019, reg 57I(1)(a)). The meaning of 'owned or controlled directly or indirectly' is set out in regulation 7. 'Beneficial interest' means 'any beneficial interest, however arising (whether held by trustee or nominee or arising under a contract or otherwise), other than an interest held by any person as mortgagee', and the reference to a 'legal title' and 'beneficial interest' includes 'one held jointly with any other person or persons' (reg 57I(3)–(4)).

[29] A ship is 'controlled' by a person 'who is able to take decisions about its operation, including (but not limited to) decisions about the route the ship may take and the appointment of master or crew'. However, a ship is not controlled by its master or crew unless that master or crew are designated persons under regulations 57A (prohibition on port entry), 57C (movement of ships), 57D (detention of ships), and 57E (registration of ships in the UK) (Russia Regulations 2019, reg 57I(1)(b), (2), and (4)).

[30] A ship is 'chartered' by a person if it is hired for a stipulated period on terms which give the person possession and control of the ship, including the right to appoint the master and crew (Russia Regulations 2019, reg 57E(3)(c)).

[31] A ship is not 'operated' by its master or crew unless that master or crew are designated persons under regulations 57A (prohibition on port entry), 57C (movement of ships), 57D (detention of ships), and 57E (registration of ships in the UK) (Russia Regulations 2019, reg 57I(2A)).

[32] In broad terms, the Secretary of State may designate a person by name or by description for the purposes of shipping sanctions in the Russia regime if the Secretary of State has reasonable grounds to suspect that the person is an 'involved person', which is a person who '(a) is or has been involved in—(i) destabilising Ukraine or undermining or threatening the territorial integrity, sovereignty or independence of Ukraine, or (ii) obtaining a benefit from or supporting the Government of Russia, (b) is owned or controlled directly or indirectly [ . . . ] by a person who is or has been so involved, (c) is acting on behalf of or at the direction of a person who is or has been so involved, or (d) is a member of, or associated with, a person who is or has been so involved' (Russia Regulations 2019, regs 5(1)(ba) and (1A)(e), 5A(1)–(4) and (12), 6(2), and 6A(1)–(3), (8)–(9), and (13)). See Chapter 8, 'Designations and Challenges'.

- a ship owned, controlled, chartered, or operated by persons connected with Russia;[33]
- a ship flying the flag of Russia; or
- a ship registered in Russia.

A ship may be 'specified' by the Secretary of State[34] if the Secretary has reasonable grounds to 'suspect that the ship is, has been, or is likely to be' used for any activity whose object or effect is: 6.12

(a) to destabilise Ukraine or undermine or threaten the territorial integrity, sovereignty or independence of Ukraine,
(b) to obtain a benefit from or support the Government of Russia, or
(c) to contravene or circumvent, or to enable or facilitate the contravention or circumvention of, any provision of these Regulations.[35]

Activities whose object or effect is set out in (a) or (b) include carrying: 6.13

(a) dual-use goods or military goods—
    (i) from a place in Russia to a [country that is not the UK, the Isle of Man, Russia, or non-government controlled Ukrainian territory (third country)],
    (ii) from a third country to a place in Russia or non-government controlled Ukrainian territory, or
    (iii) from one third country to another third country for use in Russia or non-government controlled Ukrainian territory,
(b) oil and oil products that originated in Russia—
    (i) from a place in Russia to a third country, or
    (ii) from one third country to another third country,
(c) any other goods or technology that could contribute to destabilising Ukraine or undermining or threatening the territorial integrity, sovereignty or independence of Ukraine—
    (i) from a place in Russia to a third country,
    (ii) from a third country to a place in Russia or non-government controlled Ukrainian territory,
    (iii) from one third country to another third country for use in Russia or non-government controlled Ukrainian territory, or

[33] A person is to be regarded as 'connected with Russia' if the person is '(a) an individual who is, or an association or combination of individuals who are, ordinarily resident in Russia, (b) an individual who is, or an association or combination of individuals who are, located in Russia, (c) a person, other than an individual, which is incorporated or constituted under the law of Russia, or (d) a person, other than an individual, which is domiciled in Russia' (Russia Regulations 2019, reg 57I(5)).

[34] If the Secretary of State specifies a ship, the Secretary must do so by its International Maritime Organization number or, where it is not reasonably practicable to identify it by that number, by any other appropriate means (Russia Regulations 2019, reg 57F(2)).

[35] Russia Regulations 2019, reg 57F(1), (3)(a), and (4). Pursuant to s 61(3)(d) of the Economic Crime (Transparency and Enforcement) Act 2022, regulation 57F(3) is to be read without regulation 57F(3)(b).

(iv) from a place in non-government controlled Ukrainian territory to a place in Russia or a third country.[36]

**6.14** In broad terms, there are two groups of shipping sanctions in the Russia regime: those which apply without directions from the Secretary of State or a harbour authority;[37] and those which depend on directions from the Secretary of State or a harbour authority. Each is addressed in turn below. We then identify the two general exceptions which apply to shipping sanctions in the Russia regime and consider shipping sanctions imposed in respect of Russia's 'shadow fleet'.

(i) Shipping sanctions which apply without directions

**6.15** Two types of shipping sanctions apply without directions from the Secretary of State or a harbour authority: port entry prohibitions, and the prohibition on registration in the Registry of Shipping and Seamen (the 'UK Ship Register').[38]

*a) Port entry prohibitions*

**6.16** A person must not provide a Russian or specified ship with access to a port in the UK[39] if the person knows, or has reasonable cause to suspect, that the ship is a Russian or specified ship.[40] In *Vneshprombank LLC* the High Court set out 'some uncontentious relevant law on [ ... ] the test of "reasonable cause to suspect" '.[41] Inter alia:

- 'the test imports an objective element requiring an evidential foundation';
- the suspicion 'must be fact-based and genuinely reasonable';
- the test 'requires that on the available information, a reasonable person would, not might or could, suspect';

[36] Russia Regulations 2019, reg 57F(5) and (7).

[37] The expression 'harbour authority' means, in relation to a harbour, '(a) the person who is the statutory harbour authority for the harbour, or (b) if there is no statutory harbour authority for the harbour, the person (if any) who is the proprietor of the harbour or who is entrusted with the function of managing, maintaining or improving the harbour' (Russia Regulations 2019, reg 57I(6); SAMLA 2018, s 7(14); Merchant Shipping Act 1995 (the 'Shipping Act'), s 313(1)). In relation to Great Britain, the expression 'statutory harbour authority' means 'any person in whom are vested under [the Harbours Act 1964], by another Act or by an order or other instrument (except a provisional order) made under another Act or by a provisional order powers or duties of improving, maintaining or managing a harbour' (Shipping Act 1995, s 313(1); Harbours Act 1964, s 57(1)). In relation to Northern Ireland, the expression 'statutory harbour authority' means 'any person in whom are vested under [the Harbours Act (Northern Ireland) 1970], or by or under another Act, functions of improving, maintaining or managing a harbour' (Shipping Act 1995, s 313(1); Harbours Act (Northern Ireland) 1970, s 38(1)).

[38] For context, the UK Ship Register is a traditional, or national, registry which requires ships to be owned, at least in part, by national interests. This is in contrast to open or international registers, which are open to all ships regardless of the place of business of the owner. The 2024 UK shipping fleet statistics show the UK registered trading fleet to be the 26th largest in the world by deadweight tonnage (0.4 per cent of the world total). For completeness, the trading fleet of ships directly owned, beneficially owned, managed, or operated by a UK person is considerably larger than the UK registered trading fleet (the former comprising 5 per cent of the world fleet by deadweight tonnage). See DfT, 'Shipping Fleet Statistics: 2024' (Official Statistics, 26 February 2025) <https://www.gov.uk/government/statistics/shipping-fleet-statistics-2024/shipping-fleet-statistics-2024> accessed 24 August 2025.

[39] Which includes the territorial sea (Russia Regulations 2019, reg 57I(6); SAMLA 2018, s 7(11)).

[40] Russia Regulations 2019, reg 57A(1).

[41] *Vneshprombank LLC v Bedzhamov* [2024] EWHC 1048 (Ch), [2024] 1 WLR 4674 [54].

- the 'question whether there are reasonable grounds to suspect must be considered in the round, in a fair-minded review which takes into account all relevant information including undermining material[,] and initial suspicions may be dispelled by information or evidence which undermines what might otherwise be reasonable grounds';
- it 'is necessary to guard against making unreliable assumptions and to exercise caution in treating complexity of corporate structures as grounds for suspicion'; and
- the 'accuracy and credibility of the sources of evidence relied upon should be evaluated and verified, although such evidence is not limited to that which would be admissible in court'.[42]

The prohibition is not contravened by providing a ship with access to a port if (1) the Secretary of State has given a direction requiring the ship to proceed to or enter the port (a port entry direction) or (2) access is needed by the ship in a case of emergency.[43] A person who breaches the prohibition commits an offence[44] and is liable on conviction on indictment to imprisonment for a term not exceeding seven years or a fine (or both).[45] **6.17**

The prohibition on port access is supplemented by an obligation on the master[46] or pilot[47] of a Russian or specified ship not to 'cause or permit the ship to enter a port in the [UK] if the master or pilot knows, or has reasonable cause to suspect, that the ship is a [Russian or specified ship]'.[48] However, this prohibition is not contravened by the entry into port of a ship if (1) there is a port entry direction or (2) entry is needed by the ship in a case of emergency.[49] A person who breaches the prohibition commits an offence[50] and is liable on conviction on indictment to imprisonment for a term not exceeding seven years or a fine (or both).[51] **6.18**

*b) The prohibition on registration in the UK Ship Register*

The registrar of the UK Ship Register must refuse to register a ship in the UK Ship Register if, on the basis of the information given to the registrar by the Secretary of State or accompanying the application for registration, the ship appears to the registrar to be owned, controlled, chartered, or operated by a designated person or a person connected with Russia.[52] The Secretary of State may also direct the registrar to terminate **6.19**

[42] ibid.
[43] Russia Regulations 2019, regs 57A(3) and 61A(1).
[44] Russia Regulations 2019, reg 57A(4).
[45] Russia Regulations 2019, reg 80(1)(d).
[46] The term 'master' includes 'every person (except a pilot) having command or charge of a ship and, in relation to a fishing vessel, means the skipper' (Russia Regulations 2019, reg 57I(6); SAMLA 2018, s 7(14)).
[47] The term 'pilot' means 'any person not belonging to the ship who has the conduct of the ship' (Russia Regulations 2019, reg 57I(6); SAMLA 2018, s 7(14)).
[48] Russia Regulations 2019, reg 57A(2).
[49] Russia Regulations 2019, regs 57A(3) and 61A(2).
[50] Russia Regulations 2019, reg 57A(4).
[51] Russia Regulations 2019, reg 80(1)(d).
[52] Russia Regulations 2019, reg 57E(1) and 3(a).

the registration of (1) a ship that is owned, controlled, chartered, or operated by a designated person or a person connected with Russia, or (2) a specified ship.[53]

(ii) Shipping sanctions which depend on directions

6.20 Four types of shipping sanctions depend on directions from the Secretary of State or a harbour authority. These are port barring, port entry and movement, detention, and cruise ship directions.

*a) Port barring directions*

6.21 The Secretary of State or a harbour authority may give to the master or pilot of a specified ship a direction prohibiting the ship from 'entering a port or ports specified in the direction, or any port in the [UK]'.[54] Substantively, it is unclear what a port barring direction would add to the prohibition on port entry, save that (1) the Secretary of State may direct a harbour authority further to a port barring direction to take such steps as are reasonably practicable to secure that a ship mentioned in the direction complies with that direction,[55] and (2) a master or pilot who receives a port barring direction will know, or have reasonable cause to suspect, that the ship is a specified ship.

6.22 A person who fails to comply with a direction given to them commits an offence[56] and is liable on conviction on indictment to imprisonment for a term not exceeding seven years or a fine (or both).[57]

6.23 Confidentiality obligations may attach to a port barring direction. In particular, the Secretary of State may notify a person that the existence of a port barring direction, or any part of the content of or anything done under the direction, is to be treated as confidential.[58] A person who discloses information having been notified of its confidential nature commits an offence[59] and is liable on summary conviction to imprisonment for a term not exceeding six months or a fine (or both).[60]

*b) Port entry directions and movement directions*

6.24 The Secretary of State may give to the master or pilot of a Russian or specified ship a port entry direction or a direction requiring the ship '(a) to leave a port specified in the direction, (b) to proceed to a place specified in the direction, or (c) to remain where it is'.[61] The Secretary of State may also direct a harbour authority to take such steps as are

53 Russia Regulations 2019, reg 57E(2).
54 Russia Regulations 2019, reg 57B(1)–(2) and (7).
55 Russia Regulations 2019, reg 57B(3).
56 Russia Regulations 2019, reg 57B(4).
57 Russia Regulations 2019, reg 80(1)(d).
58 Russia Regulations 2019, reg 57B(5).
59 Russia Regulations 2019, reg 57B(6).
60 Russia Regulations 2019, reg 80(4).
61 Russia Regulations 2019, reg 57C(1) and (6).

reasonably practicable to secure that a ship mentioned in a direction complies with the direction.[62]

A person who fails to comply with a direction given to them commits an offence[63] and is liable on conviction on indictment to imprisonment for a term not exceeding seven years or a fine (or both).[64] **6.25**

Similar confidentiality obligations and offences may attach to a port entry or a movement direction as to a port barring direction.[65] The penalties are the same.[66] **6.26**

### *c) Detention directions*

The Secretary of State or a harbour authority may give to the master of a Russian or specified ship a direction requiring the detention of the ship at a port or anchorage in the UK.[67] The Secretary of State may also direct a harbour authority to give a detention direction to the master of a Russian or specified ship.[68] The power to give a detention direction is discretionary: it need not be exercised in respect of every Russian and specified ship at a port or anchorage in the UK.[69] Further, the power to give a detention direction is not a secondary power, incidental to the power to give a movement direction requiring a ship to leave a port. There is 'no hierarchy' in the Russia regime.[70] **6.27**

A ship may be detained by any of the following: a commissioned naval or military officer; an officer of a Minister of the Crown or Northern Ireland department who is authorized by the Secretary of State to exercise detention powers; an officer of customs and excise; or a British consular officer.[71] Any detention direction must (1) be in writing, (2) be delivered to the master of the ship by the person who detains the ship, (3) state the grounds on which the ship is detained, and (4) state that it is given under regulation 57D and that any requirements imposed by the direction must be followed.[72] In *Dalston Projects Ltd v Secretary of State for Transport*, the Supreme Court found that the requirement to state the grounds on which the ship is detained was satisfied by the following: '[t]he Phi is being detained on the grounds that it is owned, controlled or operated by Sergei Georgievich Naumenko, a person connected with Russia'.[73] No more was required by way of the giving of reasons.[74] In rejecting the challenge to the **6.28**

[62] Russia Regulations 2019, reg 57C(2). A direction from the Secretary of State may be given to any harbour authority or to harbour authorities generally (reg 57H(5)).

[63] Russia Regulations 2019, reg 57C(3).

[64] Russia Regulations 2019, reg 80(1)(d).

[65] Russia Regulations 2019, reg 57C(4)(5).

[66] Russia Regulations 2019, reg 80(4).

[67] Russia Regulations 2019, reg 57D(1) and (4). However, a harbour authority may only give to the master of a specified ship a detention direction if it has been directed to do so by the Secretary of State (reg 57D(2)).

[68] Russia Regulations 2019, reg 57D(3).

[69] *Dalston Projects Ltd v Secretary of State for Transport* and *Shvidler v Secretary of State for Foreign, Commonwealth and Development Affairs* [2024] EWCA Civ 172, [2024] 1 WLR 3327 (*Dalston Projects CA*) [68].

[70] *Dalston Projects CA* [70].

[71] Russia Regulations 2019, reg 57D(8).

[72] Russia Regulations 2019, reg 57D(5).

[73] *Shvidler v Secretary of State for Foreign, Commonwealth* and *Development Affairs and Dalston Projects Ltd v Secretary of State for Transport* [2025] UKSC 30 (*Dalston Projects SC*) [225], [228]–[9].

[74] *Dalston Projects SC* [229]–[31].

adequacy of the stated grounds, the Supreme Court found that the Secretary of State did not have to specify whether the Phi was being detained because it was (1) owned by Mr Naumenko, (2) controlled by Mr Naumenko, or (3) operated by Mr Naumenko:[75]

> To require the Transport Secretary to specify which of the [...] possible links he or she relies on in relation to any given vessel would be a pointless exercise. It would serve only to prompt meritless challenges to directions based on a technicality arising from ownership structures which may have been designed to obscure this very point.[76]

**6.29** Where the ship is not a British ship,[77] and there is a consular officer for the 'country to which the ship belongs' in the UK, a copy of the detention direction must be sent as soon as practicable to the nearest consular officer for the 'country to which the ship belongs'.[78] The expression 'country to which the ship belongs' is not defined in the Russia Regulations. The expression is used, inter alia, in sections 12(5) and 95(4) of the Shipping Act (see also sections 6(1) and 190(6)(b)) but also not defined. In our view, the expression should be read to mean the flag state. This interpretation is consistent with the reasoning of the Court of Appeal in *The Industrie* (where the Court equated a contract 'made under the flag' with a contract 'made in the country to which the ship belongs'),[79] and of the Court for Crown Cases Reserved in *R v Seberg* (where the Court found that a ship was British because she was sailing under a British flag, notwithstanding that there was no proof that the ship had been registered as a British ship).[80]

**6.30** The master of a ship who has been given a detention direction commits an offence if:

- the ship proceeds to sea, otherwise than in accordance with the direction, before it is released by a competent authority;[81] or
- the ship fails to comply with any requirement imposed by the direction.[82]

**6.31** If the master of a ship commits either of these offences, the owner of the ship[83] also commits an offence if party or privy to the master's offence.[84]

**6.32** The offences carry a sentence of a fine on conviction on indictment.[85]

[75] *Dalston Projects SC* [232]–[3].
[76] *Dalston Projects SC* [233].
[77] A 'British ship' is a ship which (1) is registered under Part 2 of the Shipping Act, (2) is a Government ship within the meaning of the Shipping Act, (3) is registered under the law of any of the Channel Islands, the Isle of Man, or any British overseas territory, (4) is not registered under the law of a country outside the UK but is wholly owned by persons each of whom is (a) a British citizen, a British overseas territories citizen, or a British Overseas citizen, (b) an individual who is habitually resident in the UK, or (c) a body corporate which is established under the law of a part of the UK and has its principal place of business in the UK, or (5) is registered under an Order in Council under section 1 of the Hovercraft Act 1968 (Russia Regulations 2019, reg 57I(6); SAMLA 2018, s 7(12)–(14)).
[78] Russia Regulations 2019, reg 57D(6)–(7).
[79] *The Industrie* [1894] P 58 (CA) 72.
[80] *R v Seberg* (1865–72) LR 1 CCR 264.
[81] Russia Regulations 2019, reg 57D(8); Shipping Act 1995, s 284(2).
[82] Russia Regulations 2019, reg 57D(8); Shipping Act 1995, s 284(2A).
[83] And 'any person who sends to sea' the ship.
[84] Russia Regulations 2019, reg 57D(8); Shipping Act 1995, s 284(3).
[85] Russia Regulations 2019, reg 57D(8); Shipping Act 1995, s 284(2B)–(3).

*d) Cruise ship directions*

The Secretary of State may give to a master or pilot of a British cruise ship[86] a direction prohibiting the ship from entering a port or any ports located in (1) Crimea, (2) the non-government controlled areas of the Donetsk and Luhansk Oblasts, or (3) the non-government controlled areas of the Kherson and Zaporizhzhia Oblasts.[87] A person who fails to comply with a direction given to them commits an offence[88] and is liable on conviction on indictment to imprisonment for a term not exceeding seven years or a fine (or both).[89] 6.33

(iii) General exceptions

There are two general exceptions which apply to shipping sanctions in the Russia regime. In particular, an act which would be prohibited under or by virtue of the shipping regulations in the Russia regime is not prohibited if the act is one which a person in the service of the Crown or holding office under the Crown, acting in the course of that person's duty, has determined would be in the interests of (1) national security or (2) the prevention or detection of serious crime in the UK or elsewhere.[90] 6.34

(iv) Russia's 'shadow fleet'

On 18 July 2024, at a summit of the European Political Community, the UK issued 'a call to action' in respect of Russia's 'shadow fleet', which is said to comprise 'ships engaged in illegal operations for the purposes of circumventing sanctions, evading compliance with safety or environmental regulations, avoiding insurance costs or engaging in other illegal activities'.[91] The 'call to action' has been endorsed by 45 other states and the EU. Inter alia, it provides: 6.35

> We have agreed to share information on the practices and operations of the 'shadow fleet', to coordinate our responses to the risks posed by its ships and facilitators, and to work with the private sector and other maritime stakeholders to address the threat. We have asked our relevant officials and experts to meet together, as a group and in regional formats, in order to take forward concrete measures to those ends with the greatest urgency.[92]

Part of the UK's response to the risks posed by the 'shadow fleet' has been to impose shipping sanctions. By 25 November 2024, the number of oil tankers stated to be the 6.36

[86] A 'cruise ship' is a 'ship providing cruise services' (Russia Regulations 2019, reg 57(6)).
[87] Russia Regulations 2019, reg 57(1)–(2B). Such a direction 'may be given to any master or pilot of a British ship which is a cruise ship, or to masters and pilots of British ships which are cruise ships generally' (reg 57(4)(a)).
[88] Russia Regulations 2019, reg 57(3).
[89] Russia Regulations 2019, reg 80(1)(d).
[90] Russia Regulations 2019, reg 63(1) and (3).
[91] Prime Minister's Office, Foreign, FCDO, and The Rt Hon Sir Keir Starmer KCB KC MP, 'The "Shadow Fleet": A Call to Action' (Policy Paper, 19 July 2024).
[92] ibid.

subject of sanctions, whether by virtue of being a Russian ship or a specified ship, stood at 73.[93] This compared to 39 oil tankers said to have been 'sanctioned by the United States and 19 by the European Union'.[94] Of the 73 oil tankers stated to be the subject of UK shipping sanctions, 15 of them 'transport[ed] more than $4.3bn worth of oil and oil products like gasoline' between November 2023 and November 2024.[95] The designation by the UK of ships forming part of Russia's 'shadow fleet' has continued apace since November 2024,[96] and we expect the UK to continue to impose shipping sanctions on the 'shadow fleet' in the near term.

## 2. Aircraft Sanctions

**6.37** Aircraft sanctions can be found in four of the five regimes (there are no aircraft sanctions in the Iran regime). The aircraft sanctions in the Belarus regime and the Russia regime are broadly the same. They are also the most wide-ranging. This section accordingly focuses on the Belarus regime by way of illustration.

**6.38** Aircraft sanctions in the Belarus regime apply to 'Belarusian aircraft'. According to regulation 29A(7), a 'Belarusian aircraft' is an aircraft[97]

(a) owned,[98] chartered or operated by—
  (i) a designated person,
  or (ii) a person connected with Belarus, or
(b) registered in Belarus.

**6.39** The aircraft sanctions in the Belarus regime can be grouped in a similar way to the shipping sanctions in the Russia regime: those which apply without directions; and those which depend on directions. Each is addressed in turn below. We then consider briefly aircraft sanctions in practice.

[93] FCDO and The Rt Hon David Lammy MP, 'UK Imposes New Wave of Sanctions to Choke Russian oil Revenues as Foreign Secretary Arrives in Italy for G7' (Press Release, 25 November 2024) ('FCDO 25 November 2024 Press Release'). Subject to limited exceptions, the Secretary of State must take steps to publicize the specification of a ship (Russia Regulations 2019, reg 57G).

[94] FCDO 25 November 2024 Press Release (n 93).

[95] FCDO 25 November 2024 Press Release (n 93).

[96] For example, see FCDO and The Rt Hon David Lammy MP, 'UK Announces Major Sanctions in Support of Ukraine' (Press Release, 20 May 2025).

[97] The term 'aircraft' does not include the naval, military, or air-force aircraft of any country, but it does include unmanned aircraft and aircraft capable of spaceflight activities, provided they do not constitute the naval, military, or air-force aircraft of any country (Belarus Regulations 2019, reg 29E(3); SAMLA 2018, s 6(9)).

[98] An aircraft is 'owned' by a person if '(a) the legal title to the aircraft, or to any share in the aircraft, is vested in the person, or (b) the person has a beneficial interest in the aircraft or in any share in the aircraft' (Belarus Regulations 2019, reg 29E(2)). 'Beneficial interest' means 'any beneficial interest, however arising (whether held by trustee or nominee or arising under a contract or otherwise), other than an interest held by any person as mortgagee', and the reference to a 'legal title' and 'beneficial interest' includes 'one held jointly with any other person or persons' (reg 29E(1)–(2)).

### (i) Aircraft sanctions which apply without directions

Two types of aircraft sanctions apply without directions: the overfly and landing prohibitions, and the prohibition on registration in the register kept by the Civil Aviation Authority (CAA). **6.40**

#### a) *The overfly and landing prohibitions*

A Belarusian aircraft must not overfly or land in the UK.[99] However: **6.41**

- the landing prohibition is not contravened by the landing of a Belarusian aircraft in the UK if failing to land would endanger the lives of persons on board or the safety of the aircraft (an emergency landing);[100] and
- the overfly prohibition is not contravened by the flight of a Belarusian aircraft in the airspace over the UK preparatory to an emergency landing.[101]

Further, the overfly and landing prohibitions are not contravened by the movement of a Belarusian aircraft if: **6.42**

- air traffic control[102] has directed the operator[103] or pilot in command[104] of the aircraft to leave the airspace over the UK by a specific route, and the movement of the aircraft is in accordance with that direction;
- an airport operator[105] has directed the operator or pilot in command of the aircraft to take off, or to require the aircraft to take off, from an airport the operator manages, and the movement of the aircraft is in accordance with that direction; or
- the Secretary of State has directed an airport operator to secure the movement of the aircraft to a specified airport, and the movement of the aircraft is in accordance with that direction.[106]

In addition to the exceptions to the overfly and landing prohibitions, the Secretary of State may issue a licence, pursuant to which the prohibitions do not apply to anything done under the authority of the licence.[107] The Secretary of State takes the view that a licence may be granted for the overflight of UK airspace, or for the landing in the UK, of a Belarusian aircraft where it is necessary: **6.43**

[99] Belarus Regulations 2019, reg 29A(A1). The prohibition applies in respect of the UK's territorial sea (Belarus Regulations 2019, reg 29E(3); SAMLA 2018, s 6(8)).

[100] Russia Regulations 2019, regs 29A(A2) and 31H(1).

[101] Russia Regulations 2019, regs 29A(A2) and 31H(2).

[102] 'Air traffic control' is a person who holds a licence to provide air traffic services pursuant to Chapter I of Part I of the Transport Act 2000 (Belarus Regulations 2019, reg 29E(1)).

[103] The 'operator' is 'the person having the management of the aircraft, and cognate expressions are to be construed accordingly' (Belarus Regulations 2019, reg 29E(3); SAMLA 2018, s 6(10)).

[104] The 'pilot in command' is 'the pilot designated by the operator as being in command and charged with the safe conduct of [the aircraft's] flight, without being under the direction of any other pilot in the aircraft' (Belarus Regulations 2019, reg 29E(3); SAMLA 2018, s 6(10)).

[105] An 'airport operator' is a person who manages an airport (Belarus Regulations 2019, reg 29E(3); SAMLA 2018, s 6(10)).

[106] Belarus Regulations 2019, reg 31H(4).

[107] Belarus Regulations 2019, reg 33A.

- for the delivery of humanitarian assistance, or
- for the official purposes of a diplomatic mission or consular post in Belarus or the UK, or of an international organisation enjoying immunities in the UK in accordance with international law, or
- for testing the aircraft for the purposes of providing technical assistance.[108]

**6.44** The operator and pilot in command of a Belarusian aircraft commit an offence if the overfly or landing prohibition is breached,[109] and they are liable on conviction on indictment to imprisonment for a term not exceeding seven years or a fine (or both).[110] Further, a person commits an offence and is liable on conviction on indictment to imprisonment for a term not exceeding two years or a fine (or both), if, (1) for the purpose of obtaining an aircraft licence, they knowingly or recklessly (a) provide information that is false in a material respect or (b) provide or produce a document that is not what it purports to be, or (2) they purport to act under the authority of an aircraft licence but fail to comply with any condition of the licence.[111]

*b) The prohibition on registration in the register kept by the CAA*

**6.45** The CAA must refuse to register an aircraft in its register if, on the basis of the information given to the CAA by the applicant, the Secretary of State or a third person, the aircraft appears to be (1) owned or operated by a designated person, or (2) chartered by demise by a designated person (a relevant aircraft).[112] The Secretary of State may also direct the CAA to terminate the registration of a relevant aircraft.[113]

(ii) Aircraft sanctions which depend on directions

**6.46** Three types of aircraft sanctions depend on directions from the Secretary of State, air traffic control, or an airport operator: Air Navigation Order 2016 (ANO) directions, airspace directions, and movement and restriction directions.

*a) ANO directions*

**6.47** To understand ANO directions in the Belarus regime, regard must be had to articles 250 and 252 of the ANO. Pursuant to article 250(1) and (2) of the ANO, 'an aircraft registered elsewhere than in the [UK] must not take on board or discharge any passengers or cargo in the [UK] where valuable consideration is given or promised for the carriage of such persons or cargo', unless (1) the operator or charterer of the aircraft, or the Government of the country in which the aircraft is registered, has been granted permission to do so by, inter alia, the CAA, and (2) any conditions, to which

108 FCDO, DfT, Home Office, ECJU, OFSI, and OTSI, 'Republic of Belarus Sanctions: Guidance' (Statutory guidance, 15 January 2020) s 3.6. Updated 7 March 2025.

109 Belarus Regulations 2019, reg 29D(A1).

110 Belarus Regulations 2019, reg 48(1)(d).

111 Belarus Regulations 2019, regs 36A(1)–(2) and 48(3)(d).

112 Belarus Regulations 2019, reg 29CA(1) and (4).

113 Belarus Regulations 2019, reg 29CA(2). In so far as a direction from the Secretary of State to the CAA conflicts with the provisions of Part 3 of the ANO 2016, those provisions are to be disregarded (reg 29CA(3)).

such permission may be subject, are satisfied. Article 252(1) of the ANO provides that (subject to two exceptions):

> aircraft registered elsewhere than in the [UK] must not fly over the [UK] for the purpose of commercial operations unless—(a) the CAA has granted permission to do so to the operator or charterer of the aircraft; and (b) any conditions, to which such permission may be subject, are satisfied.

Under regulation 29A(1) of the Belarus regime, the Secretary of State may direct the CAA to: **6.48**

(a) refuse permission under article 250 of the ANO in respect of Belarusian aircraft;
(b) refuse permission under article 252 of the ANO in respect of Belarusian aircraft;
(c) suspend or revoke any permission granted under article 250 of the ANO in respect of Belarusian aircraft;
(d) suspend or revoke any permission granted under article 252 of the ANO in respect of Belarusian aircraft.

*b) Airspace directions*

Air traffic control may direct the operator or pilot in command of a Belarusian aircraft (1) not to enter the airspace over the UK or (2) to leave the airspace over the UK by a specified route (each, an airspace direction).[114] The Secretary of State may also direct air traffic control to give an airspace direction.[115] **6.49**

*c) Movement and restriction directions*

An airport operator may direct the operator or pilot in command of a Belarusian aircraft (1) not to take off, or not to permit the aircraft to take off, from an airport the operator manages,[116] (2) to take off, or to require the aircraft to take off, from an airport the operator manages, or (3) not to land, or not to permit the aircraft to land, at an airport the operator manages (each, a movement direction).[117] Further, the Secretary of State may direct an airport operator to (1) give a movement direction, (2) secure the detention of a Belarusian aircraft at an airport, or (3) secure the movement of a Belarusian aircraft to a specified airport (each, a Secretary of State restriction direction).[118] **6.50**

None of the foregoing directions are contravened by conduct necessary to (1) avoid endangering the lives of persons on board or the safety of the aircraft, (2) protect the safety of another aircraft, or (3) protect the safety of persons on the ground.[119] **6.51**

[114] Belarus Regulations 2019, reg 29A(2).
[115] Belarus Regulations 2019, reg 29A(3).
[116] An airport operator giving such a direction must take such steps as are reasonably practicable to detain the aircraft (Belarus Regulations 2019, reg 29A(6)).
[117] Belarus Regulations 2019, reg 29A(4).
[118] Belarus Regulations 2019, reg 29A(5). Any such direction from the Secretary of State may be given 'to any airport operator or to airport operators generally' (Belarus Regulations 2019, reg 29B(2)).
[119] Belarus Regulations 2019, regs 29B(7) and 31H(3).

6.52 A failure to comply with certain of these directions constitutes an offence. In particular, it is an offence for:

- an operator or pilot in command of a Belarusian aircraft to fail to comply with an airspace direction;[120]
- an operator or pilot in command of a Belarusian aircraft to fail to comply with a movement direction;[121] and
- an airport operator to fail, without reasonable excuse, to comply with a Secretary of State restriction direction.[122]

6.53 A person who commits such an offence is liable on conviction on indictment to imprisonment for a term not exceeding seven years or a fine (or both).[123]

6.54 Finally, confidentiality obligations may attach to any of the directions under regulation 29A: '[t]he Secretary of State may notify a person that the existence, any part of the content of a direction under regulation 29A, or anything done under the direction, is to be treated as confidential'.[124] A person who discloses information having been notified of its confidential nature commits an offence[125] and is liable on summary conviction to imprisonment for a term not exceeding six months or a fine (or both).[126]

(iii) Aircraft sanctions in practice

6.55 There is little by way of publicly available information on aircraft sanctions directions. Publicly available information does indicate that in December 2021, the Secretary of State directed all airport operators to direct operators or pilots in command of Belarusian aircraft not to land.[127] The direction was revoked in July 2022 in tandem with the entry into force of section 29A(A1) of the Belarus Regulations in July 2022 which, as stated above at 6.41, prohibits Belarusian aircraft from landing in the UK.

6.56 That being said, there has been notable, recent activity outside of any domestic transport sanctions regime. On 10 September 2024, the UK announced that it would, '[i]n coordination with our international partners, cancel its bilateral air services arrangements with Iran, which will restrict Iran Air's ability to fly in to the UK'.[128] The announcement was made 'following the Iranian regime's transfer of ballistic missiles to Russia for use on the battlefield in Ukraine'.[129] It remains to be seen whether the UK's decision will lead to litigation.

[120] Belarus Regulations 2019, reg 29D(3).
[121] Belarus Regulations 2019, reg 29D(2).
[122] Belarus Regulations 2019, reg 29D(1).
[123] Belarus Regulations 2019, reg 48(1)(d).
[124] Belarus Regulations 2019, reg 29C(5).
[125] Belarus Regulations 2019, regs 29C(6) and 29D(4).
[126] Belarus Regulations 2019, reg 48(4).
[127] Airport Operators (Republic of Belarus (Sanctions) (EU Exit) Regulations 2019) Direction 2021. Withdrawn 26 July 2022.
[128] FCDO, DfT, The Rt Hon David Lammy MP, The Rt Hon Louise Haigh MP, and The Rt Hon John Healey MP, 'UK and Partners Respond to Iran's Transfer of Ballistic Missiles to Russia' (Press Release, 10 September 2024) ('FCDO 10 September 2024 Press Release').
[129] FCDO 10 September 2024 Press Release (n 128).

## C. Reporting Obligations and Information Requests

On 10 October 2024, TASSCER came into force. Inter alia, it (1) imposes obligations on various persons in certain circumstances to report breaches, or suspected breaches, of transport sanctions to the Secretary of State, and (2) empowers the Secretary of State to request persons to provide it with certain information. **6.57**

### 1. Reporting Obligations

Two classes of persons may be the subject of reporting requirements under TASSCER: (1) shipping persons (i.e. persons that charter ships by way of business, masters, pilots, and harbour authorities); and (2) aircraft persons (i.e. pilots in command, operators, airport operators, and person that charter aircraft). **6.58**

A shipping person must inform the Secretary of State 'as soon as practicable' when: **6.59**

- the shipping person knows, or has reasonable cause to suspect, that a person has breached a prohibition or failed to comply with an obligation under shipping sanctions regulations; and
- the information or other matter on which the knowledge or cause for suspicion is based came to the shipping person in the course of:
  - chartering a ship by way of business;
  - carrying on business in connection with acting as a harbour authority; or
  - carrying on activities, whether paid or unpaid and whether for business or leisure, in connection with acting as (1) a master or (2) a pilot.[130]

Similarly, an aircraft person must inform the Secretary of State 'as soon as practicable' when: **6.60**

- the aircraft person knows, or has reasonable cause to suspect, that a person has breached a prohibition or failed to comply with an obligation under aircraft sanctions regulations; and
- the information or other matter on which the knowledge or cause for suspicion is based came to the aircraft person in the course of:
  - chartering an aircraft by way of business;
  - carrying on business in connection with acting as an airport operator; or
  - carrying on activities, whether paid or unpaid and whether for business or leisure, in connection with acting as (1) a pilot in command or (2) an operator.[131]

[130] TASSCER 2024, reg 16(1) and (4).
[131] TASSCER 2024, reg 16(1) and (4).

**6.61** 'As soon as practicable' is not defined in TASSCER. Plainly, the speed with which a person must report to the Secretary of State will turn on the circumstances: a 'person may need a period of time to establish the facts of the case before contacting the [Secretary of State] in relation to a breach or suspected breach (or failure to comply with an obligation).'[132]

**6.62** Any report by a shipping person or aircraft person to the Secretary of State must state (1) the information or other matter on which the knowledge or suspicion is based and (2) any information it holds about the person by which the person can be identified.[133]

**6.63** TASSCER makes clear that the reporting requirement does not require a person who has acted or is acting as counsel or solicitor for a shipping person or aircraft person to disclose any privileged information.[134] However, the Department for Transport (DfT) 'expects legal professionals to carefully ascertain whether privilege applies, and which information it applies to. [ ... ] DfT may challenge a blanket assertion of legal professional privilege where it is not satisfied that such careful consideration has been made.'[135] TASSCER also makes clear that the reporting requirement does not authorize the disclosure of information that would be prohibited under data protection legislation or the Investigatory Powers Act 2016.[136]

**6.64** A shipping person or aircraft person who fails to comply with a reporting requirement commits an offence[137] and is liable on summary conviction to imprisonment for a term not exceeding six months or a fine (or both).[138]

**6.65** Information obtained by the Secretary of State further to a report from a shipping person or aircraft person may be disclosed to a broad range of persons (including any regulatory body in any country, the UN, the Council of the EU, and the government of any country) for, or in connection with, a number of purposes, including (1) facilitating, monitoring, or ensuring compliance with SAMLA and sanctions regulations or directions, and (2) facilitating the exercise by an authority outside the UK of functions which correspond to functions under sanctions regulations.[139] The power of the

[132] DfT, 'Transport Sanctions: Civil Monetary Penalties' (Guidance, 13 September 2024) s 9.

[133] TASSCER 2024, reg 16(2).

[134] TASSCER 2024, reg 29(3). For further discussion of legal professional privilege in the context of sanctions, see Rachel Barnes et al., 'UK Financial Sanctions Enforcement and the Developing Role of OFSI' in Rachel Barnes et al. (eds), *The Guide to Sanctions* (6th edn, Global Investigations Review 2025).

[135] FCD, DBT, DfT, and OTSI, 'Trade, Aircraft and Shipping Sanctions, Civil Enforcement: Guidance' (Statutory guidance, 12 September 2024) s 1. Updated 19 March 2025.

[136] TASSCER 2024, reg 29(2).

[137] TASSCER 2024, reg 16(3).

[138] TASSCER 2024, reg 22. TASSCER also permits the Secretary of State to impose a monetary penalty (on which, see the text to nn 159–70 below) on a shipping person or aircraft person who breaches a reporting obligation (regs 2 and 5(1)). However, a person is not liable for a monetary penalty in respect of conduct amounting to an offence if (1) proceedings have been brought against the person for that offence in respect of that conduct and the proceedings are ongoing, or (2) the person has been convicted of that offence in respect of that conduct (reg 12(1)). Similarly, no proceedings may be brought against a person in respect of conduct amounting to an offence if the person has been given a monetary penalty in respect of that conduct (reg 12(2)).

[139] TASSCER 2024, reg 27(1)–(3).

Secretary of State to share information with third parties is consistent with the UK's broader approach to sanctions, which is founded on multilateral coordination:

> We take action alongside others for maximum impact. Where we can secure timely international agreement, we initiate or support sanctions proposals at the UN given the strength of the global signal that UN sanctions send and their reach across all 193 UN Member States. Where this is not possible, we work to co-ordinate sanctions approaches and activity with our allies, such as the G7 and EU, to maximise collective impact—both in terms of the signal we send and increasing the practical reach of sanctions across multiple jurisdictions.[140]

## 2. Information Requests

The Secretary of State may request any person to provide it with information it may reasonably require for a prescribed purpose if the Secretary of State believes the person may be able to provide the information.[141] The prescribed purposes are (1) the exercise of functions under TASSCER, (2) monitoring compliance with, or detecting evasion of, sanctions regulations, and (3) investigating a suspected breach of a prohibition, or a suspected failure to comply with an obligation, imposed by or under sanctions regulations.[142] By way of example, the Secretary of State may request information 'about the ownership structure of a ship or an aircraft' or information of assistance 'in obtaining a valuation of an asset at the time of a breach'.[143] **6.66**

The Secretary of State may also request a person acting under a shipping or aircraft licence to provide information about any matter to which the licence relates for one of the prescribed purposes or for the purpose of monitoring compliance with, or detecting evasion of, any condition of that licence.[144] **6.67**

Finally, the Secretary of State may request a person subject to a direction made under shipping or aircraft sanctions regulations to provide information about any matter to which the direction relates for one of the prescribed purposes or for the purpose of monitoring compliance with, or detecting evasion of, that direction.[145] **6.68**

As part of each of these three requests for information: **6.69**

- The Secretary of State may request the production of specified documents or documents of a specified description.[146] When requested, the person must (1) take

[140] FCDO and the Rt Hon Lord Cameron, 'Deter, Disrupt and Demonstrate – UK Sanctions in a Contested World: UK Sanctions Strategy' (Policy Paper, 22 February 2024) para 11 <https://www.gov.uk/government/publications/deter-disrupt-and-demonstrate-uk-sanctions-in-a-contested-world-uk-sanctions-strategy> accessed 20 February 2025. Emphasis omitted.
[141] TASSCER 2024, reg 17(1).
[142] TASSCER 2024, reg 17(2).
[143] DfT, 'Transport Sanctions: Civil Monetary Penalties' (n 132) s 10.
[144] TASSCER 2024, reg 19(1).
[145] TASSCER 2024, reg 19(3).
[146] TASSCER 2024, reg 20(1).

reasonable steps to obtain the documents (if they are not already in the person's possession or control), and (2) keep the documents under the person's possession or control (except for the purpose of providing them to the Secretary of State or as the Secretary of State may otherwise permit).[147] When producing a document, the Secretary of State may request the person to explain it and, when produced, she may take copies of (or extracts from) any document.[148]

- The Secretary of State may specify the way in which, and the period within which, information is to be provided.[149] However, if no such period is specified, the information which has been requested must be provided within a reasonable time.[150]
- There may be a continuing obligation to keep the Secretary of State informed 'as circumstances change, or on such regular basis as the Secretary of State may specify'.[151]

**6.70** However, as is the position in the context of the reporting requirements under TASSCER, there is no requirement for counsel or solicitors to disclose privileged information, and no authorization to disclose information or documents that would be prohibited under data protection legislation or the Investigatory Powers Act 2016.[152]

**6.71** TASSCER creates four broad offences in connection with the Secretary of State's requests:[153]

- refusing or failing within the time and in the manner specified (or, if no time has been specified, within a reasonable time) to comply with a request for information (including a request for the production of documents) without a 'reasonable excuse';[154]
- 'knowingly or recklessly' giving any information, or producing any document, which is false in a material particular in response to a request;
- destroying, mutilating, defacing, concealing, or removing any document with intent to evade requirements under a request for information (including a request for the production of documents);

[147] TASSCER 2024, reg 20(3).
[148] TASSCER 2024, reg 20(2)(a)–(b).
[149] TASSCER 2024, regs 17(3) and 19(5).
[150] TASSCER 2024, regs 17(4) and 19(5).
[151] TASSCER 2024, regs 17(5) and 19(5).
[152] TASSCER 2024, reg 29(2)–(3).
[153] TASSCER 2024, reg 21(1).
[154] There is no definition of 'reasonable excuse' in TASSCER. Section 42 of the Banking Act 1987 provided a regime for the furnishing of information and the production of documents where the Bank of England had reasonable grounds for suspecting that a person was guilty of contravening various sections of that Act. In that context, the Court of Appeal considered the ambit of the 'reasonable excuse' defence. Ralph Gibson LJ, with whom Dillon LJ agreed, approved the conclusion of Morritt J in the High Court, who interpreted the defence very restrictively: 'the concept of "reasonable excuse" [...] cover[s] such matters as physical inability to comply with a requirement for information or documents arising from illness or accidental destruction of papers, etc' (*Bank of England v Riley* [1992] Ch 475 (CA) 481–2, 484–5).

- otherwise intentionally obstructing the Secretary of State in the exercise of their powers to request information and the production of documents.[155]

A person who commits any of these offences is liable on summary conviction to imprisonment for a term not exceeding six months or a fine (or both),[156] and the court may make an order requiring the person, within such period as may be specified in the order, to comply with the request for information or documents.[157] **6.72**

As with information obtained by the Secretary of State from a shipping person or aircraft person pursuant to a reporting requirement, information obtained by the Secretary of State under a request for information may be disclosed to a broad range of persons for, or in connection with, a number of purposes.[158] **6.73**

## D. Enforcement of Transport Sanctions

The Secretary of State has the power to respond to breaches of transport sanctions by taking action with increasing levels of severity, ranging from pursuing low-level outcomes (such as issuing a warning or a compliance letter with recommendations, naming and shaming without further penalty, or referring concerns to relevant regulatory bodies) to imposing a civil monetary penalty or, in the most serious cases, referring the case for criminal investigation and prosecution.[159] Criminal prosecutions can only be brought where a prosecutor has determined that the proceedings would meet the 'Full Code Test', namely that in respect of each defendant, there is sufficient evidence to provide a realistic prospect of conviction on each charge and that prosecution would be in the public interest.[160] **6.74**

This section begins with an overview of DfT's monetary penalty regime. It then briefly considers criminal proceedings relating to transport sanctions offences. We do not provide an analysis of the use of deferred prosecution agreements or 'SOCPA agreements'[161] in the enforcement of sanctions, or the potential ancillary orders and consequences flowing from sanctions breaches (such as asset recovery, monitorships, serious **6.75**

[155] This conduct would amount to a common law offence of perverting the course of justice in the context of an anticipated criminal investigation or when one is known to have commenced. See *R v Vreones* [1891] 1 QB 360; *Government of the USA v Dempsey* [2018] EWHC 1724 (Admin), [2018] 4 WLR 110.

[156] TASSCER 2024, reg 22. TASSCER also permits the Secretary of State to impose a monetary penalty (on which, see the text to nn 162–73 below) on a person who breaches an information or document production request obligation (regs 2 and 5(1); see also reg 12).

[157] TASSCER 2024, reg 21(2).

[158] TASSCER 2024, reg 27(1)–(3).

[159] DfT, 'Transport Sanctions: Civil Monetary Penalties' (n 132) s 2.

[160] The 'Full Code Test' is set out in the Code for Crown Prosecutors, available at <https://www.cps.gov.uk/publication/code-crown-prosecutors> accessed 20 February 2025.

[161] An agreement in which an offender offers assistance to a prosecuting authority with a view to securing immunity or a significantly reduced sentence pursuant to Serious Organised Crime and Police Act 2005 (SOCPA) ss 71–5.

crime prevention orders, debarment from tendering for public sector contracts, and director disqualification orders). (See Chapter 4, 'Director Disqualification Sanctions'.)

## 1. Civil Monetary Penalties

**6.76** As of 10 October 2024, the Secretary of State may impose a monetary penalty on a person on a strict liability basis if satisfied, on the balance of probabilities, that the person has breached a prohibition or failed to comply with an obligation imposed by or under transport sanctions regulations.[162]

**6.77** When deciding how to dispose of a case and the size of any monetary penalty, DfT applies a three-stage process: (1) appropriateness; (2) penalty matrix; and (3) penalty recommendation.[163]

**6.78** Having established, on the balance of probabilities, that a person has breached a prohibition or failed to comply with an obligation imposed by or under transport sanctions regulations, DfT 'will determine whether a monetary penalty should be imposed on a case-by-case basis'. It may, for example, 'consider other enforcement actions to be more appropriate (including referring the matter to law enforcement for investigation of potential criminal enforcement)'.[164]

**6.79** If DfT determines it is appropriate in principle to impose a monetary penalty, a 'matrix' is used to calculate the penalty.

**6.80** First, where it is possible to estimate the value of the aircraft or ship (transport asset) involved in the breach or failure to comply, DfT will calculate the statutory maximum it could impose: the greater of £1 million or 50 per cent of the estimated value of the transport asset.[165]

**6.81** Second, within this maximum, DfT will identify a 'fair, proportionate, and reasonable' penalty based on its view of the 'overall seriousness of the breach'.[166] When assessing the overall seriousness of the breach, DfT will generally take into account: whether the breach is intended and deliberate, reckless, negligent, or the result of a mistake; whether the person took steps to conceal the breach; the level of actual and expected knowledge of transport sanctions held by the person; the harm or risk of harm to the purposes and/or objectives of the transport sanctions regime; voluntary self-disclosure of the

[162] TASSCER 2024, regs 2, 5(1), and 7. If a monetary penalty is payable by a body corporate, the Secretary of State may also impose a monetary penalty on an officer of the body corporate if satisfied, on the balance of probabilities, that the body corporate's breach or failure took place with the consent or connivance of the officer or was attributable to their neglect (regs 5(1) and 8(1)–(2) and (4)).

[163] DfT, 'Transport Sanctions: Civil Monetary Penalties' (n 132) s 3.

[164] ibid.

[165] TASSCER 2024, reg 10(1)–(2); DfT, 'Transport Sanctions: Civil Monetary Penalties' (n 132) s 3. If it is not possible to estimate the value of the transport asset involved in the breach or failure to comply, the statutory maximum is £1,000,000 (reg 10(3)).

[166] DfT, 'Transport Sanctions: Civil Monetary Penalties' (n 132) s 3.

breach; the size, function, and complexity of any business and/or entity; the person's sanctions history; the person's behaviour when under investigation; and whether the person has taken remedial steps to avoid further breaches.[167]

Third, DfT will consider whether a penalty reduction is warranted. In less serious cases, the reduction can be up to 50 per cent where there has been 'prompt and complete voluntary disclosure of a breach'. In serious cases, the reduction can be up to 50 per cent for 'voluntary disclosure' but, in the most serious cases, the reduction is capped at 30 per cent.[168] **6.82**

The application of the matrix results in a penalty recommendation. If, further to a recommendation, the Secretary of State intends to impose a monetary penalty, they must (1) provide the person with notice of the Secretary of State's intention to do so;[169] and (2) explain the grounds for imposing the penalty, specify the amount of the penalty, explain that the person is entitled to make representations on any relevant matter ('such as legal issues, the facts, DfT's findings on the facts, adherence to its procedures, ability to pay and the appropriateness and proportionality' of the penalty), and specify the period within which any representations must be made.[170] If a monetary penalty is imposed,[171] the person has the right to a ministerial review.[172] There is then a right of appeal to the Upper Tribunal.[173] **6.83**

We cannot predict with any certainty how the Secretary of State will exercise these new powers. If the imposition of monetary penalties by OFSI in connection with breaches of financial sanctions provides a marker, then the Secretary of State can be expected to impose monetary penalties relatively infrequently,[174] but the penalties may be substantial.[175] That said, Government funding was pledged in 2023 to increase **6.84**

[167] DfT, 'Transport Sanctions: Civil Monetary Penalties' (n 132) s 4.

[168] ibid s 3.

[169] TASSCER 2024, reg 11(1).

[170] TASSCER 2024, reg 11(2); DfT, 'Transport Sanctions: Civil Monetary Penalties' (n 132) s 3. DfT requires written representations to be made within 28 days of the Secretary of State's notice of its intention, although DfT may extend this period at its discretion. If no representations are made, DfT will decide whether to impose formally the penalty as soon as practicable after the expiration of the 28-day period for representations. If representations are made, DfT will endeavour to decide whether to impose formally the proposed penalty within 28 days of receipt of the representations. A penalty becomes due for payment when DfT issues the formal penalty notice (s 6).

[171] The Secretary of State may be satisfied that a person has breached a prohibition, or failed to comply with an obligation, imposed by or under transport sanctions regulations, but nonetheless decide not to impose a monetary penalty. In these circumstances, DfT may publish a report to this effect (TASSCER 2024, reg 13(2)).

[172] TASSCER 2024, reg 11(3)(b). See Chapter 2.I ('Right of Review') for the process of seeking review against monetary penalties.

[173] TASSCER 2024, reg 11(5). The Upper Tribunal may quash the Secretary of State's decision to impose the penalty, or uphold the decision but substitute a different amount for the amount determined by the Secretary of State (reg 11(6)).

[174] OFSI imposed 10 monetary penalties between 2017 and 2024, but in the first seven months of 2025, OFSI imposed four monetary penalties, suggesting an escalation in its enforcement workload. Details can be found in OFSI and HM Treasury, 'Financial Sanctions Enforcement: Decisions and Monetary Penalties Imposed' (Collection, 25 February 2019) <https://www.gov.uk/government/collections/enforcement-of-financial-sanctions> accessed 24 August 2025.

[175] For example, OFSI imposed two penalties (£7,693,233.50 and £12,778,576.33) on Standard Chartered Bank on 18 February 2020 for breaching Article 5(3) of Council Regulation (EU) 833, SI 833/2014 of 31 July 2014 concerning restrictive measures in view of Russia's actions destabilizing the situation in Ukraine and Regulation 3B of the Ukraine (European Union Financial Sanctions) (No 3) Regulations 2014, SI 2054/2014 by making loans totalling £97,484,808.71 to a subsidiary of a designated person (the penalties reflected a 30 per cent reduction for voluntary disclosure in a case considered 'most serious', and were reduced (from £11.9 million and £19.6 million,

enforcement capacity, which includes developing specialist capabilities within the Joint Maritime Security Centre and the National Crime Agency (NCA) to detect and respond to breaches of transport sanctions, and there remains political impetus for that to translate into concrete enforcement actions.[176]

## 2. Criminal Proceedings

**6.85** As illustrated above, transport sanctions regulations prohibit or require certain conduct, creating offences when (with any requisite mental element) the prohibited conduct occurs or the required conduct does not occur. There are also related licence and confidentiality offences. Further, TASSCER establishes reporting and information offences.

**6.86** The ordinary criminal law principles of secondary liability, inchoate liability, and corporate liability (the identification principle, now broadened by the Economic Crime and Corporate Transparency Act 2023) apply in the context of transport sanctions offences—as does Part 2 of the Serious Crime Act 2007, which created three standalone offences of encouraging or assisting crime.

**6.87** To date, enforcement of sanctions by way of criminal prosecution has been limited. Two groups of prosecutions, the *Mabey & Johnson* and *Weir Group* cases, concerned bribes paid in the context of the UN Iraq Oil-For-Food programme.[177]

**6.88** However, there are indications that the prospects of enforcement by way of prosecution are increasing. In particular:

- A new cell was established within the NCA in 2022 to target 'kleptocracy' and sanctions evasion, with one of the cell's purposes to 'support, alongside other agencies and departments, criminal cross-HMG sanctions delivery and enforcement'.[178]
- In early 2024, Dmitry Ovsyannikov, a former governor of Sevastopol, was arrested by the NCA and charged with sanctions circumvention offences contrary to the Russia Regulations and money laundering offences contrary to the Proceeds of Crime Act 2002. Dmitry Ovsyannikov's wife and brother-in-law were also charged. Mr Ovsyannikov was convicted of sanctions circumvention offences and money laundering on 9 April 2025 and received a custodial sentence of 40 months. His brother was also convicted of sanctions circumvention offences and received

respectively) following a ministerial review because Standard Chartered Bank 'did not wilfully breach the sanctions regime, had acted in good faith, had intended to comply with the relevant restrictions, had fully co-operated with OFSI and had taken remedial steps following the breach'.

[176] FCDO and the Rt Hon Lord Cameron, 'Deter, Disrupt and Demonstrate – UK Sanctions in a Contested World: UK Sanctions Strategy' (n 140) Annex 3 para 4.

[177] The case against the three senior executives of Mabey & Johnson Ltd was subject to interlocutory appellate proceedings (*R v Forsyth* [2011] UKSC 9, [2011] 2 AC 69). The parent company was later subject to High Court civil recovery proceedings. For details of the prosecution of Weir Group Plc, see Crown Office and Procurator Fiscal Service, 'Bribery Prosecutions in Scotland' (updated 26 April 2024) <https://www.copfs.gov.uk/crime-info/bribery-and-corruption/bribery-prosecutions-in-scotland/> accessed 20 February 2025.

[178] National Crime Agency, 'SARs in Action' (issue 15 March 2022) 5.

a custodial sentence of 15 months, suspended for 15 months. Mr Ovsyannikov's wife was acquitted.[179]

- In August 2025, the director of a charity was convicted of failing adequately to respond to a request for information from OFSI in relation to her ties to a pro-Hamas news outlet. She was sentenced to a suspended sentence of imprisonment.[180]
- Since July 2022, His Majesty's Revenue and Customs (HMRC) has increased its sanctions enforcement capacity with the recruitment of 40 additional criminal investigators and more policy and legal advisers and analysts, and the provision of sanctions training for existing staff. With that increased capacity, HMRC has increased the number of criminal investigations into potential trade sanctions offences: 14 were opened in 2022, 22 were opened in 2023, and 29 were opened in 2024.[181]

## E. Maritime Enforcement Powers

'Maritime transport serves as the main artery of global trade',[182] with ships carrying over 80 per cent of the volume of global trade.[183] Global maritime trade reached 12,292 million tonnes in 2023.[184] Given the UK's rich history of targeting shipping trade as part of economic warfare, it is perhaps unsurprising that SAMLA enables the making of regulations which confer maritime powers on prescribed persons for the purpose of enforcing a broad spectrum of trade sanctions.[185] **6.89**

At the time of writing, the Secretary of State has made 23 sanctions regimes which confer maritime enforcement powers.[186] By way of example, this section briefly outlines the powers conferred in the Russia regime and the circumstances in which those powers may be exercised. **6.90**

[179] Crown Prosecution Service, 'Sentencing: The First Ever UK Prosecution of Russian Sanction Breaches' (11 April 2025) <https://www.cps.gov.uk/cps/news/sentencing-first-ever-uk-prosecution-russian-sanction-breaches> accessed 24 August 2025; Sentencing Remarks of Mrs Justice Cockerill of 11 April 2025 <https://www.judiciary.uk/wp-content/uploads/2025/04/R-v-Ovsiannikov-D-and-A-sentencing-remarks-.pdf> accessed 24 August 2025.

[180] Ronan Barnard, 'Charity Director Avoids Prison in Terrorism Sanctions Case' (*Law360*, 15 August 2025) <https://www.law360.co.uk/articles/2376530/charity-director-avoids-prison-in-terrorism-sanctions-case> (accessed 28 August 2025).

[181] Letter from Sir Jim Harra KCB (HMRC) to Dame Meg Hillier (Chair of the Treasury Select Committee) (17 February 2025) <https://committees.parliament.uk/publications/46714/documents/240633/default/> (accessed 28 August 2025).

[182] UN Conference on Trade and Development (UNCTAD), '2024 Review of Maritime Transport: Navigating Maritime Chokepoints' (2024) xiii–xiv <https://unctad.org/system/files/official-document/rmt2024_en.pdf> accessed 20 February 2025.

[183] UNCTAD, '2022 Review of Maritime Transport: Navigating Stormy Waters' (2022) xv <https://unctad.org/system/files/official-document/rmt2022_en.pdf> (accessed 20 February 2025).

[184] UNTAD, '2024 Review of Maritime Transport' (n 182) 1.

[185] SAMLA 2018, ss 19–20.

[186] Venezuela (Sanctions) (EU Exit) Regulations 2019, SI 2019/135, pt 9; North Korea Regulations 2019, pt 12; Democratic Republic of the Congo (Sanctions) (EU Exit) Regulations 2019, SI 2019/433, pt 9; South Sudan (Sanctions) (EU Exit) Regulations 2019, SI 2019/438, pt 9; Iran (Sanctions) (Nuclear) (EU Exit) Regulations 2019, SI 2019/461, pt 9; ISIL (Da'esh) and Al-Qaida (United Nations Sanctions) (EU Exit) Regulations 2019, SI 2019/466, pt 9; Counter-Terrorism (International Sanctions) (EU Exit) Regulations 2019, SI 2019/573, pt 9; Belarus Regulations 2019, pt 9; Zimbabwe (Sanctions) (EU Exit) Regulations 2019, SI 2019/604, pt 9; Syria Regulations 2019, pt 10; Russia Regulations 2019, pt 10; Lebanon (Sanctions) (EU Exit) Regulations 2020, SI 2020/612,

**6.91** The Russia regime confers powers on 'maritime enforcement officers' for the purpose of (1) enforcing various trade sanctions and/or (2) investigating the suspected carriage on a ship of 'relevant goods'[187] or preventing the continued carriage on a ship of goods suspected to be relevant goods[188] (collectively, enforcing trade sanctions at sea). 'Maritime enforcement officers' include British commissioned naval officers, Ministry of Defence police officers, port constables, UK police officers more generally, designated customs officials, and designated NCA officers.[189]

**6.92** The powers conferred may only be exercised in certain circumstances:

- With respect to British ships and unflagged ships in international waters, a maritime enforcement officer may only exercise a power if they have reasonable grounds to suspect that a ship is carrying prohibited goods[190] or relevant goods.[191]
- With respect to British ships in foreign waters and foreign ships in international waters, a maritime enforcement officer may only exercise a power if (1) they have reasonable grounds to suspect that a ship is carrying prohibited or relevant goods, and (2) the Secretary of State has authorized the exercise of the officer's power.[192] The Secretary of State may only give that authorization if:
  - in respect of British ships in foreign waters, the State in whose waters the power would be exercised consents to the exercise of the power;[193] and
  - in respect of foreign ships in international waters, (1) the home State has requested the assistance of the UK for the purpose of enforcing trade sanctions at sea, (2) the home State has authorized the UK to act for the purpose of enforcing trade sanctions at sea, or (3) the 1982 UN Convention on the Law of the Sea or a UN Security Council resolution permits the exercise of the power in relation to the ship.[194]

pt 6; Central African Republic (Sanctions) (EU Exit) Regulations 2020, SI 2020/616; Somalia (Sanctions) (EU Exit) Regulations 2020, SI 2020/642, pt 9; Iraq (Sanctions) (EU Exit) Regulations 2020, SI 2020/707, pt 8; Sudan (Sanctions) (EU Exit) Regulations 2020, SI 2020/753, pt 9; Afghanistan (Sanctions) (EU Exit) Regulations 2020, SI 2020/948, pt 8; Syria (United Nations Sanctions) (Cultural Property) (EU Exit) Regulations 2020, SI 2020/1233, pt 6; Yemen (Sanctions) (EU Exit) (No 2) Regulations 2020, SI 2020/1278, pt 9; Libya Regulations 2020, pt 11; Myanmar (Sanctions) Regulations 2021, SI 2021/496, pt 9; Haiti (Sanctions) Regulations 2022, SI 2022/1281, pt 8; Iran Regulations 2023, pt 11.

[187] 'Relevant goods' are goods in relation to which there has been (or continues to be) conduct outside the UK by a person other than a UK person which would constitute a contravention of a prohibition in specified trade sanctions regulations (or a related trade licence) if the conduct had been (or was ongoing) in the UK or by a UK person (Russia Regulations 2019, reg 94; SAMLA 2018, s 20(11)–(12)).

[188] Russia Regulations 2019, reg 89(1)–(3).

[189] Russia Regulations 2019, reg 90.

[190] 'Prohibited goods' are goods which have been, or are being, dealt with in contravention of a prohibition in specified trade sanctions regulations (or a related trade licence) (Russia Regulations 2019, reg 94; SAMLA 2018, s 19(13)).

[191] Russia Regulations 2019, regs 89(1) and 91(1).

[192] Russia Regulations 2019, regs 89(1) and (5), 91(1), and 93(1).

[193] Russia Regulations 2019, reg 93(2).

[194] Russia Regulations 2019, reg 93(3).

Where a maritime enforcement officer has reasonable grounds to suspect that a ship is carrying prohibited or relevant goods, and subject to receipt of any authorization required from the Secretary of State, they may stop the ship, board the ship, and/or require the ship to be taken to (and remain in) a port or anchorage in the UK or any other State willing to receive it.[195] Where the officer boards the ship, they may, inter alia, search the ship, require those on board to provide information or produce documents, and seize any suspected prohibited or relevant goods.[196] If necessary, the officer may use reasonable force in the exercise of any power conferred on them.[197] **6.93**

Maritime enforcement activities by the UK are rare but have occurred. For example, in 2019, Royal Marines assisted authorities in Gibraltar to board and detain a tanker carrying Iranian oil suspected to be travelling to Syria in breach of EU sanctions.[198] In May 2024, the UK announced that it conducted joint maritime patrols with the Republic of Korea in the waters around the Korean peninsula to enforce UN sanctions against the Democratic People's Republic of Korea.[199] **6.94**

## F. Conclusion

Transport sanctions are significant measures designed to disrupt trade. They have long been a cornerstone of the UK's foreign policy. Today, these sanctions invariably co-exist with trade sanctions and are increasingly paired with asset freezes. This convergence is evident in the case of Russia where, for example, on 25 November 2024, the UK pointed to the 'vital' need to constrain oil revenues funding the Kremlin and announced the specification of 30 ships in Russia's 'shadow fleet', as well as the designation of two alleged 'dubious Russian insurers' who are said to be 'enabling the shadow fleet'.[200] **6.95**

While the policy goals behind transport and transport-related sanctions are clear, it is essential not to overlook the potential unintended consequences. For instance, has Russia's 'shadow fleet'—with its 'older ships [ … ] having substandard maintenance, unclear ownership and a severe lack of insurance'[201]—expanded as a result of **6.96**

[195] Russia Regulations 2019, reg 91(1)–(2).

[196] Russia Regulations 2019, regs 91(3)(b) and (4)(a), and 92(1)–(2)(a).

[197] Russia Regulations 2019, regs 91(7) and 92(3).

[198] Tom Bateman, 'Royal Marines Used Brute Force, Says Tanker Captain' *BBC* (London, 30 July 2019) <https://www.bbc.co.uk/news/uk-49162256> accessed 20 February 2025.

[199] Ministry of Defence and The Rt Hon Grant Shapps, 'UK and Republic of Korea Conduct Joint Sanctions Enforcement Patrols' (Press Release, 14 May 2024).

[200] FCDO 25 November 2024 Press Release (n 93). No mention is made of 'enabling the shadow fleet' in the statement of reasons for either insurer. Rather, each insurer is said to be an involved person on the ground that each 'is or has been involved in obtaining a benefit from or supporting the Government of Russia by carrying on business in a sector of strategic significance to the Government of Russia, namely the Russian financial services sector'.

[201] International Maritime Organization, 'Addressing Ship-to-Ship Oil Transfers and Tankers in the "Dark Fleet"', Meeting Summary of the Legal Committee, 110th session (LEG 110) 27–31 March 2023 <https://www.imo.org/en/MediaCentre/MeetingSummaries/Pages/Legal-Committee%2c-110th-session.aspx> (accessed 20 February 2025).

sanctions? If so, the risks associated with these ships, including oil spills, collisions, and unaccountable shipowners, may have grown.[202] Policymakers must carefully consider these emerging challenges as they continue to assess the effectiveness and broader impact of transport and transport-related sanctions.

202 ibid.

# 7
# Human Rights Sanctions

*Amanda Pinto KC and Charles McCombe*



## A. Introduction

In response to human rights violations and abuses worldwide, human rights sanctions regimes allow governments to impose measures such as asset freezes and travel bans. This chapter provides an overview of the UK's current human rights sanctions regime, adopting the following structure: **7.01**

a. First, we discuss the emergence of global human rights sanctions regimes, which arose from the passing of the 'Magnitsky Act' by the United States Congress, following the death of Russian tax and accountancy expert, Sergei Magnitsky.
b. Second, we address the two key pieces of primary legislation in the UK which can properly be placed under the 'Magnitsky' heading: (i) section 13 of the Criminal Finances Act 2017 (CFA), which amended Part 5 of the Proceeds of Crime Act 2002 (POCA); and (ii) the inclusion of Magnitsky-style purposes for which sanctions regulations could be made in the Sanctions and Anti-Money Laundering Act 2018 (SAMLA).
c. Third, we discuss the UK's autonomous global human rights sanctions regime introduced on 6 July 2020 by the Global Human Rights Sanctions Regulations 2020 (the '2020 Regulations'). In particular, we focus on the purposes of those regulations and the test for designation.
d. Finally, we close the chapter by considering which additional rights may be added to the current regime in the future.


Amanda Pinto KC and Charles McCombe, *Human Rights Sanctions* In: *UK Sanctions Law and Practice*. Edited by: Amanda Pinto KC, Alexandre Haines, and Sophie O'Sullivan, Oxford University Press. © Oxford University Press 2026. DOI: 10.1093/oso/9780198964179.003.0007

## B. Background to the UK's Human Rights Legislation: The 'Magnitsky Affair'

**7.02** In 2012, the United States Congress passed the Russia and Moldova Jackson-Vanik Repeal and Sergei Magnitsky Rule of Law Accountability Act, known as the 'Magnitsky Act'.[1] Amongst other things, the Magnitsky Act sought to impose sanctions (financial measures[2] and travel bans[3]) on Russian officials determined to have been responsible for the detention, abuse, and/or death of Sergei Magnitsky,[4] or others who carried out extrajudicial killings, torture, or other gross violations of internationally recognized human rights committed against those seeking to expose illegal activity carried out by the Russian Government or those seeking to promote internationally recognized human rights and freedoms in Russia.[5]

**7.03** The circumstances surrounding the death of Sergei Magnitsky, and the role of the Russian State in his detention and death, were described by Lord Anderson, Rapporteur to the Council of Europe's Committee on Legal Affairs and Human Rights, in his Explanatory Memorandum to a 2018 report entitled 'Sergei Magnitsky and Beyond—Fighting Impunity by Targeted Sanctions':[6]

> The Assembly was appalled by the death in pretrial detention, in 2009, of the Russian tax and accountancy expert, Sergei Magnitsky. Mr Magnitsky had carried out investigations into a massive tax reimbursement fraud against the Russian State budget perpetrated by the abuse of investment vessels captured from Mr Magnitsky's client, Mr William Browder, by criminals benefiting from the collusion of corrupt police and tax officials. After the complaints he had prepared were entrusted for investigation to the very officials whom he had accused of complicity in the suspected fraud, Mr Magnitsky was himself detained for alleged tax evasion. When he refused to change his testimony, he faced increasingly harsh conditions of detention despite his declining health, including acute pancreatitis for which he was refused necessary surgery. Mr Magnitsky finally died in terrible circumstances in pretrial detention after he was beaten with rubber batons, which were used to 'pacify' him when he screamed in agony. The Assembly was further appalled that none of the officials responsible for Mr Magnitsky's death had been punished. On the contrary, some enjoyed promotions and public praise by senior representatives of the State, whilst Mr Magnitsky himself

[1] Russia and Moldova Jackson-Vanik Repeal and Sergei Magnitsky Rule of Law Accountability Act of 2012 (the 'Magnitsky Act') (Pub L No 112-208) (14 December 2012) <https://www.govinfo.gov/content/pkg/PLAW-112publ208/pdf/PLAW-112publ208.pdf> accessed 19 September 2025.

[2] See Magnitsky Act 2012, s 406.

[3] See Magnitsky Act 2012, s 405.

[4] See Magnitsky Act 2012, s 404(a)(1).

[5] See Magnitsky Act 2012, s 404(a)(2).

[6] Doc 14661 Report (30 October 2018) <https://www.europarl.europa.eu/cmsdata/161078/6%20-%2005%20CoE%20doc%2014661%20-%20Report%20Committee%20Legal%20Affairs%20and%20Human%20Rights%20on%20Sergei%20Magnitsky%20and%20Beyond.pdf> accessed 19 September 2024.

was prosecuted posthumously, something which may properly be considered as the ultimate absurdity.

In 2016, building upon the foundations laid by the Magnitsky Act, Congress passed further legislation in the form of the Global Magnitsky Human Rights Accountability Act ('Global Magnitsky Act') which permits the Government of the United States to sanction certain individuals anywhere in the world who are, according to the Act's preface, 'responsible for gross violations of internationally recognized human rights'.[7] The key test which must be satisfied before sanctions can be imposed under the Global Magnitsky Act requires the President to determine, based on 'credible evidence', that 'any foreign person': **7.04**

(1) is responsible for extrajudicial killings, torture, or other gross violations of internationally recognized human rights committed against individuals in any foreign country who seek—
  (A) to expose illegal activity carried out by government officials; or
  (B) to obtain, exercise, defend, or promote internationally recognized human rights and freedoms, such as the freedoms of religion, expression, association, and assembly, and the rights to a fair trial and democratic elections;
(2) acted as an agent of or on behalf of a foreign person in a matter relating to an activity described in paragraph (1);
(3) is a government official, or a senior associate of such an official, that is responsible for, or complicit in, ordering, controlling, or otherwise directing, acts of significant corruption, including the expropriation of private or public assets for personal gain, corruption related to government contracts or the extraction of natural resources, bribery, or the facilitation or transfer of the proceeds of corruption to foreign jurisdictions; or
(4) has materially assisted, sponsored, or provided financial, material, or technological support for, or goods or services in support of, an activity described in paragraph (3).

Since the introduction of the Magnitsky Act and the Global Magnitsky Act in the United States, other jurisdictions, including Canada,[8] Australia,[9] and the European Union,[10] have introduced their own Magnitsky laws. **7.05**

The focus of this chapter, however, is on the UK's Magnitsky-style measures. Initially, some Parliamentarians held the view that sufficient legal powers already existed in the **7.06**

[7] Global Magnitsky Human Rights Accountability Act ('Global Magnitsky Act'), Title XII, Subtitle F of Pub L No 114-328, as amended; 22 U.S. Code §§10101 ff. The Global Magnitsky Act was ultimately incorporated into the National Defense Authorization Act for Fiscal Year 2017 (NDAA FY), which came into force on 23 December 2016. See Pub L 114-328: <https://www.govinfo.gov/content/pkg/PLAW-114publ328/pdf/PLAW-114publ328.pdf> accessed 19 September 2025.

[8] Justice For Victims of Corrupt Foreign Officials Act (Sergei Magnitsky Law) SC 2017, c 21.

[9] Autonomous Sanctions Amendment (Magnitsky-style and Other Thematic Sanctions) Regulations 2021.

[10] cf EU Global Human Rights Sanctions Regime enacted on 7 December 2020 and prolonged until 8 December 2026.

UK to deal with human rights abuses and that specific Magnitsky-style legislation was unnecessary. For example, in a debate on 21 January 2016 in the House of Commons over the publication of the Litvinenko Inquiry's report, Prime Minister Theresa May made the following statements:[11]

> The right hon. Gentleman asked a number of other questions, including about a potential Magnitsky Act. [ … ] There are a number of actions we can take in preventing individuals from coming to the United Kingdom, but in this case, of course, we actually want Lugovoy and Kovtun to be in the United Kingdom to be able to face justice. The right hon. Gentleman said that there were reports of them travelling. There are Interpol red notices and European arrest warrants in place, which will lead to their being arrested if they travel outside Russia.
>
> [ … ]
>
> In respect of the two individuals whom the inquiry found committed this murder on the streets of London, it is important that we take every step to bring them to the UK, rather than stop them coming here, because we wish to see them brought to justice.
>
> [ … ]
>
> I say once again to those who think that the creation of a Magnitsky Act and a list of people who are excluded will, in some sense, add to the strength of measures that we already have that it is already possible for us to exclude people from the United Kingdom.
>
> [ … ]
>
> The [Magnitsky] Act excludes or stops certain individuals from coming into a country, in this case the United States. We already have powers that are at least as robust, if not more so, than the powers in the Magnitsky Act. It is on that basis that I think we have the powers we need to exclude people. I repeat the point I made earlier: if people think that introducing the Magnitsky Act will mean that those who perpetrated this heinous crime will be brought to justice, they are very wrong.

**7.07** However, the Government's position changed over time[12] and two key pieces of primary legislation were introduced. First, section 3 of CFA 2017 amended the definition of 'unlawful conduct' in Part 5 of POCA 2002 to permit an initial freeze and, later, civil recovery of property obtained through conduct which constitutes or is connected with the commission of a gross human rights abuse or violation. Second, section 1 of SAMLA 2018 permits an appropriate Minister to make sanctions regulations for

[11] HC Deb 21 January 2016, cols 1569–82 <https://publications.parliament.uk/pa/cm201516/cmhansrd/cm160121/debtext/160121-0002.htm#16012124000411> accessed 19 September 2025.

[12] See e.g. the House of Commons Library Briefing Paper by Ben Smith and Joanna Dawson, 'Magnitsky Legislation' (CBP 8374, 13 July 2020) (the 'Magnitsky Briefing Paper') <https://researchbriefings.files.parliament.uk/documents/CBP-8374/CBP-8374.pdf> accessed 19 September 2025. The Briefing Paper summarizes the background to the introduction of Magnitsky legislation in the United Kingdom at pp 3–6, including reference to Prime Minister May's comments cited in para 7.06 above.

specific purposes, including, (i) to provide accountability for or to be a deterrent to gross violations of human rights, (ii) otherwise promote compliance with international human rights law, and (iii) respect for human rights.

We address each of these statutory provisions below, before turning to the key piece of secondary legislation – namely the 2020 Regulations – introduced under section 1 of SAMLA. **7.08**

## C. Section 13 of the Criminal Finances Act 2017

Part 5 of POCA provides for the civil recovery of property which is, or represents, property obtained through unlawful conduct, or which is intended to be used in unlawful conduct.[13] **7.09**

Section 13 CFA inserted subsection 2A into section 241 of POCA, thereby expanding the definition of 'unlawful conduct' as follows: **7.10**

> (2A) Conduct which—
> (a) occurs in a country or territory outside the United Kingdom,
> (b) constitutes, or is connected with, the commission of a gross human rights abuse or violation (see section 241A), and
> (c) if it occurred in a part of the United Kingdom, would be an offence triable under the criminal law of that part on indictment only or either on indictment or summarily,
> is also unlawful conduct.

Section 241A of POCA[14] provides that conduct will constitute the 'commission of a gross human rights abuse or violation' if each of the following three conditions is met: **7.11**

a. The first condition concerns conduct which constitutes torture[15] or other cruel, inhuman or degrading treatment or punishment of a person who has either sought to expose illegal activity carried out by a public official or a person acting in an official capability, or to obtain, exercise, defend, or promote human rights and fundamental freedoms.[16]
b. The second condition is that the conduct is carried out in consequence of the person having sought either of the two broad categories of aims set out in the first condition.[17]

[13] See Proceeds of Crime Act 2002 (POCA), s 240.
[14] Inserted by s 13 of the Criminal Finances Act 2017 (CFA).
[15] Torture, for these purposes, includes the intentional infliction (whether it be through an act or omission) of severe pain or suffering (physical or mental) on another person; see POCA 2002, s 241A(6)–(7).
[16] See POCA 2002, s 241A(2).
[17] POCA 2002, s 241A(3).

c. The third condition is, in short, that the conduct is carried out by a public official, or a person acting in an official capacity, in the (purported) performance of their official duties, or someone else at the instigation of such a person.[18]

**7.12** In addition, conduct is to be regarded as 'connected with' the commission of a gross human rights abuse or violation if it is conduct by a person that involves (i) acting as an agent for another in connection with activities relating to conduct which constitutes the commission of such abuse or violation;[19] (ii) directing or sponsoring such activities;[20] (iii) profiting from such activities;[21] or (iv) materially assisting such activities.[22]

**7.13** Section 241A of POCA was briefly considered by the Court of Appeal in *R (World Uyghur Congress) v National Crime Agency.*[23] The World Uyghur Congress (WUC) presented a body of evidence to the NCA that suggested the Government of the People's Republic of China was committing human rights abuses against the Uyghur people relating to the production of cotton being brought into the UK from China.[24] The NCA declined to open an investigation with a view to bringing prosecutions for money laundering offences[25] or civil recovery proceedings in the UK.[26] The WUC judicially reviewed the NCA's decision not to commence investigations.

**7.14** The Court of Appeal allowed the WUC's appeal. The court held that the NCA's decision not to commence the investigations was unlawful, being premised on two material errors of law: (1) the NCA wrongly considered it was necessary to be able to identify recoverable or criminal property before commencing an investigation; and (2) the NCA wrongly considered that the provision of 'adequate consideration' anywhere in the supply chain would prevent the product from being characterized as 'recoverable property' or 'criminal property'. Even if one person in the chain were to avail themselves of the defence, it would not apply to others.[27] The Court of Appeal therefore remitted the question of whether to investigate back to the NCA, applying the correct tests.

**7.15** While a detailed analysis of this judgment is outside the scope of this chapter, it is important to recognize that the Court of Appeal's judgment, on its face, set a relatively low bar to be met before the NCA may be required to investigate alleged gross human rights abuses in similar situations within the context of Parts 5 and 7 of POCA. That

[18] POCA 2002, s 241A(4).
[19] POCA 2002, s 241A(5)(a).
[20] POCA 2002, s 241A(5)(b).
[21] POCA 2002, s 241A(5)(c).
[22] POCA 2002, s 241A(5)(d) 'Material assistance' is defined (non-exhaustively) in POCA 2002, s 241A(8).
[23] *R (World Uyghur Congress) v National Crime Agency* [2024] EWCA Civ 715, [2024] 1 WLR 4532 (CA) ('*World Uyghur Congress*').
[24] See the headnote to the judgment in *World Uyghur Congress* (n 23).
[25] Contrary to POCA 2002, pt 7.
[26] Under POCA 2002, pt 5, to recover money obtained through unlawful conduct.
[27] See *World Uyghur Congress* (n 23) [48]–[59].

is to say, if the NCA was presented with evidence suggestive of conduct which may fall within the scope of section 241A of POCA, neither the inability to identify particular recoverable or criminal property nor the provision of adequate consideration at any point in the supply chain would necessarily relieve the investigative body of its responsibility to commence what may be a complex, multi-jurisdictional investigation into alleged human rights violations. On one view, the Court of Appeal's decision supplies section 241A of POCA 2002 with 'teeth'; it may prevent an investigative authority from relying on evidential complexity to justify it *not* commencing an investigation.

## D. SAMLA 2018

Section 1(1) of SAMLA permits an appropriate Minister to make sanctions regulations where considered to be appropriate for the purposes of (i) compliance with a UN obligation, (ii) compliance with any other obligation, or (iii) for a purpose specified in section 1(2). **7.16**

Section 1(2)(f) is the most explicitly Magnitsky-style purpose for which regulations may be made: **7.17**

> (2) A purpose is within this subsection if the appropriate Minister making the regulations considers that carrying out that purpose would –
> [...]
> (f) provide accountability for or be a deterrent to gross violations of human rights, or otherwise promote –
> (i) compliance with international human rights law, or
> (ii) respect for human rights.

Section 1(7) further defines the purpose: **7.18**

> (7) In this Act any reference to a gross violation of human rights is to conduct which—
> (a) constitutes, or
> (b) is connected with,
> the commission of a gross human rights abuse or violation; and whether conduct constitutes or is connected with the commission of such an abuse or violation is to be determined in accordance with s.241A of POCA.

Therefore, the meaning of 'gross violation of human rights' in SAMLA is consistent with that as set out in POCA.[28] **7.19**

[28] As inserted by the CFA 2017. See para 7.11 above.

**7.20** Beyond section 1(2)(f) of SAMLA, which refers specifically to 'gross violations of human rights', a number of additional purposes are consistent with the general policy aims of Magnitsky-style legislation, including the following:

> (2) [...]
> (d) further a foreign policy objective of the government of the United Kingdom,
> (e) promote the resolution of armed conflicts or the protection of civilians in conflict zones,
> [...]
> (g) promote compliance with international humanitarian law.
> (h) contribute to multilateral efforts to prevent the spread and use of weapons and materials or mass destruction, or
> (i) promote respect for democracy, the rule of law and good governance.

**7.21** Interestingly, the purposes addressed in sub-subsections (e), (g), (h), and (i) above were originally introduced in the form of an amendment by Lord Collins, on behalf of the Opposition, during the report stage of the Bill in the House of Lords. The amendment was ultimately agreed.[29] Then, during the third reading of the Bill in the House of Commons, Sir Alan Duncan (on behalf of the Government) proposed further amendments to make the legislation more explicitly Magnitsky-related in style.[30] These examples—reflected generally in the debates in Hansard—indicate there was all-party consensus to achieve that end.

**7.22** It is important to note the relationship between the direct Magnitsky purpose in section 1(2)(f) of SAMLA—namely to provide accountability for, or to be a deterrent to, gross violations of human rights—and the other Magnitsky-related purposes set out in section 1(2) (see paragraph 7.20 above). The expanded list provides for sanctions regulations, including for the purposes of promoting respect for human rights;[31] complying with international humanitarian law;[32] promoting respect for democracy, the rule of law, and good governance;[33] and furthering a foreign policy objective.[34] The practical effect of these separate purposes is to restrict the definition of 'gross violation of human rights' found in section 241A of POCA. However, while on their face, the three conditions in section 241A of POCA reduce the situations which may be considered a 'gross human rights abuse or violation', it is very likely that conduct which falls outside this restrictive definition will, nonetheless, be caught by the far-reaching and broad purposes in section 1(2). In particular, such

[29] HL Deb, 15 January 2018, vol. 788 <https://hansard.parliament.uk/Lords/2018-01-15/debates/B590A93A-CA86-441C-AD56-5CD088B3A0C3/SanctionsAndAnti-MoneyLaunderingBill(HL)#contribution-BC4F7D3E-E14B-4E2F-839F-BA7A501570B9> accessed 19 September 2025. See the Magnitsky Briefing Paper, pp 9–10, which makes references to and discusses this legislative history, from which we have drawn.

[30] See the Magnitsky Briefing Paper, pp 10–11.

[31] Sanctions and Anti-Money Laundering Act 2018 (SAMLA), s 1(2)(f)(ii).

[32] SAMLA 2018, s 1(2)(g).

[33] SAMLA 2018, s 1(2)(i).

[34] SAMLA 2018, s 1(2)(d).

conduct is likely to breach section 1(2)(f)(ii) of SAMLA relating to the promotion of respect for human rights.

## E. Global Human Rights Sanctions Regulations 2020

The 2020 Regulations made under section 1(1) of SAMLA came into force on 6 July 2020.[35] According to the Explanatory Memorandum to the 2020 Regulations, their purposes are to 'deter, and provide accountability for, activities which, if carried out by or on behalf of a State, would amount to a serious violation of certain human rights by that State', enabling 'the Secretary of State to impose asset freezes and travel bans on persons involved in such conduct'.[36] From the outset, the Government signalled that the human rights which the 2020 Regulations seek to target are specific and exhaustive. The policy background which led to identification of these specific rights is addressed in the Explanatory Memorandum in the following terms: **7.23**

> ***What is being done and why?***
>
> 7.1 HMG seeks to champion human rights, good governance and the rule of law. Serious human rights violations by State actors, and similar conduct by non-State actors, leads to unstable and less prosperous societies. Such conduct perpetuates violent conflict, creates a world where terrorism flourishes and where democratic institutions are weakened. It has a devastating impact on individuals and places the safety of individuals and societies at risk. Successfully deterring such conduct would help create fairer and more just societies, which support the long-term global conditions most conducive to security, economic growth and the safety of all.
>
> 7.2 This instrument will enable HMG to designate persons who are involved in certain activities which, had they been carried out by or on behalf of a State within the territory of that State, would amount to a serious violation by that State of certain human rights. These are: an individual's right to life; an individual's right not to be subjected to torture or cruel, inhuman or degrading treatment or punishment; and an individual's right to be free from slavery, not to be held in servitude or required to perform forced or compulsory labour. Such persons are able to be designated for the purpose of a travel ban or an asset freeze. The designation of such persons is intended to deter, and provide accountability for, such activities. The activities could be carried out by a State or a non-State actor.[37]

[35] The EU Global Human Rights Sanctions Regime was enacted shortly after, on 7 December 2020.

[36] Explanatory Memorandum to the Global Human Rights Sanctions Regulations 2020, 2020 No 680, s 2 ('Explanatory Memorandum'). The purposes of the Explanatory Memorandum are to be distinguished from the purposes of the 2020 Regulations, as set out in reg 4.

[37] Explanatory Memorandum (n 36), paras 7.1–7.2. Emphasis added.

7.24 Upon introduction of the regime, the Secretary of State announced 49 new designations under the 2020 Regulations. The 'first wave' of sanctions targeted people and organizations that were described in the Foreign and Commonwealth Office's press release as:

a. 25 Russian nationals who were 'involved in the mistreatment and death' of Sergei Magnitsky, 'who uncovered widespread Russian corruption by a group of Russian tax and police officials';
b. 20 Saudi Arabian nationals 'involved in the death of journalist Jamal Khashoggi';
c. '2 high-ranking Myanmar military generals involved in the systematic and brutal violence against the Rohingya people and other ethnic minorities';
d. '2 organisations involved in the forced labour, torture and murder that takes place in North Korea's gulags'.[38]

7.25 By the end of 2020, a further 29 designations were made in six stages, with an average of 6.5 designations per month.[39] As of July 2021, Belarus, China, Ukraine, The Gambia, and Venezuela were also represented in new designations.[40] As of 5 September 2025, there are 128 designated individuals and 24 designated entities.[41]

## 1. The Purposes of the 2020 Regulations

7.26 Regulation 4 of the 2020 Regulations states the purposes of the regime in the following terms:

**Purposes**

4.— (1) The purposes of the regulations contained in this instrument are to deter, and provide accountability for, activities falling within paragraph (2).
(2) An activity falls within this paragraph if it is an activity which, if carried out by or on behalf of a State within the territory of that State, would amount to a serious violation by that State of an individual's—
(a) right to life,[42]
(b) right not to be subjected to torture or cruel, inhuman or degrading treatment or punishment, or

[38] Foreign and Commonwealth Office (FCO) and The Rt Hon Dominic Raab, 'UK Announces First Sanctions Under New Global Human Rights Regime' (News story, 6 July 2020) <https://www.gov.uk/government/news/uk-announces-first-sanctions-under-new-global-human-rights-regime> accessed 19 September 2025.
[39] Charlie Loudon and Celeste Kmiotek, 'The Global Human Rights Sanctions: Year One in Numbers' (Royal United Services Institute, 20 July 2021) <https://rusi.org/explore-our-research/publications/commentary/uk-global-human-rights-sanctions-year-one-numbers> accessed 19 September 2025.
[40] ibid.
[41] Whereas the EU Global Human Rights Sanctions Regime currently applies to 116 individuals and 33 entities.
[42] Interestingly, the EU Global Human Rights Sanctions Regime refers to genocide and crimes against humanity, which the UK framework does not.

(c) right to be free from slavery, not to be held in servitude or required to perform forced or compulsory labour, whether or not the activity is carried out by or on behalf of a State.

(3) An activity falls within paragraph (2) if it is carried out—

(a) outside the United Kingdom by any person, or

(b) in the United Kingdom by a person who is not a United Kingdom person.

(4) In paragraph (2), an 'activity' includes an omission.

The significance of the purposes in regulation 4 is twofold. First, they guide the operation of the test for designation as set out in regulation 6 (discussed below in paragraphs 7.33–40). Second, they must correspond with one or more of the purposes for which regulations may be made as set out in section 1(2) of SAMLA. **7.27**

When the 2020 Regulations were introduced, the appropriate Minister was required by section 2(4) of SAMLA[43] to lay a report before Parliament which explained why, amongst other things, the purpose of the regulations met one or more of the conditions in section 1(2) of SAMLA, and why there were good reasons to pursue that purpose. The report under section 2(4) laid before Parliament (the 'Section 2(4) Report')[44] by the Rt Hon Dominic Raab MP, the Secretary of State for Foreign and Commonwealth Affairs, addressed these requirements. Four purposes in section 1(2) are identified: **7.28**

a. to provide accountability for or be a deterrent to gross violations of human rights, or otherwise promote (i) compliance with international human rights law, or (ii) respect for human rights (section (2)(f));
b. to promote respect for democracy, the rule of law, and good governance (section (2)(i));
c. to further a foreign policy objective of the government (section (2)(d));
d. to be in the interests of national security (section (2)(b)).

As to the first two purposes, the Section 2(4) Report provides the following reasons for pursuing them: **7.29**

> There are good reasons for pursuing these purposes. Inherent to all human beings by virtue of their dignity, human rights are the universal concern of all States. Human rights form an integral part of the rules-based international system, which the UK seeks to promote and defend by encouraging fulfilment by States of their international human rights obligations, increasing pressure on repressive and authoritarian States, and holding States to account for human rights violations. Protection and promotion of human rights is in the UK national interest. Human rights violations and abuses

[43] Section 2 of SAMLA 2018 was repealed by section 57(3) of the Economic Crime (Transparency and Enforcement) Act 2022 (ECTEA) on 15 March 2022.

[44] Report under Section 2(4) of SAMLA 2018 ('Section 2(4) Report') <https://www.legislation.gov.uk/uksi/2020/680/pdfs/uksiod_20200680_en.pdf> accessed 19 September 2025.

> perpetuate violent conflict, create a world in which terrorism can flourish and weaken democratic institutions and inclusion. They have a devastating impact on individuals and place the safety of societies at risk. Successfully deterring human rights violations and abuses can help create fairer and more just societies, which support the long-term global conditions most conducive to security, economic growth and the safety of all.[45]

**7.30** As to section (2)(d), the Section 2(4) Report notes a number of the UK's foreign policy goals, which include promoting and protecting human rights worldwide and joining a 'global network of like-minded jurisdictions that work together to tackle those who commit gross human rights violations'.[46] Existing human rights sanctions regimes in particular states[47] are also recognized in the report.[48]

**7.31** As to section (2)(b), tackling the root causes of terrorism and other national security problems and sending 'strong messages to those who perpetrate serious human rights violations or abuses, including those involved in terrorism' are relied upon, amongst other things.[49]

**7.32** Finally, the Section 2(4) Report justifies the targeting of serious human rights violations or abuses carried out in the UK by non-UK persons, in addition to those carried out abroad. The possibility of those carrying out activity in the UK on behalf of another state, or visiting from another state, and then leaving the jurisdiction 'making traditional forms of law enforcement ineffective' is the example given.[50]

## 2. The Test for Designation Under the 2020 Regulations

**7.33** Regulation 6 of the 2020 Regulations sets out the test for designation that must be satisfied before a person may be designated under regulation 5, which must always be read pursuant to SAMLA. A number of features of the designation test are noteworthy.

**7.34** The threshold originally set by the test in regulation 6(1) was:

> (1) The Secretary of State may not designate a person under regulation 5 unless the Secretary of State—
> (a) has reasonable grounds to suspect that that person is an involved person, and
> (b) considers that the designation of that person is appropriate, having regard to—
> (i) the purposes stated in regulation 4, and

[45] ibid para 5. Reasons why the focus is placed on three human rights and why acts by both state and non-state have been included are set out at paras 6 and 7 of the Section 2(4) Report, respectively.
[46] Section 2(4) Report, paras 8–10. The Section 2(4) Report cites directly from the Secretary of State's contribution to the Public Bill Committee Debate on 1 March 2018 in the House of Commons.
[47] Democratic Republic of Condo, Iran, Libya, Myanmar, South Sudan, Venezuela, and Zimbabwe.
[48] Section 2(4) Report, para 10.
[49] Section 2(4) Report, para 11.
[50] Section 2(4) Report, para 12.

(ii) the likely significant effects of the designation on that person (as they appear to the Secretary of State to be on the basis of the information that the Secretary of State has).

However, this test was omitted on 18 April 2025[51] and substituted by regulation 6(2), which defines an 'involved person' for the purposes of regulation 5A ('Conditions for the designation of persons by name') in the following terms, mirroring the test set down in other sanctions regulations, such as the Russia Regulations 2019: **7.35**

(2) In this regulation an 'involved person' means a person who—
 (a) is or has been involved in an activity falling within regulation 4(2),
 (b) is owned or controlled directly or indirectly (within the meaning of regulation 7) by a person who is or has been so involved,
 (c) is acting on behalf of or at the direction of a person who is or has been so involved, or
 (d) is a member of, or associated with, a person who is or has been so involved.

Notwithstanding this amendment, there may be little substantive change to the nature of the discretion to designate. The purposes of the regulations and the effects of the designation on the person in question remain relevant considerations, albeit recent cases confirm that the Secretary of State will be given a wide margin of appreciation in respect of these considerations. (See Chapter 8, 'Designations and Challenges', paragraphs 8.47, 8.57–8.) **7.36**

In Jay J's judgment in *LLC Synesis v Secretary of State for Foreign, Commonwealth and Development Affairs*, the first case to consider an application under section 38 of SAMLA (in relation to the Russian sanctions regime), he stated:[52] **7.37**

> Given that possible HRA compliance and proportionality were considered by the Defendant in relation to the Claimant's designation, the removal of Regulation 6(1)(b) makes little or no practical difference in the circumstances of this particular case. Even under the new regime, the Defendant clearly has a discretion to designate, and the inquiry does not notionally cease as soon as he has reasonable grounds to suspect that the entity at issue is an involved person. But a list of all the factors potentially

[51] The Sanctions (EU Exit) (Miscellaneous Amendments) Regulations 2025, SI 2025/394, regs 1(2) and 21(4)(b). Before the 18 April 2025 amendment, the requirement that the designation be appropriate had been omitted by section 58(3) of the ECTEA 2022. When first enacted, SAMLA required the Minister to find that designation of the relevant person was appropriate, having regard to the purpose of the relevant regulations engaged and the likely significant effects of the designation on that person. This criterion, however, was removed by amendments made to SAMLA by section 58(3) of the ECTEA 2022. It follows that between 1 August 2022 when the ECTEA 2022 came into force and 18 April 2025 when The Sanctions (EU Exit) (Miscellaneous Amendments) Regulations 2025 came into force, regulation 6(1)(b) is to be treated as statutorily abrogated, in other words, deemed never to have had effect. See *Synesis* (n 52) [22].

[52] *LLC Synesis v Secretary of State for Foreign, Commonwealth and Development Affairs* [2023] EWHC 541 (Admin) [23].

relevant to the exercise (or non-exercise) of the discretion under these provisions is not required for current purposes.

**7.38** In *Phillips v Secretary of State for Foreign, Commonwealth and Development Affairs*,[53] the court confirmed that designations will be permitted to impact on a designated person's rights where this is proportionate to a legitimate aim; and in *Shvidler v Secretary of State for Foreign, Commonwealth and Development Affairs*, the Supreme Court ruled that ministers:[54]

> [S]hould be accorded a wide margin of appreciation in making their judgments about whether the objectives of the measures [ … ] are sufficiently important to justify the limitation of a fundamental right; whether there is a rational connection between the measures and those objectives; whether a less intrusive measure could have been used; and whether a fair balance has been struck between the relevant Convention rights of the individuals and others concerned and the interests of the community

**7.39** The meaning of 'involved in an activity falling within regulation 4(2)' provided by regulation 6(3) is notably broad. The definition ranges from responsibility for or engagement in the activity (regulation 6(3)(a)); to the provision of 'financial services, or [making] available funds, economic resources, goods or technology, knowing or having reasonable cause to suspect that those financial services, funds, economic resources, goods or technology will or may contribute to such an activity' (regulation 6(3)(d)); '[profiting] financially or [obtaining] any other benefit from an activity falling within regulation 4(2)' (regulation 6(3)(f)); or 'intentionally or recklessly' failing to investigate or prosecute such an activity, where the person has such a responsibility (regulation 6(3)(g)). If the apparent breadth of 'involvement in an activity falling within regulation 6(2)' was not already clear on the face of the wide-ranging and broad list of conduct in regulation 6(3), regulation 6(4) provides that '[n]othing in sub-paragraph (3) is to be taken to limit the meaning of any of the other sub-paragraphs of that paragraph'.

**7.40** Finally, on 6 July 2020, the Government published a policy paper containing a non-exhaustive list of considerations relevant to designation, with commentary.[55] The seven considerations are: (i) His Majesty's human rights priorities; (ii) the nature of the victim; (iii) the seriousness of the conduct; (iv) the international profile and collective action; (v) the degree of control, authority, and organization of relevant non-state actors over people or an area; (vi) the status and connections of the involved person; and (vii) the effectiveness of other measures.

[53] *Phillips v Secretary of State for Foreign, Commonwealth and Development Affairs* [2024] EWHC 32 (Admin) [167].

[54] *Shvidler v Secretary of State for Foreign, Commonwealth and Development Affairs* [2025] UKSC 30 [130].

[55] FCO and Foreign, Commonwealth and Development Office (FCDO), 'Global Human Rights Sanctions: Consideration of Designations' (Policy paper, 6 July 2020) <https://www.gov.uk/government/publications/global-human-rights-sanctions-factors-in-designating-people-involved-in-human-rights-violations/global-human-rights-sanctions-consideration-of-targets> accessed 19 September 2025.

## F. The Future: Should Further Rights be Included in the 2020 Regulations?

The decision to introduce Magnitsky-style sanctions requires the government to take a view on a number of theoretical questions which arise. We consider one such issue concerning the substantive human rights that are targeted by such a regime. **7.41**

As noted above in paragraph 7.23, the Explanatory Memorandum which accompanied the 2020 Regulations repeatedly made it clear that the new sanctions regime sought to target serious violations of *certain* human rights by foreign states.[56] Those rights, in summary, are the right to life (regulation 4(2)(a)); the right not to be subjected to torture or cruel, inhuman, or degrading treatment or punishment (regulation 4(2)(b)); and an individual's right to be free from slavery and related conduct (regulation 4(2)(c)). **7.42**

When the 2020 Regulations were enacted, the Secretary of State made a statement to the House of Commons explaining that '[the Government] will continue to explore expanding this regime to include other human rights'[57]. Further, he made the following broader comment on the Government's commitment to human rights: **7.43**

> As we forge a dynamic new vision for a truly global Britain, this Government are absolutely committed to the United Kingdom becoming an even stronger force for good in the world: on climate change, as we host COP26; as we champion 12 years of education for every girl in the world, no matter how poor their background; and on human rights, where we will defend media freedoms and protect freedom of religious belief; and, with the measures we are enacting and announcing today, hold to account the perpetrators of the worst human rights abuses.[58]

Although no other rights have been added, a reasonable starting point for possible contenders may be the further rights specified in the Global Magnitsky Act, such as freedoms of religion, expression, association and assembly, and the rights to a fair trial and democratic elections (see paragraph 7.4, above). **7.44**

The most recent Human Rights Programme summary for 2022–2023, published on 30 March 2023, lists a number of issues on which the 'FCDO human rights objectives currently place a particular emphasis'.[59] It included the following: **7.45**

> [...]
> - standing up for the freedom of people of any or no religion to practise their beliefs in peace and safety, including for the freedom of religion or belief conference that took place in London in July 2022

[56] See the Explanatory Memorandum (n 36), paras 2.1 and 7.2.

[57] HC Deb 6 July 2020, vol 678, col 664 <https://hansard.parliament.uk/commons/2020-07-06/debates/24B78A01-061C-48A8-AA92-8E53C17516E3/GlobalHumanRightsSanctionsRegime> accessed 19 September 2025.

[58] ibid col 663.

[59] FCDO, 'Human Rights Programme Summary 2022 to 2023' (Transparency data, 30 March 2023) <https://www.gov.uk/government/publications/official-development-assistance-oda-fcdo-internatio

- supporting the right of human rights defenders to carry out their work, and be able to voice their opinions freely and safely
- promoting the development and strengthening of democracy

[...]

- continuing the UK's commitment to defend and support media freedom internationally, building on commitments made at the 2019 global conference

## G. Conclusion

**7.46** Despite the change in government since the publication in 2023 of the UK's human rights priorities, a significant shift in those priorities appears unlikely. The rights outlined in previous policy objectives—such as freedom of religion, speech (including press freedom), and fair-trial rights—are broadly uncontroversial and align closely with the UK's longstanding foreign policy commitments. They also reflect the purposes set out in section 1(2) of SAMLA. These priorities extend beyond narrowly defined 'gross human rights violations or abuses' to encompass broader objectives, including the promotion of human rights generally,[60] respect for democracy and the rule of law, and the advancement of good governance.[61] Consequently, what began as a targeted effort to address severe human rights abuses has evolved into a more expansive framework, incorporating broader objectives. To what extent the UK will deploy this tool of foreign policy remains to be seen, but the current regime allows for the possibility of far-reaching measures to address global human rights abuses and violations, in the wider sense.

nal-programme-spend-objectives-2022-to-2023/human-rights-programme-summary-2022-to-2023> accessed 19 September 2025.

[60] SAMLA 2018, s1(2)(f)(ii).

[61] SAMLA 2018, s 1(2)(i).

# 8

# Designations and Challenges

*Amanda Pinto KC, Alexandre Haines, and Sophie O'Sullivan*



## A. Power to Designate

Sections 9 to 13 of the Sanctions and Anti-Money Laundering Act 2018 (SAMLA) set out the UK Government's key designation powers. Section 9 introduces the term 'designated persons' to mean persons (individuals and entities) who are specifically subjected to sanctions. Section 10 permits for persons to be designated either by name or by description and enables the Minister to set out in regulations how the designation powers must or may be exercised (section 10(2)).[1] **8.01**

[1] See Foreign, Commonwealth and Development Office (FCDO), 'Post-Legislative Scrutiny Memorandum: Sanctions and Anti-Money Laundering Act 2018' (CP 1024, March 2024) 13. The Memorandum states that, as of 31 December 2023, 669 individuals and 193 entities were designated under UN-only regimes and 37 ships were specified under UN-only regimes (899 total); 2,758 individuals and 625 entities were designated under autonomous regimes (3,383 total); and eight individuals were designated under mixed UK/UN regimes (eight total).

Amanda Pinto KC, Alexandre Haines, and Sophie O'Sullivan, *Designations and Challenges* In: *UK Sanctions Law and Practice*. Edited by: Amanda Pinto KC, Alexandre Haines, and Sophie O'Sullivan, Oxford University Press.
 DOI: 10.1093/oso/9780198964179.003.0008

## 1. Designation by Name

8.02 Following amendments to SAMLA by the Economic Crime (Transparency and Enforcement) Act 2022 (ECTEA), an appropriate Minister has the power to designate a person by name under either the standard or urgent procedure.[2]

8.03 Under the standard procedure, section 11 of SAMLA empowers an appropriate Minister to designate a person where they have 'reasonable grounds to suspect' that the person is involved in, or otherwise connected to, an activity prohibited in the regulations for a specific sanctions regime.[3] That person is an 'involved person'.[4] Section 11(3) of SAMLA defines 'an involved person' as a person who—

(a) is or has been involved in an activity specified in the regulations,
(b) is owned or controlled directly or indirectly by a person who is or has been so involved,
(c) is acting on behalf of or at the direction of a person who is or has been so involved, or
(d) is a member of, or associated with, a person who is or has been so involved.

8.04 When first enacted, SAMLA also required the Minister to find that designation of the relevant person was 'appropriate, having regard to the purpose of the relevant regulations engaged and the likely significant effects of the designation on that person'.[5] However, this criterion was removed by amendments made to SAMLA by section 58(3) of ECTEA.

8.05 Notwithstanding this amendment to section 6 and the resultant weakening of the designation criteria, the High Court in *Dalston Projects Ltd v Secretary of State for Transport* ('*Dalston I*')[6] recognized the continued obligation on the Government to establish a 'rational connection between the sanctions measure and the aim'.[7] Similarly, in *R (on the application of Mikhail Fridman) v HM Treasury* ('*Fridman*'),[8] whilst recognizing that the Government had a residual discretion to refuse a licence even where the licence

[2] In the EU, by contrast, designation of individuals and entities is not performed by each Member State at government level but by unanimous decision of the Council of the European Union, followed by the enactment of an appropriate Council regulation, which is directly binding throughout the EU with no need for transposition into domestic law (unlike the position for EU directives).

[3] Under EU Regulation 269/2014, the criteria for designation are set forth specifically for each sanctions regime. For instance, the EU sanctions regime against Russia provides for asset freeze measures against, i.e., 'natural persons responsible for supporting or implementing actions or policies which undermine or threaten the territorial integrity, sovereignty and independence of Ukraine, or stability or security in Ukraine, or which obstruct the work of international organisations in Ukraine', as well as 'legal persons, entities or bodies supporting, materially or financially, actions which undermine or threaten the territorial integrity, sovereignty and independence of Ukraine' (Council Regulation (EU) 269/2014, Art 3(1)).

[4] Sanctions and Anti-Money Laundering Act 2018 (SAMLA), s 11(2A), as amended.

[5] See SAMLA 2018, s 11(2)(b), as originally enacted.

[6] The case involved a legal challenge brought against the then-Secretary of State for Transport for detention of a superyacht under the powers in regulation 57D of the Russia (Sanctions) (EU Exit) Regulations 2019 (the 'Russia Regulations'), on the basis that the detention was disproportionate under Article 1 Protocol 1 of the ECHR.

[7] *Dalston I* (n 6) [86].

[8] *R (on the application of Mikhail Fridman) v HM Treasury* [2023] EWHC 2657 (Admin) (17 October 2023).

application met the criteria, the court noted that the discretion 'must be exercised consistently with the purposes of the primary legislation and the Russia Regulations' in accordance with established public law principles.[9]

Because general public law principles are applicable to all judicial review proceedings, the Government must still have regard to the *purpose* of the relevant regulation (as per section 11(2)(b) of SAMLA, as originally enacted) in exercising its designation powers. This is so notwithstanding the removal of the 'appropriate' criterion from section 11 of SAMLA by ECTEA. **8.06**

Under the urgent procedure,[10] a Minister may designate a person on an expedited basis if two conditions are met: **8.07**

1. that individual or entity has already been designated by the US, EU, Australia, Canada, or any other country specified in the relevant regulation for the purposes of the urgent procedure, and
2. it is in the public interest to make a designation under the expedited procedure.[11]

Where a person is designated under the urgent procedure, the designation expires after 56 days unless the Minister either certifies that the individual or entity continues to be sanctioned by another applicable jurisdiction and it remains in the public interest for the designation to continue for a further 56 days (the urgent procedure conditions) or has reasonable grounds to suspect that the individual or entity is an involved person (the standard procedure conditions).[12] **8.08**

Where an individual or entity has been designated by name, the relevant authority must provide a 'Statement of Reasons' setting out in brief terms the reasons for the designation decision.[13] **8.09**

An entity, although not designated by name on the UK Sanctions List, may nevertheless be subject to the same financial restrictions and prohibitions as a designated person by virtue of the rules on ownership and control. Under regulation 7 of the Russia (Sanctions) (EU Exit) Regulations 2019 (the 'Russia Regulations') (and equivalent provisions in other regimes), an entity is treated as being designated if it is owned or controlled, directly or indirectly, by a designated person. **8.10**

OFSI's General Guidance emphasizes that the UK 'will look to designate owned or controlled entities/individuals in their own right where possible';[14] however, the guidance **8.11**

[9] ibid [60].

[10] Interestingly, there is no urgent procedure in place for the expedited designation of individuals or legal entities under EU sanctions regimes, hence designation always follows the complex two-step process (EU Council decision followed by the enactment of EU regulation).

[11] SAMLA 2018, s 11(2B) and (2D), as amended.

[12] SAMLA 2018, s 11, as amended.

[13] SAMLA 2018, s 10(3) and (4), as amended.

[14] Office of Financial Sanctions Implementation (OFSI), 'UK Financial Sanctions General Guidance' (13 February 2024) s 4.1 <https://www.gov.uk/government/publications/financial-sanctions-general-guidance/uk-financial-sanctions-general-guidance> accessed 11 September 2025.

also recognizes that this is not always feasible. In practice, there are numerous entities which are not expressly named on the UK Sanctions List but which are deemed designated because they fall within the scope of the ownership and control provisions.

**8.12** 'Ownership' includes situations where a designated person holds, directly or indirectly, more than 50 per cent of the shares or voting rights, or has the right to appoint or remove a majority of directors. 'Control' is broader still: it extends to circumstances where it is *reasonable to expect* that a designated person is able to ensure that the entity acts in accordance with their wishes. (See Chapter 3.D.4, 'Ownership and Control'.)

**8.13** The High Court in *Hellard v OJSC Rossiysky Kredit Bank*[15] ('*Hellard*') identified four relevant categories of control:

1. de jure control (formal legal control)
2. actual present de facto control
3. potential future de jure control
4. potential future de facto control.

**8.14** This wide interpretation of control means that even minority shareholdings, state influence, or indirect means of exerting influence may suffice, provided there is evidence that the designated person can direct the entity's affairs. By contrast, in *Hellard*, the court concluded that mere supervisory influence by a Russian state agency chaired by a designated person was not enough to amount to control, underlining that the test remains fact-sensitive.

**8.15** The position is mirrored under EU sanctions. Article 2 of Council Regulation (EU) 269/2014 (Russia) provides that funds and economic resources must be frozen where they belong to, are owned, held, or controlled by designated persons. Both the EU and the UK regimes thus apply a comprehensive approach: entities not expressly designated may still be treated as such, leading to a practical landscape where the number of restricted persons is significantly greater than the number of names in the published list. There is, as a result, a greater onus on the private sector to determine—usually through specialist legal advice—whether an entity ought to be deemed designated.

## 2. Designation by Description

**8.16** Section 12 of SAMLA provides the additional power for a Minister to designate a person by description.[16] It is a condition of this type of designation that the description

[15] *Hellard v OJSC Rossiysky Kredit Bank* [2024] EWHC 1783 (Ch).

[16] While designation by description does not exist per se under EU regulations, a similar approach has been adopted through the association criteria. Council Regulation (EU) 2022/330 of 25 February 2022 introduced the reference to 'natural or legal persons, entities or bodies associated with them' (i.e. associated with persons

of persons specified is such that a reasonable person would know whether a person fell within the description.[17]

As with designation by name, designation by description may be made under the standard or urgent procedure.[18] **8.17**

Where an individual or entity has been designated by description, the relevant authority must provide a 'Statement of Reasons' setting out the reasons for the designation decision.[19] **8.18**

## B. The Statutory Threshold to Designate

The Minister must have 'reasonable grounds to suspect' that the person is an involved person for the purposes of the relevant regulation. In *LLC Synesis v Secretary of State for Foreign, Commonwealth and Development Affairs*, the first designation challenge brought before the UK courts under section 38 of SAMLA, Jay J held that the reasonable grounds to suspect threshold did not import any standard of proof and that the Foreign, Commonwealth and Development Office (FCDO) was not required to make a finding of fact.[20] Rather, the FCDO must assess or evaluate the information and material available, draw inferences, and adopt a 'good faith state of mind' in respect of that exercise. Information and material that can be considered by the decision-maker is widely drawn; Jay J held that:[21] **8.19**

> [...] 'material' or 'information' is not limited to evidence that would be admitted in a court of law. The net goes far wider. The decision-maker is certainly entitled to take hearsay into account; he is also entitled to consider other information which might be described as 'allegations', 'multiple hearsay' or (in the appropriate case) 'intelligence'. The weight to be given to this information and material, possessing as it does a weaker character than evidence properly so called, is for the decision-maker to assess; although the Court will normally expect that at least some recognition has been given to its inherent quality.

listed under Annex I pursuant to Article 1(a) to (g)). The EU Commission has clarified that asset freeze measures may de facto apply to persons not directly listed but mentioned in the 'reason' section under the association criterion: 'Strictly speaking, only the persons and entities who/which appear under the column "Name" in Annex I to Council Regulation (EU) 269/2014 are directly subject to an asset freeze and a prohibition to make funds and economic resources available to them or for their benefit. However, these restrictions can affect transactions with natural or legal persons, entities or bodies associated with them, some of which happen to be mentioned in the "Identifying information" and/or "Reasons" columns of Annex I to Council Regulation (EU) 269/2014.' (EU Commission Consolidated FAQs on the implementation of Council Regulation No 833/2014 and Council Regulation No 269/2014, s B.1, question 2.)

[17] SAMLA 2018, s 12(3), as amended.
[18] SAMLA 2018, s 12, as amended. See paras 8.02–8 above.
[19] SAMLA 2018, s 12(7), as amended.
[20] *LLC Synesis v Secretary of State for Foreign, Commonwealth and Development Affairs* [2023] EWHC 541 (Admin).
[21] ibid [73].

**8.20** The UK courts have broadly interpreted the 'reasonable grounds to suspect' threshold for lawful designation decisions. This interpretation differs from the 'reasonable cause to suspect' standard applied to criminal sanctions offences, such as dealing with funds or economic resources owned, held, or controlled by a designated person.[22] The distinction was clarified in the High Court case of *Vneshprombank LLC v Bedzhamov*.[23] In this case, the defendant, Georgy Bedzhamov, sought a declaration on whether there was reasonable cause to suspect that the claimant was funded by a company owned or controlled by designated persons under the Russia Regulations 2019. The court considered whether the offence of dealing with funds or economic resources requires only a reasonable suspicion that they are owned, held, or controlled by a designated person, or whether it must also be proved that they are, in fact, owned, held, or controlled by such a person. The applicant argued that the existence of a reasonable suspicion was enough to make out the relevant offence and that it was not also necessary to prove that, as a matter of fact, the funds or economic resources in issue were so owned, held, or controlled. The court held that even if a 'reasonable cause to suspect' is established, an offence will only occur if the entity is factually owned or controlled by a designated person subject to a UK asset freeze. This ruling aligns with Council Regulation (EU) No 833/2014 (from which the Russia Regulations derive). As noted in *PJSC National Bank Trust v Mints*, Article 2 of Council Regulation (EU) 269/2014 mandates freezing 'all funds and economic resources belonging to, owned, held or controlled by' designated persons and prohibits making such resources available to them.[24] The court in *Vneshprombank* emphasized that this is a purely factual test of ownership or control, not merely a suspicion-based one.[25]

**8.21** In the FCDO's Post-Legislative Scrutiny Memorandum: Sanctions and Anti-Money Laundering Act 2018 (published in March 2024), the Government endorsed Jay J's approach in the following terms:[26]

> [T]he judge confirmed that in order to establish whether there are reasonable grounds to suspect that a designated person has met the designation criteria, 'the decision-maker must consider all the material or information known to him or ought to have been within his knowledge following reasonable inquiry. [ … ] [T]hat "material" or "information" is not limited to evidence that would be admitted in a court of law. The net goes far wider [ … ] although the Court will normally expect that at least some recognition has been given to its inherent quality.' The overall decision that there are 'reasonable grounds to suspect' must still be rational.

22 See e.g. regulation 11(1) of the Russia Regulations 2019.
23 *Vneshprombank LLC v Bedzhamov* [2024] EWHC 1048 (Ch).
24 *PJSC National Bank Trust v Mints* [2023] EWHC 118 (Comm) [189].
25 *Vneshprombank* (n 23) [70].
26 FCDO, 'Post-Legislative Scrutiny Memorandum' (n 1) 18.

The Public Interest Disclosure (Prescribed Persons) (Amendment) Order 2025, enacted on 26 June 2025, expanded whistleblower protections to include reports of sanctions breaches. As a result, employees who reasonably believe that wrongdoing has occurred at their place of work, such as breach of financial, trade, or transport sanctions, can now make protected disclosures to relevant Government departments with safeguards against consequential workplace detriment. Were such a report made, the whistleblower information would almost certainly form part of the material considered by the Government in its decision to impose, maintain, vary, or remove a designation. **8.22**

## C. Interim Relief

Although there is no specific provision for interim relief under SAMLA, the court has jurisdiction to order such relief under section 37 of the Senior Courts Act 1981, applying the Civil Procedure Rules (CPR), Part 25.[27] **8.23**

The applicable principles to the determination of any interim relief application in this context were confirmed by Linden J in *Mazepin v Secretary of State for Foreign Commonwealth and Development Affairs*.[28] At the time of writing, this is the only application for interim relief arising from a designation made under SAMLA that the courts of England and Wales have determined. In *Mazepin*, the court confirmed that the principles applicable to such an interim relief application were those summarized by the Court of Appeal in *R (Public and Commercial Services Union) v Secretary of State for the Home Department*.[29] In dismissing the application, the court held that: **8.24**

> 75. The grant of interim relief is governed by the well-known test and principles set out by the House of Lords *in American Cyanamid Co v Ethicon Ltd* [1975] AC 396. The questions that arise are usually:
>
> (1) Is there a serious question to be tried?
> If the answer to that question is 'yes', then two further related questions arise; they are:
>
> (2) Would damages be an adequate remedy for a party injured by the court's grant of, or its failure to grant, an injunction?

[27] Similarly, interim measures may also be sought before EU Courts pursuant to Articles 278 and 279 of the Treaty on the Functioning of the European Union. See e.g. Case T-743/22 *Mazepin v Council*, order of the President of the General Court of 1 March 2023.

[28] *Mazepin v Secretary of State for Foreign Commonwealth and Development Affairs* [2023] EWHC 1777 (Admin). Nikita Mazepin is a Russian racing driver. He is the son of Belarusian-Russian oligarch Dmitry Mazepin. In March 2022, both Nikita Mazepin and his father were included on the EU and UK sanctions lists. In September 2023, the EU sanctions against Nikita Mazepin were partially lifted by the General Court allowing him to visit the EU for activities related to motorsport. In March 2024, the General Court found that the link to his father was not enough for the driver to remain on the EU's list, stating that the association criteria used in the sanctions require the existence of a link beyond a simple family relationship.

[29] *R (Public and Commercial Services Union) v Secretary of State for the Home Department* [2022] EWCA Civ 840.

(3) If not, where does the 'balance of convenience' lie? The first question indicates a threshold requirement.

76. It is acknowledged that the test is modified in the public law context. As Sir Clive Lewis puts it in Judicial Remedies in Public Law:

> 'Further, the adequacy of damages as a remedy will rarely determine whether or not it is appropriate to grant or refuse an interim injunction. For that reason, the courts will normally need to consider the wider balance of convenience and in doing so, the courts must take the wider public interest into account.'[30]

## D. Routes to Challenge Designation

**8.25** A key distinction between the UK's sanctions framework before and after its departure from the EU is the way in which a designated person can challenge their designation. Under the pre-Brexit framework, the only route by which persons designated under EU sanctions (either by virtue of a UN listing or an EU listing) could challenge their designation was at EU level and, to a much more limited extent, UN level (see Chapter 1.D, 'UK Sanctions Framework Pre-Brexit').

**8.26** Under SAMLA, designated persons can challenge their designation in the UK under its domestic procedure, or, where the designation is made by the UN, they can request the assistance of the UK Secretary of State to seek their removal from a UN sanctions list. Section 25 of SAMLA provides the right of an UN-named person to request a review of their designation. This provision gives the designated person the right to request that the Secretary of State uses their best endeavours to secure that the person's name is removed from the relevant UN list; however, as one can anticipate, the Secretary of State retains the discretion to decline the request for assistance and, indeed, what amounts to 'best endeavours' remains vague. See also *Youssef, R (On the Application Of) v The Secretary of State for Foreign, Commonwealth and Development Affairs*,[31] in which the court held that while it can review a Secretary of State's decision whether to use best endeavours to seek removal of a designated person's name from a UN sanctions list and could order the use of best endeavours, it remains the position that the court cannot revoke or require revocation of UN listings.

**8.27** Chapter 2 of SAMLA provides the administrative route for designation challenges and de-listing applications: by section 23, a person may request a review, variation, or revocation of their designation by an appropriate Minister. (See Chapter 2, 'The Post-Brexit UK Sanctions Framework'.)

[30] ibid [75]–[6], citing Clive Lewis, *Judicial Remedies in Public Law* (6th edn, Sweet & Maxwell 2020) para 8-024.
[31] *Youssef, R (On the Application Of) v The Secretary of State for Foreign, Commonwealth and Development Affairs* [2021] EWHC 3188 (Admin) (26 November 2021).

It is only once an applicant has exhausted the administrative review procedure for applying for relief that they may appeal the decision of the Minister by applying to the High Court of England and Wales (or Court of Session in Scotland) for the decision to be set aside.[32] **8.28**

Where such an application for review is made to the High Court under section 38 of SAMLA, in determining whether the decision should be set aside, the court must apply the principles applicable on an application for judicial review.[33] As such, a designation challenge under section 38 of SAMLA is a public law proceeding, governed by public law principles, and the core grounds upon which a listing challenge is based are illegality, irrationality, and procedural impropriety.[34] **8.29**

The Administrative Court's judgment in *KP v FCDA*,[35] though not a sanctions case, provides valuable clarity on the fundamentals of substantive judicial review. The case involved KP, a refugee from Diego Garcia—the largest island in the Chagos Archipelago, part of the British Indian Ocean Territory. Under a May 2025 agreement, the UK will transfer sovereignty of the territory to Mauritius, while retaining a 99-year lease on Diego Garcia. KP challenged his exclusion from relocation to the UK due to prior criminal convictions. In the judgment, Chamberlain J sets out the standard of review for rationality in a manner that reaffirms the principle that the Wednesbury doctrine is not rigid.[36] This underscores the flexible nature of rationality review in judicial proceedings. **8.30**

[32] By contrast, in the EU seeking a delisting directly with the Council of the European Union is not a procedural prerequisite to filing an action for annulment of the legal act grounding the designation before the Court of Justice of the European Union. In practice, arguments raised before the Council of the EU seeking revocation of sanctions are often used to improve the statement of reasons against said designated person during the revision of restrictive measures, thus questioning the strategic utility of raising compelling arguments at this stage.

[33] SAMLA 2018, section 38(4).

[34] The principles that have emerged from EU jurisprudence are (i) effective judicial protection (where the relevant authority must disclose the grounds for the sanctions decision when the measure is adopted or as swiftly as possible); (ii) rights of defence; (iii) obligation to state reasons; (iv) unjustified or disproportionate restrictions of fundamental rights; (v) unsubstantiated reasons and manifest error of assessment (the most common ground for successful challenges to EU acts imposing sanctions); (vi) infringement of the applicant's legitimate expectations; and (vii) abuse of powers.

[35] *KP v FCDA* [2025] EWHC 370 (Admin).

[36] ibid [75]–[8]. See also Professor Mark Elliott, 'KP v Foreign Secretary: A Primer on Rationality Review' (*Public Law for Everyone*, 10 March 2025) <https://publiclawforeveryone.com/2025/03/10/kp-v-foreign-secretary-a-primer-on-rationality-review/> accessed 11 September 2025. Elliott states that '[i]t has long been recognised that the Wednesbury doctrine is not monolithic, in that the court's approach—and, with it, the intensity of review—may vary depending on the circumstances of the case'. *KP* demonstrates that 'the "proportionality versus rationality" debate is ultimately a distraction from the real business of substantive review namely, setting the justificatory burden the decision-maker should be placed under and determining the appropriate role of the reviewing court in deciding whether that burden has been discharged' and 'the importance of conceptually distinguishing between different forms of deference, recognising the possibility of combining a heavy burden of justification with substantial adjudicative deference, and acknowledging that the role of the court in substantive review cases must be understood by reference to due analysis of what is at stake in the case rather than by resorting to crude distinctions between (for example, cases that do and do not involve rights)'.

## 1. Administrative Review

**8.31** Pursuant to section 23(1) of SAMLA, a person may request a review, variation, or revocation of their designation by the appropriate Minister.[37] Any such request for review can only be made once,[38] 'unless the grounds on which the further request is made are or include that there is a significant matter which has not previously been considered by the Minister'.[39]

**8.32** The Minister has the power to revoke or vary a designation at any time, and they must revoke the designation if they consider that the required conditions are not met. Where a designation has been made pursuant to the standard procedure (section 11 of SAMLA; see paragraphs 8.02–15) and the Minister later determines that the person is no longer 'an involved' person for the purposes of the relevant regulation, the designation must be revoked.[40]

**8.33** The process of administrative review[41] is set out in the Sanctions Review Procedure (EU Exit) Regulations 2018. The applicant must complete a Sanctions Review Request Form[42] setting out the reasons why they consider the designation should be varied or revoked,[43] together with evidence[44] supporting such a variation or revocation.[45] The application in its entirety must be submitted via email to the FCDO.[46] Where the applicant's evidence is not in English, they must provide an official translation in order for the evidence to be considered. The translation must include a signed declaration by the translator that the translation is accurate, the date of the translation, and the full name and contact details of the translator.[47]

**8.34** The FCDO has a duty to consider an application for review 'as soon as reasonably practicable'.[48] In practice, however, this is likely to take several months.

[37] The request is to be dealt with by the appropriate Minister, i.e. the Minister who made the decision or, in the case of UN listings, the Secretary of State. See the Explanatory Note to The Sanctions Review Procedure (EU Exit) Regulations 2018, SI 2018/1269.

[38] There is no such limitation under EU sanctions regimes. In practice, the designated person files observations with the EU Council seeking to obtain revocation of sanctions. Upon each response from the EU Council, the designated person is granted a time window to file new observations. This is also the case when the EU Council conducts its periodic review of restrictive measures.

[39] SAMLA 2018, s 23(2).

[40] SAMLA 2018, s 22.

[41] In the EU, there is no formal process and the request for revocation of sanction can be freely drafted by the designated person or their counsel.

[42] Sanctions Review Request Form: Designated Persons and UN Listed Persons <https://www.gov.uk/government/publications/sanction-challenge-form-designated-persons> accessed 11 September 2025.

[43] The Sanctions Review Procedure (EU Exit) Regulations 2018, reg 4(5).

[44] With regard to seeking revocation with the EU Council, the preliminary step to be taken is to seek communication of the bundle of evidence used by the Council to justify sanctions. In practice, this bundle is rapidly communicated to the designated person.

[45] The Sanctions Review Procedure (EU Exit) Regulations 2018, reg 4(6).

[46] Administrative review applications are submitted via email to sanctions.reassessment@fcdo.gov.uk. Similarly, communication with the Council of the European Union is done by email at sanctions@consilium.europa.eu.

[47] The Sanctions Review Procedure (EU Exit) Regulations 2018, reg 4(7).

[48] The Sanctions Review Procedure (EU Exit) Regulations 2018, reg 7.

The FCDO must provide reasons for its review decision in writing; however, it may exclude any information that it considers appropriate to exclude in the interest of national security, international relations, justice, or for reasons connected with the prevention or detection of serious crime in the United Kingdom or elsewhere.[49] **8.35**

In its March 2024 Post-Legislative Scrutiny Memorandum on SAMLA, the FCDO stated that 45 of its designations have been the subject of administrative review; of the 28 completed reviews, 9 designations were revoked (the number of designation variations was not provided).[50] **8.36**

## 2. Court Challenges

Where the designated person disagrees with the decision of the Minister pursuant to the section 23 SAMLA review procedure, they may then seek court review of the Minister's decision pursuant to section 38 of SAMLA.[51] **8.37**

Section 38(2) of SAMLA permits 'the appropriate person' to apply to the High Court (or Court of Session in Scotland) for the Minister's decision to be set aside. The appropriate person is the person named in the designation or, where the designation is made by specified description, the appropriate person is any person of that specified description.[52] **8.38**

At the time of writing, there have been a handful of designation challenges made pursuant to section 38 of SAMLA, the vast majority of which have related to the Russia Regulations 2019, or, as with the first designation challenge to come before the UK courts, *Synesis*, the Republic of Belarus (Sanctions) (EU Exit) Regulations 2019. Given the relative infancy of the UK's autonomous sanctions laws, how the UK courts are likely to interpret and apply the sanctions legislative framework in accordance with judicial review principles and public law proceedings continues to develop with each judgment. **8.39**

## 3. Appeals

Where a designated person's application to the High Court under section 38 of SAMLA is refused, they may seek permission to appeal that decision to the Court of Appeal and, thereafter, the Supreme Court, in accordance with Part 52 CPR.[53] **8.40**

[49] The Sanctions Review Procedure (EU Exit) Regulations 2018, reg 8(3).
[50] FCDO, 'Post-Legislative Scrutiny Memorandum' (n 1).
[51] Under EU proceedings, challenging a designation before EU courts (namely the General Court (Tribunal) of the CJEU) requires filing an action for annulment against the underlying legislative act, relying on five limited grounds: (i) lack of competence of the EU institution that adopted the contested act; (ii) infringement of an essential procedural requirement; (iii) infringement of the Treaties; (iv) infringement of any rule of law relating to the application of the Treaties; and (v) misuse of powers.
[52] SAMLA 2018, ss 23(1) and 38(3)(a).
[53] In contrast, the decisions issued by the Tribunal of the CJEU may only be appealed on challenges pertaining to the application of the law, within two months following issuance of the Tribunal's decision.

8.41 At the time of writing, there have been three substantive appeals to the Court of Appeal under section 38 SAMLA: *Dalston Projects Ltd v Secretary of State for Transport* and *Shvidler v Secretary of State for Foreign, Commonwealth and Development Affairs* ('*Shvidler II*') heard together,[54] and *Khan v Foreign, Commonwealth and Development Affairs*.[55] All three appeals were dismissed. *Shvidler* and *Dalston Projects* were then taken to the Supreme Court, for its first consideration of challenges brought under SAMLA. In its judgment, *Shvidler v Secretary of State for Foreign, Commonwealth and Development Affairs; Dalston Projects Ltd v Secretary of State for Transport* ('*Shvidler III*'), the court—by a majority of 4:1 (Lords Reed, Sales, Rose, and Richards; Lord Leggatt dissenting as to Shvidler's appeal)—upheld the dismissals and confirmed the designations.[56] As discussed in more detail in paragraphs 8.51–8, the Supreme Court decision in *Shvidler III* is significant in confirming that proportionality challenges require the court to conduct its own assessment rather than simply defer to the executive, although weight is accorded to ministerial expertise in foreign policy. The court also endorsed the principle that sanctions may be justified if they make a plausible cumulative contribution to statutory objectives, even where the individual effect of a designation is limited.

8.42 Following the Court of Appeal decision to uphold the High Court decision in *Khan*, the appellant appealed to the Supreme Court arguing that her designation breached human rights law. On 30 July 2025, the Supreme Court refused permission to appeal.

## E. Key Principles to Section 38 Court Review Proceedings

### 1. Proportionality

8.43 The *Bank Mellat* test, established in *Bank Mellat v HM Treasury (No 2)*, serves as the cornerstone for evaluating proportionality when state measures, including sanctions, interfere with ECHR rights.[57]

8.44 In *Bank Mellat (No 2)*, the UK Supreme Court addressed the proportionality of financial restrictions imposed on an Iranian bank under Schedule 7 of the Counter-Terrorism Act 2008, due to alleged links to Iran's nuclear program. The Treasury's direction barred UK financial institutions from dealing with Bank Mellat, interfering with its property rights under Article 1 of Protocol 1 (A1P1) to the European Convention on Human Rights (ECHR). By a 6-3 majority, the court found the measure

[54] *Dalston Projects Ltd v Secretary of State for Transport* and *Shvidler v Secretary of State for Foreign, Commonwealth and Development Affairs* [2024] EWCA Civ 172 (CA) ('*Shvidler II*') (27 February 2024).

[55] *Khan v Foreign, Commonwealth and Development Affairs* [2025] EWCA Civ 41 (24 January 2025).

[56] *Shvidler v Secretary of State for Foreign, Commonwealth and Development Affairs* and *Dalston Projects Ltd v Secretary of State for Transport* [2025] UKSC 30 (29 July 2025) ('*Shvidler III*').

[57] *Bank Mellat v HM Treasury (No 2)* [2013] UKSC 39 (19 June 2013).

disproportionate, emphasizing the need for rational justification when targeting specific entities amid broader risks.

Lord Reed, agreeing with Lord Sumption at [20], confirmed the four-limb proportionality test with the following key criteria: **8.45**

(1) whether the objective of the measure is sufficiently important to justify the limitation of a protected right;
(2) whether the measure is rationally connected to the objective;
(3) whether a less intrusive measure could have been used without unacceptably compromising the achievement of the objective; and
(4) whether, balancing the severity of the measure's effects on the rights of the persons to whom it applies against the importance of the objective, to the extent that the measure will contribute to its achievement, the former outweighs the latter.[58]

*Bank Mellat (No 2)* established a structured proportionality test that, post-Brexit, has become central to assessing the lawfulness of measures interfering with fundamental rights, including in the context of financial sanctions and designations under SAMLA. This test is routinely invoked in section 38 SAMLA challenges, where designated persons seek to set aside ministerial decisions on grounds such as disproportionality under the ECHR, particularly Article 8 (right to private life) and A1P1 (peaceful enjoyment of possessions). **8.46**

Courts have applied the *Bank Mellat* test in cases involving a section 38 challenge where the designation interferes with ECHR rights; see, for example, *Synesis*.[59] Courts conduct an 'objective' review (per Lord Reed in *R (Begum) v Special Immigration Appeals Commission*[60]) but afford ministers a 'wide margin of appreciation' in foreign policy and security matters. **8.47**

Recent section 38 SAMLA challenges demonstrate the *Bank Mellat* test's application in a UK sanctions law context: **8.48**

- In *Shvidler III,* the Supreme Court (majority) upheld Russia-related designations, applying *Bank Mellat (No 2)* to find rational connections and fair balance despite impacts on property rights: 'The question under this part of the proportionality test "is whether a less intrusive measure could have been used without unacceptably compromising the achievement of the objective." '[61]
- In *Dana Astra IOOO v Secretary of State for Foreign, Commonwealth and Development Affairs*, applying *Bank Mellat (No 2)*, the High Court found a Belarus designation proportionate, noting that although there was minimal UK impact, it was outweighed by deterrence objectives: 'The four questions are: (i) whether the

[58] ibid [74].
[59] *Synesis* (n 20).
[60] *R (Begum) v Special Immigration Appeals Commission* [2021] UKSC 7 (26 February 2021) [69].
[61] *Shvidler III* (n 56) [203], citing *Bank Mellat v HM Treasury* (No 2) [2013] UKSC 39.

objective is sufficiently important [... and] (iv) whether "a fair balance has been struck"'.[62]

## 2. The Standard of Court Review

8.49 In *Synesis*, Jay J held 'that this Court cannot stand in the shoes of the Defendant when conducting this review exercise under section 38 of SAMLA. Instead, the Court's role is to examine whether the Defendant's decision was either based on no evidence or was irrational.'[63]

8.50 That approach was nuanced in *Anzhelika Khan v SoSFCDO* ('*Khan*').[64] In *Khan*, Cockerill J identified central principles that have been historically emphasized in respect of 'testing decisions which impact on fundamental human rights (such as asylum and nationality claims as well as sanctions)',[65] namely:

> 26. In testing decisions which impact on fundamental human rights (such as asylum and nationality claims as well as sanctions) in the past a number of principles have been emphasised:
>
> 1) A review adopts administrative law concepts of lawfulness, reasonableness, and procedural fairness including: '*whether the decision-maker has acted in a way in which no reasonable decision-maker could have acted, or whether he has taken into account some irrelevant matter or has disregarded something to which he should have given weight, or has erred on a point of law*': *R (Begum) v Special Immigration Appeals Commission* [2021] AC 765;
> 2) Where a decision is taken which affects fundamental rights, an 'anxious scrutiny' standard applies. While derided by Carnwath LJ as an uninformative expression, the important point is that the invocation of that standard '*underlin[es] the very special human context in which such cases are brought*' and requires '*decisions to show by their reasoning that every factor which might tell in favour [of the person affected] has been properly taken into account*': *R (YH) v Secretary of State for the Home Department [2010] 4 All ER 448*, [24]; see also *Begum [2023] HRLR 6* at [46–49] where it was elided with using a '*more powerful microscope*'.
> 3) When considering whether a measure is compatible with the Convention, the Court must 'determine that matter objectively on the basis of its own assessment': *R (AAA (Syria)) v Secretary of State for the Home Department* [2013] 1 WLR 4433 [38–41] (Lord Reed and Lord Lloyd-Jones); *Begum* at [69] (Lord Reed).

[62] *Dana Astra IOOO v Secretary of State for Foreign, Commonwealth and Development Affairs* [2025] EWHC 289 (Admin) (11 February 2025) [275].
[63] *Synesis* (n 20) [81].
[64] *Anzhelika Khan v SoSFCDO* [2024] EWHC 361 (Admin) (20 February 2024).
[65] ibid [26]-[27].

> 27. As to the review of sanctions decisions under SAMLA, there is some guidance in the existing cases. In *R (Youssef) v Secretary of State for Foreign, Commonwealth and Development Affairs* [2022] 1 WLR 2454 [68–102] Garnham J explained that the review mechanism in s 38 of SAMLA is the means by which the State guarantees the minimum threshold of access to a court required to render the scheme compatible with Articles 6 and 8 of the Convention.[66]

In *Shvidler III,* the Supreme Court held that when a reviewing court carries out a proportionality assessment it must decide for itself if there has actually been a violation of Convention rights. The court's function is therefore not merely a secondary, reviewing function, dependent on establishing that the primary decision-maker misdirected itself, or acted irrationally or was guilty of procedural impropriety, stating: **8.51**

> 120. The Court of Appeal stated the law in relation to assessment of proportionality correctly. It is well established that the court has to make its own assessment whether a measure is proportionate to a legitimate aim. If a measure is not proportionate to a legitimate aim, it will be incompatible with the relevant Convention right and its adoption by the relevant public authority will be unlawful as contrary to section 6(1) of the HRA. The question of whether the action taken by the public authority is lawful or not is what the court has to decide on a challenge. As Singh LJ put it in his judgment (para 11), citing *Belfast City Council v Miss Behavin' Ltd* [2007] UKHL 19; [2007] 1 WLR 1420 ('*Miss Behavin' Ltd*'), paras 13–15, the question whether an act is incompatible with a Convention right is a question of substance for the court itself to decide; the court's function is not the conventional one in public law of reviewing the process by which a public authority reached its decision. As Lord Hoffmann explained in *Miss Behavin' Ltd* (para 15), the question is whether there has actually been a violation of Convention rights 'and not whether the decision-maker properly considered the question of whether [the applicant's] rights would be violated or not'. Other recent authorities which make this point include *R (Begum) v Special Immigration Appeals Commission* [2021] UKSC 7; [2021] AC 765, para 69, and *R (AAA (Syria)) v Secretary of State for the Home Department* [2023] UKSC 42; [2023] 1 WLR 4433 ('*AAA (Syria)*'), paras 56–57 and 71. In this sense, it can be said that the court's function is not merely a secondary, reviewing, function dependent on establishing that the primary decision-maker misdirected itself or acted irrationally or was guilty of procedural impropriety.
>
> 121. However, in a challenge based on Convention rights under the HRA to action by a public authority, it is not accurate to say that the court becomes the primary decision-maker in the full sense of that term: see *R (Daly) v Secretary of State for the Home Department* [2001] UKHL 26; [2001] 2 AC 532 ('*Daly*'), paras 26–28; *Huang*, para 13 ('although the Convention calls for a more exacting standard of review, it remains the case that the judge is not the primary decision-maker'); *Bank Mellat*, para 21 (Lord

[66] ibid.

Sumption) and paras 70–71 (Lord Reed: '[t]he intensity of review varies considerably according to the right in issue and the context in which the question arises'); *R (Lord Carlile of Berriew) v Secretary of State for the Home Department* [2014] UKSC 60; [2015] AC 945 ('*Lord Carlile*'), paras 20, 22, 31 and 34 (Lord Sumption: 'no review, however intense, can entitle the court to substitute its own decision for that of the constitutional decision-maker'; 'a court of review does not usurp the function of the decision-maker, even when Convention rights are engaged'). The court's role is to assess the lawfulness of the authority's action against the substantive legal criteria which are inherent in the Convention rights, including the criterion of proportionality. The public authority decides on the action it will take, and hence is the primary decision-maker; but the court makes its own assessment whether such action is proportionate, and hence lawful, or not.

**8.52** The Supreme Court stated that they may either apply a 'review approach', assessing whether the lower court's proportionality evaluation was arrived at properly and reasonably, or a 'fresh determination approach,' where the appellate court conducts its own full assessment. The choice depends on context, particularly the novelty or general significance of the case.[67]

**8.53** In *Shvidler III*, the Supreme Court unanimously held that the appeals warranted the 'fresh determination' approach, given their role as test cases under the sanctions regime. Applying the *Bank Mellat* test:

- Legitimate aim (limb i): The court recognized the aim of deterring Russian aggression as 'one of the most vital aims that the UK government has been called upon to pursue in recent years', entirely justifying interference with Convention rights.[68]
- Rational connection (limb ii): The court rejected the appellants' contention that sanctions having minimal individual effect cannot be justified, finding that, generally, where there is a very important public interest at stake, a less direct connection may be sufficient.[69] The court also observed that it is difficult to assess whether any particular sanction measure, or indeed any of the other measures put in place by the UK and its international partners, has had or may in the future have an influence or effect.[70] Further, there was no need to show that the particular sanctions imposed would by themselves achieve such purposes; it is important to have regard to the cumulative effect of all the measures taken.[71] All that is needed is for the Secretary of State to show some plausible contribution made to that effect by the measure in question.[72] In *Shvidler*, the appellant's ties with prominent Russian

[67] *Shvidler III* (n 56) [44], [160], and [165].
[68] *Shvidler III* (n 56) [166]–[73].
[69] *Shvidler III* (n 56) [177].
[70] *Shvidler III* (n 56) [179].
[71] *Shvidler III* (n 56) [188]–[92].
[72] *Shvidler III* (n 56) [193]–[4].

oligarchs Abramovich and Evraz justified a rational connection; in *Dalston*, even indirect economic symbolism—the detention of the superyacht—contributed to the regime's impact: 'some plausible contribution [has been] made'.[73]

- Less intrusive means (limb iii): The court concluded that there were no less intrusive measures available that would achieve the objective without compromising effectiveness.[74]
- Fair balance (limb iv): The majority recognized that the sanctions in *Shvidler* had a 'severe, open-ended and drastic effect' on a British citizen but held that essential interests and needs could still be met via licensing mechanisms, and that sanctions must necessarily be severe to be effective. Thus, a fair balance had been struck. In *Dalston*, the limited financial impact from the yacht's detention[75] and its symbolic value as conspicuous consumption[76] supported proportionality.

Lord Leggatt, in his vigorous dissent in Shvidler's case, stated that the rational connection requirement (limb ii) was not satisfied. He described the measures imposed against Eugene Shvidler as 'unjust and disproportionate', saying that the Government's reasons did 'not come close to justifying such a drastic curtailment of his liberty', and decried the limitations on Shvidler's access to his own funds as 'Orwellian'.[77] **8.54**

## 3. Judicial Deference

On the question of what weight the court is to place on the decision maker's assessment in the context of reviewing its proportionality analysis, in *Shvidler I* (the second delisting challenge brought to the High Court under SAMLA), Garnham J, with reference to the proportionality test in *Bank Mellat v HM Treasury (No 2)*, held that:[78] **8.55**

> 91. Undoubtedly, this is a case where close scrutiny is necessary in order to adjudicate on a complaint that Convention rights have been infringed. And it is the structured analysis articulated in *Bank Mellat* that must be applied. But the court does not assume the role of primary decision maker on issues that turn on the exercise of judgment or the determination of policy, limiting itself instead to asking whether the decision was one properly open to the executive. It will recognise the constitutional competence of the Secretary of State and his officials on matters of foreign affairs, attaching particular

[73] *Shvidler III* (n 56) [174]–[80], [195]–[201].
[74] *Shvidler III* (n 56) [203]
[75] *Shvidler III* (n 56) [204]–[209].
[76] *Shvidler III* (n 56) [190].
[77] *Shvidler III* (n 56) [300]–[19], [324].
[78] *Shvidler v Secretary of State for Foreign, Commonwealth and Development Affairs* [2023] EWHC 2121 (Admin) ('*Shvidler I*') [91] and [92]. See also *Graham William Phillips v The Secretary of State for Foreign, Commonwealth and Development Affairs* [2024] EWHC 32 (Admin); *Shvidler II* (n 54) [138], adopting the approach in *Shvidler I*.

weight to the judgments of a primary decision-maker with special institutional competence who has considered all the relevant material.

92. Applying that approach, the Court must consider closely the particular question that falls for decision so as to gauge the extent to which it should defer to the expertise of the Secretary of State and the extent to which it can itself form a judgment. In my view, the question as to how far the evidence relied upon by the Secretary of State supports the contention that the Claimant's designation could contribute to achieving that objective (Limb 2 of *Bank Mellat*) is not entirely a question of United Kingdom foreign policy on which the Court is unqualified to form a view, nor is it a subject on which the Court should necessarily be slow to interfere on grounds of institutional competence. The Secretary of State is the primary decision-maker under the statute but the Court is well placed to judge the reasonableness of his analysis. The other limbs of *Bank Mellat* require a similar approach.

**8.56** In *Shvidler III*, by ruling that the 'court's task is to assess the proportionality of the measure for itself',[79] the Supreme Court thereby rejected an approach of blanket deference to ministerial decision-making. However, it also stated that the weight accorded to the Secretary of State's judgment will vary according to context. In areas of institutional competence, such as foreign affairs and national security, the executive's assessment will command particular respect; but this does not relieve the courts of their duty to decide for themselves whether a fair balance has been struck between individual rights and community interests.[80]

**8.57** When applying the *Bank Mellat* test afresh, the court in *Shvidler III* gave weight to the Secretary of State's expertise, especially on the second limb of rational connection, accepting by majority that the connection between the appellant's designation and the statutory objective was 'plausible', despite arguments about limited individual effect. This approach emphasizes that the sanctions regime must be assessed cumulatively.[81]

**8.58** Lord Leggatt's dissenting judgment criticized the majority for excessive deference to the executive, stating that courts must rigorously scrutinize encroachments on fundamental rights without a wide margin of appreciation which has the effect of abdicating judicial responsibility.[82] He noted the 'catastrophic impact' on Shvidler and his family, including open-ended asset freezes with no end in sight, and rejected the fair balance metaphor as misleading: '[i]t embodies a false assumption that there is some common system of measurement which enables benefits to society as a whole to be weighed against costs to the affected individual to decide which outweighs the other and so should have priority.'[83] Lord Leggatt described the proper approach to proportionality in the following terms:

[79] *Shvidler III* (n 56) [120].
[80] *Shvidler III* (n 56) [120]–[125].
[81] *Shvidler III* (n 56) [174]–[80], [195]–[201].
[82] *Shvidler III* (n 56) [256], [286].
[83] *Shvidler III* (n 56) [292], [297], [278].

What is required in deciding whether an interference with a fundamental right or freedom is proportionate is a judgment about whether the interference is just, having regard to its impact on the individual's rights and the nature and strength of the reasons relied on to justify it. That is a judgment which under the division of responsibilities in the UK constitution is allocated to the courts.[84]

## 4. Compatibility with Convention Rights

The case of *Graham William Phillips v The Secretary of State for Foreign, Commonwealth and Development Affairs* was the first in England and Wales to consider the relationship between financial sanctions and freedom of expression.[85] The claimant, a journalist, sought court review of his designation on the basis that, inter alia, he was designated because of his political views which, it was submitted, was *ultra vires* the powers given to the UK Government under SAMLA. In rejecting the application, Johnson J held that SAMLA was intended to permit the Secretary of State (in certain circumstances) to make regulations that authorize the imposition of sanctions in response to the exercise of free speech and that impact on freedom of expression,[86] and that it 'authorises the making of regulations that interfere with common law and Convention rights'.[87] Additionally, the court held that there was power in SAMLA and the regulations made under it to impose financial sanctions on someone in his position (a journalist) for acts of 'expression'.[88] **8.59**

The February 2025 decision of *Dana Astra IOOO v Secretary of State for Foreign, Commonwealth and Development Affairs* further explored the compatibility of UK sanctions with ECHR rights, specifically addressing whether the designation of a foreign entity with no UK assets fell within the UK's jurisdiction under Article 1 ECHR.[89] Saini J held that it did not, as jurisdiction is primarily territorial and no exceptional extraterritorial circumstances applied. He rejected arguments based on Swiss ECtHR cases like *Nada v Switzerland* and *Al-Dulimi v Switzerland*.[90] Assuming there had been jurisdiction, the designation was proportionate under the *Bank Mellat* test: it was rationally connected to the sanctions objectives of encouraging Belarus to respect human rights and democracy, with no less intrusive measures being sufficient, and it struck a fair balance given the public interest and minimal UK impact on the claimant.[91] This reinforces that SAMLA designations may interfere with property rights abroad **8.60**

[84] *Shvidler III* (n 56) [280].
[85] *Graham William Phillips v The Secretary of State for Foreign, Commonwealth and Development Affairs* [2024] EWHC 32 (Admin) (12 January 2024).
[86] ibid [91].
[87] ibid [167].
[88] ibid [125] and [126].
[89] *Dana Astra* (n 62) [46]–[62].
[90] *Nada v Switzerland* App no 10593/08 (ECtHR, 12 September 2012); *Al-Dulimi v Switzerland* App no 5809/08 (ECtHR, 21 June 2016).
[91] *Dana Astra* (n 62) [64]–[83].

without necessarily engaging ECHR protections unless the entity is within UK jurisdiction, building on the *Phillips* ruling by clarifying limits on Convention applicability in autonomous UK sanctions regimes.

**8.61** *Dana Astra* demonstrates that SAMLA designations of foreign entities without UK ties will likely evade ECtHR scrutiny, reducing successful challenges based on extraterritorial rights. This aligns with post-Brexit autonomy, prioritizing foreign policy flexibility over expansive human rights obligations. However, it underscores the need for evidence of UK 'possessions' to engage A1P1, potentially encouraging claimants to demonstrate local impact. For practitioners, it reinforces that administrative routes must be exhausted first and robust proportionality arguments must be presented.

**8.62** Compared to *Phillips*, *Dana Astra* shifts focus from freedom of expression to property, but both affirm SAMLA's broad powers. Future cases may test hybrid claims (e.g. expression plus property) or appeal to the ECtHR for wider extraterritoriality.

### 5. Admissibility of Evidence

**8.63** In *Fridman,* the court held that it will be very slow to allow a party to adduce post-decision evidence in a judicial review context, unless it is considering proportionality in the context of a human rights challenge. The admission of such evidence is inconsistent with the proper role of judicial review which is only to consider the lawfulness of a decision and the process leading up to it.[92]

### 6. Damages

**8.64** Where a court would otherwise have the power to award damages, it may not do so in relation to relevant sanctions claims, unless it is satisfied that the decision concerned was made in bad faith.[93] Given the outcome of court reviews in the section 38 SAMLA context thus far, and the repeated confirmation of the extent of the Government's discretion in making designations, it is uncontroversial to consider that the prospect of the Administrative Court making findings of bad faith—leading to an award of damages against the Government—is low.

## F. Disclosure and Closed Material Proceedings

**8.65** A designated person may not always be informed of all or some of the reasons why a revocation request has been refused by the Minister, as the Minister has the discretion

[92] *Fridman* (n 8) [65] and [66].
[93] SAMLA 2018, s 39.

to exclude any matter(s) in the interests of national security or international relations, for reasons connected with the prevention or detection of serious crime, or in the interests of justice. Regulation 8(3) of the Sanctions Review Procedure (EU Exit) Regulations 2018 enables the Minister to withhold such information (see paragraph 8.35, above).

The same is true in respect of challenges to the courts made under section 38 of SAMLA as, by virtue of section 40(1), the court may hear sensitive evidence not disclosed to the applicant/claimant in a 'closed material' procedure. This closed material procedure has been imported from domestic anti-terrorist legislation, specifically sections 66 to 68 of the Counter-Terrorism Act 2008 which enable courts to consider sensitive material (e.g. intelligence or foreign policy data) in closed sessions, with special advocates representing the claimant's interests without disclosing the material to them.[94] The use of closed material procedures reflects the balance between ensuring a fair hearing under Article 6 ECHR and protecting national security, a tension central to sanctions litigation given designations' severe impacts on property and personal rights. **8.66**

As of August 2025, no court has substantively considered disclosure in the context of designation challenges under section 38 of SAMLA. However, recent cases provide indirect guidance, and principles from broader judicial review, counter-terrorism, and pre-SAMLA sanctions cases illuminate the likely approach courts will adopt. These emphasize sufficient disclosure to enable 'meaningful and focused representations' while permitting restrictions where security demands. **8.67**

## 1. General Disclosure Principles in Judicial Review

The test for the level of disclosure required in judicial review proceedings generally is that the level of detail required must be such as to enable the claimant to make 'meaningful and focused representations'.[95] *De Smith's Judicial Review*, 9th edition, at 9-084, provides as follows: **8.68**

> In order to protect their interests, the person must also be enabled to controvert, correct or comment on other evidence or information that may be relevant to the decision and influential material on which the decision-maker intends to rely; including, in certain cases, disclosure of representations or information provided by third parties. At least in some circumstances, there will also be a duty on the decision-maker to

[94] See Part 2 of the Justice and Security Act 2013 and CPR Part 82 for the current framework on closed material procedures. See also *Bank Mellat v HM Treasury (No.1)* [2013] UKSC 38 and *Bank Mellat v HM Treasury (No. 2)* [2013] UKSC 39.

[95] *R v Secretary of State for the Home Department, ex parte Harry* [1998] 1 WLR 1737 [1748]; *R (on the application of Breckland DC) v Electoral Commission Boundary Committee for England* [2009] EWCA Civ 239, [2009] PTSR 1611 [44], [46] (important to enable 'effective representations' to be made and to publish enough material to enable all those interested to respond intelligently). But see *R (on the application of O) v Independent Appeal Panel for Tower Hamlets LBC* [2007] EWHC 1455 (Admin), [2007] ELR 468 [42] (no general duty to draw attention to every provision that might be relevant to the conduct of an appeal).

disclose information favourable to the applicant, as well as information prejudicial to their case.[96]

## 2. Pre-SAMLA Sanctions and Disclosure

**8.69** *R (John Arnold Bredenkamp) v Secretary of State for Foreign and Commonwealth Affairs* concerned the claimant's application for disclosure in relation to their challenge to a decision of the Foreign Secretary to recommend the claimant and his companies for sanctions designation and listing under Annex III to Regulation EC 314/2004.[97] The court held:

> [I]t is established that the Court can order disclosure to be provided by the Defendant in appropriate cases. Orders for disclosure are not automatic. They should be made only where 'disclosure appears to be necessary in order to resolve the matter fairly and justly', see *Tweed* at paragraph 3. Cases involving proportionality reviews are one type of case where disclosure may be necessary but, even in such cases, disclosure orders are likely to remain exceptional, see *Tweed* at paragraph 56. The decision for disclosure must be made on the facts of each individual case.[98]

**8.70** This case underscores that disclosure decisions are fact-specific, with courts balancing fairness against security. In *Bredenkamp*, partial disclosure was ordered to clarify the Foreign Secretary's reasoning, suggesting courts considering section 38 applications may similarly order limited disclosure to ensure fairness without compromising sensitive intelligence.

## 3. Counter-Terrorism and Fairness Standards

**8.71** In *SoSHD v AF (No 3)*, the House of Lords addressed disclosure in control order cases under the Prevention of Terrorism Act 2005, which, like SAMLA, involve closed material procedures.[99] In *AF (No 3)*, the court held that a controlee must be given sufficient information about the allegations against them to enable them to give effective instructions. In *Bank Mellat v HM Treasury*, which involved an application to set aside restrictive measures imposed against the claimant under section 63 of the Counter-Terrorism Act 2008, the court confirmed that where the restrictive measures in issue severely limited a person's ability to function normally, the approach taken by the House of Lords in *AF (No 3)* was correct.[100]

[96] Catherine Donnelly SC, Dr Joanna Bell, and Ivan Hare KC, *De Smith's Judicial Review* (9th edn, Sweet & Maxwell 2024) para 9-084.

[97] *R (John Arnold Bredenkamp) v Secretary of State for Foreign and Commonwealth Affairs* [2013] EWHC 2480 (Admin).

[98] ibid [18].

[99] *SoSHD v AF (No 3)* [2010] 2 AC 269.

[100] *Bank Mellat v HM Treasury* [2014] EWHC 3631 (Admin).

### 4. Judicial Observations on Sanctions' Impact

As Cockerill J noted in *Khan,* 'the effects of being designated are capable of being very significant.'[101] This underscores the need for robust disclosure to enable challenges, as designations can disrupt livelihoods and reputations. In *Khan* the court referenced *AF (No 3)* indirectly, emphasizing 'anxious scrutiny' in cases which impact human rights, suggesting disclosure must be sufficient to meet this heightened standard.[102] **8.72**

### 5. Developments in 2025

Recent SAMLA cases provide tangential insights into disclosure practices. In *Dana Astra* the court heard an application to redact civil servant names in disclosure documents, granting it under CPR 79.23 for national security reasons.[103] The Secretary of State relied on *R (IAB) v Secretary of State for the Home Department*, in which the Court of Appeal considered whether a defendant in judicial review proceedings was entitled routinely to redact disclosed documents so as to remove the names of civil servants (including junior civil servants).[104] The court in that case held that a defendant was not permitted to apply such redactions as a matter of routine.[105] Instead, 'good and specific reasons' would be required for redactions, for example where the redaction of names was justified for reasons of national security or where there was evidence of a real risk to the personal safety of the individual concerned. In granting the application, Saini J held that, 'in my judgment, this evidence amply satisfies the requirement to show "good and specific reasons" of the type and nature contemplated by IAB'.[106] While not a substantive disclosure dispute, this illustrates the role of the closed material procedure in protecting sensitive material. **8.73**

Against this backdrop, we can readily anticipate future section 38 SAMLA challenges in which courts will determine whether the disclosure that is necessary for fair and just resolution has been provided, thereby ensuring claimants can give effective instructions in line with *AF (No 3)*. **8.74**

[101] *Khan* (n 64) [24], citing *Ahmed v HM Treasury* [2010] 2 AC 534 [37]–[9].
[102] *Khan* (n 64) [26].
[103] *Dana Astra* (n 62) [97]–[101].
[104] *R (IAB) v Secretary of State for the Home Department* [2024] EWCA Civ 66.
[105] ibid [36].
[106] *Dana Astra* (n 62) [101].

# 9

# Sanctions in Commercial Disputes

*Francis Bond and Tom Cornell*



## A. Introduction

**9.01** For as long as there have been sanctions, there have been sanctions disputes. Trade and other economic sanctions are by no means a recent invention and, unsurprisingly, have always generated commercial litigation in some form or another. For example, in the case of *Millar & Co Ltd v Taylor & Co Ltd*,[1] which was decided in 1916, the claimant argued that its obligations under a contract for the supply of confectionery for export had been discharged as a result of British Government proclamations outlawing the export of foodstuffs from the UK after the outbreak of the First World War. However, the nature, volume, and scope of sanctions measures have proliferated at an incredible speed in recent years and particularly since the Russian invasion of Ukraine in 2022. The Russian invasion also came shortly after the UK had effectively rewritten its sanctions legislation in the wake of the decision to leave the EU. The Sanctions and Anti-Money Laundering Act 2018 (SAMLA) came into full force on 31 December 2020, at the end of the Brexit transition period.

**9.02** The combination of an entirely new and independent UK sanctions framework and its extensive and fast-moving deployment in respect of the Russian invasion of Ukraine

[1] *Millar & Co Ltd v Taylor & Co Ltd* [1916] 1 KB 402.

Francis Bond and Tom Cornell, *Sanctions in Commercial Disputes* In: *UK Sanctions Law and Practice*. Edited by: Amanda Pinto KC, Alexandre Haines, and Sophie O'Sullivan, Oxford University Press. 
DOI: 10.1093/oso/9780198964179.003.0009

has led to a sharp increase in sanctions litigation in the UK courts. The cases relating to the UK's Russia sanctions—i.e. the Russia (Sanctions) (EU Exit) Regulations 2019 (the 'Russia Regulations')—started to come through the courts in 2023 and continued apace throughout 2024. At the time of writing, the Supreme Court has recently handed down its decision in the *Shvidler* case,[2] with another appeal to the Supreme Court regarding the Russia Regulations pending.[3] The law in this area is therefore still developing and likely to continue doing so in the coming years. This chapter aims to provide an overview of how the UK courts have dealt with commercial litigation involving sanctions issues to date.

Importantly, the English courts have upheld the right of access to the courts in the UK sanctions context, emphasizing, for example, that designated persons retain the right to issue proceedings and obtain judicial determination of their claims before the courts: '[t]he court system in England and Wales does not have outlaws or [ … ] pariahs'.[4] The courts have also held that the principle of legality—whereby fundamental rights can only be curtailed by express wording or necessary implication—applies in this context and that sanctions legislation must be construed accordingly.[5] As a result, the English courts remain open both to designated persons seeking to vindicate their claims,[6] and to those seeking to bring claims against designated persons.[7] Notwithstanding the openness of the courts, there are a number of practical, procedural, and substantive issues that would-be litigants and their legal representatives should be aware of before instituting proceedings before the English courts which involve either designated persons specifically or sanctions issues more broadly. **9.03**

The remainder of this chapter is divided into three broad sections as follows: (i) practical and procedural issues, including the courts' interpretation of certain problematic sanctions provisions (section B); (ii) key trends in commercial litigation involving substantive sanctions issues (section C); and (iii) sanctions issues in commercial arbitration (section D). **9.04**

## B. Practical Issues and Key Sanctions Provisions

The prohibitions imposed by UK sanctions regimes create significant practical and procedural difficulties for commercial litigation involving or relating to designated persons. For example, almost all UK sanctions regulations impose a prohibition on 'dealing with' funds and economic resources owned by designated persons.[8] That prohibition has been treated as imposing an obligation to freeze funds received from **9.05**

[2] *Shvidler v Secretary of State for Foreign, Commonwealth and Development Affairs* [2025] UKSC 30.
[3] *UniCredit Bank AG, London Branch v Celestial Aviation Services Limited* (UKSC 2024/0103).
[4] *Mints v PJSC National Bank Trust and PJSC Bank Okritie Financial Corporation* [2023] EWCA Civ 1132 [178] (Sir Julian Flaux PC).
[5] ibid [179] and [187].
[6] See *Mints* (n 4).
[7] See (e.g.) *Fortenova Grupa DD v LLC Shushary Holding* [2023] EWHC 1165 (Ch).
[8] See e.g. the Russia Regulations 2019, reg 11(1).

designated persons,[9] which means that, ordinarily, any payment received from a designated person must be frozen by the recipient. For practical purposes, this amounts to a prohibition on UK lawyers receiving payment from designated persons in respect of legal services. Interestingly, the High Court recently reached the view, albeit obiter, that the receipt of funds owned by a designated person would not, without more, amount to a breach of the prohibition on dealing.[10]

**9.06** There are also prohibitions on making funds or economic resources available to designated persons, so that, among other things, there is a prohibition on paying a designated person's costs of litigation. There are therefore certain baseline difficulties to contend with. These difficulties are exacerbated by the breadth of the language used—including the terms 'dealing with', 'making available', 'funds', and 'economic resources'—which raises the question of how far-reaching Parliament intended the relevant prohibitions to be and whether it intended an encroachment on certain fundamental common law rights. Some of these issues have now been addressed by the courts, in particular in the *Mints* case, discussed at paragraphs 9.08–11 below. Moreover, the Office of Financial Sanctions Implementation (OFSI) has issued a number of general licences and published guidance in order to clarify the scope of the restrictions and, to a certain extent, facilitate litigation.[11]

## 1. Legal Representation

**9.07** The first practical issue that arises is legal representation. As noted in paragraph 9.05, there is a prohibition in practice on UK law firms and counsel receiving payment for the provision of legal services. That prohibition is mitigated, however, by two factors. The first is the existence of a specific licensing ground in most UK sanctions regimes authorizing the 'payment of (a) reasonable professional fees for the provision of legal services, or (b) reasonable expenses associated with the provision of legal services'.[12] Designated persons may therefore apply for a licence authorizing the payment of legal fees and associated expenses. The second factor is that OFSI has issued a general licence under the UK Autonomous Sanctions Regulations allowing lawyers to receive payment from persons designated under those sanctions regimes for the provision of legal advice, provided that they have met the terms of the licence.[13] On that basis, UK

[9] HM Treasury adopted a policy in 2014 whereby any funds received directly or indirectly by a UK person from a designated person outside the EU must be frozen. Although that policy was adopted pursuant to changes in EU law, there is nothing at present to suggest that OFSI has abandoned the policy since the UK left the EU.

[10] *Celestial Aviation Trading Ltd v Volga-Dnper Logistics BV* [2025] EWHC 1156 (Comm) [40(ii)].

[11] See e.g. OFSI, 'UK Financial Sanctions FAQs' (1 May 2024) <https://www.gov.uk/government/publications/uk-financial-sanctions-faqs/uk-financial-sanctions-faqs> accessed 5 December 2024.

[12] See e.g. the Russia (Sanctions) (EU Exit) Regulations 2019 ('Russia Regulations'), sch 5, para 3; the Democratic People's Republic of Korea (Sanctions) (EU Exit) Regulations 2019, sch 3, para 2; and the Myanmar (Sanctions) Regulations 2021, sch 4, para 3.

[13] General Licence INT/2025/7323088 came into force on 29 October 2025 and is granted under the UK Autonomous Sanctions Regulations listed in Annex 1 of the General Licence. Previously, the legal services General Licence—the last one being General Licence INT/2025/6160920 which expired on 28 October 2025—applied only to the Russia and Belarus Regulations.

law firms and counsel may not have to apply for a specific licence in order to represent certain designated persons and receive payment for those legal services. The terms of the general licence include a cap on legal fees and expenses and a requirement to report any payments received under the general licence to HM Treasury.

## 2. Judgment for a Designated Person

The second issue is whether a UK court can enter judgment in favour of a designated person. This was the key issue in *PJSC National Bank Trust v Mints* before the Administrative Court, [14] which involved a fraud claim brought by two Russian banks, one of which was a designated entity, against a group of non-designated individuals. The non-designated defendants argued that the court was prohibited from entering judgment in favour of designated persons, and made an application for a stay of the proceedings on that basis. In particular, the defendants argued that entering judgment in favour of a designated person would infringe the prohibition on making funds available to a designated person,[15] as well as the prohibition on dealing with funds or economic resources owned, held, or controlled by a designated person.[16] The High Court dismissed the Appellant's application for an indefinite stay, but granted permission to appeal to the Court of Appeal. The Court of Appeal rejected that argument and held that, as a matter of statutory construction, a claim or a cause of action is not a 'fund' for the purpose of the applicable sanctions restrictions, although it is an 'economic resource'. Further, the entry of a judgment did not constitute 'making funds available', because 'the words "make funds available" are simply not apt to describe the exercise by the court of one of its prime judicial functions in administering justice, of entering judgment on a valid cause of action'.[17] The same was found to be true in respect of the prohibition on 'dealing with' economic resources: '[t]he court would not receive anything in exchange for the causes of action. Furthermore, the words "dealing with" are simply not apt to describe the exercise by the court of its judicial function of entering judgment on a valid cause of action.'[18] **9.08**

Although these conclusions were reached irrespective of the principle of legality, the Court of Appeal emphasized the importance of that principle and found that there were no express words in the relevant sanctions legislation to displace it: 'the principle of legality is engaged in this case and needs to be considered as one of the principles of construction in construing the meaning of SAMLA'.[19] The court held that the right of access to the court, which includes the right to have a claim adjudicated upon and to obtain judgment in one's favour, is a fundamental common law right which would be **9.09**

[14] *PJSC National Bank Trust v Mints* [2023] EWHC 118 (Comm); see also Court of Appeal *Mints* judgment (n 4).
[15] Russia Regulations 2019, reg 12.
[16] Russia Regulations 2019, reg 11.
[17] *Mints* (n 4) [202].
[18] *Mints* (n 4) [208].
[19] *Mints* (n 4) [179] and [187].

curtailed by an indefinite stay of the proceedings.[20] When applied to the relevant provisions of the Russia Regulations, the court found that the principle of legality rendered the interpretation advanced by the non-designated individuals 'unarguable'.[21] Finally, the court observed that the existence of section 44 SAMLA—which provides a defence to liability in civil proceedings where an act is 'done in the reasonable belief that the act is in compliance with' sanctions regulations—militated in favour of the legislation preserving a designated person's right of access to the courts, 'since otherwise the statutory defence under that section would be unnecessary'.[22] Section 44 of SAMLA is dealt with at paragraphs 9.12–14 below.

**9.10** Separately, the claimants in *Mints* argued that the court was an emanation of the Crown and therefore not a 'person' for the purpose of compliance with UK sanctions prohibitions. The Court of Appeal did not deal with this point so it remains open:

> [I]t is not necessary to determine whether other ways in which the claimants put their case, that the court is not a person or that, as an emanation of the Crown it is not bound by the Regulations, are correct. It would seem more sensible to leave determination of those issues to another case where they are necessary for the decision.[23]

## 3. Costs of Litigation

**9.11** The third issue concerns other costs and expenses associated with litigation. These costs might include, for example, the payment of adverse costs orders by designated persons or the payment of funds into court as security for costs. The issue of whether OFSI has the power to grant licences for the payment of these types of costs and expenses was also considered in *Mints*.[24] In particular, the defendants argued that OFSI could not issue licences for these costs and expenses on the basis that they fell outside the scope of any of the licensing grounds contained in the Russia Regulations. Both the first instance court and Court of Appeal disagreed and found that the payment of adverse costs orders and security for costs was covered by the wording of Schedule 5, paragraph 3 of the Russia Regulations ('payment of (a) reasonable professional fees for the provision of legal services, or (b) reasonable expenses associated with the provision of legal services'). In respect of adverse costs orders, the Court of Appeal held that the wording of Schedule 5, paragraph 3 was 'wide enough to cover an opposing party's fees' and covered both the voluntary payment of legal fees and the court-ordered payment of legal fees.[25] It was common ground that if paragraph 3 covered adverse costs orders, it must also cover security for costs.[26] The court held that OFSI was also able to issue a

[20] *Mints* (n 4) [178], [182], and [187].
[21] *Mints* (n 4) [203] and [209].
[22] *Mints* (n 4) [210].
[23] *Mints* (n 4) [211].
[24] *Mints* (n 4).
[25] *Mints* (n 4) [217]–[18].
[26] *Mints* (n 4) [222].

licence enabling compliance with costs orders in favour of a designated person.[27] First, there was no question of a 'net gain' to a designated person's funds; and second, if it were otherwise, then 'an opposing party could take every unmeritorious point with impunity safe from any costs liability, which obviously cannot have been the intention of Parliament in passing the Regulations'.[28]

## 4. The S 44 Defence

The fourth issue that practitioners should be aware of in this area is section 44 of SAMLA. As mentioned above, section 44 of SAMLA states that a person will not be liable to any civil proceedings for an act or omission 'done in the reasonable belief that the act is in compliance with' sanctions regulations imposed under section 1 of SAMLA. The section therefore provides a substantive defence to civil claims brought in the UK courts relating to steps taken (or not taken) in the reasonable belief that they were taken (or not taken) in compliance with UK sanctions obligations. Further, the Explanatory Notes to section 44 state that the provision 'aims to protect people from any adverse results generated by compliance (for example, a breach of a contract to supply goods that are prohibited from export by sanctions)'. Section 44 was considered by the Court of Appeal in *Celestial Aviation Services Ltd v UniCredit Bank GmbH, London Branch*, which involved a claim brought for the non-payment of a debt incurred under letters of credit.[29] The defendant bank argued that it was prohibited from paying the debt pursuant to regulation 28(3) of the Russia Regulations, which prohibits the provision of financial services in pursuance of or in connection with an arrangement whose object or effect is, inter alia, the export of restricted goods. The bank also argued that section 44 protected it from civil liability because it had failed to pay the debt in compliance with regulation 28(3) of the Russia Regulations. 9.12

The Court of Appeal confirmed that in order to rely on section 44, a defendant must show both (i) a subjective belief that the relevant act was done in compliance with applicable sanctions regulations, and (ii) that its belief was objectively reasonable. Here, the court emphasized that it 'is important to avoid viewing the position with the benefit of hindsight, having heard argument from well-prepared leading Counsel and with the benefit of judicial consideration that might ultimately appear to make clear what was in fact not at all clear at the relevant time'.[30] 9.13

The Court of Appeal concluded that the defendant bank in the case did believe that payment under the letters of credit would breach regulation 28(3), and that its belief was reasonable in the circumstances. This conclusion was unsurprising given that the court 9.14

[27] *Mints* (n 4) [222].
[28] *Mints* (n 4) [222].
[29] *Celestial Aviation Services Ltd v UniCredit Bank GmbH, London Branch* [2024] EWCA Civ 628.
[30] ibid [73].

had previously concluded that the bank's belief about the relevant sanctions prohibition was not only reasonable, but correct. However, having found that the bank's belief was reasonable, the court then considered the scope of section 44, including the question of the type of civil proceedings to which it could apply. Ultimately, the court found that section 44 protects against 'a liability which is created as a result of something done (or not done) in the reasonable belief that it is in compliance with a sanctions regulation. It is not concerned to protect against pre-existing liabilities'.[31] On that basis, section 44 cannot preclude liability for civil proceedings in respect of a claim to recover a debt, because the debt is not created as a result of the defendant's non-compliance with sanctions regulations; rather, the debt is a pre-existing liability.[32] That is an important limitation to the scope of the section, albeit that the court also confirmed that section 44 would preclude liability in damages (in, for example, those resulting from a failure by the defendant to supply goods that are prohibited from export by sanctions).

## 5. Ownership and Control

**9.15** The meaning of the legislative term 'owned or controlled directly or indirectly' has become a key point of contention in sanctions-related disputes. Such a term is found in each jurisdictional regime (e.g. regulation 7 of the Russia Regulations). Chapter 3, paragraphs 3.48–71 set out in detail the key examples of judicial comment on the term thus far: in *Mints* (at the High Court and in the Court of Appeal),[33] *Litasco*,[34] and, most recently, *Hellard*.[35]

**9.16** All global sanctions regimes tend to function through the application of asset freezes, not just against the persons on the respective sanctions lists, but also against any entities they own or control. The intention—which was a broad requirement of United Nations sanctions resolutions, but which each UN Member State interprets in their own way—is to ensure that the sanctions apply as comprehensively against their targets as possible, and that designated persons cannot avoid their effects through holding assets at arm's length.

**9.17** The UK's current ownership and control regime is built on the previous guidance provided by the EU, solidifying that non-binding guidance into a legislative provision. We use regulation 7 of the Russia Regulations to demonstrate the inherent ambiguity that arises from a provision being drafted as broadly and vaguely as possible in a bid to prevent circumvention of the asset freeze. Regulation 7's ambiguity has led to the proliferation of judicial interpretations of its meaning. Regulation 7(4) is worth quoting in full, as the ambiguity is plain in its construction:

[31] ibid [87].
[32] ibid [90].
[33] See *Mints* (n 4) and (n 14).
[34] *Litasco SA v Der Mond Oil* [2023] EWHC 2866 (Comm).
[35] *Hellard v OJSC Rossiysky Kredit Bank* [2024] EWHC 1783 (Ch).

> The second condition is that it is reasonable, having regard to all the circumstances, to expect that P would (if P chose to) be able, in most cases or in significant respects, by whatever means and whether directly or indirectly, to achieve the result that affairs of C are conducted in accordance with P's wishes.

The words 'if P chose to' in parenthesis were central to the four recent cases referred to in paragraph 9.15 above. 9.18

The UK is not alone in struggling towards an agreed definition of ownership and control: the Canadian Government recently issued guidance in a bid to bring clarity to the concept, and EU Member States have often differed over their own national interpretations. But the ongoing inability to settle a question of interpretation so fundamental to every UK jurisdictional regime (from Afghanistan to Zimbabwe) has increasingly undermined a central pillar of any sanctions framework: the clarity on which the system depends, regarding whom must be treated as sanctioned by those seeking to comply with it. 9.19

If Parliament is hoping that the courts can provide such clarity on its behalf—for instance through Supreme Court cases—it is likely to be disappointed. The lack of clarity stems from the drafting of the legislative text itself and is unlikely to dissipate without the UK Government taking action to amend it and, in doing so, embarking on a fraught and delicate process which would impact the whole sweep of UK sanctions. 9.20

## 6. Reasonable Cause to Suspect

The concept of 'reasonable cause to suspect' often precedes the question of ownership and control, as it does many other key provisions of UK sanctions, central as it is to the question of a party's knowledge that they may be acting in breach of sanctions. Nonetheless, the phrase has been the subject of far less judicial consideration than the controversies over 'ownership and control'. 9.21

The concept did, however, receive extended consideration in the case of *Vneshprombank LLC v Bedzhamov*.[36] In that case the claimants sought an interim declaration from the court that there was reasonable cause to suspect that A1 LLC—an entity funding two of the parties' (Vneshprombank and the Trustee's) participation in the litigation—was owned or controlled by designated persons, and that, therefore, any payments to Vneshprombank/the Trustee would be prohibited by the Russia Regulations. A1 LLC's major investors included multiple UK designated persons (Mikhail Fridman, Petr Aven, German Khan, and Alexei Kuzmichev) and the claimants professed concerns that the entity was effectively controlled by them. The questions raised at court were therefore highly practical, and ones which private sector actors must regularly assess in their due diligence on high-risk counterparties. What is the requisite level of 'suspicion' 9.22

[36] *Vneshprombank LLC v Bedzhamov* [2024] EWHC 1048 (Ch).

necessary to commit an offence under the legislation? How should such suspicion be determined?

**9.23** Firstly, the judgment helpfully cited what it called 'uncontentious relevant law' on the test for 'reasonable cause to suspect', including inter alia that the test imports an objective standard requiring an evidential foundation;[37] that such a standard must be fact-based and genuinely reasonable;[38] and that it is necessary to guard against making unreliable assumptions treating complexity of corporate structures as grounds for suspicion.[39]

**9.24** Secondly, the judgment focused on the key sentence in regulation 11 (emphasis added):

> (1) A person ('P') *must not deal with funds or economic resources owned, held or controlled by a designated person* if P knows, or has reasonable cause to suspect, that P is dealing with such funds or economic resources.

**9.25** In doing so, the court dismissed the claimant's contention that, where a person has *prima facie* reasonable cause to suspect that they are dealing with the assets of a designated person, they must freeze those assets unless that suspicion is subsequently dispelled (e.g. by a court or an arbitrator). Rather, a person is either a designated person, and subject to sanctions, or they are not. This is a question of fact and law that can be determined. If, for example, a company concludes that a counterparty should not be treated as a designated person, and it later turns out that the party is in fact subject to sanctions, the company may commit a criminal offence. However, the court concluded, it cannot be the case that the company commits such an offence even in the event that the counterparty turns out not to be subject to sanctions (because e.g. ownership and control could not be established) simply because the company continued to deal with that counterparty, despite having reasonable cause to suspect that they were sanctioned. To allow the claimant's argument would 'represent a monumental extension of criminal liability', offending against the principle of strict interpretation of criminal legislation.

**9.26** The court's conclusion should not, it must be emphasized, lead to the assumption that commercial parties need not exercise caution when dealing with funds which they suspect may derive from a sanctioned party. Rather, the judgment makes clear that there is no legal obligation to freeze funds, or refrain from dealing with a counterparty, merely because of the existence of a reasonable cause to suspect that a counterparty is sanctioned; the obligation is only incurred in the event such a person is *actually* subject to sanctions in practice. Making that determination based on the facts should be the key focus during due diligence.

[37] *R v Lane and Letts* [2018] UKSC 36.
[38] *R (Ahmed) v HM Treasury* [2009] 3 WLR 25 [135] (Sedley LJ).
[39] *National Crime Agency v Baker* [2020] EWHC 822 [95]–[100].

In this instance, the court determined that there was 'reasonable cause to suspect' that A1 LLC was owned or controlled by designated persons, citing the 'multiple overlapping indications' in respect of its designated investors and their relationship with the entity. The court therefore made a declaration to that effect, but declined to determine whether ownership and control was exercised over A1 LLC in practice and, therefore, whether the entity was sanctioned as a matter of the UK law. It emphasized that this point would only need to be determined in the event of an actual movement of funds. **9.27**

### 7. Pre-Existing Obligations

Finally, practitioners should be aware of the exception to sanctions prohibitions that applies in respect of pre-existing obligations. For example, regulation 58(5) of the Russia Regulations states as follows (emphasis added): **9.28**

> The prohibitions in regulations 12 and 13 are not contravened by the transfer of funds to a relevant institution for crediting to an account held or controlled (directly or indirectly) by a designated person, *where those funds are transferred in discharge (or partial discharge) of an obligation which arose before the date on which the person became a designated person.*

The scope of this provision was recently debated in the case of *Chanana v Khan*,[40] where one party sought to set aside a statutory demand for unpaid rent on the basis that the landlady was a designated person. The respondent landlady argued that the applicant's liability to pay rent had arisen pursuant to the lease agreement, which was entered into pre-designation, thus engaging the exception under regulation 58(5). The applicant, on the other hand, argued that the obligation to *pay* the rent had arisen after the designation. The High Court concluded that the exception was wide enough to apply, mainly because that was the effect of the equivalent provision under EU law and there was no reason to consider that it was intended to have a narrower scope under UK law post-Brexit: 'both were essentially intended to allow for payments in **discharge of obligations the source of which pre-dated designation.**'[41] **9.29**

## C. Key Trends in Judicial Interpretation

Because the autonomous, post-Brexit UK sanctions framework is still in its infancy, analysing broad trends in judicial treatment requires caution. Many of its provisions, particularly those in the Russia Regulations, are being adjudicated for the first time, and the pace of change in the underlying legislation has created a more unpredictable judicial environment than is typical when key pieces of legislation are interpreted, debated, **9.30**

[40] *Chanana v Khan* [2025] EWHC 1472 (Ch).
[41] ibid [24]. Emphasis added.

and developed by judges over years and decades. However, certain broad themes have begun to emerge.

### 1. Sanctions Are Not an Excuse to Avoid Obligations

**9.31** Chief amongst these themes is a broad, pragmatic attitude from the English courts that commercial parties should not be permitted to use sanctions as an excuse to escape contractual obligations to which they previously signed up, nor to evade their statutory duties or other obligations.

**9.32** The vast increase in sanctions regulations in the last three years has put strain on commercial obligations throughout the global economy. Many of those obligations are governed by English law and subject to the jurisdiction of the English courts. Whilst the courts have upheld the importance of strict compliance with UK sanctions and permitted parties to rely upon the contractual principle of illegality where appropriate, they have also been alert to increasing attempts by commercial actors to 'hide behind' sanctions. This often takes the form of masking commercial considerations behind a purported attempt to comply with the new legislation without having exhausted alternate routes to fulfilling their obligations. The cases on ownership and control[42]—*Mints, Litasco,* and *Hellard*—can all be said to demonstrate this basic approach by the courts.

**9.33** In *Mints*, whilst the Court of Appeal's obiter remarks—dissenting from the lower court's determination on ownership and control—have already gained notoriety, on the actual point in issue, the Court of Appeal upheld the lower court's decision: the effect of sanctions was not to prohibit the claimants from bringing their action for fraud, nor the court from entering judgment upon it. Generally, where sanctions had a practical impact on litigation, a licence could be obtained to let that litigation continue (see paragraphs 9.5–9 above).

**9.34** Similarly, in *Litasco*, a Swiss energy company owned by PJSC Lukoil made an application for summary judgment in an unpaid debt claim, against two Senegalese companies, Der Mond Oil and Gas Africa Sa ('Der Mond') and Locafrique Holding SA ('Locafrique'). The defendant companies argued inter alia that the trade sanctions provisions of the contractual documentation had been triggered, because PJSC Lukoil—although not sanctioned in the UK—was controlled by either its founder and ex-CEO Vagit Alekperov, or Russian President Vladimir Putin, both of whom were sanctioned in the UK. It would therefore be prohibited to make funds available to Litasco, as that would constitute 'making funds available directly or indirectly to a designated person' contrary to regulation 12 of the Russia Regulations. The court rejected these submissions, pointing to the low (in the case of Mr Alekperov) and non-existent (in the case of President Putin) shareholdings of the two men, and determining that the defendants

[42] See Chapter 3, paras 3.48–71.

had failed to provide evidence that either exercised control over the entity or that Lukoil 'functions as an organ of the Russian state'.[43] Litasco's application in respect of its debt claim was therefore granted, and the sanctions arguments made by the defendants deemed insufficient to prevent payment.

This broad approach was followed in the context of statutory duties in *Hellard*.[44] In this case, the trustees in bankruptcy of a Russian individual named Alatoly Motylev applied to the court under section 303(2) of Insolvency Act 1986 for directions, including as to whether the respondents (referred to as the 'Russian Bank Creditors') should be treated as subject to sanctions under the Russia Regulations. The trustees expressed concern to the court that, if they did not treat the Russian Bank Creditors as subject to sanctions, the trustees could be exposed to civil or criminal liability in the event that the Creditors were later found to be sanctioned. Notably, OFSI itself was added by the trustees as a respondent, even though the agency had unsuccessfully requested that the court remove it as a party. Although the court eventually concluded that there was insufficient evidence to definitively declare whether the Russian Bank Creditors should be regarded as 'owned or controlled' by designated persons, it practically directed the trustees to proceed as if they were not, unless new evidence came to light. It also emphasized that, even if the Russian Bank Creditors were to be regarded as sanctioned, trustees exercising their duties in the insolvency (including exercising their voting rights) would not be in breach of the Russia Regulations. **9.35**

This pragmatic approach by the English courts—seeking to uphold duties and obligations where possible, despite the impact of sanctions—can perhaps most clearly be seen through the innovative judicial approach in *Fortenova Grupa D.D. v LLC Shushary Holding*.[45] Fortenova, an EU company, wished to redeem loan notes held by a Russian subsidiary of UK, EU, and US-designated PJSC VTB Bank. Due to the sanctions, Fortenova could not make the necessary payments to redeem the notes without making funds available to or for the benefit of the subsidiary. Notably, the court made an order at Fortenova's request that the funds could be paid into the court itself and held for the period of the subsidiary's designation, to be released upon an application by the subsidiary in the event sanctions were later removed. Such an order was described in the judgment as 'relatively straightforward as a way of dealing with the unfortunate situation in which the Company [Fortenova] finds itself'.[46] **9.36**

The pragmatic judicial approach has a long history in the context of UK sanctions, going back to some of the earliest pre-Brexit leading cases, like that of *R v R*.[47] *R v R* remains one of the only examples of judicial assessment of the notoriously elusive concept of sanctions 'circumvention'. It concerned an appeal by an EU-sanctioned Russian **9.37**

[43] *Litasco* (n 34) [68].
[44] *Hellard* (n 35).
[45] *Fortenova Grupa D.D. v LLC Shushary Holding* [2023] EWHC 1165 (Ch).
[46] ibid [5].
[47] *R v R* [2015] EWCA Civ 796.

citizen, against an English court order requiring him to make maintenance payments to his UK-resident ex-wife's bank account in Russia. The appellant, citing circumvention concerns, had argued that the payments may be remitted by his ex-wife to the UK in breach of sanctions, causing a criminal offence on his part. The court disagreed, concluding that the proposed structure was a 'lawful route to a lawful objective', and observing that the aim of the UK sanctions regime was not to prevent orders being made in favour of a party entitled to receive the underlying payments.[48]

**9.38** That the courts have broadly adopted such a pragmatic approach should not, however, be interpreted as meaning that they will 'read down' sanctions legislation, nor that the terms of a contract will be stretched in order to encourage offending payments to take place. *MUR Shipping BV v RTI Ltd* was an appeal from an arbitral award, which was appealed in the High Court and the Court of Appeal, before being considered by the Supreme Court.[49] It has significant implications for the interpretation of reasonable endeavours provisos and force majeure clauses. In *MUR*, the Supreme Court specifically rejected the Court of Appeal's conclusion that the contractual force majeure clause could have been 'overcome' by 'reasonable endeavours', namely the payment of an obligation in Euros, rather than US dollars as specified in the contract, thereby avoiding the effect of US sanctions against RTI's parent company. The Supreme Court held that the 'reasonable endeavours' proviso should not be interpreted as including non-contractual performance by the other party and, therefore, MUR Shipping was entitled to reject RTI's offer to pay in Euros as a route to fulfilling its payment obligation, even if that led to adverse consequences for the performance of the contract.

**9.39** Similarly, in *LLC Eurochem North-West-2 v Societe Generale SA*, the High Court dismissed the Russian claimant's interim application for an order that the defendants (a group of European banks) make payments into court or a frozen account in order to fulfil their outstanding payment obligation, despite those banks' purported concerns that doing so would breach sanctions.[50] The court emphasized that it was at least arguable that the payments could breach sanctions if the defendants were required to make them, and that therefore that risk must be properly taken into account. It was by no means certain that the claimant would obtain judgment at trial, a condition relied upon by the claimant.

**9.40** A comparable conclusion was reached in *Lamesa Investments Ltd v Cynergy Bank Ltd*,[51] which is examined in further detail in paragraphs 9.41–4 below.

[48] ibid [57].
[49] *MUR Shipping BV v RTI Ltd* [2024] UKSC 18.
[50] *LLC Eurochem North-West-2 v Societe Generale SA* [2023] EWHC 2720 (Comm).
[51] *Lamesa Investments Ltd v Cynergy Bank Ltd* [2020] EWCA Civ 281.

## 2. The English Courts Are Increasingly Required to Assess the Impact of Foreign Sanctions

*MUR Shipping, Eurochem,* and *Lamesa* are all examples of how the English courts have sought to deal with the challenge of foreign sanctions regimes. Further to the growth of 'unilateral' sanctions[52] in recent years, not least resulting from Brexit and the UK subsequently establishing its own sanctions framework effective from January 2021, the judiciary has increasingly had to assess the impact of the sanctions regimes of foreign states on contracts governed by English law or adjudicated through the English courts. The extra-territorial reach of most national sanctions regimes—applying, like the UK framework, not just on home territory but also to their companies and citizens acting anywhere in the world—creates an inherent potential for conflicts of laws, as well as difficult questions of interpretation for the English courts when examining multi-jurisdictional transactions. **9.41**

The Court of Appeal's decision in *Lamesa* in June 2020 illustrates these complexities. The defendant, Cynergy Capital Ltd ('Cynergy'), a UK retail bank, had borrowed £30 million from Lamesa, a Cypriot entity, under a Facility Agreement governed by English law and with exclusive English jurisdiction. In 2017, Lamesa's ultimate beneficial owner, Viktor Vekselberg, was added to the US Specially Designated Nationals (SDN) list (although he was not sanctioned in the UK). Cynergy declined to repay interest due on the loan on the basis that it risked being subject to US secondary sanctions which, under US law, can apply to any global transaction. Cynergy argued that by making payment to Lamesa it could be deemed by US authorities to be 'facilitating a significant transaction' with a US-designated person under US law, and could therefore be subjected to US sanctions itself. **9.42**

Cynergy relied on clause 9.1 of the Facility Agreement, which stated that it would not be in default where sums were withheld: '[i]n order to comply with any mandatory provision of law, regulation or order of any court of competent jurisdiction'. Lamesa, by contrast, submitted that clause 9.1 was not intended to be construed so broadly as to cover US secondary sanctions; that the risk of Cynergy being sanctioned by the US Government was extremely remote; and that US secondary sanctions (as opposed to UK sanctions) were not 'directly binding' on Cynergy as a UK company. **9.43**

The court agreed with Cynergy that the parties intended clause 9.1 to apply to 'a foreign statute that would otherwise be triggered' and that included the US secondary sanctions. The court determined that 'context and commercial common sense' dictated that Cynergy's withholding of payments was done in compliance with US secondary sanctions and permitted in accordance with the Facility Agreement. **9.44**

[52] Typically opposed to 'multilateral' sanctions, being those derived from the UN Security Council and implemented by all UN Member States.

9.45 Similarly, in *Celestial Aviation*,[53] letters of credit were issued by Sberbank, which subsequently became a designated entity, and confirmed by UniCredit (the appellant) in favour of certain Irish-incorporated leasing companies (the respondents), which included Celestial Aviation Services Ltd. The respondents made demands for payment under the letters of credit in March 2022, but UniCredit declined to pay on the basis of UK, EU, and US sanctions imposed on Sberbank. UniCredit did go on to apply for licences in all three jurisdictions, and these were granted except in the US by the time of the Court of Appeal hearing. The High Court had ruled that a payment by UniCredit in US dollars would not necessarily be prohibited by US sanctions, because the involvement of US jurisdiction (e.g. through a correspondent bank) could theoretically be avoided through payment in cash, despite the obvious practical issues this might pose. The Court of Appeal rejected this conclusion. It also ruled against UniCredit's argument that it could rely on the principle in *Ralli Bros*, under which non-payment can be justified where performance is not illegal under English law but is in the place of performance of the contract (here, the US).[54] The court held that UniCredit's OFAC licence application did not constitute the 'reasonable efforts' required of a party relying on *Ralli Bros* to avoid illegality in the place of performance, because the licence application was narrowly framed on processing a payment by Sberbank and had not sought to cover all of the relevant payment obligations.

## 3. Anti-Suit Injunctions Are on the Rise

9.46 Perhaps the most extreme jurisdictional interplay of UK sanctions with its foreign equivalents has been with Russia itself, manifested in a significant increase in anti-suit injunctions (ASIs)[55] and anti-enforcement injunctions issued by the English courts. This trend is a reaction to the growing use of article 248 of Russia's Arbitrazh Procedure Code, which permits Russian parties in disputes impacted by sanctions—a broad definition that goes beyond merely the involvement of designated parties—to petition the Russian courts to repatriate their disputes to Russia, effectively granting the Russian courts exclusive jurisdiction in such matters. The provision therefore allows Russian parties to override contractual clauses on jurisdiction which they previously agreed.

9.47 Russia's introduction of article 248 was justified by the perceived impact of western sanctions on Russian parties attempting to receive a fair hearing in foreign courts, and the accompanying access to justice concerns for Russian persons seeking legal representation. As noted by the Court of Appeal in *UniCredit Bank*

[53] See paragraphs 9.12–14.

[54] *Celestial Aviation* (n 29), citing *Ralli Bros v Compañia Naviera Sota y Aznar* [1920] 2 KB 287.

[55] Ordinarily, anti-suit injunctions are granted by the English Court if (i) England is the natural forum, and (ii) further pursuit of the foreign proceedings would be vexatious and oppressive or unconscionable, per *Deutsche Bank AG v Highland Crusader Offshore Partners LP* [2009] EWCA Civ 725.

*GmbH v RusChemAlliance LLC*,[56] the provision has increasingly been 'applied broadly by the Russian courts', and is currently impacting a number of active disputes before the English courts:

- In September 2024, the UK Supreme Court affirmed the Court of Appeal's decision to issue an anti-suit injunction in the *UniCredit* case. The injunction prevents RusChemAlliance LLC from continuing the legal proceedings they initiated in Russia under article 248. RusChemAlliance was seeking payment of €448 million in bonds issued by UniCredit, which UniCredit contended was affected by EU sanctions.
- In June 2024, the High Court issued both an anti-suit and an anti-enforcement injunction in favour of Airbus Canada (*Airbus Canada Limited Partnership v Joint Stock Company Ilyushin Finance Co (No 2)*).[57] This decision was one of numerous post-Ukraine war disputes in the English courts related to the supply of aircraft to and from Russia. The court required the defendant, JSC Ilyushin Finance, to discontinue its article 248 proceedings in Russia, ruling that it could have access to justice by applying for licences from the UK sanctions authority covering its legal costs and participation in the arbitration.
- In July 2024, the High Court granted an anti-suit and anti-enforcement injunction in favour of Barclays Bank Plc (Barclays) which prevented PJSC Sovcombank from pursuing its Russian court proceedings against Barclays in relation to the latter's failure to make payments under a facility agreement after sanctions were imposed on Sovcombank (*Barclays Bank PLC v PJSC Sovcombank*).[58]

As an aside, it is worth noting that judgments in the EU have faced similar challenges, **9.48** and EU policymakers have thus far taken a more explicitly hard line in seeking to push back against the Russian courts than their UK equivalents. The EU's 14$^{th}$ package of sanctions measures, unveiled in July 2024, incorporated a 'transaction ban'[59] prohibiting EU persons from engaging commercially with Russian parties that have initiated claims before Russian courts on the basis of article 248, where the party has done so citing the restrictions imposed upon them by EU sanctions.

The increase in such jurisdictional clashes portends a highly unstable future envir- **9.49** onment for cross-border disputes involving sanctions, and raises concerns over the reliability of contractual arrangements between western parties and Russian counterparties. The most ominous endpoint would be a reciprocal breakdown of trust in either judicial system's ability as an impartial arbiter in contractual disputes. The dystopian

[56] *UniCredit Bank GmbH v RusChemAlliance LLC* [2024] EWCA Civ 64 [22].
[57] *Airbus Canada Limited Partnership v Joint Stock Company Ilyushin Finance Co (No 2)* [2024] EWHC 790 (Comm).
[58] *Barclays Bank PLC v PJSC Sovcombank* [2024] EWHC 1338 (Comm).
[59] Council of the EU, 'Russia's War of Aggression Against Ukraine: Comprehensive EU's 14th Package of Sanctions Cracks Down on Circumvention and Adopts Energy Measures' (Press release, 24 June 2024) <https://www.consilium.europa.eu/en/press/press-releases/2024/06/24/russia-s-war-of-aggression-against-ukraine-comprehensive-eu-s-14th-package-of-sanctions-cracks-down-on-circumvention-and-adopts-energy-measures/> accessed 26 August 2025.

alternative might be western and Russian parties bypassing agreed contractual clauses and separately seeking redress from their respective national courts in order to enforce judgment over their counterparty's assets in that jurisdiction. Recent developments in the *UniCredit* case indicate a step in that direction, following the Commercial (Arbitrazh) Court of St Petersburg's decision to seize UniCredit's Russian-based assets whilst proceedings in the English courts were ongoing.[60]

**9.50** Such 'weaponization' of court judgments would not necessarily stop at the countries' respective borders. The recent legal battle between the Russian state and Google illustrates the potential for such jurisdictional clashes to become internationalized; whilst Google successfully obtained an anti-suit injunction in the English courts, Russia sought to have the decision of a Moscow judge enforced over Google's assets in South Africa, perceived as a country broadly friendly to Russia.[61] This rise in 'legal nationalism' puts third countries in a difficult position when presented with contradictory court judgments from both sides of a dispute.

**9.51** However, there is evidence of less extreme reactions: in *Magomedov v PJSC Transneft*, the High Court showed signs of being receptive to article 248 claims from Russian parties, so long as those claims were made in good faith.[62] Although an anti-suit injunction was granted against the Russian court, the judgment notably sought to emphasize that article 248 had been invoked entirely legitimately by Transneft, and that even if the provision had been 'applied very broadly' by the Russian courts of late, 'including in situations where no such juridical problem really arises', the provision '[ ... ] was introduced with the intention of addressing a real juridical problem, namely that Russian parties cannot get access to justice because of the impact of sanctions'.[63]

## D. Sanctions and Arbitration

**9.52** The proliferation of sanctions measures in recent years has had a similarly profound impact on the resolution of disputes via arbitration. In fact, many of the sanctions disputes that have ended up before the English courts—including *MUR Shipping* (see paragraph 9.38 above)—started as arbitral disputes. The practical issues created by sanctions are arguably more far-reaching in the arbitration context given that the arbitral process is entirely private and governed by contract. Moreover, arbitrators are undoubtedly 'persons' (see paragraph 9.10 above regarding the argument that the courts are not 'persons' for the purpose of sanctions compliance) and therefore subject to sanctions prohibitions, and possibly in multiple jurisdictions. For example, a

[60] Anastasia Stognei, Silvia Sciorilli Borrelli, and Joshua Franklin, 'Russian Court Seizes €700mn Assets from UniCredit, Deutsche Bank and Commerzbank' *Financial Times* (17 May 2024) <https://www.ft.com/content/481d418e-9366-4152-8ec5-92b81d020991> accessed 31 October 2025.

[61] *Google LLC & Google Ireland Limited v NAO Tsargrad Media* [2025] EWHC 94 (Comm).

[62] *Magomedov v PJSC Transneft* [2024] EWHC 1176.

[63] ibid [100].

US national presiding over an arbitral tribunal seated in London will have to consider and take into account both US and UK sanctions measures. Sanctions prohibitions also apply to arbitral institutions, although the latter have emphasized that UK and EU sanctions do not generally prevent parties from referring disputes to UK or EU-based arbitral institutions.[64] OFSI has also issued a general licence allowing the London Court of International Arbitration (LCIA) to process payments from designated persons subject to the Russia and Belarus sanctions regimes.[65] Notwithstanding the fact that arbitration, as with litigation before the courts, remains open to all, the increase in sanction measures has had a chilling effect, for example, on the number of UK-seated arbitrations involving Russian parties.[66] There has unsurprisingly been a concomitant increase in the number of disputes being pursued in jurisdictions without wide-ranging sanctions regimes, including Hong Kong and Singapore. This trend has been exacerbated by an increasing divergence between the sanctions measures imposed in different jurisdictions (e.g. between UK and EU sanctions) and by the imposition of Russian countersanctions.

## 1. Practical Issues and Arbitrability

Many of the practical issues raised in section B above also arise in relation to arbitral disputes. The legal representation of designated persons in arbitration proceedings, for example, is subject to exactly the same restrictions, and the same mitigating factors apply. Similar administrative issues also arise in respect of the payment of arbitrators and arbitral institutions. Although it is unclear to what extent the answers given by the Court of Appeal in *Mints* can be directly transposed to the arbitration context, some of the court's reasoning is plainly relevant in respect of similar issues. **9.53**

On the question of whether an arbitral tribunal can issue an award in favour of a designated person, for example, the Court of Appeal's reliance on the prior position under EU sanctions legislation—permitting payments to designated persons under judicial or arbitral decisions[67]—supports the view that an arbitral tribunal is not prohibited from issuing an award in favour of a designated person. **9.54**

[64] See (e.g.) the joint statement published by the ICC International Court of Arbitration, London Court of International Arbitration (LCIA), and Arbitration Institute of the Stockholm Chamber of Commerce (SCC), 'The Potential Impact of the EU Sanctions Against Russia on International Arbitration Administered by EU-Based Institutions' (17 June 2015): '[ . . . ] the Russian sanctions – while they may result in some additional administrative steps – do not preclude parties from referring their disputes to arbitration at an EU-based institution. As such, it is very much business as usual for both the institutions and the parties.'

[65] General Licence INT/2022/1552576 – LCIA Arbitration Costs, issued on 17 October 2022 and revoked on 28 March 2025. See also the current General Licence INT/2025/5787748 – Arbitration Costs, issued on 28 March 2025.

[66] See e.g. Satindar Dogra, Kerstin Wilhelm, and Joanne Denton, 'Crucial Sanctions Challenges in Civil Litigation and Arbitration' in Rachel Barnes et al. (eds), *The Guide to Sanctions* (5th edn, Global Arbitration Review 2024).

[67] See e.g. *Mints* (n 4) [190], discussing Article 7(2)(c) of Regulation (EU) 269/2014: '[t]hat the pursuit of proceedings is permitted is really borne out by Article 7(2)(c), since that permits payments to a designated person under a judicial or arbitral decision, again provided that the money is paid into a frozen account.'

9.55 Moreover, the licensing regimes under the various UK sanctions regimes can be used by arbitrators and arbitral institutions to mitigate some of the administrative and practical difficulties created by sanctions measures. In any event, arbitrators, arbitral institutions, and legal representatives should, at the very least, conduct due diligence before accepting roles in arbitration proceedings involving designated persons in order to satisfy themselves either that their engagement will not infringe applicable sanctions prohibitions or, if it does, that they can obtain a licence. Where multiple sanctions jurisdictions are involved (e.g. because an arbitrator has dual UK/EU nationality), applications for licences may have to be made in numerous jurisdictions, thus increasing the overall administrative burden in relation to the arbitration.

9.56 As for arbitrability, it has in the past been argued that disputes involving sanctions measures are fundamentally incapable of resolution by arbitration and fall within the narrow category of 'non-arbitrable' disputes (e.g. in *Fincantieri-Cantieri Navali Italiani SpA v ATF*). That approach has, however, been rejected by most jurisdictions and the prevailing view is that disputes involving sanctions measures are arbitrable.[68]

9.57 In the *Fincantieri* case, which involved issues arising as a result of UN sanctions on Iraq, the International Chamber of Commerce (ICC) upheld the arbitrability of the dispute, and found that the application of the UN sanctions regime went to the merits of the dispute and not the issue of arbitrability.[69] On an application challenging the ICC award, the Swiss Federal Tribunal also rejected the argument that the dispute was inarbitrable because of sanctions issues.[70] That approach is reflected in the results of an arbitration survey published in 2022, with 80 per cent of respondents expressing the view that arbitration is a suitable method for resolving sanctions-related disputes.[71]

## 2. Substantive Sanctions Issues in Arbitration

9.58 Where the arbitration is governed by the law of a sanctioning state as the *lex causae*, sanctions may also have an impact on the substance of the dispute. Where an arbitration is substantively governed by English law, moreover, the trends and issues discussed in section C above—including issues relating to contractual performance, termination, frustration, and illegality—will be just as relevant in the arbitration context. Where a

[68] See e.g. Eric De Brabandere and David Holloway, 'Sanctions and International Arbitration' in Larissa van de Herik et al. (eds), *Research Handbook on UN Sanctions and International Law* (Edward Elgar Publishing 2017); Elliott Geisinger et al., 'Les Conséquences des Sanctions Économiques sur les Obligations Contractuelles et l'Arbitrage' (2012) *Intl Business L J* 405.

[69] *Fincantieri-Cantieri Navali Italiani SpA v ATF* (25 November 1991) ICC Award Nr 6719 (Interim Award) Journal du droit international (1994) 1074.

[70] *Fincantieri-Cantieri Navali Italiani SpA v M and Arbitral Tribunal* (23 June 1992) ATF 118 II 353 (Tribunal Fédéral Suisse), 1993(1) ASA Bull 58, XX YB Com Arb 766 (1995). Note, however, that the Genoa Court of Appeal took a different approach in a parallel claim brought in the Italian courts, holding that the dispute could not be submitted to arbitration under Italian law (*Fincantieri-Cantieri Navali Italiani SpA v Iraq* (1994) Riv Dell'arb 4 (1994) (Genoa Court of Appeal, Italy) 505).

[71] Queen Mary University of London and Pinsent Masons, 'Future of International Energy Arbitration Survey Report' (2022).

contractual dispute involving sanctions issues is referred to arbitration and the arbitration is seated in England and Wales, the parties may also make applications to the courts in support of the arbitration. In *O v C*,[72] for example, a party to an arbitration dispute concerning the impact of US sanctions on a charterparty made an application to the English court under section 44 of the Arbitration Act 1996 for an order for sale. The court granted the application in support of the arbitration and ordered that the proceeds of sale be paid into court. In doing so, the court held that the importance of the order for payment into court, including the 'desirability of supporting the arbitration', outweighed what it found to be the 'very low risk of prosecution' for a potential breach of US sanctions.[73]

## 3. Enforcement of Arbitral Awards

Perhaps the most common issue raised by sanctions in the arbitration context arises in respect of the enforcement of arbitral awards. For example, the enforcement of an award is susceptible to challenge on the grounds that it would infringe sanctions law and therefore would be contrary to public policy for the purpose of the 1958 New York Convention on the Recognition and Enforcement of Foreign Arbitral Awards.[74] In this context, UN sanctions are often considered to constitute international public policy.[75] This was the approach taken by the Paris Court of Appeal in rejecting a public policy objection in the *Sofregaz* case.[76] The applicant argued that the arbitral award was contrary to public policy on the basis that the arbitral tribunal had failed to take into account the impact of US sanctions against Iran. However, the Paris Court of Appeal upheld the award, holding that although UN sanctions form part of transnational or international public policy, and can therefore prevent the recognition and enforcement of an arbitral award in the French courts, US sanctions do not form part of international public policy. **9.59**

In *Türkmengaz v National Iranian Gas Company*,[77] the losing party in the arbitration sought to set aside the award on the basis that it was contrary to public policy. The party argued that it could not comply with the order to pay interest on the award in view of applicable US sanctions. The Swiss Federal Tribunal rejected that argument and held that there were no applicable UN or EU sanctions, meaning that the interest could be paid in euros. **9.60**

[72] *O v C* [2024] EWHC 2838 (Comm).
[73] ibid [40].
[74] See e.g. *Sofregaz v Natural Gas Storage Company* (3 June 2020) Paris Court of Appeal (Chamber 5-16) No 19-07261.
[75] See e.g. Andrea Carlevaris and Veit Öhlberger (eds), 'Economic Sanctions and Arbitration: A Practical Guide for Parties, Counsel and Arbitrators' (International Association of Lawyers 2023) para 123.
[76] *Sofregaz* (n 74).
[77] *Türkmengaz v National Iranian Gas Company*, ICC Case No 23312/MHM/HBH, Final Award (18 June 2020).

9.61 Regardless of these decisions upholding the enforcement of arbitration awards in Western Europe, the real enforcement risk relates to hostile jurisdictions, including Russia, where a foreign arbitral award is far less likely to be enforceable, particularly against a person or company designated under western sanctions regimes. It has been observed, for example, that some Russian respondents in arbitration proceedings have commenced proceedings in the Russian courts in order to obtain favourable judgments and pre-empt the risk of any arbitral award subsequently being enforced in Russia.[78] That has been exacerbated by legislation passed in Russia in 2020 allowing the Russian courts to assume jurisdiction over disputes potentially affected by sanctions.[79] Unsurprisingly, the Russian courts take a rather different approach to public policy when it comes to the enforcement of arbitral awards. Strikingly, the Russian Supreme Court issued a judgment in July 2024 denying the enforcement of an arbitral award issued by a tribunal seated in London on the basis that the tribunal comprised arbitrators from 'unfriendly' jurisdictions and was therefore contrary to public policy under the New York Convention.[80] This is a demonstration of the growing risk that the Russian courts will prevent the enforcement of international arbitration awards against Russian parties.

## 4. Investment Arbitration and Sanctions

9.62 Finally, the imposition of sanctions has formed the basis of numerous investment arbitration claims against sanctioning states, both before and since the Russian invasion of Ukraine. In 2020, for example, Qatar Airways filed four investment arbitration claims against the United Arab Emirates, Bahrain, Egypt, and Saudi Arabia in relation to the denial of access to airspace by those states.[81] Similarly, an investor brought a claim against South Korea under the Iran-South Korea bilateral investment treaty, claiming that the State's implementation of certain UN sanctions exceeded the scope of the relevant UN Security Council Resolution, thus constituting a breach of the fair and equitable treatment standard.[82] More recently, Mikhail Fridman, a designated person, including under UK and EU sanctions law, filed an UNCITRAL claim against Luxembourg under the Belgium-Luxembourg bilateral investment treaty in respect of his assets frozen in Luxembourg.[83] These claims may represent the start of a more

[78] Amaryllis Bernitsa, 'The Impact of Sanctions on International Arbitration – Key Issues' (*BIICL Blog*, 15 December 2023) <https://www.biicl.org/blog/72/the-impact-of-sanctions-on-international-arbitration-key-issues> accessed 26 August 2025.

[79] Article 248 of the Arbitration Procedure Code (see further at section C above).

[80] *C. Thywissen v Novosibirskhleboproduct*, Supreme Court of the Russian Federation, Case No A45-19015/2023, Decision (26 July 2024).

[81] Tom Jones, 'Qatar Airways Launches Treaty Claims Over Blockade' *Global Arbitration Review* (22 July 2020) <https://globalarbitrationreview.com/article/qatar-airways-launches-treaty-claims-over-blockade> accessed 26 August 2025.

[82] *Dayyani v South Korea*, Paris Court of Appeal, Case No 2015-38.

[83] Susannah Moody, 'Sanctioned Businessman Files Mega-claim Against Luxembourg' *Global Arbitration Review* (13 August 2024) <https://globalarbitrationreview.com/article/sanctioned-businessman-files-mega-claim-against-luxembourg> accessed 26 August 2025.

concerted attempt by individuals and companies to hold states accountable under international law for the harm caused by their sanctions.

## E. Conclusion

Until recently, the imposition of economic sanctions by states and international organizations had only sporadically given rise to issues in English commercial litigation. Now that sanctions play a central role in the foreign policy of the UK and other western states, however, sanctions issues are routinely being considered by the English courts and are likely to remain a part of the litigation landscape for the foreseeable future. That is all the more so given that the English courts have emphasized that sanctions do not generally preclude commercial claims; any sanctions issues in this context can and should be managed or resolved by litigants and/or the court. The key for practitioners will be to identify any sanctions issues, whether procedural or substantive, as early as possible in the litigation process. **9.63**

As for specific provisions of UK sanctions law, the courts—including the UK Supreme Court—will no doubt continue to grapple with the interpretation of SAMLA and related legislation. There are, however, limits to what the courts can do in this context. The 'ownership and control' test, for example, remains fraught with difficulty despite several decisions attempting to impose some degree of intelligibility and pragmatism. The solution may well be, as the Court of Appeal suggested in *Mints*, that it is for the legislature to reconsider the breadth of the language used in the relevant provisions. It remains to be seen whether sufficient political will exists to amend those provisions, particularly where that could be perceived as 'softening' the applicable sanctions regimes. **9.64**

All in all, there is likely to be much more sanctions litigation to come. The issues and cases discussed in this chapter will no doubt be relevant in that context. **9.65**

# 10

# Looking Forward

## A Global Perspective

*Charles Steele*



## A. Introduction

**10.01** Russia's February 2022 invasion of Ukraine prompted sanctions on an unprecedented scale. More than 40 countries (many not previously known for vigorous use of sanctions) joined in a generally co-ordinated effort to impose economic costs and pain on Russia in the hope of inducing some positive change in its behaviour. This has been a historic high point for multilateralism in the sanctions arena. However, three and a half years on (this chapter having been written in mid-2025) and with no significant change in behaviour by Russia—and with a new US president in office—it is not entirely clear what the short-term future holds. There are, however, reasons to expect there will be less focus on multilateralism going forward. This chapter considers the prospects for multilateralism generally as well as a few specific issues, some against an international background and others with more of a US focus, given the US has always been the most expansive and aggressive deployer of economic sanctions and often drives sanctions considerations worldwide.

Charles Steele, *Looking Forward* In: *UK Sanctions Law and Practice*. Edited by: Amanda Pinto KC, Alexandre Haines, and Sophie O'Sullivan, Oxford University Press. © Oxford University Press 2026.
DOI: 10.1093/oso/9780198964179.003.0010

## B. The Prospects for Multilateralism

Most sanctions practitioners and observers agree that multilateral sanctions are generally preferable to unilateral sanctions. The more countries that impose sanctions in a particular scenario, the more powerful the sanctions will be overall. They will have greater impact and will serve as a stronger statement of international condemnation of the target's actions. **10.02**

Even so, we are likely to see less emphasis on multilateral approaches going forward than we saw in the sanctions against Russia after February 2022. Even if there is another cataclysmic event that similarly implicates global stability, there may well not be a similarly co-ordinated international sanctions response, at least until there is a change in US presidential administrations in January 2029. **10.03**

The US will drive this dynamic. That the US dollar is still the world's principal reserve currency and remains heavily favoured globally for international financial transactions is a key reason for the powerful impact of US sanctions. For these reasons, and because the US has always used sanctions more aggressively and expansively than any other country, the US tends to have a leading and outsized impact in the global sanctions arena. **10.04**

The first Trump administration (2017–21) was much less concerned with achieving multilateral consensus than its predecessors, and it became clear within a few months of President Trump's January 2025 inauguration that his second administration will take the same approach. The president's 'America First' campaign and his general willingness to disregard and even criticize long-standing international consensus (e.g. his harsh criticisms of NATO allies for what he said was their failure to pay their fair share of defence costs) are examples. We should not assume the current administration will reject all efforts at multilateralism—it may be happy to have other countries join forces with the US in particular situations, if the consensus can be achieved without, in the administration's view, compromising US interests—but will be unlikely to prioritize multilateralism and consensus-building generally. Because the US is often the de facto global driver of sanctions considerations, any US retreat from prioritizing multilateralism may well have ripple effects leading to similar approaches in other countries. **10.05**

President Trump will also enjoy the considerable benefit of having his party (the Republican Party) control both houses of Congress (the Senate and the House of Representatives) for at least the first two years of his administration, and possibly all four (depending on the results of the mid-term congressional elections in November 2026). This will give the president a substantial advantage, and a much better chance at quickly moving his agenda than if one or both houses were controlled by the opposition (the Democrats). Those Republican majorities most likely share, or at least are unlikely to significantly impede, the America First underpinnings of President Trump's agenda. They will be unlikely to criticize US sanctions initiatives as being insufficiently multilateral. On the contrary, members of Congress in both houses and from both **10.06** parties, who seem to be able to agree on very little, tend uniformly to favour aggressive use of economic sanctions; if anything, the chief complaint from both parties for the past several years has been that they want sanctions to be used even more aggressively than they already are.

**10.07** With this in mind, one of the great unknowns is how other governments will react if and to the extent the US pulls back from consensus-building. Perhaps, if the facts of a particular situation merit it, the EU[1] and/or the UK will try to fill the void and take the lead. A further question will then be how the US will react if these other actors succeed in beginning to develop a multilateral consensus—will the US join in or stay out?

**10.08** Aside from Russia, two other countries in particular might trigger global anxiety and offer early tests in the sanctions arena. The first is China. If China threatens or takes military action against Taiwan, for example, then countries will face to some degree the same choice they faced when Russia invaded Ukraine. The other is Iran. There was a multilateral approach to Iran beginning several years ago, which was prompted by its nuclear programme and lasted through the initiation of the Joint Comprehensive Plan of Action (JCPOA), agreed among Iran and the five permanent members of the UN Security Council (China, France, Russia, the UK, and the US), Germany, and the EU. Under the first Trump administration, the US withdrew from the JCPOA in 2018, and reimposed (and expanded) sanctions under its new policy, expressly calling for 'maximum pressure' on Iran. Iran's subsequent resumption of nuclear programme efforts might prompt a resurgence of multilateral efforts, and that some countries view Iran as a supporter of terrorism around the world and a destabilizing force in the Middle East may add to this incentive. Prospects for sanctions have also been potentially complicated by the strong military strikes by Israel and the US against Iran, which occurred shortly before this chapter was completed in mid-2025.

**10.09** However, short of dramatic events such as these, with clear global implications, it seems more likely than not that the post-2022 Russia sanctions will mark a high point—and perhaps the last hurrah—for serious proactive efforts to achieve broad multilateralism in the sanctions arena, at least while the Trump administration is in place.

**10.10** Countries' willingness to launch new sanctions efforts will also likely be affected by their perceptions of the efficacy of sanctions going forward. In the case of Russia, the global sanctions substantially achieved (as they almost always do) the first-stage goal of inflicting economic and financial pain and damage on the targets, but they have not yet achieved anything like the ultimate goal, which is to induce the Russian Federation Government to change its behaviour; ideally to abandon the war, or at least to draw back significantly. Some critics note that Iran has likewise weathered sanctions for the most part, and that even Cuba has managed to live with US sanctions (and an embargo) for more than 50 years.

[1] The EU is, of course, a multilateral body by definition, but it acts in practice as a single authority for the purpose of imposition of sanctions (as distinct from enforcement for violations and circumvention, which is handled at the national level).

To the extent that countries come to doubt the efficacy of sanctions, particularly when deployed against an entire country, they may become less willing to use them in the future, especially against targets like China that are strong and important players in the global economy and are able to deploy their own effective countermeasures. **10.11**

## C. Example of the New US Approach: The International Criminal Court

It took less than three weeks to see concrete evidence of the second Trump administration's lack of interest in multilateralism, when President Trump issued sanctions against the International Criminal Court (ICC) on 6 February 2025, just 17 days after his inauguration. Notably, this occurred notwithstanding the absence of concurrence or any similar approach by any other country (except Israel). **10.12**

Some background is helpful and illustrates both that US presidents enjoy extremely broad powers in sanctions matters (discussed further in paragraphs 10.20–27), and also that US sanctions are primarily functions of policy, and not a traditional legal regulatory regime. On 11 June 2020, in the waning months of his first administration, President Trump imposed sanctions on the ICC with Executive Order (EO) 13928, 'Blocking Property of Certain Persons Associated With the International Criminal Court'. The EO declared a national emergency arising from the ICC's 'illegitimate assertions of jurisdiction over personnel of the United States and certain of its allies'.[2] The EO declared that the ICC threatened 'to subject current and former United States Government and allied officials to harassment, abuse, and possible arrest', and to 'infringe upon the sovereignty of the United States and impede the critical national security and foreign policy work of United States Government and allied officials'. This was deemed a 'threat to the national security and foreign policy of the United States'. **10.13**

The EO further determined 'any attempt by the ICC to investigate, arrest, detain, or prosecute any United States personnel without the consent of the United States, or of personnel of countries that are United States allies and who are not parties to the Rome Statute or have not otherwise consented to ICC jurisdiction, constitutes an unusual and extraordinary threat to the national security and foreign policy of the United States'.[3] President Trump formally declared a national emergency to deal with that threat. As discussed below, this triggered his ability—and the ability of certain presidential subordinates such as the Secretary of the Treasury and the Secretary of State—to impose a broad variety of sanctions on the ICC and its personnel. **10.14**

[2] The EO stated that the illegitimate assertions of jurisdiction included 'the ICC Prosecutor's investigation into actions allegedly committed by United States military, intelligence, and other personnel in or relating to Afghanistan'.

[3] Executive Order No 13928, 'Blocking Property of Certain Persons Associated With the International Criminal Court' 85 Fed Reg 36139 (11 June 2020) <https://www.federalregister.gov/documents/2020/06/15/2020-12953/blocking-property-of-certain-persons-associated-with-the-international-criminal-court> accessed 26 August 2025.

**10.15** The move seemed to have been prompted by the ICC Appeals Chamber's 5 March 2020 decision permitting an investigation into what it characterized as alleged war crimes committed by US personnel in Afghanistan. The EO broadly authorized (amongst other things) blocking (that is, freezing) sanctions on any person determined to have directly engaged in any effort by the ICC to investigate, arrest, detain, or prosecute any US personnel without the consent of the United States, or of personnel of countries that are US allies and who are not parties to the Rome statute or have not otherwise consented to ICC jurisdiction.[4] The Secretary of State thereafter designated and subjected to blocking sanctions the then ICC Prosecutor, Fatou Bensouda for having directly engaged in efforts to investigate US personnel, and Head of Jurisdiction Phakiso Mochochoko for having materially assisted Bensouda.

**10.16** Less than three months after President Biden took office in January 2021, he revoked EO 13928 and terminated the national emergency, in EO 14022, 'Termination of Emergency With Respect to the International Criminal Court'.[5] As a result, the blocking of and travel restrictions against Bensouda and Mochochoko were lifted. This was entirely a policy decision; President Biden did not declare that there had been an insufficient factual or legal basis for President Trump's declaration of the national emergency. In fact, the new EO took no issue with the nature and scope of the declaration of emergency in President Trump's EO. President Biden confirmed that the United States 'continues to object to the [ICC's] assertions of jurisdiction over personnel of such non-States Parties as the United States and its allies absent their consent or referral by the United Nations Security Council', and declared only that economic sanctions against the Court and its personnel 'are not an effective or appropriate strategy for addressing the United States' concerns with the ICC'.

**10.17** Then, as many predicted, President Trump reimposed sanctions very soon after his inauguration, with EO 14203, 'Imposing Sanctions on the International Criminal Court' (6 February 2025). The EO referenced not only 'illegitimate and baseless actions targeting America', but also the targeting of 'our close ally' Israel (with specific reference to the ICC having issued 'baseless' arrest warrants for Israeli Prime Minister Benjamin Netanyahu and former defence minister Yoav Gallant). The ICC itself was not immediately designated and blocked, but the EO designated one individual (Karim Khan, ICC Prosecutor and British national) and five more individuals have been designated as of August 2025. This course was taken without any indication of consultation with, or concern for contrary views of, any other country, including close allies such as the UK, of which Mr Khan is a citizen. This confirms that the US under President Trump will not hesitate to deploy sanctions unilaterally, even in potentially polarizing ways, when it determines it is in US interests to do so.[6]

[4] EO 13928, section 1(a)(i)(A).

[5] Executive Order No 14022, 'Termination of Emergency With Respect to the International Criminal Court' 86 Fed Rg 17895 (1 April 2021) <https://www.federalregister.gov/documents/2021/04/07/2021-07239/termination-of-emergency-with-respect-to-the-international-criminal-court> accessed 26 August 2025.

[6] Another example was OFAC's mid-2025 designation of Brazilian Supreme Federal Court Justice Alexandre De Moraes under the Global Magnitsky sanctions for alleged human rights abuses ('Treasury Sanctions Alexandre

This does not mean the US will never seek or welcome bilateral or multilateral approaches. As the day-to-day administrator of US sanctions, the Treasury Department's Office of Foreign Assets Control (OFAC), which is composed entirely of career civil servants (there are no political appointees in its ranks), recognizes that such approaches can add value. In the last couple of years, for example, OFAC and the UK Treasury's sanctions agency (the Office of Financial Sanctions Implementation, or OFSI) have formalized and broadened their relationship to permanently enable regularized bilateral co-ordination.[7] As another example, on 16 May 2025, OFAC and Switzerland's State Secretariat for Economic Affairs (SECO) announced a 'Memorandum of Understanding Regarding Enhanced Sanctions Enforcement Through Information Sharing'.[8] These initiatives might, in turn, lead naturally to broader multilateral efforts in cases in which countries' policy goals overlap. These viewpoints are not limited to civil servants; US political appointees likewise often see the value in such efforts and work to establish or support them. **10.18**

These are signs that bilateral and multilateral approaches can still prevail where appropriate and not inconsistent with the plans of high-level political policy makers. As always, though, there are some caveats. Most importantly, the degree of receptivity to seeking multi-country consensus, at least in the US, depends heavily on the particular people occupying political (and even civil servant) positions at any particular time. Momentum for or interest in such initiatives can wane when new leaders have other philosophies or priorities, or otherwise give the efforts limited attention, let alone when they affirmatively disfavour the initiatives. This is especially true in the US, given the broad unilateral authority afforded to the president in the sanctions realm (discussed below in paragraphs 10.20–27). Because of this, high-level political appointees in the US have greater ability to initiate and abandon initiatives, and to change policy directions much more easily and quickly than might be possible in more structured US legal regimes. **10.19**

de Moraes' (Press Release, 30 July 2025) <https://home.treasury.gov/news/press-releases/sb0211> accessed 26 August 2025). I will not address the merits or demerits of the allegations and designation; I note only that it was another example of the Trump administration being unconcerned with developing any degree of multilateral consensus for the action.

[7] In October 2022, for example, OFAC and OFSI launched their new 'Enhanced Partnership,' described as an 'ongoing commitment from two of the world's leading financial sanctions implementation authorities to deepen their collaboration' ('OFAC-OFSI Enhanced Partnership' (*OFSI Blog*) <https://ofsi.blog.gov.uk/2022/10/17/ofac-ofsi-enhanced-partnership/> accessed 26 August 2025). One and two years later, in November 2023 and November 2024, the agencies publicly proclaimed that the partnership was moving along well, and that the agencies were working closely together to exchange best practices and align sanctions implementation. They also instituted quarterly virtual and in-person exchanges of personnel, and have undertaken enhanced information sharing and joint industry engagement and guidance on a wide variety of topics. The partnership is intended to be permanent, not only in relation to the post-2022 Russia sanctions but, also, across other common sanctions regimes.

[8] OFAC, 'Memorandum of Understanding between OFAC and the Swiss State Secretariat for Economic Affairs' (16 May 2025) <https://ofac.treasury.gov/recent-actions/20250516> accessed 26 August 2025.

## D. US Legal Authorities for Sanctions

**10.20** When trying to predict how the US under President Trump might use sanctions, it is helpful to understand that US law gives the president enormous discretion and authority to declare foreign origin 'national emergencies' and then to impose sanctions to deal with the emergencies. The US president probably has substantially more discretion and authority than do governments of most, if not all, other (non-authoritarian) countries in this regard. The goal of the US legal framework is to enable extremely broad, nimble, flexible, and powerful use of sanctions by the executive branch, for the most part unilaterally. Congress generally defers heavily to the president with respect to sanctions, and for 40 years US courts have likewise given considerable deference to the executive branch, although that has recently begun to change to some degree (see the discussion of the Supreme Court's June 2024 *Loper Bright* decision, in paragraphs 10.28–36).

**10.21** Almost all US sanctions programmes (including those involving Russia and Iran) are based on a statute called the International Emergency Economic Powers Act (IEEPA).[9] When the president formally declares a national emergency with respect to an 'unusual and extraordinary' foreign threat to the 'national security, foreign policy, or economy of the United States', certain broad authorizations under IEEPA are triggered to enable the president to deal with the threat. Presidents have used those authorities to impose a variety of types of sanctions, including not only the long-familiar 'blocking' sanctions, but also prohibitions against providing certain categories of services to all parties located in particular countries, and against any new investment in such countries, amongst others.

**10.22** The president makes such declarations in EOs which identify and describe the national emergency and then set forth certain criteria, tied to the emergency, for the imposition of sanctions. For example, in EO 14024, President Biden declared a national emergency based on the Russian Government's 'harmful foreign activities', specifically

> efforts to undermine the conduct of free and fair democratic elections and democratic institutions in the United States and its allies and partners; to engage in and facilitate malicious cyber-enabled activities against the United States and its allies and partners; to foster and use transnational corruption to influence foreign governments; to pursue extraterritorial activities targeting dissidents or journalists; to undermine security in countries and regions important to United States national security; and to violate well-established principles of international law, including respect for the territorial integrity of states [ . . . ].[10]

[9] 50 U.S.C. § 1701ff <https://uscode.house.gov/view.xhtml?path=/prelim@title50/chapter35&edition=prelim> accessed 26 August 2025.

[10] Executive Order 14024, 'Blocking Property With Respect To Specified Harmful Foreign Activities of the Government of the Russian Federation' 86 Fed Reg 20249 (15 April 2021) <https://www.federalregister.gov/documents/2021/04/19/2021-08098/blocking-property-with-respect-to-specified-harmful-foreign-activities-of-the-government-of-the> accessed 26 August 2025.

The EO then authorized the imposition of sanctions against (amongst many others) persons who operate or who have operated in the financial services sector of the Russian Federation economy.[11] The EOs also typically authorize specified executive branch officers subordinate to the president, such as the Secretaries of the Treasury and State, to designate foreign persons and parties for sanctions upon determining that they meet one or more of the EO's criteria.

IEEPA gives the president vast authority to deal with the threats. A key provision states that upon declaration of the emergency, **10.23**

> [t]he President may [ ... ] investigate, block during the pendency of an investigation, regulate, direct and compel, nullify, void, prevent or prohibit, any acquisition, holding, withholding, use, transfer, withdrawal, transportation, importation or exportation of, or dealing in, or exercising any right, power, or privilege with respect to, or transactions involving, any property in which any foreign country or a national thereof has any interest by any person, or with respect to any property, subject to the jurisdiction of the United States [ ... ].[12]

This language is so broad as almost to appear open-ended. The president can impose on any 'dealings' (a term which is undefined) with sanctioned parties any prohibitions or conditions that fairly constitute 'regulating', 'directing', 'compelling', 'preventing', 'prohibiting', 'nullifying', or 'voiding'. None of these terms are defined, either in IEEPA or in OFAC's regulations implementing the EOs. OFAC interprets undefined terms broadly, and when it does define a term such as 'property' and 'property interest', it likewise does so broadly.[13] This is all intended to provide wide scope to give the sanctions maximum effect and flexibility, including in reaction to novel (even unprecedented) circumstances. The goal is to have room to apply the sanctions measures efficiently and effectively, as strongly and quickly as needed to address the particular national **10.24**

[11] EO 14024, s 1(a)(i). The financial services sector of the Russian Federation economy was not originally specified in EO 14024 when the EO was issued on 15 April 2021. However, on 22 February 2022, that sector was included under the EO pursuant to a 'Determination Pursuant to Section 1(a)(i) of Executive Order 14024' <https://ofac.treasury.gov/media/918726/download?inline> accessed 26 August 2025. This Determination triggered authority to designate parties like Alfa-Bank (and many other Russian banks) for operating or having operated in the sector.

[12] IEEPA, 50 U.S.C. § 1702(a)(1)(B) <https://ofac.treasury.gov/media/5736/download?inline> accessed 26 August 2025.

[13] See, for example, OFAC's standard definitions of 'property' and 'property interest' in IEEPA-based regulations: 'The terms *property* and *property interest* include, but are not limited to, money, checks, drafts, bullion, bank deposits, savings accounts, debts, indebtedness, obligations, notes, guarantees, debentures, stocks, bonds, coupons, any other financial instruments, bankers acceptances, mortgages, pledges, liens or other rights in the nature of security, warehouse receipts, bills of lading, trust receipts, bills of sale, any other evidences of title, ownership or indebtedness, letters of credit and any documents relating to any rights or obligations thereunder, powers of attorney, goods, wares, merchandise, chattels, stocks on hand, ships, goods on ships, real estate mortgages, deeds of trust, vendors' sales agreements, land contracts, leaseholds, ground rents, real estate and any other interest therein, options, negotiable instruments, trade acceptances, royalties, book accounts, accounts payable, judgments, patents, trademarks or copyrights, insurance policies, safe deposit boxes and their contents, annuities, pooling agreements, services of any nature whatsoever, contracts of any nature whatsoever, and any other property, real, personal, or mixed, tangible or intangible, or interest or interests therein, present, future, or contingent.' See, for example, OFAC's Russian Harmful Foreign Activities Sanctions Regulations, 31 CFR § 587.311, and Iranian Transactions and Sanctions Regulations (ITSR), 31 CFR § 560.325. OFAC uses the same definition in its other IEEPA-based sanctions regulations.

emergency, and to sufficiently advance and protect US foreign policy and national security interests.

**10.25** OFAC then promulgates regulations, codified in 31 CFR Subtitle B, Chapter V, to implement the EOs and the corresponding sanctions programmes. The regulations typically set forth prohibitions, exemptions, definitions, interpretations, licences (i.e. authorizations to engage in otherwise prohibited conduct), statements of licensing policy, and other provisions. When the regulations define a term, they likewise do so broadly. The EOs and regulations are written to enable energetic and robust steps to address the identified national emergency and to advance and protect US foreign policy and national security goals.

**10.26** In short, US law is designed to empower the executive broadly, by giving the president very high degrees of mostly unilateral discretion, authority, and flexibility. All presidents going back at least to Bill Clinton—and including President Trump during his first term—have used sanctions with increasing frequency, often as the first response to new international problems. As always, exactly what sanctions are imposed will depend to a large degree on the particular personnel occupying key political positions in the administration. As of August 2025, the Secretary of State is former US Senator Marco Rubio, and the Secretary of the Treasury is former hedge fund manager Scott Bessent. Secretary Rubio is well versed in and a strong supporter of the vigorous use of sanctions, and a hawk on many foreign policy issues, including as to Iran, Cuba, and China. Secretary Bessent does not appear to have had exposure to sanctions prior to taking office, but unsurprisingly and immediately became a key player in advancing the president's national security and foreign policy agendas. We can therefore expect that in the second Trump administration the US will continue to turn frequently to sanctions to respond to troubling global events.

**10.27** At the same time, it is possible we may occasionally see some degree of strategic restraint from the US. Many observers and commentators, and President Trump himself, have at times cautioned that there is potential danger in overuse of sanctions, including because it can incentivize countries—even countries not unfriendly to the US—to try to find or create alternatives to the US dollar as a means of staying outside US sanctions jurisdiction. That could, in theory, result in fewer sanctions in Trump's second term than in his first (including, in particular, fewer persons and entities designated and added to the SDN List). In addition, some changes in designation patterns will flow simply from US policy changes.[14] However, this too will depend primarily on world

[14] For example, as of August 2025, OFAC had not designated a single Russian entity or individual under the post-2022 Russia sanctions. This seemed clearly to flow from President Trump's desire to maximize his chances of persuading President Putin to scale back Russia's war efforts, rather than from any general philosophical concerns about overuse of the tool. However, on 22 October 2025, OFAC imposed further sanctions 'as a result of Russia's lack of serious commitment to a peace process to end the war in Ukraine'. The designation targeted Russia's two largest oil companies, Rosneft and Lukoil and 34 of their subsidiaries, pursuant to EO 14204. (US Department of the Treasury, 'Treasury Sanctions Major Russian Oil Companies, Calls on Moscow to Immediately Agree to Ceasefire' (Press release) <https://home.treasury.gov/news/press-releases/sb0290> accessed 31 October 2025.)

events. Long-term strategy considerations can evaporate when a response must quickly be found to a new foreign policy imperative. Generally, we can expect the US will often respond to problematic global developments—for example, a country launching unprovoked military aggression against another—with vigorous sanctions.

## E. Reduced Judicial Deference to OFAC: *Loper Bright Enterprises v Raimondo*

The long-standing deference US courts had given OFAC and other executive branch administrative agencies was curtailed somewhat in the summer of 2024. It is not yet clear how and to what extent this development will affect OFAC's practices, but the legal framework is now in place for parties to more easily consider suing to challenge at least novel and forward-leaning sanctions actions. **10.28**

On 28 June 2024, the US Supreme Court issued a decision in *Loper Bright Enterprises v Raimondo*).[15] The decision has significant import for administrative agencies in the US. It reversed a 40-year-old principle of law—called 'Chevron deference' (because the principle was most clearly articulated in a 1984 Supreme Court decision in a case brought by Chevron)—pursuant to which courts were obliged to defer to an agency's interpretation of ambiguous statutory and regulatory terms so long as the agency's interpretation was a reasonable and permissible interpretation, even if not the best interpretation. OFAC, like all US administrative agencies, benefitted greatly from that discretion over the years; it is widely considered one of the principal reasons, and perhaps the primary reason, that OFAC has very rarely been sued (because parties often fear they have little chance of success in challenging an OFAC designation, enforcement action, or other action). The Supreme Court in *Loper Bright* did away with Chevron deference, holding that under the US Constitution it is for the judicial branch, not the executive branch, to say what the law is. **10.29**

It is not yet entirely clear how much impact this new rule will have on OFAC's administration of sanctions programmes. However, a decision of the Fifth US Circuit Court of Appeals[16] on 26 November 2024, just five months after *Loper Bright* and the First Circuit Court decision to apply the new rule, sheds some light.[17] The case involved OFAC's 8 August 2022, designation of Tornado Cash, an open-source, crypto-transaction software protocol that facilitates anonymous transactions of virtual currency. As a result, all of Tornado Cash's property and interests in property were blocked (i.e. frozen). **10.30**

[15] *Loper Bright Enterprises v Raimondo* 603 US 369 (2024) <https://www.supremecourt.gov/opinions/23pdf/22-451_7m58.pdf> accessed 26 August 2025.

[16] Which sits one level below the Supreme Court.

[17] *Van Loon v Department of the Treasury* No 23-50669 (5th Cir, 26 November 2024). <https://www.ca5.uscourts.gov/opinions/pub/23/23-50669-CV0.pdf>accessed 26 August 2025.

10.31 In connection with its designation of Tornado Cash, OFAC imposed the usual prohibition against any US-linked dealings involving any property of Tornado Cash. OFAC defined 'property' in this case to include Tornado Cash's 'smart contracts'—software or computer programmes uploaded onto the blockchain network and that function automatically, without direction from any person or party. Some of them are immutable, meaning they cannot be altered in any way or removed from the blockchain. Several users of Tornado Cash sued, asserting among other things that OFAC had exceeded its statutory authority in designating the smart contracts as property.

10.32 The Fifth Circuit Court of Appeals agreed with the plaintiffs, holding that immutable smart contracts are not 'property', principally because they are not capable of being owned by any person. The court probably would not have been able to reach this decision when Chevron deference prevailed, because it would have been bound to accept OFAC's definition of 'property' as long as the definition was reasonable, even if the court thought another definition was better. The court probably would have been reluctant to find OFAC's definition unreasonable.

10.33 Freed, however, from that restraint by the recent *Loper Bright* decision, the Fifth Circuit had no difficulty ruling against OFAC. Because IEEPA does not define the term 'property', the court looked first to the ordinary, common meaning of the term at the time IEEPA was passed (in 1977). The court looked to contemporary dictionary definitions. The court also considered OFAC's regulatory definition of the term (without conceding that it was required to do so). The court found that the common, ordinary meaning (as reflected in contemporaneous dictionary definitions) and OFAC's regulatory definition both required that 'property' be capable of being owned by someone; and, since immutable smart contracts are not capable of being owned, they cannot constitute 'property' in either case. Further, because they are not property, IEEPA does not provide authority to block or regulate them, and so OFAC's designation—which was authorized only by IEEPA—failed.

10.34 The specific holding seems unlikely to have broad consequences for OFAC, since it was quite fact-specific and will apply only in the narrow category of cases involving cryptocurrency and other items that, like the immutable smart contracts, are consequential to transactions and movements of funds but are not capable of being owned. The other types of property on which OFAC has typically focused—for example, money, wire transfers, bank accounts, real property, vessels, etc.—all easily fit any reasonable definition of 'property' and so will presumably not be affected by this decision.

10.35 However, the broad new principle that courts no longer need defer to OFAC's definitions and interpretations of terms, and can instead look first to the common, ordinary meaning of those terms at the time of IEEPA's enactment, could cause problems for the agency. For example, OFAC's sanctions programmes rely heavily not only on broadly defined terms, but also on some terms it does not define at all, such as 'blocking' and 'dealing'. It may not go well for OFAC if a party subject to designation or an enforcement action sues in a case whose unusual facts leave OFAC vulnerable to a judicial finding of overreach.

There are already signs that we may see such rulings. In the first weeks of his second administration, President Trump issued various tariffs, including some under IEEPA, declaring that the latter were needed to deal with national emergencies arising from trade deficits and flows of fentanyl into the US from Mexico and other countries. Certain small businesses and importers of consumer goods sued, asserting amongst other things that IEEPA, notwithstanding its breadth, does not authorize tariffs, which are governed by other statutes. The US Court of International Trade and the US District Court for the District of Columbia had ruled for the plaintiffs. They held amongst other things that the Constitution gives Congress exclusive authority to impose tariffs, and that even if movements of fentanyl into the US validly constituted a national emergency under IEEPA, the president's tariffs did not actually 'deal with' that emergency, as required by the statute. Many practitioners believe that the president overreached and that the lower courts' decisions are correct. Time will soon tell because, at the time of writing, the cases had moved up to higher courts which will render the final judgments. In any event, given President Trump's expansive and assertive views of executive authority, these cases might not be the last in which courts are called upon to delineate IEEPA's boundaries. **10.36**

## F. Russia

As of August 2025, it is not entirely clear how US sanctions against Russia will proceed under the second Trump administration, nor how other countries are likely to respond to any US changes. In just the first few months of his current administration, President Trump's public statements swung between musings about possibly starting to lift some sanctions to expressions of frustration with Russian President Putin accompanied by statements that the US might intensify the sanctions. **10.37**

By way of background, the US, characteristically, led the way in the international community's dramatic and expansive use of sanctions in response to the invasion of Ukraine. Beginning on the very day of the invasion (22 February 2022), the US began imposing a series of waves of broad sanctions, including amongst others blocking sanctions on large numbers of Russian individuals, banks, and other types of entities; prohibitions on new investment in Russia; and prohibitions on exporting to or importing from Russia an increasing number of types of services (starting with accounting, trust and corporate formation, and management consulting services, and moving on to, among others, quantum computing services, services related to maritime transport of crude oil and petroleum products of Russian origin, IT and software services, and others). The US also laid out its 'secondary sanctions' regime, authorizing blocking of any non-US persons determined to have provided material support or assistance to any person blocked under EO 14024. **10.38**

**10.39** The EU, UK, and dozens of other countries also imposed their own sanctions, in the most extensive and co-ordinated manner ever, marking a historic highpoint for multilateral use of the tool. This was perhaps not surprising given the rare and profound implications of Russia's action (a military invasion of a neighbouring country intended to change borders). However, although the sanctions have inflicted some economic damage, they have not yet achieved anything like their ultimate aim of inducing Russia to abandon, or even scale down, its war efforts. Russia has not meaningfully abandoned its efforts and not surprisingly has undertaken prodigious efforts to evade the sanctions. It is also increasingly receiving assistance and support from China, as well as Iran and North Korea.

**10.40** Now, almost three and a half years later and with the war still dragging on, President Trump appears to be taking a soft approach to those sanctions, at least so far. He has not imposed any new sanctions under the Russia sanctions programme. This appears to reflect his desire to avoid or forestall adversarial action while he tries to intercede personally with President Putin. At the same time, however, President Trump occasionally makes public statements that the lack of progress toward peace may lead him to ratchet up the sanctions. As of August 2025 it is not possible to predict whether and how the course of events might change.

**10.41** It is likewise hard to foresee how other countries will respond if the US does more formally and officially relaxes its sanctions. However, and particularly if doubts about efficacy dampen countries' enthusiasm for sanctions as a policy tool, US relaxation may have a compounding effect.

## G. Iran

**10.42** The current Trump administration quickly reinstated the 'maximum pressure' campaign against Iran.[18] This will include aggressive use of sanctions. Iran's continuing support for Israel's enemies, its general role, from a US perspective, as a destabilizing force in the Middle East, its support of international terrorism, news reports[19] (which Iran denies) of Iran's plotting to assassinate Trump during the campaign, and the military strikes between Israel and Iran which began in mid-June 2025 will serve as ongoing grounds for broad and aggressive sanctions.

**10.43** Other countries do not necessarily share US policy views on Iran, at least not as comprehensively and intensely. It therefore seems unlikely that there will be a return to a

[18] The White House, 'Fact Sheet: President Donald J. Trump Restores Maximum Pressure on Iran' (4 February 2025) <https://www.whitehouse.gov/fact-sheets/2025/02/fact-sheet-president-donald-j-trump-restores-maximum-pressure-on-iran/> accessed 26 August 2025.

[19] Dan De Luce, 'Iran "Never" Plotted to Kill Trump During Campaign, Iran's President Tells NBC News' *NBC News* (14 January 2025) <https://www.nbcnews.com/investigations/iran-never-plotted-kill-president-elect-donald-trump-irans-president-t-rcna187644> accessed 26 August 2025.

broad international consensus for strong sanctions. Again, however, the Trump administration will not be discouraged by that and will be happy to act unilaterally.

## H. China

China could test the practicalities and efficacy of economic sanctions in unprecedented ways. **10.44**

Many countries see China as posing foreign policy and national security threats and challenges. This certainly includes the US, where many members of Congress and recent presidents from both parties have agreed that China presents such threats. Sanctions typically follow such wide and bipartisan agreement. **10.45**

Sanctions, however, depend on the economic strength of the issuer as compared to that of the target. The US, for example, has been able easily to impose harsh sanctions on countries with much smaller and weaker economies, such as Iran, North Korea, and Cuba, which cannot easily absorb the resulting damage or find economic and commercial alternatives that will enable them to avoid US sanctions altogether. **10.46**

China is quite another matter: it has the world's second-largest economy and is deeply intertwined with countries around the world, very much including the US. China is not vulnerable to other countries' offensive use of economic power in the ways smaller countries have been. And given China's deep economic relationships with other countries, there would be far-reaching and profound collateral consequences to any extensive sanctions, perhaps at least as painful and damaging to innocent third parties (such as China's trading partners and commercial counterparties) as the sanctions would be to China. Furthermore, China can impose its own countermeasures and, unlike those imposed by smaller countries, China's would have real bite. **10.47**

China would also have better avenues to avoid or minimize the impact of Western sanctions than other countries historically have had. It would be able to look to and band together with a small but significant number of countries that have started to work around US and international sanctions to a meaningful degree. This includes Russia, India, North Korea, and Iran. **10.48**

For these reasons it is unlikely that we will see anything like the volume and types of sanctions against China that we have seen against Russia, let alone against Iran and other smaller countries. **10.49**

Further, any doubts as to the efficacy of sanctions will likely influence governments' calculations as to China to a greater degree than they have with respect to other countries. To the extent governments doubt how much impact the sanctions will have and, accordingly, how likely they will be to prompt China to change behaviour, they will be less likely to want to use sanctions, even if the US jumps in first. **10.50**

10.51 Notwithstanding these general points, though, even countries otherwise harbouring such doubts might feel compelled to join in an international sanctions movement if China invades Taiwan or takes other military action against it or another country. In that case, as in the case of Russia and Ukraine, countries may feel they have no choice but to take some action, especially once other countries do.

## I. Prospects for New Sanctions Programmes?

10.52 Finally, it will be interesting to see whether President Trump creates and/or Congress calls for any new sanctions programmes during the next few years. Anything a president characterizes as a foreign policy or national security threat—and as to which the president is willing to formally declare a national emergency—could serve as a basis for a new programme. In his first administration, for example, President Trump created the Global Magnitsky sanctions programme,[20] targeting foreign human rights abuse and corruption, and what he called the 'Communist Chinese Military Company' sanctions, targeting what he alleged to be China's exploitation of US capital to resource nominally private-sector Chinese companies that aided the development and modernization of its military, intelligence, and other security apparatuses.[21] As noted above in paragraphs 10.21–4, IEEPA provides the president very broad sanctions authorizations upon the formal declaration of a national emergency. If President Trump or his senior advisors someday perceive a new foreign threat, then economic sanctions, as demonstrated over the past several decades in the US, will be readily available to use in response.

[20] <https://ofac.treasury.gov/sanctions-programs-and-country-information/global-magnitsky-sanctions> accessed 26 August 2025. The sanctions implemented the Global Magnitsky Human Rights Accountability Act, which was signed into law by President Obama in December 2016, after President Trump's election but before his inauguration in January 2017.

[21] <https://ofac.treasury.gov/sanctions-programs-and-country-information/chinese-military-companies-sanctions> accessed 26 August 2025. President Biden refined those sanctions, which are now called the 'Chinese Military Companies Sanctions'. Ibid.

# Appendix

| Name | Date (Last Updated) | Link |
|---|---|---|
| **General** | | |
| Starter Guide to UK Sanctions (FCDO, OFSI, OTSI, DfT, HMT, DBT) | 13 October 2025 | https://www.gov.uk/guidance/starter-guide-to-uk-sanctions |
| UK Sanctions Guidance for Non-UK Businesses Operating Outside the UK (FCDO) | 27 June 2025 | https://www.gov.uk/government/collections/uk-sanctions-guidance-for-non-uk-businesses-operating-outside-the-uk |
| How 'Ownership and Control' Applies to Public Officials Under Financial Sanctions (OFSI and FCDO) | 20 August 2024 | https://www.gov.uk/government/publications/ownership-and-control-public-officials-and-control-guidance |
| Deter, Disrupt and Demonstrate—UK Sanctions in a Contested World (HM Government) | 2024 | https://assets.publishing.service.gov.uk/media/65d720cd188d770011038890/Deter-disrupt-and-demonstrate-UK-sanctions-in-a-contested-world.pdf |
| Russia Sanctions Regime: Industry and Specialist Guidance (FCDO) | 27 June 2025 | https://www.gov.uk/government/collections/uk-sanctions-on-russia |
| **HMT (OFSI): Financial Sanctions** | | |
| UK Financial Sanctions FAQs | 24 October 2025 | https://www.gov.uk/government/publications/uk-financial-sanctions-faqs/uk-financial-sanctions-faqs |
| UK Financial Sanctions Guidance | 18 August 2025 | https://www.gov.uk/guidance/uk-financial-sanctions-guidance |
| Financial Sanctions Enforcement: Decisions and Monetary Penalties Imposed | 30 September 2025 | https://www.gov.uk/government/collections/enforcement-of-financial-sanctions |
| Financial Sanctions Targets by Regime | 23 July 2025 | https://www.gov.uk/government/collections/financial-sanctions-regime-specific-consolidated-lists-and-releases |
| OFSI General Licences | 28 October 2025 | https://www.gov.uk/government/collections/ofsi-general-licences |
| Who is Subject to Financial Sanctions in the UK? | 30 October 2025 | https://www.gov.uk/government/publications/financial-sanctions-consolidated-list-of-targets |
| Financial Sanctions Guidance for Russia | 17 July 2025 | https://www.gov.uk/government/publications/financial-sanctions-guidance-for-russia/financial-sanctions-guidance-for-russia |
| Financial Sanctions Enforcement and Monetary Penalties Guidance | 14 November 2024 | https://www.gov.uk/government/publications/financial-sanctions-enforcement-and-monetary-penalties-guidance/financial-sanctions-enforcement-and-monetary-penalties-guidance |

| Name | Date (Last Updated) | Link |
|---|---|---|
| Reporting Information to OFSI—What to Do | 17 July 2025 | https://www.gov.uk/guidance/suspected-breach-of-financial-sanctions-what-to-do |
| OFSI Blog | 17 July 2025 | https://ofsi.blog.gov.uk/ |
| Monetary Penalties for Breaches of Financial Sanctions | 3 May 2024 | https://www.gov.uk/government/publications/monetary-penalties-for-breaches-of-financial-sanctions |
| OFSI Financial Services Threat Assessment | February 2025 | https://assets.publishing.service.gov.uk/media/67f3f2467ed82b90fcf5bffc/OFSI_Financial_Services_Threat_Assessment_Report.pdf |
| OFSI Legal Services Threat Assessment | April 2025 | https://assets.publishing.service.gov.uk/media/67ee635698b3bac1ec299c3e/OFSI_Legal_Services_Threat_Assessment.pdf |
| OFSI Cryptoassets Threat Assessment | July 2025 | https://assets.publishing.service.gov.uk/media/687e637292957f2ec567c625/OFSI_Cryptoassets_Threat_Assessment.pdf |
| OFSI Property and Related Services Threat Assessment | April 2025 | https://assets.publishing.service.gov.uk/media/67f7d42804146682e61bc80f/OFSI_Property_and_Related_Services_Threat_Assessment.pdf |
| OFSI Art Market Participants and High Value Dealers Threat Assessment | June 2025 | https://assets.publishing.service.gov.uk/media/6852a572235ba1380b6aa684/OFSI_Art_Market_Participants_and_High_Value_Dealers_Threat_Assessment_1.pdf |
| OFSI Annual Review 2023 to 2024: Engage, Enhance, Enforce | 21 March 2025 | https://www.gov.uk/government/publications/ofsi-annual-review-2023-24-engage-enhance-enforce/ofsi-annual-review-2023-24-engage-enhance-enforce |
| OFSI Annual Review 2024 to 25: Effective Sanctions | 15 October 2025 | https://www.gov.uk/government/publications/ofsi-annual-review-2024-25-effective-sanctions |
| **DBT (OTSI): Trade Sanctions** | | |
| Report a Suspected Breach of Trade Sanctions | 27 June 2025 | https://www.gov.uk/guidance/report-a-suspected-breach-of-trade-sanctions |
| UK Strategic Export Controls | 21 November 2023 | https://www.gov.uk/guidance/uk-strategic-export-controls |
| Trade, Aircraft and Shipping Sanctions, Civil Enforcement: Guidance | 19 March 2025 | https://www.gov.uk/government/publications/trade-aircraft-and-shipping-sanctions-civil-enforcement-guidance/trade-aircraft-and-shipping-sanctions-civil-enforcement-guidance |
| How Suspected Breaches of Trade Sanctions are Assessed by OTSI | 31 July 2025 | https://www.gov.uk/guidance/how-suspected-breaches-of-trade-sanctions-are-assessed-by-the-office-of-trade-sanctions-implementation-otsi |
| Appealing a Civil Monetary Penalty for a Breach of Trade Sanctions | 10 October 2024 | https://www.gov.uk/guidance/appealing-a-civil-monetary-penalty-for-a-breach-of-trade-sanctions |
| Information You Must Provide in Response to a Trade Sanctions Information Request | 10 October 2024 | https://www.gov.uk/guidance/information-you-must-provide-in-response-to-a-trade-sanctions-information-request |

| Name | Date (Last Updated) | Link |
|---|---|---|
| Mandatory Reporting for Suspected Breaches of Trade Sanctions | 10 October 2024 | https://www.gov.uk/guidance/mandatory-reporting-for-suspected-breaches-of-trade-sanctions |
| Navigating Trade Sanctions with Guidance | 21 October 2024 | https://otsi.blog.gov.uk/2024/10/21/navigating-trade-sanctions-with-guidance/ |
| **Solicitors Regulation Authority (SRA)** | | |
| Complying with the UK Sanctions Regimes | 1 May 2025 | https://www.sra.org.uk/solicitors/guidance/financial-sanctions-regime/ |
| Sanctions Regime—Firm-Wide Risk Assessments | 23 January 2024 | https://www.sra.org.uk/solicitors/guidance/sanctions-regime-firm-wide-risk-assessments/ |
| Government Sanctions Regime—How All Firms Can Stay Compliant | 3 May 2023 | https://www.sra.org.uk/news/events/on-demand-events/government-sanctions-regime-stay-compliant/ |
| Sectoral Risk Assessment—Anti-Money Laundering and Terrorist Financing (and Sanctions) | 31 July 2025 | https://www.sra.org.uk/pdfcentre/?type=Id&data=697721737 |
| New Guidance Issued on Trade Sanctions | 5 February 2025 | https://www.sra.org.uk/news/news/sra-update-136-trade-sanctions/ |
| **Law Society** | | |
| Financial Sanctions: How to Comply | 4 February 2024 | https://www.lawsociety.org.uk/topics/anti-money-laundering/financial-sanctions-how-to-comply |
| Q&A: My Client is a Possible Sanctions Match. What Should I Do? | 26 August 2025 | https://www.lawsociety.org.uk/contact-or-visit-us/helplines/practice-advice-service/q-and-as/my-client-is-a-possible-sanctions-match-what-should-i-do |
| Financial Sanctions FAQs (Law Society of Scotland) | Undated | https://www.lawscot.org.uk/members/regulation-and-compliance/financial-compliance/anti-money-laundering/financial-sanctions-faq/ |
| **Bar Standards Board (BSB) and Bar Council** | | |
| Compliance with Your Obligations: Sanctions (BSB) | 29 July 2025 | https://www.barstandardsboard.org.uk/for-barristers/compliance-with-your-obligations/sanctions.html |
| Sanctions Guidance (Bar Council) | June 2025 | https://www.barcouncilethics.co.uk/wp-content/uploads/2024/07/Sanctions-guidance-June-2024.pdf |
| FCA | | |
| Memorandum of Understanding Between FCA and OFSI | 21 November 2023 | https://www.fca.org.uk/publication/mou/mou-fca-ofsi.pdf |
| Joint Statement from UK Financial Regulatory Authorities: Sanctions and the Cryptoasset Sector | 11 March 2022 | https://assets.publishing.service.gov.uk/government/uploads/system/uploads/attachment_data/file/1060448/Statement_from_UK_authorities_on_Cryptoassets_-_March_2022.pdf |
| **DBT (Export Control Joint Unit)** | | |
| Export controls: Dual-Use Items, Software and Technology, Goods for Torture and Radioactive Sources | 7 July 2025 | https://www.gov.uk/guidance/export-controls-dual-use-items-software-and-technology-goods-for-torture-and-radioactive-sources |

| Name | Date (Last Updated) | Link |
|---|---|---|
| Export Controls: Military Goods, Software and Technology | 10 April 2024 | https://www.gov.uk/guidance/export-controls-military-goods-software-and-technology |
| Applying for Export Licences Using SPIRE | 7 July 2025 | https://www.gov.uk/government/publications/spire-online-export-licensing-guidance |
| Open General Export Licences (OGELs) | 13 October 2025 | https://www.gov.uk/government/collections/open-general-export-licences-ogels |
| OGEL and Goods Checker Tools | Undated | https://www.ecochecker.businessandtrade.gov.uk/spirefox5live/fox/spire/OGEL_GOODS_CHECKER_LANDING_PAGE/new |
| Notices to Exporters | 29 October 2025 | https://www.gov.uk/government/collections/notices-to-exporters |
| **Sector-Specific Guidance** | | |
| Financial Sanctions Guidance for Charities and Non-Governmental Organisations (NGOs) | 21 June 2024 | https://www.gov.uk/government/publications/financial-sanctions-guidance-for-charities/financial-sanctions-guidance-for-charities-and-non-governmental-organisations-ngos |
| Transport Sanctions: Civil Monetary Penalties | 13 September 2024 | https://www.gov.uk/government/publications/transport-sanctions-civil-monetary-penalties/transport-sanctions-civil-monetary-penalties |
| Financial Sanctions Guidance for Maritime Shipping | 18 March 2025 | https://www.gov.uk/government/publications/financial-sanctions-guidance-for-maritime-shipping/financial-sanctions-guidance-for-maritime-shipping |
| UK Maritime Services Ban and Oil Price Cap Industry Guidance | 18 July 2025 | https://www.gov.uk/government/publications/uk-maritime-services-ban-and-oil-price-cap-industry-guidance?utm_medium=email&utm_campaign=govuk-notifications-topic&utm_source=79b63d57-e8f2-4f44-b449-dbb43bf97c71&utm_content=immediately |

Note: All webpages were last accessed 30 October 2025. This Appendix reflects the latest updates at the time of writing.

# Index